cover design by Jonathan Green-Armytage. Printed and
bound by David Neil & Co. (TU), South Street, Dorking,
Surrey.   ISBN 7163 4003 8 (cloth), 7163 4004 6 (paper)

Labour and inequality

1. introduction: the need for radical policy

Peter Townsend and Nicholas Bosanquet

Judging by events following the Labour Party's defeat in 1951, there is a risk that socialists may refrain from submitting the Labour Government's achievements and shortcomings during 1964-70 to searching analysis. New decisions and problems are apt to divert interest and attention from the past record. The corpse of the dead government lies in the no-man's land between today's newspapers and tomorrow's history books. It is certainly difficult soon after a government's fall to come to an overall view of the record. Much information which would allow a clearer judgment to be made of the underlying social and economic situation and the alternative courses of action which the Government might have been able to pursue has still to be published. But it is possible to review the record in particular policies in considerable detail and to draw some lessons for the future. This kind of work helps to free a party from stultifying subservience to its own past and contributes to the constructive job of developing a new policy programme. Certainly the Labour Party would have been very much better equipped for government in 1964 had it carried out such a review in the early 1950s. As R. H. S. Crossman wrote in 1963 in the *New Statesman*: "After 1951, as contrasted with 1931, no attempt was made to assess the achievements of the Labour Government and to analyse the reasons for its defeat . . . It has taken twelve years to purge the Labour Party of the disease of "ex-ministeritis" which first crippled our parliamentary leadership in the early fifties and then blighted the self-criticism which should have made the political wilderness blossom with Socialist ideas" (reprinted in *Towards socialism*, pp149-150).

This volume represents an attempt by a number of authors working in a common pattern and a common vein to assess the Labour record on social policy. Such policy is deliberately defined more broadly than is conventionally understood and includes incomes, wealth and fiscal policy, work situations, civil rights and urban and social planning, as well as policy covering the social services: health, education, welfare, housing and social security. It is offered in the hope that it will help both to stimulate discussion and establish standards of progress towards socialism.

There are of course disadvantages as well as advantages in examining the record so soon after the event. The disadvantages include a possible loss of confidence in certain principles of action as well as in key policies and personnel. Moreover, a party in defeat needs quickly to restore morale and gather strength for future political battles. Many ex-ministers and loyal supporters of the Labour Government are naturally watchful about over-exposure to criticism, especially from their own ranks. Loyalty is a precious commodity and yet loyalty to Party can sometimes conflict with loyalty to socialist objectives. And although the Labour Party has to be on its guard against any threat to its chances of winning or maintaining power it has to encourage self-criticism in order to demonstrate its freedom from the exercise of arbitrary power.

As a general rule parties, and leaders, make the mistake of being over-restrictive. They demand allegiance and tend to inhibit the creative interplay of ideas and hence the fulfilment of the principles of democracy. Self-criticism, on the contrary, can be a source of moral and political strength. It is one of the major means by which power and responsibility can be gradually diffused and the class hierarchy dismantled. An early discussion of the record prevents criticism from being pushed underground and allowed to fester for several years. Grievances can be aired and more closely defined. Argument can be encouraged in the belief that a more enduring consensus within the Labour movement is important and might be reached. Just as important, any intelligent analysis of the sequence as well as the substance of decisions taken by Labour Ministers, and of the inter-relationships between different policies, is likely to produce fresh understanding about strategy. In particular, there may be valuable lessons to be learned for organisation as well as planning, and for morale as well as administration.

equality

There are dangers in any historical analysis of over generalised enquiry and in our planning it seemed important to concentrate on a single theme. Equality has long been the central objective of the Labour movement. It had been the theme of one of the planning documents produced under Hugh Gaitskell's leadership (*Freedom and equality*, Labour Party, 1956). It was in large part the theme of the 1964 manifesto. Shortly after June 1970, therefore, the Executive Committee of the Fabian Society approved a proposal made by its Social Services Sub-Committee that a conference should be held in January 1971 on the theme of equality.

For many years the Labour Party had treated the expansion of the social services and the reform of the tax system as perhaps the major means of reducing inequality. But there was a need to descend from the level of generality and to examine the assumptions in detail, especially as they applied to 1964-70. What had Labour achieved in practice? How far had the social policies of the Labour Government in fact reduced inequality? The papers in this book attempt to answer these questions. First, they examine certain major fields of policy. Second, they analyse the dynamic factors at work in the country which make for greater and new inequalities. Finally, they put forward some of the lessons for a re-vitalised Labour Party. No attempt is made to present detailed policy programmes, but only to draw the implications for principle and illustrate the directions in which Labour might move. The book does not pretend to deal with Tory policies. An examination of these is, of course, an urgent task, but a separate one. The book deals with the actions and policies of the Labour Government of 1964-70, with the relationship of these policies to those worked out by the Labour Opposition before 1964, and with the germination of new policies in the early 1970s.

the problem of support

The authors have concentrated on policy rather than political morale and action. There are very real problems of political organisation, education and morale which deserve to be the subject of separate books. What was the importance and influence during these six years of Transport House, the Parliamentary Left, the Party Conference, the constituency parties, the TUC and other Labour groups and organisations? Was there a failure to use the

Labour movement itself as an instrument of change in order to educate mass support and maintain enthusiasm for particular policies and reforms? Certainly the experience of those who travelled about the country to Labour meetings of various kinds was that some of the most ardent activists were discouraged from helping the cause at critical moments, and did not believe any longer that the Government was capable of introducing really radical socialist change.

During 1969-70, in particular, there was dismay among many Labour supporters over incomes, fiscal and social service as well as industrial relations policies. Although most activists rallied to the cause again during the general election, the loss of some support (for example, in helping to get voters to the polls) may have contributed in some measure to the fall in the Labour turn out. The analysis of the election by David Butler and Michael Pinto-Duschinsky failed to deal with this factor (*The British general election of 1970*, MacMillan, 1971). Morale is linked, inevitably, with policy and it is the possible failings in policy to which this book is primarily devoted.

the problem of making redistribution real

Certain themes run through many of the papers. In some areas the pattern of spending during the six years was uneven, growing rapidly or as steadily as in preceding years at the beginning of the period in office and then tailing off towards the end. It proved difficult for the Government to increase expenditure on the social services within a context of general economic stagnation. But other problems would have arisen, although in a less acute form, whatever the general fortunes of the economy. There was the growing conflict between decisions affecting expenditure and those affecting finance. The expenditure decision led to improved health care, housing and pensions which, as the data in *Economic Trends* show, preserved the general redistributive functions of the social services from young to old and from employed to unemployed as well as from rich to poor. Although redistribution remained oblique poorer families benefited relatively more from these services (in total in cash and kind) than the better off. But these services, along with the other expenditure requirements of government, were financed through a tax and national insurance system which was far from progressive. The national insurance contribution was highly regressive, and even at the end of Labour's period in office was still a most important source of revenue for social security. During this period there was an increased emphasis on indirect taxation, the burden of which fell with disproportionate weight on poorer families. The *expenditure* decision was pulling, though perhaps haphazardly, in one direction, towards social equality, while the *financing* decision was pulling in quite the other direction. The lesson here for a future Labour Government is simple—of the need to calculate the *net* effect of the expenditure and financing decisions on households. This illustrates a point made about planning repeatedly in these pages.

The Labour Government's record cannot be defended simply by quoting (usually in money terms) a few chosen examples of increases in aggregate expenditure on schools, housing and hospitals. It can be defended only by a careful accounting of the net effect of all expenditure and financing decisions on households. We have to look at the inequality of post-tax incomes calculated to include the social wage. And one of the problems, as Michael Meacher shows later, is that accretions of certain kinds of wealth to some families are hazardous to estimate, if not incalculable.

Another painful dilemma is inherent in the faster rates of growth of spending on some social services compared with others. Priorities are harder, and more difficult to identify. In the pre-war and immediate post-war period it could be claimed that an increase in social service spending of almost any type would have benefited the poor. A main reason for the growth of the social services, as argued by Tawney in his *Equality*, was to deal with the human consequences of poverty. But that was when social policy was primarily conceived as establishing a national minimum and before public health and national insurance services were extended to the better-off. Today the problem has already shifted from establishing services which are designed to be used more or less evenly by most groups in the population to that of preventing the more prosperous sections from benefiting disproportionately from increases in public expenditure. Some of the fastest growing areas of social spending have been in fact for services which are little used by the poor. Thus few people in the lowest income groups use motorways. Relatively few children from Sparkbrook or Scotland Road go on to a university or poly-technic. Improvement grants chiefly benefit owner occupiers. Places in new towns tend to be reserved for skilled manual workers and are hard for the unskilled to come by. There was and is a growing conflict of priorities between providing social services for the poor and providing them for the middle classes. Yet society is largely unconscious of the growth of services for the latter and, by operating means tested schemes for the former is ensuring that many of them do not in fact receive certain services to which they would be entitled. Many of the differences in standards between different parts of the education system, for example, are closely correlated with the class identity of the ultimate consumers. Under the Labour Government social spending for the affluent rose at a very rapid rate. This is not to deny that there are economic and social arguments for the provision of such services—in terms both of economic growth and of social amenity. But there is an underlying conflict of priorities which has not been properly expressed and which the rather ambiguous concept of "positive discrimination"—enunciated by the Plowden Committee to justify special expenditures on schools in deprived areas—goes only a small part of the way towards resolving.

socialist objectives and tests of achievement

Four long term gains from the kind of exercise attempted in this book might be claimed. First, social objectives are reviewed. There are of course many different meanings of "equality." There is the extension of political rights, the development of justice at work and in law; equality of respect and dignity of man; the encouragement of "minimum" standards of housing, health and welfare; the attempt to create equality of opportunity, especially for children and young people; and the establishment of equal incomes and collective ownership. We have to look at these objectives in relation to particular events and decisions if they are to have meaning.

Second, measures of achievement and of need are developed which might be of value for Labour politics. Strictly, there are three separate types of evaluation: subjective, collective and objective. The individual makes subjective judgments of progress, and if he commands widespread respect he is listened to attentively. One man might argue that education is the paramount leveller; or that strong unions are more important than anything else in bringing about an equality of incomes. But others may disagree. Subjective opinions are, of course, frequently shared and often there are general if not universal opinions about ideas and achievements just as there are about dress and food. A society can come to believe that, say, a wage freeze is beneficial, or that the rate of income tax is "punitive" or that the flow of immigrants is worsening the availability of housing. Myths can have widespread currency despite government denials, or they can be given an aura of respectability. The sociologist is aware that all societies tend to exaggerate their progress. The idea that life is improving all the time is functional for society in current world conditions. It is a source of comfort and of reassurance to the middle aged and elderly when they look askance at the novelties introduced by the young. Politicians in particular want to believe that the practice of their profession has a constructive effect, and whatever their party, tend to assume that the greater is the volume of Parliamentary activity the greater is the outside impact upon the life and structure of the nation. Yet the laws enacted by Parliament, like treaties between nations, can become symbols of intention rather than practice.

We need to develop sounder criteria of progress based on a careful examination of statistics and policy. This is of particular importance to a party of the left. It can be a method of accelerating change. The balance of subjective evaluation, as expressed in popular beliefs and views on social issues, tends to favour the right. A political debate conducted largely on the basis of these views can damage Labour in two main ways. First, it reflects a choice of terrain on which Labour is likely to lose. Second, it means that Labour is neglecting areas of concern to a crucial group of potential supporters, especially better educated and younger voters who would welcome a more developed examination of the underlying problems of society. Political debate in Britain tends to be conducted in terms of simple moral precepts involving "truth," "keeping promises," "honesty," "consistency" or "paying our way." It is not based as often as it might be on an open and well informed examination of trends, and options. If the Labour Party and its leadership over a period of years could work to establish new standards of policy discussion in British life, and encourage debates of a more penetrating kind, it would have greatly increased the chances of radical change in Britain. This is not an argument for pomposity or pretension which together with a surprising lack of any sense of humour tend to characterise the current tone of British public life. Statistics over time have to be developed, conditions and policies have to be compared cross nationally and some attempt has to be made to analyse the society by contrasting different regions and different classes as well as by comparing the resources devoted to different parts of national endeavour. The following papers are a contribution to the development of these tests.

the problem of deradicalisation

Third, the papers raise the choice of strategy. Historically there have been both the insurrectionary and Parliamentary roads to socialism. Is the long history of democratic socialism one of earnest and humane but rather meagre reformism? Can a social democratic party do little more than introduce watery improvements over a long period of time? The implication is uncomfortable for many people within the Labour movement, yet it is a question to which they need to have an answer. Is there a permanent disjunction between Labour Party members' ideals and the Party's performance in office, such that no democratic socialist government will ever live up to, or *can* live up to, popular hopes? Fabians are implacable democrats. But are they naive in believing that democracy is reconcilable with radical, structural change in society? Or should they, in the light of experience, face up to realities and settle for a philosophy of very slow change? This question is raised indirectly by several authors in this book. The choice can be a frightening one for the socialist. Sociology and history teach that achievement is inevitably measured with out-dated tools and the concepts and preoccupations of previous generations. Just when evidence of achievement and obstacles overcome seems to have been produced, new problems and new inequalities arise to mock complacency. So Parliamentary socialism has to prove itself, and prove itself in terms of defending its record.

Some social scientists conclude that European social democratic parties have become deradicalised during the twentieth century (see for example, F. Parkin, *Class, inequality and political order*, MacGibbon and Kee, 1971). Whether this fate has befallen or need befall the Labour Party should be widely discussed.

Two groups of people now stand outside the Labour Party. First there are many people, both young and older of a not very ideological cast of mind, but who have gained through their personal or occupational experience a broad sympathy for social reform. Second, there are some people with strong political values who have moved further to the left of the Labour Party. In the eyes of both groups the Labour Party appears to suffer from compromised standards and halting purpose. The former want evidence of a steady and consistent improvement in social conditions, or determination to do some-thing about them. The latter are cynical about political standards, and wonder how far the ideals of socialism seem to be preached but the principles of little capitalism practised. Increasingly since 1959, General Elections have come to seem like badly acted amateur theatricals. The current climate is one in which many in both groups are turning to the Labour Party for the first time, shocked by the social policies of conservatism. The caricature conjured up by some political commentators of a Tory Tweedledum at odds with a Labour Tweedledee is recognisably false and more people might now be persuaded that Labour offers the only realistic political alternative within which to work out idealistic, humane and co-operative policies. But they will be persuaded only if they feel that the Labour Party is prepared to uncover and discuss failures in policies, procedures and institutions, and is willing to push ahead fast with radical change.

the forces of change

Finally, the attempt by the authors to apply similar questions to fields as different as, say, education policy and housing policy, or social security and income tax policy, helps to concentrate attention on the motivating forces of change. What are the respective roles of government, civil service, interested pressure groups, the Labour movement and public opinion? Are they just the unconscious agents of more deep seated industrial, economic and social changes? Any political party needs continuously to debate the respective importance to the attainment of its objectives of grass roots support, union solidarity, the sponsorship of controversy between different groups within the Labour movement, the recruitment and training of an administrative elite, and even a system of tight knit control over the party leadership by the movement. In politics it is natural to suppose that the formal political system is responsible for change, more than the changes in outside institutions and values. But the party, and the politicians, may need to develop a knowledge of the limitations of the part they play in the process. For example, in his paper, Dennis Marsden suggests that the changes in practice now being introduced by teachers in some comprehensive and other schools represent the most significant real change in the system of education in this country, more significant than anything achieved in Parliament by politicians in the last 20 years. Even if this paradox cannot be fully documented and pinned down, it needs to be discussed. No party can afford to ignore the value of deciding what are the best agents of change. Individual socialists sometimes say that they cannot live like socialists until the rest of society agrees to pass the necessary legislation. But the reverse may be nearer the truth. Until sufficient socialists are prepared to live as socialists, society will never change in structure.

In many ways this is a critical book. While noting the achievements, most of the authors have failed to find evidence of marked changes in the direction of fulfilling socialist objectives. Their analyses present a gloomy picture. They confirm the inability of the Government to use its power on behalf of the weaker members of the community.

Hope for the future depends on whether the movement can recover the purpose which it has seemed to lack since the desperate privations of unemployment and poverty in the 1930s and the immediate phase of post-war reconstruction. Events alone will not create this purpose. It depends on the willingness of individuals in all parts of the Labour movement to break with the stale rituals into which party life has fallen and believe more strongly in their socialist aspirations. It depends too on a willingness to find out the facts and face historical as well as economic and social realities. The failures have been those both of philosophy and intellectual honesty. Democratic socialism did not fail in the 1960s: it was not tried. A wide range of policies based on an assertive modern expression of socialist philosophy is required to change patterns of opportunity, income and economic and social power and they have to be spelt out in detail. The purpose of this book has been to prepare the ground. We write in the hope that the 1970s will not be another lost decade for the Labour Party.

If the Government had a hard struggle with the elements to reduce inequality and less support from outside than might reasonably have been expected that is an honourable case. It needs to be put as badly as does the case of the critics. For otherwise it will be hard to rekindle the enthusiasm and idealism of former party stalwarts and dispel the scepticism which exists among the youngest generation of voters. Whatever the verdict of the next election, it is conviction in the ability to build an equal society which has first to be restored to the Labour Party.

2. inequality and social security

A. B. Atkinson

There can be little doubt that social security received much more attention from the Labour Government of 1964-1970 than it did during the preceding thirteen years. The Labour Government introduced earnings related benefits for sickness and unemployment, re-fashioned the National Assistance Board, put forward detailed plans for a radical reform of the pension system, as well as increasing existing benefits (one of which—family allowances—had remained unchanged for twelve years). What is more controversial is whether the Labour measures were sufficiently large—or even of the right kind—to make a significant contribution to the reduction of inequality in Britain. Total social security expenditure grew substantially between 1964-65 and 1969-70, but did this represent increased benefit being channelled to those in need? Or did the increase simply reflect demographic changes, higher unemployment and the increases necessary to keep up with inflation? National insurance pensions and other benefits have increased, but have they kept pace with rising incomes elsewhere in the economy? Have the new programmes such as supplementary benefits succeeded in reaching those for whom they were intended? The aim of this chapter is to provide answers to some of these questions and to assess how far Labour's social security policy was effective in reducing inequality.

Controversy over Labour's record on social security has arisen not simply over what has been done, but also over the method by which its achievements should be judged (as was well illustrated by the debate between the Child Poverty Action Group and David Ennals). Inequality is clearly a concept that has many dimensions and a policy which reduces inequality in certain respects may appear inegalitarian when judged by other standards. In this chapter I have therefore examined Labour's policy from a number of different viewpoints. The first section takes an aggregate approach and analyses the change in total expenditure between 1964-65 and 1969-70. This may be seen as a measure of the overall "effort" made in the social security field. In contrast to this approach, the second section examines the impact of the changes during this period on the *individual*. It is concerned with the increase in national insurance benefits and family allowances in relation to incomes elsewhere, and the effect of increased national insurance contributions; the impact of the new earnings related benefits and the introduction of supplementary benefits.

The third section brings together these results in an assessment of the effect on the overall distribution of income, as can be measured from the Family Expenditure Survey. Finally, I have discussed separately the likely effect of national superannuation had it reached the statute book.

THE AGGREGATE "EFFORT"

Considerable weight was attached in Labour Party statements to the increase in total social security expenditure. In his debate with the Child Poverty Action Group, David Ennals pointed to the increase from £1,960 million in 1964-65 to an estimated £3,600 million at the post-November 1969 rates—an increase of more than 80 per cent. In this section I examine the causes of the increase in actual expenditure between 1964-65 and 1969-70. In order to allow for the general rise in money incomes, I have in most cases expressed the expenditure as a percentage of gross national product. This procedure is a rather crude one, but does provide a broad measure of aggregate "effort" which abstracts from general increases in income.

AGGREGATE SOCIAL SECURITY EXPENDITURE 1964-65* AND 1969-70

	1964-65		1969-70	
	£m	% GNP	£m	% GNP
national insurance	1,591	5.4	2.645	6.7
war pensions	115	0.4	131	0.3
national assistance/ supplementary benefits†	255	0.9	536	1.4
family allowances‡	154	0.5	367	0.9
total	2,115	7.2	3,679	9.3

* the year runs to 31 March. 1964-65 therefore includes the first six months of the Labour government, but this does not seriously affect the analysis since very few changes were introduced during this period (retirement pensions, for example, went up on 29 March 1965). The figures relate to the UK. They do not include Redundancy Fund payments.
† includes non-contributory old age pensions in 1964-65 (absorbed in Supplementary Benefits in November 1966).
‡ the figures quoted by Mr. Ennals obviously excluded family allowances.
source: *Monthly digest of statistics*, May 1970.

The basic figures given in the table above show that social security expenditure rose very substantially as a percentage of GNP—from 7.2 per cent to 9.3 per cent—or an increase of a third. The increase was common to all of the broad categories apart from war pensions (which are not discussed below). It is clear, however, that there were a number of factors contributing to the growth of expenditure which cannot be seen as reducing inequality. Three of the most important were:

1. The increase in unemployment—the rise in expenditure due to this can hardly be claimed as an achievement!

2. Demographic changes, particularly the increase in the number of old people.

3. The use of "clawback" in 1968. This involved a switch from child tax benefits to family allowances, and only part of the increase in the latter can be regarded as a *net* benefit.

In assessing the contribution that the increase in expenditure can have made to reducing inequality, we should allow for these factors. In the table overleaf I have estimated what the expenditure would have been in 1964-65 if there had been the same level of unemployment and the same number of old people as in 1970, and subtracting that part of the increase in family allowances which was "clawed-back" from child tax relief. With this adjustment the increase between 1964-65 and 1969-70 is considerably smaller—the rise being 0.7 per cent of GNP rather than 2.1 per cent of GNP—or less than half the amount suggested by the original figures. A large part of the increase in total expenditure can, therefore, be attributed to demographic and other factors.

AGGREGATE SOCIAL SECURITY EXPENDITURE ADJUSTED FOR DEMOGRAPHIC AND OTHER FACTORS (% GNP)

	1964–65 actual	1964–65 adjusted	1969–70 actual
national insurance	5.4	6.0	6.7
national assistance/ supplementary benefits*	0.9	1.1	1.4
family allowances†	0.5	1.1	0.9
total‡	7.2	8.6	9.3

* it was assumed that the expenditure on retirement pensions would have increased proportionately with the number of pensioners. It was assumed that the same proportion of new pensioners would have claimed National Assistance and that the average amount paid would have been the same as in December 1964. Similar assumptions were made in the case of the unemployed (a distinction being made between those receiving the National Insurance benefit and those not).
† the adjustment for claw-back was made on the assumption that the net cost of the increase (allowing for subsequent tax changes) was £50 million.
‡ including war pensions.

If we examine the sources of the increase in expenditure, we can identify three main areas:

1. Increases in existing benefits.

2. Re-fashioning of national assistance so that more of those eligible for assistance claim the benefit to which they are entitled.

3. Introduction of the earnings related programmes.

These three factors are discussed in detail in the next section. For the present, we may note that the first two of these reasons are likely to contribute towards greater equality in the current distribution of income, but that the expenditure on the earnings related benefits may be less effective. Expenditure on these benefits is in fact currently around £100 million—or some 0.3 per cent of GNP—so that they account for about a half of the rise in national insurance expenditure (as a per cent GNP).

Before leaving the aggregate expenditure, it may be interesting to put these figures in historical context. The table opposite presents information in the same form as the previous table but covering the period 1959-60 to 1964-65. Using the unadjusted figures there appears to have been some small increase in expenditure as a percentage of GNP, but when we adjust for the

SOCIAL SECURITY EXPENDITURE COMPARISON WITH 1959-60—1964-65 (% GNP)

	1959-60 actual	1964-65 actual	1964-65 adjusted for demographic and other factors
national insurance	4.8	5.4	5.0
national assistance	0.8	0.9	0.8
family allowances	0.6	0.5	0.5
total*	6.7	7.2	6.7

* including war pensions.
see notes to previous table.

increase in the number of old people (and the fall in unemployment) this disappears. The record of the previous Conservative Government was, therefore, even less creditable.

SOCIAL SECURITY AND THE INDIVIDUAL

The aggregate figures presented in the previous section give little indication as to who gained from the increased social security expenditure. In this section I examine the three main areas of expansion isolated in the previous section: increases in existing benefits, the introduction of the earnings related benefits and the extension of national assistance.

higher national insurance benefits

The extent to which the Labour Government's measures narrowed the gap between national insurance benefits and wages was one of the subjects of the exchange between the Child Poverty Action Group and Mr Ennals. The CPAG compared the post-November 1969 benefits with those in May 1963 (the last increase before Labour came to power) and argued that they had gone up by less than average earnings (48 per cent against 54 per cent). Mr Ennals objected to this basis for comparison, and showed that the increase since October 1964 was greater than that of earnings. It seems clear, however, that the CPAG were right in comparing dates at which the benefit had been increased. Given the system of reviewing benefits every two or three years, the national insurance benefits fall as a proportion of average earnings between reviews, and to obtain a measure of the trend one must compare "peaks." Taking October 1964 as a baseline will therefore distort the picture. On the other hand the CPAG method does not take into account the fact that prices may have risen faster or slower for different groups such as pensioners, and that the relevant standard of comparison is really *take home pay* (allowing for national insurance contributions and income tax) rather than *gross earnings*.

In the table below, I have presented a revised comparison of the real value of national insurance benefits with the real value of the take home pay of a manual worker with average earnings in manufacturing (assumed to have one child). For the purposes of argument, I have taken two representative cases—a single pensioner and an unemployed man with three children. The figures in each case relate to dates at which benefits had been increased. The results show that over the period as a whole the national insurance benefits have risen slightly faster than the take home pay of the average

INCREASES IN NATIONAL INSURANCE BENEFITS

	real take home pay for average worker*	real value of single pension†	real value of unemployment benefit (man with wife & 3 children)‡
March/May 1963	100	100	100
January/March 1965	106	111	110
October 1967	108	114	113
November 1969	110	114	116

* based on average earnings for adult male manual workers in manufacturing, allowing for income tax and national insurance contributions.

† calculated on the special price index for single pensioner households published by the *Employment and Productivity Gazette* adjusted for housing expenditure using the housing component of the retail price index. Since a disproportionate number of pensioners have controlled tenancies, this may over state the increase in prices.

‡ this column is deflated by use of the retail price index.

worker. This finding differs from that of the CPAG since income tax and national insurance contributions have increased as a proportion of gross earnings since 1963 (a point to which I return later). Most of the increase occurred, however, in March 1965, and subsequent rises in the National Insurance benefits have been less than sufficient to keep up with average take home pay.

While comparison of the "peaks" is undoubtedly the correct way of measuring the long run trend, the changes in the purchasing power of benefits between reviews is of very real importance to the individual. The extent to which the value is reduced depends on the length of time between reviews and the rate of inflation. From September 1952, the periods between reviews (for retirement pensions) under the Conservatives were 31 months, 33 months, 38 months and 26 months. In the case of the Labour Government, the reviews (counting from May 1963) took 22 months, 31 months and 24 months, which clearly represented an improvement. On the other hand, the rate of price increase has also accelerated. To give a measure of

PERCENTAGE FALL IN REAL VALUE OF NATIONAL INSURANCE BENEFITS BETWEEN REVIEWS

	%		%
April 1955	11	March 1965	6
January 1958	11	October 1967	8
April 1961	6	November 1969	12

The figures on the left are estimated using the price index given by M. F. W. Hemming (National Institute, *Economic Review*, August 1965) which is based in turn on that of T. Lynes (*National assistance and national prosperity*) adjusted to cover housing. In view of the difficulties of linking and of using an annual index, figures should be treated with caution. The figures on the right are calculated as described in footnote above. Since the two series cannot be linked, no figure is given for May 1963.

the combined effect of these factors, the table shows the percentage by which the single retirement pension had fallen in value by the time of the review. On this basis, the Labour performance appears less satisfactory (although in view of the statistical difficulties described in the notes comparisons between the 1950s and 1960s must be made with care). This table brings out the urgent need for more frequent reviews of benefits—over the period October 1967 to November 1969 a single pensioner's real income fell by 12 per cent, which is a very serious fall. By January 1971 the value of the pension fixed in November 1969 had fallen by 8 per cent.

So far I have focussed on those receiving national insurance benefits, but we must also consider the effect of the increase in family allowances. Was this increase sufficient to offset the effect on lower paid workers of higher taxes and prices? In the table below, I have shown the change in the real income of a low paid worker (earning two thirds of the average in manufacturing) with three children over the period October 1964 to October 1970.

This shows how small the increase in family allowances was for this family when we allow for the effect of claw back (which caused him to pay income tax for the first time). Allowance must also be made for the effects of the withdrawal of free school meals, re-introduction of prescription charges, and so on. The increase in 1968 was some $3\frac{1}{2}$ per cent of his take home pay. Since then the benefit has been eroded by inflation; an allowance of £1 is now (January 1971) equivalent in real terms to £0.85 in October 1968.

The table also brings out the importance for the low paid worker of the increase in national insurance contributions, and this is explored further in the table below, which shows the employee contributions (for a person contracted-in to the graduated scheme) as a proportion of earnings in 1964 and 1970, where in each case earnings are expressed as a percentage of the average in manufacturing.

FAMILY ALLOWANCES, NATIONAL INSURANCE
CONTRIBUTIONS, INCOME TAX AND THE LOW PAID WORKER*

October	earnings† £ s	national insurance £ s	income tax £ s	family allowances £ s	take home £ s	index of real take home‡
1964	12 9	15	—	18	12 12	100
1965	13 8	17	—	18	13 9	102
1966	13 17	18	—	18	13 17	101
1967	14 12	1 1	—	18	14 9	103
1968	15 14	1 3	8	1 18	16 1	109
1969	17 0	1 5	15	1 18	16 19	109
1970	17 10	1 6	10	1 18	17 13	107

* it is assumed that he has three children under eleven, and that he is contracted-in to the graduated pension scheme. All figures are rounded to the nearest 1s.

† earnings are taken as two thirds of those of the average adult male worker in manufacturing.

‡ the price index used is the retail price index.

NATIONAL INSURANCE CONTRIBUTIONS AS A PERCENTAGE OF EARNINGS

% of national average earnings	1964	1970
50	6.5	8.3
60	6.1	7.7
70	5.8	7.3
80	5.6	6.8
100	5.3	6.2
120	4.4	5.7
200	2.7	3.4
300	1.8	2.3
400	1.3	1.7

This brings out not only the extreme regressivity of the contributions, but also the fact that there has been little change in the degree of regressivity since 1964. Despite the avowed intention of moving away from flat rate contributions, and the attempt to do so in November 1969, the increase for the low paid worker earning half the national average was the same as that for someone earning four times the national average. Flat rate contributions in fact increased by 50 per cent compared with a 40 per cent rise in average gross earnings.

effect of new earnings related benefits

One important innovation of the Labour Government was the programme of short term earnings related supplements to sickness and unemployment benefits and widows' allowances. They are payable for the first six months (after twelve waiting days) at a rate of one third of average weekly earnings between £9 and £30, subject to a maximum total benefit of 85 per cent of average weekly earnings.

Any assessment of the contribution that these benefits can make to reducing inequality depends on the dimension of inequality with which one is concerned. It is clear, for example, that earnings related benefits of this type will mitigate hardship caused by a fall in income. For a man earning £30 a week, the total benefit (including the supplement) now represents 50 per cent of his earnings rather than 27 per cent with just the flat rate (for a married couple). However, it could well be argued that a man earning £15 a week has greater need should he become unemployed, since he will have been able to save less and may have less discretionary expenditure which can be reduced. It is open to debate, therefore, whether earnings related benefits represent the most effective use of resources.

Doubts about the earnings related benefits may also be raised with regard to their temporary nature. Benefits are only paid during the first six months (after the waiting period), and only 85,000 out of a total 480,000 men unemployed in November 1969 were in fact receiving the earnings related supplement. It can well be argued that those who have been unemployed longer have greater needs (as their stocks of clothing, furniture and goodwill become used up).

CHANGE IN NATIONAL ASSISTANCE/SUPPLEMENTARY BENEFIT SCALE*

	real value single pensioner	real value married man with 3 children†	real take home pay for average worker
May 1963	100	100	100
March 1965	111	112	106
November 1966	117	110	106
October 1967	122	115	108
November 1969	122	115	110

* the scale is calculated using the average discretionary addition (adjusted to spread winter fuel costs throughout the year) for retirement pensioners. It does not include any allowance for rent. The price index used for the single pensioner is that in the *Employment and Productivity Gazette*.
† it is assumed that the children are aged four, six, and eleven.

the re-modelling of national assistance

One characteristic of Labour social policy was increased reliance on means testing: rent rebates, rate rebates, prescription charges and so on. This is also reflected in the role played by supplementary benefits. The income guarantee promised when in opposition emerged in 1966 in emasculated form as the replacement of national assistance by supplementary benefits. This comprised an increase in level of benefits and administrative and other changes designed to ensure that all those eligible did claim the benefit to which they were entitled.

The change in the real level of the national assistance/supplementary benefit scale is given in the table above. Since part of the increase in November 1966 (when supplementary benefits were introduced) replaced discretionary payments made under national assistance, I have included the average discretionary payment. (The scale does not include any allowance for housing costs.) From this it is clear that the supplementary benefit scale increased rather faster than take home pay, and faster than national insurance benefits.

The raising of the supplementary benefit scale relative to national insurance benefits was a deliberate element in Labour strategy, and it clearly provided help to many of those with low incomes. However the success of this means tested approach depends crucially on people not being deterred from claiming the benefit to which they are entitled. For this reason the Labour Government laid great stress on the second plank in their platform—the administrative change (and rechristening). These changes have been widely claimed as an "outstanding success" (Mr Ennals), a "remarkable success" (Mr Houghton) and "a tremendous social change" (Mr Crossman). These claims are based primarily on the increase in the number of old people receiving assistance; however, a detailed examination of the evidence shows that a large part of the increase can be explained by the rise in the assistance scale relative to the national insurance pension. It can in fact be estimated that, on an optimistic view, the number not claiming the assistance to which they are entitled has only been reduced by a quarter. (See

PERCENTAGE OF UNEMPLOYED MEN RECEIVING NATIONAL ASSISTANCE/SUPPLEMENTARY BENEFITS SUBJECT TO WAGE STOP

year*	%	year*	%
1962	14.1	1966	13.8
1963	14.2	1967	14.6
1964	12.3	1968	13.3
1965	16.2	1969	14.0

* December 1962-66, November 1967-70.
source: Reports of the National Assistance Board and DHSS.

A. B. Atkinson, *Poverty in Britain and the reform of social security,* Chapter 4.) The introduction of supplementary benefits cannot therefore be claimed to have dealt with the problem and serious doubt remains about the wisdom of relying on means tested benefits.

Before leaving supplementary benefits, I should like to refer to one further reform introduced in 1968—the administration of the wage stop. At the end of 1967, the government published a report on the effects of the wage stop and announced a number of important changes in the way in which it was to be administered. The most significant of these were the use of local authority wage rates for assessing the normal earnings of labourers (rather than local average earnings), the abolition of a deduction for working expenses, and a review of all cases where there was an element of disability. These changes, which began to be implemented early in 1968, were designed to reduce the number of families subject to the wage stop. Figures recently published by the DHSS allow one to see whether this has in fact happened. The table above shows the proportion of unemployed men receiving assistance who were subject to the wage stop in 1962-69. This percentage has remained remarkably stable, and in November 1969 was little different from 1962. This certainly does not suggest that the new administrative procedures have had a dramatic effect on the number wage stopped (although the size of the stop may have been reduced).

EFFECT ON THE OVERALL DISTRIBUTION OF INCOME

Statistics on the overall distribution of income in Britain are seriously incomplete. The Inland Revenue figures exclude many important types of income, and do not cover all low income households; moreover, they provide little information about family size and other relevant characteristics. The Family Expenditure Survey gives more detailed information in a number of respects, but is based on a small sample and is subject to a number of biases. The conclusions that can be drawn about the effect of Labour's policy on the overall distribution of income are therefore rather limited.

The official analysis of the incidence of taxes and social service benefits published in *Economic Trends* are based on the Family Expenditure Survey. In the most recent study, an attempt was made to compare the distribution in 1968 with that in 1961. As was pointed out in this article, this comparison is rather difficult to make, since households may have been expected to move between income ranges. The table below was constructed on the assumption that the original income of all households would have increased at the same rate as total personal income (excluding government grants) *per capita,* and compares 1968 (the latest year available) with 1964.

It shows for each year the ratio of income after social security benefits, income tax and National Insurance contributions to original income. (The table does not include pensioners, whose original incomes are very small indeed.) The results show a rise in this ratio for low income households and a fall at the upper end of the income distribution. However, what is interesting is the small size of the increase for most low income households. If we take the adult household that gained most (those with original incomes between £260 and £314), the gain was about 15s a week. It is also interesting to note that many low income families with two or three children showed virtually no increase and some lost slightly.

INCOME AFTER DIRECT TAXES AND BENEFITS AS A PERCENTAGE OF ORIGINAL INCOME

original income ranges in 1968 £s (annual)	1 adult		2 adults		2 adults 1 child		2 adults 2 children		2 adults 3 children	
	1964	1968	1964	1968	1964	1968	1964	1968	1964	1968
260—	151	169	216	231						
315—	131	143	198	207						
382—	107	130	176	182						
460—	92	112	137	156						
559—	92	99	116	138						
676—	86	91	102	112	100	106	98	113		
816—	83	83	95	101	92	94	93	100	108	99
988—	81	83	89	88	89	89	94	94	97	100
1,196—	81	78	86	84	89	86	91	90	95	94
1,448—	83	78	85	83	87	84	90	87	96	92
1,752—	81	77	84	82	85	84	89	86	92	89
2,122—	—	76	83	80	81	81	86	86	—	89
2,566—	—	80	81	80	—	82	89	82	—	84
3,109—	—	—	—	—	—	85	—	79	—	85

source: calculated from *Economic Trends*, February 1970.

Moreover, as the *Economic Trends* article points out, those households in low income ranges receiving social security benefits will not have had as large an increase in original income as assumed in the table. This means that those in the lowest income ranges are *likely* to include an *increasing* proportion of sick and unemployed households and this no doubt explains part of the increase for these groups. On this basis the redistribution from high income to low income households has only been very slight over the period 1964 to 1968. One factor which will cause the redistributive effect to be under stated is that during this period the Central Statistical Office treated employers' national insurance contributions as being borne by the worker. If they are in fact passed on in higher prices, they will be slightly less regressive.

If we consider the redistribution between different types of households, this

INCOME REDISTRIBUTION BY HOUSEHOLD TYPE AFTER DIRECT TAXES AND BENEFITS* AS A PERCENTAGE OF ORIGINAL INCOME

	1964	1968
1 adult non-pensioner	96	101
2 adult non-pensioner	93	95
2 adult and 1 child	98	96
2 adult and 2 children	104	102
2 adult and 3 children	116	114
2 adult and 4 children	125	127
all households†	102	103

* including benefits in kind from NHS, education, school meals, milk and other welfare services.
† including pensioners.
source: *Economic Trends*, February 1970.

suggests that the position of families has worsened between 1964 and 1968. The table above shows that income after tax and benefits *fell* as a percentage of original income for families with one, two or three children, whereas the average for all households increased. This lends support to the view that the benefit from higher family allowances has been offset by higher taxes and (particularly) higher national insurance contributions.

THE LABOUR PLAN FOR PENSIONS

If enacted, national superannuation would have been the most far reaching change in our social security system since Beveridge. In this section I examine the contribution that it would make to reducing inequality.

The distributional consequences of the scheme can be discussed in a number of different ways. I consider first the impact on the overall distribution of income at any particular date. The initial effect will be primarily that from the new schedule of contributions, which would be at a rate of $6\frac{3}{4}$ per cent of earnings for employees up to a ceiling of $1\frac{1}{2}$ times national average earnings. The schedule would therefore be proportional for most of its range, although it would still be regressive at the top (a man earning £5,000 a year would only pay $2\frac{1}{2}$ per cent of his earnings). From the table showing national insurance contributions as a percentage of earnings, it can be seen that the change over would reduce the burden on those with below average earnings, although the amount involved would be fairly small (a man earning £12 10s a week gaining 4s 4d). The benefit to low paid workers could be made much larger by making the schedule progressive rather than simply proportional: for example, the contribution could be payable at a percentage rate on earnings above half the national average. When the scheme was in full operation, the pensions paid would in most cases be substantially larger than at present. A man who had earned the equivalent of £12 10s a week throughout his life would receive (in current terms) £7 5s—or nearly 50 per cent more than the present flat rate pension—a man with earnings of £20 a week would receive £9 1s. (One group that would not fare so well under this scheme are single women dependent on their own earnings record. At current earnings levels for women, some

THE BUILD UP OF NATIONAL SUPERANNUATION PENSIONS
PERCENTAGE WITH PENSIONS BELOW THE SUPPLEMENTARY
BENEFIT SCALE (INCLUDING AVERAGE RENT)*

	married couples	single men	single women	total
1980	79	86	95	88
1990	23	37	52	38
2000	2	5	26	13

* it was assumed that the flat rate pension, the supplementary benefit scale and the national superannuation pensions in payment would all rise in line with average earnings.
source: A. B. Atkinson, *Poverty in Britain and the reform of social security,* p 117.

would actually get less than at present.) The national superannuation pensions would, therefore, represent a major increase in the incomes of old people and would very considerably reduce their dependence on supplementary benefits. Moreover, the pensions would be inflation-proofed, so that old people would have the security of knowing that the real value would be maintained at the biannual reviews (although there are strong arguments for doing more and guaranteeing pensions as a percentage of *average earnings*).

Under the transition provisions of the scheme the pensions would be built up gradually over a 20 year period. The effect of these provisions is indicated by the table above, which shows the proportion of old people with pensions below the supplementary benefit scale (including average rent) in 1980, 1990 and 2000—assuming that the scheme had begun operation in 1972. Even in the year 2000, 13 per cent of all pensioners would still be getting less than the supplementary benefit scale and this would be particularly true of single women. Even if national superannuation is introduced speedily by the next Labour Government, it will take a long time for it to come fully into effect.

So far we have treated separately the contributions to the scheme and the resulting benefits; however, the individual will also be concerned with the relationship between them. This relationship can be expressed in terms of the rate of return that an individual is getting on his contributions, and in

PERCENTAGE RATE OF RETURN FROM NATIONAL
SUPERANNUATION AFTER TAX IN MONEY TERMS

earnings as % national average	married couple	single men	single women
50	9.3	6.3	9.0
75	8.7	5.6	8.3
100	8.3	5.2	7.9
150	7.7	4.6	7.4
250	7.0	3.9	6.7

source: A. B. Atkinson, "National superannuation: redistribution and value for money," *Bulletin of the Oxford Institute of Economics and Statistics,* August 1970. The basic assumptions are described in this article.

FLAT RATE BENEFITS AND EARNINGS RELATED CONTRIBUTIONS (MARRIED COUPLE)

% of average earnings	national superannuation	flat-rate
50	9.3	9.3
75	8.7	8.1
100	8.3	7.2
150	7.7	5.9
250	7.0	5.2

source: as previous table.

the table on the previous page estimates of this return are given. Two points of interest emerge. First, the *level* of the return is high. National superannuation represents, therefore, an opportunity for people to invest at high (and inflation proofed) rates of interest which are comparable with those of the best run occupational schemes.

Secondly, although the return is higher for those with low earnings, the difference is not especially marked: a married man with earnings equal to half the national average gets 1.6 per cent more than a man at the ceiling. The degree of redistribution in this respect cannot be described as dramatic. It is perhaps interesting to compare the national superannuation scheme with the alternative of using earnings related contributions to finance higher flat rate benefits, where the gap is 3.4 per cent as shown in the table above.

CONCLUSIONS AND FUTURE POLICY

The principal conclusions from the examination of Labour's record may be summarised as follows:

1. The claims made for the increase in aggregate "effort" in the field of social security expenditure under the Labour Government were exaggerated. A substantial part of the rise in spending was attributable to their being more old people and more unemployed.

2. In 1965 there was a definite increase in the level of national insurance benefits, but in the next five years they scarcely kept pace with rising earnings. The periods between reviews of the benefit levels were shorter than under the Conservatives, but there was still a substantial fall in the purchasing power of benefits between reviews.

3. The introduction of supplementary benefits has not had the success claimed for it by Labour ministers and has failed to eliminate the problem of people not claiming the benefits to which they are entitled.

4. The gain to low income families from the 1968 rise in family allowances has largely been offset by higher national insurance contributions and income tax.

5. National superannuation would have led to a considerable increase in pensions, but the gestation period was long and more could have been done to ease the burden of contributions on the low paid worker.

The implications of this critical review of the last Labour Government's record cannot be fully developed in the scope of this chapter. However, in my view the policy of the next Labour Government should include:

1. A change to wholly earnings-related national insurance contributions, with a progressive schedule.

2. The total revenue from contributions should be increased and used to pay substantially higher flat rate benefits. The pension for a single person should be at least £8.50 and that for a couple at least £12.50 (in 1971). This would considerably reduce dependence on supplementary benefits.

3. There should be a major redistribution of income towards families with children. The present family allowances and child tax relief should be replaced by a single (tax free) child benefit graduated according to age.

4. Social security benefits (including family allowances) should be guaranteed as a percentage of average earnings and adjusted at quarterly intervals.

These measures are only some of those necessary, and they should form part of an integrated plan to deal with the needs of all those with low incomes. Without such a plan, the next Labour Government will be no more successful in dealing with the problems of poverty and inequality.

chronology

November 1964	Increases in national insurance benefits and contributions announced—effective March 1965. Earnings rule abolished for widows.
April 1965	Redundancy Payments Bill published.
August 1966	Ministry of Social Security came into being.
October 1966	Earnings related benefits introduced and period for which flat rate unemployment benefit payable extended to twelve months.
November 1966	Supplementary benefits replaced national assistance.
June 1967	Earnings limits for retirement pensions raised and other changes made in administration of earnings rule.
July 1967	Report on the circumstances of families published.
October 1967	Family allowances increased for fourth and subsequent children.
October 1967	National insurance benefits increased.
December 1967	Report on the administration of the wage stop published.
March 1968	Budget announces introduction of clawback.
April 1968	Family allowances increased for all children.
July 1968	New restrictions on payment of supplementary benefits to unemployed announced.
October 1968	Family allowances increased for all children.
November 1968	R. H. S. Crossman appointed Secretary of State for Social Services over Department of Health and Social Security.
January 1969	White Paper on National Superannuation published.
November 1969	National insurance benefits increased.
December 1969	National Superannuation Bill published.

3. inequality in housing

Colin Crouch and Martin Wolf

Assessment of the implications for social equality of housing policy is made exceptionally difficult by two important sets of factors. First housing policy has other objectives than simply the reduction of economic equality. Secondly there are three major different sectors of housing provision in addition to such small size sectors as co-operative and co-ownership housing as well as housing provided by charitable housing associations. The complexity and uniqueness of their financing make it impracticable to discuss them in this chapter. A socialist housing policy is likely to have at least three goals: to provide everyone with a home; to provide everyone with a home which meets certain minimum standards of quality; and to provide everyone with a home which he can afford. All three of these objectives relate to equality, yet they can easily conflict. The conflict between provision and standards was shown when the Conservative Government in 1951 set about increasing the rate of house building to 300,000 a year by reducing the size of the houses. The conflict between provision and rents was long exemplified in the policies of Labour controlled local authorities in Scotland who kept council house rents exceedingly low at the expense of failing to construct new dwellings for the large number of overcrowded slum-dwellers in privately rented property. Finally, the conflict between provision and rents can be seen in the present problem of councils who are finding that many potential tenants cannot afford the rents they feel they must charge for Parker Morris standards dwellings.

In December 1969 the breakdown by tenure (England and Wales) was as follows: rented from local authority or new town corporation: 27.8 per cent; owner-occupied: 51.1 per cent; rented from private owners: 16.1 per cent; other tenures: 5 per cent (MHLG, *Handbook of statistics 1969,* June 1970).

The existence of the three major housing sectors makes it well nigh impossible to secure equity of treatment between them, or to judge whether they have in practice been treated equitably. There are inherent difficulties in comparing the purchase of a house with the payment of rent, but the situation is made more complex still by the different role of "subsidies" in each sector. It is really inaccurate to speak of "subsidy" with regard to all three sectors: rather we should speak of different means by which different categories of house-holders are protected from bearing the full cost of their housing.

An important fact about British housing policy is indicated by this combin-ation of sectors; housing is only very partly regarded as a social service. Partly it is a private consumption good and partly (in some aspects of owner occupation) it is a form of mass property investment. Welfare aspects of the situation have been grafted on in an even more *ad hoc* and unco-ordinated way than is usually the case with social policy. A series of historical accretions, reflecting different and sometimes contradictory policy intentions and changing fashions, have combined to produce a mass of anomalies. The result of this is to ensure that any attempt to remedy an injustice in one corner creates new ones in at least one other. During the course of the twentieth century we have moved from a position where the mass of ordinary people lived in privately rented dwellings to one where 51 per cent of the population live in homes which they own. In between these stages has been a varied history of rent control and more important, the dramatic rise and subsequently faltering progress of the council house. Rent control and council housing were probably the beginnings of modern "social policy" in housing. But they were not introduced as contributions towards an egalitarian society; rather, they were responses to war-time crises, desperate shortages or crying evils. Typically, throughout the inter-war period council houses were statutorily intended for "the working classes," yet nowhere was this term defined.

Unlike some other areas of social policy, housing received no major rationalisation from the post-war Labour Government. Aided by the need to grapple with the immense post-war shortages, that Government seemed to assume that henceforth the great mass of house-building for ordinary families would be in the form of council housing, and the long term aspiration for the privately rented sector was municipalisation. These ambitions were, of course, never fulfilled. Both major parties seem now to have settled for the continuing co-existence of the three sectors, and the major change since the Attlee Government left office has been the great increase in owner occupation. If the council house symbolised the post-war years, the privately owned dwelling has perhaps become the embodiment of the inegalitarian populism which has characterised our politics for the past two decades.

When Labour took office in 1964, the following were the main areas of inequality in housing:

1. There was a striking inequality in material housing standards. It has been estimated that at that time three million families were living in "slums, near slums on grossly overcrowded conditions" (MHLG, *The housing programme* 1965-70, Cmnd 2838, HMSO, 1965). In several respects, existing house building efforts and the use of Government finance were not being geared directly to meet these needs.

2. Only a minority of families in Britain had to bear the full market cost of their housing. However, the means by which households in different housing sectors were protected from bearing this cost bore no relation either to each other or to any criterion of reducing inequality or meeting needs.

3. Within the owner occupied sector, house buyers benefited from tax concessions which served a directly inegalitarian purpose; the higher one's income, the higher the concession.

4. The rents of council tenants were subsidised by both the Exchequer and local rate contributions, but the criteria for allocating subsidy both to individual authorities and to the tenants within them were so varied and anomalous that few principles of social justice can be observed in their operation. These anomalies were partly offset but partly intensified by the operation of rent rebate schemes.

5. While both owner occupiers and council tenants were protected from

their full housing costs by State finance, private tenants benefited, through rent controls, at the expense of their landlords alone. Partial rent decontrol had made more confused a system which was in any case based on no distinct criterion of providing aid where need existed. Further, landlords and their tenants suffered from certain tax disadvantages.

inequalities in housing conditions

It was the first of these inequalities which attracted most of the attention of the Labour Government when it first formulated its housing policy. Several of the anomalies in the operation of state subsidies in housing result from the fact that the major purpose of subsidies has been to get houses built in a period of prolonged shortage, rather than to subsidise rents according to criteria of need. Given this institutional structure, any Government which embarked on a course of trying to end the shortage by encouraging authorities to build houses was virtually bound to create new anomalies in the allocation of subsidy.

The Government's first contribution to this policy was the White Paper of 1965, which produced the figure of three million famlies in need and established the target of 500,000 houses a year by 1970 if the housing problem were to be resolved within "ten to fifteen years." We are here concerned with the implications of this policy for social equality alone. First, Labour planned a considerable expansion of building in the local authority sector which had declined considerably under the Conservatives, and which Labour restored to 50 per cent of total new housing (MHLG, *Housing statistics,* 19, 1970). In view of the many barriers which prevented low or moderate income families buying their own homes, this marked a movement towards removing inequalities in physical housing standards. Not only was the cost of owner occupation beyond the reach of many families, but various forms of discrimination tend

DISTRIBUTION OF HOUSHOLDS BY INCOME AND TENURE GROUP: 1968

| household income per annum | households with economically active heads | | | | households with economically inactive heads | | | |
| | privately rented | owner occupied dwellings | | | privately rented | owner occupied dwellings | | |
	local authority dwellings	unfurnished dwellings	owned with mortgage	owned outright	local authority dwellings	unfurnished dwellings	owned with mortgage	owned outright
£500	1	3	1	3	45	57	11	27
£500—	6	9		7	24	23	24	31
£800—	8	12	3	9	7	4	23	11
£1,000—	34	33	24	26	13	11	18	13
£1,500—	30	24	35	25	7	3	20	8
£2,100—	11	10	17	12	2	2	4	5
£2,600—	6	5	9	7	2			2
£3,400+	4	4	11	11	2	—		3
	100	100	100	100	100	100	100	100

to worsen the position of lower income groups. In 1961 L. Needleman estimated that something like 90 per cent of households could not afford to buy a *new* house out of income, taking account of interest rates, agents' and legal fees and similar ancillary costs ("A long-term view of housing," *National institute economic review,* November 1961). This is illustrated in the table on the previous page.

Several professions have access to housing finance at preferential rates of interest, and some firms provide a similar service for their senior staff. Building societies tend to make allowances for likely future growth in income when assessing for a mortgage an applicant in a profession, while they are most reluctant to take account of even stable overtime earnings of manual workers. In addition to these distinctions, house-buyers on higher incomes were at that time eligible for tax concessions which could not affect the position of a person on a lower income. Therefore, it is to council housing that families of lower-income workers have had to look for good quality accommodation. The table also indicates the low-income position of tenants in the private sector, where the bad housing conditions have been concentrated. It is therefore clear that, assuming existing institutional arrangements, an increase in local authority building would be required to assist the families in poor conditions in the private rented sector.

Within the local authority sector, Labour made an attempt to relate the building effort more closely to the existence of need. Priority areas were established on the basis of housing need; these included the whole of Greater London and 130 authorities in the rest of the country. These authorities were told to construct as many houses as their resources made possible, concentrating on the destruction of slums and the relief of overcrowding (see Fourth report of the Estimates Committee, *Housing subsidies* vol 1 para 24, October 1969).

STOCK OF DWELLINGS: BY CONDITION AND TENURE

	owner occupied	rented from public authority	other tenure	total
unfit	7.0%	1.9%	33.2%	11.7%
not unfit	93.0%	98.1%	66.8%	88.3%

source: *House condition survey, England and Wales,* 1967.

As an incentive to authorities to increase their building effort, subsidies were increased under the Housing Subsidies Act 1967. Instead of relating subsidy simply to the number of houses as in past, the new subsidies were aimed primarily at protecting authorities from increases in interest rates. There were additional subsidies for building on expensive sites, for building high rise flats, and so forth. Whereas under the previous Conservative legislation the Exchequer subsidy had been either £8 or £24 a house, under the 1967 Act subsidy had reached £110 a house (much higher in Greater London) by 1968-69 (*op cit,* para 86).

Finally, a variety of measures ranging from restrictions on office development in the London and Birmingham regions to means of improving efficiency in the construction industry were used in order to concentrate building resources on housing, both public and private sectors. Initially, these and other factors were sucessful—1967 and 1968 were record years for house building in Britain.

The ability of these measures to fulfil their purpose of ending bad housing conditions was vitiated by the following factors. First, of course, as 50 per cent of new building continued (outside Scotland) to be in the private sector, half the construction effort was not, in the short run, directly involved in meeting the problems in those areas defined as being in greatest need. In the long run, of course, any increase in house-building is likely to ameliorate the overall situation.

A second handicap was that, although the concept of priority areas made it possible to select the authorities in greatest need, there were few instruments available to ensure that these auhorities actually rehoused the families in the greatest need. Partly this was the fault of institutional arrangements. The only indicator most authorities have of need is their waiting list, which is simply a record of those people who have applied for housing. Beyond a general injunction to abate overcrowding and clear slums, authorities have little guidance on what needs they should be meeting. A more intractable difficulty arises in that there are genuinely conflicting criteria of need; for example, should a family which has lived many years in fairly poor conditions be rehoused before a family which has been in extremely poor conditions for a short time, or *vice versa*? (for a fuller discussion of this problem see *Council housing purposes, procedures and priorities,* ninth report of the Housing Management Sub-Committee of the Central Housing Advisory Committee (Cullingworth sub-committee) chs 1 and 7, 1969). Whatever decision an authority takes in such cases, it it bound to be criticised from one point of view. To this kind of dilemma there can be no solution, and a judgement as to whether or

NON-PARKER MORRIS (PM) STANDARD HOUSES WHICH COULD HAVE BEEN BUILT: ENGLAND AND WALES, 1964-69

year	approvals	% with PM standards	number with PM standards	extra number of non-PM houses possible
1964	143,461	14.2	20,371	4,074
1965	159,964	20.8	33,273	6,655
1966	169,489	40.2	68,135	13,627
1967	167,649	54.3	91,033	18,207
1968	151,502	94.5	143,075	28,615
1969	118,772	98.5	116,904	23,380
total	910,837	—	472,791	94,558

sources: MHLG, *Housing statistics,* 12, table 14; 18, table 15; (the cost of Parker Morris houses appear to be one-fifth more from *Housing statistics,* 3, p61. It is assumed here, therefore, that one-fifth more old houses than Parker Morris houses could have been built for the same money. This assumes that land prices would not rise as more are built, which biases the results upwards. But the exclusion of housing approved for 1964-67 with some Parker Morris standards biases the results downwards).

not a given policy is meeting needs is difficult indeed. Other inefficiencies in meeting need arise because authorities may exercise prejudices towards, for example, coloured people or families with poor financial or moral reputations (*op cit*, chs 3 and 4).

The ability of Labour's policy to meet need was further affected by another difficult decision on priorities, aggravated by the institutional anomalies of local authority housing finance. Labour decided to accept most of the recommendations of the Parker Morris Report (Central Housing Advisory Committee, *Houses for today and tomorrow*, 1961) for greatly improved space and amenity standards in new local authority dwellings. The construction of houses according to these standards has definitely brought within the reach of families on moderate incomes housing of a quality which would not otherwise be available to them. Further, the policy of building today at such advanced standards is expected to yield a return for future generations who will inherit a good stock of housing. However, the better the quality of new housing the fewer people can be rehoused. In the case of such a wide improvement in quality as that involved in the Parker Morris standards, the effect of this on total housing output can be significantly large, as is indicated by the table above.

This indicates a loss of 94,558 houses over the period 1964-69, which is about 10 per cent of the total local authority programme and means that about 300,000 people have not been re-housed who would otherwise have been re-housed. This is assuming that the saved resources could have been invested in the construction of additional new dwellings. If they had been devoted to a programme of improving existing houses, the additional number that could have been re-housed would have been greater still.

Furthermore, since council housing is subsidised, and since council tenants have overall higher incomes than private tenants while private rented accommodation is of generally poor quality, a considerable injustice is done to those remaining in the private sector. Their own re-housing is postponed while they, through rates and taxes, subsidise the rents of council tenants wealthier than themselves who are thereby enabled to occupy the high standard accommodation. However, the alternative policy, involving a reduction in the standards of council housing, could be criticised on a variety of grounds. This is a further striking instance of the virtual impossibility of conducting an egalitarian housing policy since the criteria of equality conflict.

Finally, the ability of the new housing programme to meet need was undermined by the collapse of the programme itself. Labour deserves credit for protecting the programme from the effects of economic crisis for a lengthy period. Even when the local authority building programme was cut by 15,000 in the post-devaluation statement of January 1968, the priority areas were exempted. But the higher interest rates eventually affected the overall level of local authority building, since in effect the Government imposed a limit on the extent of borrowing at the privileged rate of interest.

The Ministry identified as further causes of decline the hold-up caused by the Ronan Point disaster and the change in political control of many local authorities (MHLG, *Annual Report*, 1967-68). Although by no means all the Conservative councils which took control in 1967 and 1968 cut their local housing programmes, many of them did so.

The programme was in virtual collapse when, in 1969, the possibility of assistance from a new direction appeared. The White Paper *Old houses into new homes* (MHLG, Cmnd 3602, April 1968) had brought together the new evidence on housing conditions revealed in the House Condition Survey 1967 and the results of local experiments in an enlarged concept of housing improvement. It was proposed that many houses which it had previously been thought would need to be demolished could be brought to a satisfactory standard by extensive improvements. The Housing Act 1969 introduced new improvement grants, and the improvement programme was well under way when Labour left office. By September 1970 general improvement areas covering 23,254 dwellings had been declared, work having been completed on 683 dwellings (*Housing statistics,* 19, *op cit, table* 35).

This policy could have several implications for the housing problem, though as yet it is too early to assess its effects. Of course, local circumstances will affect the applicability of the new methods, but overall it involves considerably less disruption to people's lives than a policy of demolition and replacement. It should also involve major economies, and hence a more rapid solution to the continuing problem of inadequate housing.

One of us has attempted to compare the costs of actual improvements with those which must be reached by a programme of improvement if it is to be competitive with a policy of new building. The calculations are too complex and detailed to be given here, but will be found in M. H. Wolf, *Government housing policy* (unpublished B.Phil thesis, University of Oxford, 1971). In brief they indicate that in the great majority of cases a policy of improvement is likely to be more economic than one of new construction, particularly, as is usually the case with urban renewal, the new construction must be accompanied by demolition. Housing 40 to 60 years old will nearly always be worth preserving, and if a house is worth preserving at all it is worth keeping for a further 40 years. Although of course local conditions vary considerably, it would seem that, had calculations of this kind figured in housing policy in previous years, far more houses would have been improved rather than demolished and reconstructed, with, as a result, the country having a greater number of fit houses for the same investment. Certainly, the emphasis on scrapping and new building which dominated local authority housing until recently must have been extremely wasteful.

relations between the sectors

Assessing the amount of subsidies to the various tenure groups is an extremely complex business, and inevitably unsatisfactory. The different types of subsidy used in the various sectors are themselves a source of difficulty, but there exist additional problems. The theory is that a subsidy will represent the difference between the market price of a good and the price paid by an individual. This theory is, however, valid only for marginal changes. If the subsidy had changed all the prices operating in the market, it becomes much more difficult to assess. This is certainly the case with the non-taxation of imputed income, and with rent control. The second problem is that of the effect of a subsidy in one sector upon prices in another. In long-run equilibrium the cost of building new houses will determine the price, but the subsidy to a sector will change what people are willing to pay for the non-produced good location. Thus the subsidy to owner occupiers will change the price of land, which will affect prices in the other sectors, and, therefore, the subsidies received by those other sectors. The third problem is that of distinguishing between effects in the short and long run. If one introduced a subsidy for the purchase of goods whose supply is inelastic the first effect is that prices rise. The only people to benefit will be the original owners of the asset. In the long run, new housing will be produced, and this will determine the price of housing. The effect of the subsidy will be to allow some people who would not have purchased the goods previously to enjoy them. However, as the subsidy to housing also is a subsidy to the purchase of land, and since the quantity of that cannot be increased, the price will remain higher; a subsidy will have long run effects on prices as well as quantities. The fourth problem is that of deciding what the market price should be estimated at. Is the situation with no taxes, or with taxes, the point of reference? This question is very important, but it is not clear what the answer should be. What has been done in the following account is, broadly, to take as the base line the situation in the uncontrolled part of the private rented sector. The picture presented by this comparison must be one of the areas of government policy most riddled with anomaly and arbitrariness; and this confusion in the relationships between the housing sectors was an aspect of housing policy which did not figure on the agenda of the Labour Government at all. They did make attempts at improving the situation *within* each sector, but the only effect of the Government on inter-sector relations was perhaps to make the situation more intolerable, simply because during Labour's period of office the sums involved grew considerably.

For several years Labour writers on housing have pointed out that mortgagors of owner occupied property have enjoyed a "subsidy" through tax relief on mortage interest repayments (John Greve, *The housing problem*, Fabian research series 224, p33, 1961, D. A. Nevitt, *Housing taxation and subsidies*, 1966). Not only did this appear to be a hidden "subsidy" which was not taken into account when council house subsidies were examined, it was also (as was bound to be the case with an income tax allowance) a "subsidy" which gave most to the wealthy. However, until 1963 owner occupiers paid schedule A taxation based on their imputed earnings from rent. They were considerably under taxed, since this tax was based on a property valuation carried out in the 1930s, but it could be claimed that the mortgage interest relief was a legitimate allowance against such a tax. When schedule A tax was removed in 1963, the allowance was still granted, and thus became more obviously a "subsidy." But the final step in this direction was taken by the Labour Government when in the Budget of 1969 it abolished taxation allowances on all loan interest apart from house purchase. This left mortgage interest tax allowance as a policy measure to encourage owner occupation, and it has subsequently been acknowledged as such by the Treasury (Estimates Committee, *op cit*, Vol II, minutes of evidence, Q 5683).

The extent to which a mortgagor is protected from the market cost of his housing is therefore a complex matter. The only valid comparison can be with the position of a private tenant with an uncontrolled rent. Since the abolition of schedule A tax, private landlords have had to pay income tax on rent incomes under schedule D. They may, however, still claim tax allowance on mortgage interest. The basis of the owner occupier's protection from housing costs lies, therefore, not in the tax relief but mainly in the remission of schedule A tax. The introduction of capital gains tax added a new element to the owner occupier's privilege. The private landlord has to pay this tax when he sells a house, but owner occupiers are exempted from it. In recent years, therefore, owner occupation has become an extremely privileged form of investment, being subject to no taxation at all apart from rates. And of course the rates are a tax imposed on all types of tenure.

We estimate that a sum of around £727,000,000 is involved through owner occupiers not paying tax on imputed rental income or on capital gains. As is pointed out in the table below, which breaks down this subsidy by income

TAX BENEFITS TO OWNER OCCUPIERS BY HOUSEHOLD
INCOMES (ENGLAND AND WALES)

weekly income	under £10	£10-£15	£15-£20	£20-£25	£25-£30	£30-£35	£35-£40	£40+
numbers (1,000s)	675	572	747	1096	1128	1017	755	1954
annual benefit	£53	£62	£69	£77	£83	£90	£110	£129

source: M. H. Wolf, *Government housing policy* (unpublished) p94. The approximate nature of the evidence must be borne in mind. The distribution of owner occupiers by income is derived from the FES 1967, and of incomes by rateable values from the FES 1963. The latter are used to weight the proportions of the total benefit going to each income group, as benefits depend on the rental value of the dwelling. The total subsidy estimated at £727,000,000 is divided by weighted income group, and divided by the number in each group, which is estimated by applying the FES proportions to the 7,945,000 dwellings owner occupied in 1967. The result is an estimate of the benefit of not paying tax for each person by income. The result is too high for the first two groups who probably pay no tax. Similarly, the estimate for the highest group is probably an under-estimate, because of the number paying surtax. The figures should, therefore, be regarded very cautiously.

group, such a calculation rests on some very approximate estimates and assumptions. Nevertheless, in the absence of more precise figures it is the best assessment that can be made.

The subsidies received by council tenants are generally considered to have two sources, exchequer contributions and rate fund contributions. However, if we again compare the council tenant's position with that of the private tenant, the full extent of his protection from market cost is shown to be greater. Like the owner occupier, for example, the local authority does not pay income tax on rent earnings; whereas a private tenant's rent must reflect this tax payment by landlords, a council tenant's rent does not do so. The only valid point of comparison would therefore be between the rent which a council tenant actually pays and that which he would pay if his house were rented in a free market.

In 1967-68 the total rents of council houses were £299,366,524, and the ratio of rents to gross value was 1.01. Assuming the market rent of 1.7 gross value, and a tax of 0.325 (the standard rate on earned income), the value of the subsidy is £302,989,000. Attempts to assign council house subsidies by incomes are made impossible by the variation in council rent and rent rebate policies; however, it is possible to make a suggestive estimate based on averaging out the rent policies of the different authorities. The results of such a calculation, whose very approximate nature must be borne in mind, are given in the table below.

SUBSIDY TO COUNCIL HOUSE OCCUPANTS BY INCOME, 1967 (GREAT BRITAIN)

annual income	£500 or less	£500- £800	£800- £1,050	£1,050- £1,550	£1,550- £2,100	£2,600- £2,600	£2,100- £3,100	£3,100 and more	all house holds
mean rent	62	77	80	86	92	98	101	108	84
mean GV	72	85	86	92	95	103	106	111	90
subsidy	60	68	66	70	70	77	79	81	69
gross subsidy	76	100	98	105	103	115	118	120	103

sources: table on "Household incomes, rents and gross values" derived from FES by MHLG (unpublished). Subsidy is calculated by multiplying gross value by 1.7 (see A. G. Holmans, *A forecast of effective demand for housing in Great Britain in the 1970s; an account of sources and methods*, MHLG, unpublished) and subtracting rent. Tax is levied at 0.3275, except in the first income group, where it was 0.2.

The position of the private tenant himself is extremely varied. Many tenants still occupy dwellings with controlled rents at considerably below market values. Some of these will become "registered" rents under the Housing Act 1969. Many of those rents which were decontrolled by the Conservatives between 1957 and 1964 are now registered rents under the Rent Act 1965, and are thus set at levels somewhat higher than controlled rents but below market rents. Finally, some property is exempted entirely from control, either because it has a gross value higher than the limit covered by the 1965 Act, or because tenants are ignorant of, or afraid to use, their rights of registration. Meanwhile, the small number of furnished lettings are, rather inadequately, covered by a rent fixing machinery under separate legislation altogether. Unlike the owner occupier and the council tenant, the private tenant whose rent is in some respect less than market value is not receiving a subsidy from the general body of taxpayers, but from his landlord alone. This factor has, indirectly, been responsible for much of the tension there has been in relations between landlord and tenant in past years. In addition to this problem, the landlord suffers certain disadvantages at taxation. Reference has already been made to the landlord's liability for income tax on his rent earnings, a tax not borne by local authorities or council tenants. But he is also unable to claim a tax allowance for depreciation on his property. Since owner occupiers are also unable to make such claims, this does not represent a handicap in the private rented sector in comparison with other sectors. But it is a peculiarity suffered by investment in *residential* property alone in Britain, based on an antiquated assumption that residential property lasts for ever (Nevitt, *op cit*). This lack of a depreciation allowance has been one of the causes of the physical deterioration of much privately rented property.

In drawing attention to the varied and confusing ways in which different types of householder are protected from bearing the market cost of their housing, one is not necessarily advocating that people should bear such costs. However, if we seek to subsidise housing costs on social policy grounds, the difference between market cost and the price actually paid should be the result of deliberate acts of policy. A Labour Government presumably seeks to vary such subsidy with income, family circumstances and perhaps some other special criteria of need. At present, as is clear from the above, our structure fails entirely to do this, for a confusion of different mechanisms apply to different sectors, and the sector containing the poorest people in the worst housing gets the worst outcome.

It would presumably be possible to compute how these different "subsidies" have moved during the period Labour was in office, but although the figures might provide a useful debating point, they would have little real significance as a comment on what Labour did. For example, the amount of income tax revenue foregone under the continuing absence of schedule A will have risen because of the rise in gross values and in incomes. But this can hardly be classed as an "increase" in subsidy as the result of the actions of the Labour Government. More strikingly, this foregone revenue will have increased as a result of the increase in income tax rates. If we call this an increase in subsidy, we reach the paradoxical position where a government which reduced income tax rates on high incomes will be judged to have reduced housing inequality, because the amount of imputed schedule A tax foregone will thereby have fallen and the advantages of the owner occupier *vis-a-vis* the private tenant reduced. This latter point also applies to the popular but rather inaccurate comparison between owner occupiers' tax relief and council tenants' subsidies. If the former have increased, it is partly as a result of increases in tax rates. And the latter have risen because of the protection now given from rising interest rates.

It is therefore impossible to speak in simple terms of the actions of the Labour Government *vis-a-vis* inequalities of taxation and subsidy between the different housing sectors. Without massive changes in institutional structures, it would have been impossible for the Labour Government to proceed according to any criterion of overall equity. And here we encounter a further conflict of goals.

It is unlikely indeed that a government making such institutional reforms would at the same time be able to carry out the urgent and large scale change in the overall direction of housing activity which Labour had made its priority. In the short run, facing the institutional problem would probably have frustrated the house building programme, while in the long run the arrangements made necessary by the latter will only worsen the impact of the former's iniquities.

owner-occupation

Within each of the sectors of housing tenure it is possible to reach more precise conclusions. Within the sphere of owner occupation, Labour's policy had two major objectives relevant to the reduction of inequality. First, it sought to ease the cost of house purchase for low income house buyers, and second it sought to make access to home ownership available to some groups who could not previously afford it.

The White Paper *Help towards home ownership* (MHLG, Cmnd 3163, 1966) was the first official document to claim that the tax relief on mortgage interest represented assistance with the cost of house purchase, though it did not refer to the advantages conferred on the owner occupier by the abolition of schedule A. It went on to point out that householders whose income and family circumstances were such that they paid no income tax (or paid at less than standard rate) were unable to take advantage of this concession (or could only benefit partly from it). The White Paper therefore proposed the introduction of option mortgages, under which house buyers could forego any future tax relief on mortgage interest for which they may be eligible in exchange for a 2 per cent reduction in the interest rate, a subsidy roughly equivalent to the tax advantage of people paying tax at the standard rate. By mid 1970, 7 per cent of the mortgages granted by building societies and 12.6 per cent of those granted by local authorities were option mortgages (*Housing statistics*, 19, *op cit*, tables 46, 53). This measure remedied some of the injustice of the tax relief system at the point where it was most important. However, the general structure of the tax concession remains considerably inegalitarian, giving the most relief to those with the most incomes and smallest families but buying the biggest houses. The fact that the tax concession became officially regarded as a housing subsidy only makes the inequality more striking. Further, by introducing yet a new principle into reducing the cost of housing, the option mortgage scheme has made the structure of housing finance that much more anomalous and comprised of contradictory principles. However, it should be remembered that the true estimate of the owner occupier's tax relief consists of the remission of taxation on imputed rental income and capital gains, the effect of which on different income groups is sharply regressive.

Option mortgages, together with increased availability of 100 per cent mortgages, were part of the Labour Government's programme for improving access to home ownership. It is possible that the option mortgages were among the factors which led to the increase in private house building from 1966-68.

However, in the subsequent years, when house building was in decline, the only effect of a subsidy of this kind can have been markedly to increase the cost of housing. The history of 100 per cent mortgages is a sad one, since they declined overall during the period of Labour Government (*op cit*, table 53). The value of such a mortgage is that it enables people who cannot afford to save for a deposit to take on a mortgage; it thus helps those without capital to compete with those who have it.

These were Labour's main attempts to improve social equality within the field of home ownership. No action was taken over the preferential access to mortgages enjoyed by various professional and other groups to which reference was made above. The only improvement in the situation under Labour was therefore the extension of tax concessions to lower income house buyers through the option mortgage. But overall the full extent of the tax concessions from which owner occupiers benefited was not even fully comprehended by the policy makers.

local authority housing

If tax concessions among owner occupiers have had a directly inegalitarian effect, the allocation of council house subsidies has been simply riddled with anomaly. It is not even possible to draw accurate general conclusions on the extent to which the subsidies reduce or accentuate income inequalities, because their impact varies so much between local authorities. If one examines not only the formal subsidies but the full extent to which council tenants are protected from market rents, the situation would be yet more complex. Bearing in mind the limitations of the data mentioned above, the value of subsidy increases with income because of the higher gross value of accommodation inhabited by the more affluent. Its proportional value, however, declines with higher income. Nevertheless, it is clear that the benefits of subsidy do not all go to the poorest. Specific account is not taken of rent rebates because the family expenditure survey data would have already taken them out. It is clear that they make very little difference.

Within the formal subsidies, these variations are partly the result of a conflict of aims in housing policy, partly the product of historical anomaly, and partly the result of different policies by local authorities.

The first of these is the most intractable. The essential purpose of subsidies has been to encourage local authorities to build houses, not to subsidise rents, and a further purpose has been to ensure standards of accommodation. But of course the fact that they have the effect of subsidising rents is of considerable importance. This problem was a central one when Labour embarked on the expansion of local authority building in 1965, introducing the generous new subsidies in order to encourage authorities to build many more houses and to build them to Parker Morris standards. Whereas the early efforts at council house building had been carried out when most council tenants comprised society's poor, Labour was now extending increased subsidies to a group whose incomes were rather similar to those of the country as a whole, while the poorest members of the population were living in unsubsidised slums. Further, as the family expenditure survey of 1967 revealed, low income council tenants were spending a far higher proportion of their incomes on rent than both higher income council tenants and low income tenants in the private sector. Of local authority tenants with a head of household income of under £15 a week, 35 per cent paid more than one-fifth of their income in rent, whereas 77 per cent of those with weekly incomes of over £20 paid less than one-tenth of their income in rent. Tenants of local authority dwellings with incomes of below £15 a week paid a significantly larger proportion of their income in rent than did similar private tenants (Estimates Committee, *op cit*, para 126, and Vol III, appendix 27, evidence of IMTA). An additional problem was created by the high standards of the new housing; even when subsidised the rents of these new dwellings would often be beyond the reach of some potential tenants. The Government therefore decided to place a stronger emphasis on the use of rent rebates, and the 1965 White Paper encouraged local authorities to use their subsidies primarily to offset the housing burden of lower income tenants (*op cit*, Cmnd 2838, para 41).

Differential rents, usually in the form of rent rebates, had been the policy of central Government since 1956, but little had been done to secure uniformity or to ensure that individual authorities' schemes effectively met needs (see R. A. Parker, *The rents of council houses*, occasional papers in social administration, 22, ch 4, 1967). In 1967 the Labour Government issued a circular urging authorities to adopt and publicise rebate schemes and setting out a model plan (MIILG, Circular 46/67). There has been some response to the circular. The number of authorities adopting schemes grew from the two-fifths that it had been before publication of the circular to 53 per cent by March 1968 (MHLG, *Annual Report*, 1967-68). However, this does not necessarily mean that all these authorities had adopted the recommended Ministry scheme, though the Ministry "believed" that there was a "steady movement" towards adoption of its scheme (Estimates Committee, *op cit*, para 136). In fact, during the period 1967-68 only 16.2 per cent of the exchequer subsidy was spent on rebates; the £9.5 million total rebate went to over a quarter of a million tenants, representing nearly 12 per cent of the total housing stock (*op cit*). Since then the figures have probably improved, but it would appear that the effectiveness of rebates is still of limited significance.

But even if rebates have had some effect in reducing inequalities among tenants within individual authorities, there is no possibility of their meeting some overall criterion of distribution. The total amount of subsidy available to an individual authority is only partly based on its current housing needs, and not at all on the incomes and circumstances of its tenants. The major source of variation in authorities' receipt of exchequer subsidy is history; subsidies have been allocated on many different bases since they began after the first World War, and once a house has been subsidised under a particular Act of Parliament it continues to be so for sixty years. The subsidy received by an authority therefore depends on the legislation in force at the time that it built up its housing stock. The 1967 Act increased subsidies on new houses to such an extent that it is already the second biggest individual source of subsidy (the first being the Act of 1946), but its effect is not sufficient significantly to alter the overall distribution (*op cit*, para 6).

Finally, the extent to which the rent of an individual tenant is subsidised depends on the policy of the particular authority. In addition to the exchequer subsidy, councils may further subsidise their housing from the rate fund. Policy on this varies widely, some authorities making no contribution at all while others provide subsidies bigger than their income from rents (NBPI, *Increases in rents of local authority housing*, report 62, Cmnd 3604, para 12, 1968). There is considerable difference in policies between Scottish and English authorities. The NBPI found that all Scottish local authorities made a rate contribution, the average being 35 per cent of total costs (*op cit*, para 31). In England and Wales 38 per cent of authorities made no contribution at all; of the remainder more than half made a contribution of less than 5 per cent of total costs and one-third made a contribution of between 5 and 10 per cent. This is not simply a source of variety in the rents of council tenants; it also affects the relationship between council tenants and other ratepayers in an individual authority's area. When an authority, many of whose ratepayers are low income families in uncontrolled privately rented accommodation, makes a large rate subsidy to the housing revenue account, the private tenants are helping to pay the rents of council tenants who are better housed than themselves. This was for long an issue of controversy in Scotland (see R. D. Cramond, *Housing policy in Scotland 1919-1964,* University of Glasgow social and economic research studies papers 1, 1966).

There are further sources of variation in the principles local authorities use to establish rent levels. Since the cost of providing new housing is now much higher than in earlier years, the tenants of new housing are rarely expected to pay the full rent of their accommodation. The rent pooling system usually ensures that, in effect, the tenants of older property pay disproportionately more for their housing. They therefore "subsidise" the rents of occupants of new dwellings. However, attempts to end this injustice only serve to create another. Since, as a result of land costs, interest charges and Parker Morris standards, the cost of new houses has risen considerably in the last few years, several authorities have started to charge significantly higher rents for new dwellings. As a result a new and growing problem is emerging in council housing, that of people who cannot be re-housed because they cannot afford the rent. Where there are rebate schemes the problem is not so severe, although there have been cases of authorities refusing to extend their rebates to new property.

This question is considered in the report of the Estimates Committee (*op cit,* paras 126-130) and in the Cullingworth Report (*op cit,* paras 43-46). The latter concluded that the rent policies of a number of authorities were such as to constitute "an insurmountable barrier" to low income families. Concern was also expressed on this issue by the Seebohm Committee.

Two further important aspects of inequality between council tenants need to be noted. First, the system of council house allocation favours the immobile against the mobile. Apart from re-housing following demolition programmes, the main means of acquiring a council house is to remain on a waiting list for several years. It is therefore difficult for workers who, for various reasons, have had to move to different parts of the country, to obtain local authority housing.

Second, the structure of subsidies now in force introduces certain distortions into the allocation of subsidy between different parts of the country. Extra subsidy is granted for high-rise building and the purchase of particularly expensive sites. Both these subsidies favour the large urban areas of the South East and the West Midlands, especially the London area. This has the result that taxpayers in economically less favoured parts of the country subsidise the housing of those in the most prosperous areas.

It is evident that the present means of allocating subsidy to local authorities gives rise to increasing anomalies and injustices. Labour made a small start at unravelling the problem through the concept of priority areas and by encouraging rebate schemes. But, ironically, the very process of seeking an expanded building programme of council housing of particularly high quality has led to an intensification of several of the anomalies. The table below gives an indication of the kind of variation in rents for similar properties which this whole structure has produced.

VARIATIONS IN TYPICAL STANDARD RENTS FOR POST-WAR
THREE-BEDROOM HOUSES, OCTOBER 1967

lowest	lower quartile	medium	upper quartile	highest
s d	s d	s d	s d	s d
16 2	32 3	37 7	45 3	86 9

source: Institute of Municipal Treasurers and Accountants. Quoted in NBPI,
report 62, *Increases in rents of local authority housing*, Cmnd 3604, p5, 1968.

A final element of Labour housing policy affecting council rents was the
action taken on the report of the NBPI. For a period, as part of the prices and
incomes standstill, local authorities were not permitted to increase rents.
Thereafter, a limit was set on the extent of increases permitted. In part the
sudden move to increase council rents was the result of the large successes of
the Conservative Party in local elections in 1967 and 1968, but many of these
councils were able to produce reasonable cases for their increases. The
restraint was imposed for wider purposes of prices and incomes policy, not
because the increases were in themselves unjustified. The NBPI report lay stress
on the need for rent rebate schemes and proposed various means of rational-
ising the subsidy structure (*op cit*, para 85). The argument against increases in
council rents was not helped by the chaos of the present basis of allocation.

the privately rented sector

The privately rented sector was a further area of considerable activity under
the Labour Government, the cornerstone of the policy being the Rent Act
1965 (later consolidated with other legislation as the Rent Act 1968). The Act
was concerned partly with rent assessment and partly with security of tenure
and protection from harassment, and in the latter area was preceded by the
emergency Protection from Eviction Act 1964. This small Act did much to
stem the rising tide of homelessness, particularly in London, which had been
the direct consequence of the Conservative Rent Act of 1957.

From 1962-64 about 2,000 homeless families had been taken into welfare
accommodation each year in the LCC area. This dropped to 1,300 in 1965 and
1,500 in 1966 (MHLG, Annual report, 1965-66). In itself this restoration of
security of tenure must count as a contribution to social equality; it enabled
private tenants to enjoy something approaching that security possessed by
other types of occupier. However, in more recent years, the numbers of
people made homeless has begun to increase again (see DHSS, Annual reports).
Partly this is probably the result of landlords discovering more subtle means
of harassment, and an ironical source of a landlord's incentive to evict a
tenant has come through the increase in local authority slum clearance
activity. Authorities frequently offer such high prices for houses with vacant
possession when acquiring property prior to demolition that landlords will find
it worth while to defy provisions of the Rent Act.

A further development since the Rent Act which has had a number of
unfortunate side effects is the considerable growth in furnished as opposed to
unfurnished lettings (see *Report of committee on the rent act* (Francis Committee), Cmnd 4609 March 1971). Following the advice of the Milner Holland
Committee (*Report of the committee on housing in Greater London*, Cmnd

2605, 1965) the Rent Act did not extend the same security of tenure to furnished tenants. As a result many landlords now rent their property furnished, even though many of the families concerned would have preferred to use their own furniture. Whereas formerly furnished tenants were normally mobile people who did not expect to remain long in their accommodation (this was an important reason for their not being given full security of tenure), there are now many "reluctantly" furnished tenants. Unfortunately, local authorities frequently continue to regard furnished tenants as "mobile" (possibly implying "feckless") and in a few cases will not re-house them when slum clearing an area (Cullingworth report, *op cit*, table 10, p81). Although this problem only affects a small number of people, it is particularly disturbing since it results from two otherwise worthy acts of housing policy: the Rent Act and the council slum clearance programme. The Government became aware that certain loopholes may be vitiating the effect of the Rent Act, and established the Francis Committee to examine the problem. The committee reported after Labour had left office, and advocated no basic change in the position of furnished tenants on the grounds of its likely effect on the supply of furnished lettings.

The major part of the Rent Act concerned rent restriction. It sought to avoid the errors of both the rigid and unrealistic control of the pre-1957 period and also the disruption and exploitation which had followed the 1957 Act in the areas of housing stress in major cities (Milner Holland report, *op cit*, chs 7 and 8). The Act provided for a system of rent fixing between landlord and tenant under the supervision of a rent officer and with rights of appeal to a rent assessment panel. The general intention was to agree at a reasonable rent taking account of the state of the property, but not taking account of "scarcity." As such the Act probably provided a more reasonable means of settling rents than had existed since the first World War, but as a means of subsidising rents it left much to be desired. It failed to end the extraordinary situation where landlords are called upon to bear the full weight of the "subsidy" of their tenants' rents. It did nothing to change the unfair tax disadvantages of the private sector. And the notion of a "fair rent" involved in the Act bore no relation at all to the income and circumstances of the tenant, except in so far as the most expensive property was excluded from its provisions.

Somewhat surprisingly, perhaps, the overall effect of the Act has been to increase the level of rents. The following conclusions are some that can be drawn from the available data (*viz* MHLG, *Housing statistics*, 18 August 1970, tables vii and 60). First, we can assume that the tenants who have benefited from the Act are mainly those on very low incomes, since among properties of the smallest gross value rents have tended to be decreased by the rent assessment machinery. Second, there has been a tendency over time for an increasing proportion of registered rents to be increased. This may partly reflect inflation, but partly it may be a result of the third noteworthy point in that landlords have made greater use of the Act than tenants, *and increasingly so over the years*. This last fact is of considerable concern to the egalitarian, and is an important cause of the tendency for rents to be increased by the rent officers and assessment panels. It is the very familiar problem of the inability of the people in need to take advantage of legislation passed in their interest. This is not so much a housing inequality as that wider inequality at law which, whatever the formal rhetoric, pervades our legal system.

improvement grants and social security benefits

Two final sources of financial assistance towards housing costs need to be mentioned, though they are of minor importance in comparison with the major structure of the housing system as it has been outlined above. First, improvement grants have been available for several years from Government finance to enable an owner occupier or a private landlord to carry out certain specified improvements to his property. Similar facilities are also available to local authorities. Owner occupiers have taken advantage of these grants to a much fuller extent than landlords, even though the housing which would be eligible for such improvement is concentrated in the latter sector.

IMPROVEMENT GRANTS MADE 1965-69

year	owner occupiers	private landlords and housing associations
1965	60,282	28,718
1966	54,288	27,281
1967	58,664	29,298
1968	59,123	27,833
1969	56,653	26,800

source: Housing statistics, 19, *op cit*; based on tables 28, 29, 26.

There was a tendency for this disparity to decline under Labour, which may possibly reflect the publicity campaigns carried out by the Government. But the effect of improvement grants is inegalitarian in further ways than the simple inequality of uptake. An owner occupier not only receives an improved house but an appreciation in its capital value. The tenant of a local authority or a private landlord will never be able to gain an equivalent reward even on improvents which he carries out at his own expense. Further, a private landlord is entitled to increase his rent by a certain amount once he has carried out grant aided improvements. These inequalities are partly a reflection of the continuing conflict of goals in housing policy.

Improvement grants improve the general housing stock, which is in the common interest, and contribute to welfare, but it seems to be in the nature of the case that their uptake is inegalitarian in effect. Obviously, an owner occupier has an economic incentive to make use of a grant, while a private tenant has an economic incentive to persuade his landlord not to do so. As has been mentioned above, Labour's major initiative in the field of improvement grants was to introduce the concept of the general improvement area. So far it is too early to assess its effects, but it is likely, given the concentrations of below standard property, that it will involve the improvement of many more privately rented dwellings.

Finally, mention must be made of the assistance with rent which is available through the Department of Health and Social Security for tenants of both local authorities and private landlords eligible for supplementary benefit. In 1968-69, £446,000,000 was paid in supplementary benefit, of which perhaps a fifth can be assumed to have been for housing. There were 2,296,000 householders in receipt of benefit, of whom 385,000 were owner occupiers, 1,131,000 local authority tenants, and 780,000 private tenants. In addition some 392,000 non-householders received benefit, of whom a large number must have received the 11s per week supplement for rent, an annual rate of £29. If one subtracts from the total of £436,000,000 what seems to be the proportion going to non-householders, one is left with £389,000,000, of which £78,000,000 can be imputed to housing. Divided among all recipients, this gives an average of £34 per annum. This sum which goes entirely to the poor is quite substantial, but it does not compare with the other sources of subsidy discussed above.

conclusion

The factors which impeded Labour's efforts to reduce inequalities in housing included the continuing economic crisis; the difficulty of ensuring that measures of central policy have their intended impact in areas of chronic social need; the chaos of the means by which different tenure groups are protected from bearing the full cost of their housing; and the co-existence of inevitably conflicting goals of policy.

The first of these took its toll in the reductions enforced in the house building programme from January 1968 onwards, partly by direct Government decision and partly by the continuing increases in interest rates. Solutions for these wider economic problems obviously lie beyond the scope of housing policy which must, however, be dependent on them. The Labour Government had gone further than previous administrations in seeking to protect the housing programme from wider economic difficulties, partly by its general policy of safeguarding the spending programmes in the social sector, and partly by the reduction of interest rates for local authority house building provided in the Housing Subsidies Act 1967.

The most urgent issue remains now as it was in 1964: the urban areas of chronic need. The problem is one of low income families being forced, because of the location of employment, to live in crowded and unfit housing in central areas. In nearly every case these areas have records of poor landlord tenant relations. There is some hope for change in the policies for urban priority areas started when Labour was in office, and further alleviation may result from adoption of the various proposals which have been made for legal advice services in the areas of need. However, several of the points in the foregoing analysis of the housing problem lead to more radical proposals.

First, it must be recognised that the confusion of controlled, regulated, uncontrolled and uncontrollable rents in the private sector marks no final solution to the problems of this declining source of housing provision, nor does it represent a rational form of housing subsidy. Second, it is extremely unlikely that the private landlord will ever re-emerge as a major source of housing. The Labour Party is unlikely in the extreme to foster such a revival, and given modern rates of inflation it is unlikely that new resources can be attracted into rented housing which could be made available at rents which the poor can afford. Given present policies, therefore, the private landlord will continue his lingering death in circumstances which will have unfortunate consequences for his tenants.

This evidence points to the need for a more radical solution to the private sector, and further weighty evidence may be found in the arguments presented above on the relative cost of house improvement and new construction by local authorities. If the financial and political structure of local authorities' housing activities were so changed that it became their task to produce housing at or above a certain standard, whether by improvement or new construction, depending on what was the more economic in any given case, there would be an important change. There would be a considerable increase in the number of improvements carried out. But for local authorities to act in this way, they must obviously maintain the ownership of the houses improved so that they could receive the rent income. In other words, to argue that local authorities should be allowed to make a rational economic choice between house construction and house improvement is to argue for the gradual municipalisation of private rented property in poor condition. This is the first major area where new policy initiatives need to be made by the Labour Party in housing. Given the acceptance of such a policy of gradual local authority control of the private rented sector, the remaining parts of this sector would be luxury provision and a marginal provision by isolated landlords. In the latter case the sector would be of a size where a policy of rent subsidy for private tenants became manageable.

The problem of the overall chaos of subsidy in the owner occupied sector and local authority housing is less amenable to change. We cannot in the scope of this study spell out the details of an alternative policy. We can, however, stress an overall objective for Labour in this area, and raise some of the questions which will need to be faced by a detailed policy. In the face of the gross anomalies and injustices, and the massive size of the overall sums involved in existing forms of "subsidy," the major objective of egalitarian reform must be as follows: receipt of assistance with housing costs should be broadly related to income and family circumstances. This is not a question of selectivity versus universality, because housing is far from being a universal social service. Neither does allocation of subsidy on an income basis raise the problem normally associated with means tests; since such large numbers of owner occupiers and council tenants have become accustomed to receiving various kinds of assistance with their housing, it is not politically feasible to propose that subsidy be allocated solely to those in extreme need.

The principles of a system of housing allowances which allocate according to need but without the complexities of means testing have been set out by Della Nevitt in an earlier Fabian publication ("A national housing allowance scheme" in *Social services for all?*, Fabian Society 1969). The crucial issue concerns which existing benefits should be abolished in order to finance such a scheme. Miss Nevitt's proposals excluded consideration of the tax benefits enjoyed by wealthy owner occupiers, largely on grounds of political acceptability. But it must be remembered that the larger the scale of existing concessions withdrawn, the greater the scope and size of the housing allowance would be; and that it is the concessions to owner occupiers which are the most regressive and anti-egalitarian. The boldest (and most radically egalitarian) plan would be to re-impose schedule A tax, tax local authority rent income and instruct local authorities to charge replacement cost rents. This would make possible a generous system of housing allowances. Less radical schemes would tackle only the owner occupiers' mortgage interest relief and not re-impose schedule A tax, while also not taxing local authorities' rent income. The political decision on the precise nature of the reform would depend on the balance desired between certain important variables. These include the concern of a government for avoiding controversial tax changes as compared with its interest in reducing inequality and decreasing market distortion; and the appropriate balance to be struck in the public sector between encouraging the production of certain kinds of dwellings and the subsidising of the rents of individual families. All we can do here is to indicate the implications of a policy which would reduce inequality, and to remind those who are reluctant to make radical changes in taxation or introduce an element of means testing that they do so at the expense of the poorest and the worst housed.

chronology

December 1964	Protection from Eviction Act.
April 1965	Publicity campaign for housing improvements launched.
July 1965	Postponement of plans for specially favourable interest rates for owner occupiers; and reduction in the volume of local authority loans for house purchase.
November 1965	Publication of national housing plan, with adoption of target of 500,000 houses a year by 1970 and introduction of priority area concept.
December 1965	Rent Act 1965 in operation.
April 1967	Publication of new standards for local authority housing, based on Parker Morris report.
May 1967	Housing Subsidies Act 1967.
June 1967	Publication of house condition survey, indicating scope for house improvement.
June 1967	MHLG Circular 46/67 on rent rebate schemes.
October 1967	Leasehold Reform Act.
December 1967	Over 400,000 houses completed in Britain for first time.
January 1968	Cuts in housing programme announced as part of post-devaluation measures.
April 1968	Option mortgage scheme and mortgage guarantee scheme in operation. Publication of White Paper *Old houses into new homes*. Restrictions imposed on public and private sector rent increases under Prices and Incomes Act 1968.
July 1968	Restrictions imposed on local authorities' rights to sell council houses.
December 1968	Another record year for house construction (over 413,000).
July 1969	Housing Act 1969 (new plans for improvements).
December 1969	House construction drops to below 370,000.

4. inequalities in health

Nicholas Bosanquet

In some of its enterprises, the Labour Government met total success—in others, total failure. But no single clear cut judgement fits to its work for the NHS. It was a story of promising initiatives not quite carried through, bold spending decisions which achieved less than they might, new procedures which seemed uncannily like the old ones, advocacy for the weak yet suppression of criticism—some wasted years and some glowing hope. Ideally the Labour record in the NHS should be reviewed from the point of view of patients. We want to know about the "outputs" of the service in terms of better health. In practice this method poses many difficulties. It may be possible to measure the quantity of output—in terms of numbers of patients treated in hospital or of visits to General Practitioners. But it is difficult to assess its quality. Nor do we have the detailed epidemiological information, by region and by social class which would be needed to assess changes in inequality of outputs. We have therefore to fall back on a less satisfactory method of assessing movements in inequality. This is to look at changes in "inputs"—in levels of spending and of staffing in different regions and types of hospital. Such comparisons form a large part of this paper. But to be useful they have to be preceded by a look at the setting of pressures and priorities within which decisions were taken.

priorities in care

An assessment of Labour policies has to begin by an assessment of the needs. Needs in 1964 were rather different from needs in 1950. Between 1950 and 1964 certain great advances were made in care. New drugs and inoculations had almost eliminated deaths from diptheria, pneumonia, tuberculosis and poliomyelitis. But most of the improvements—associated with the new antibiotics—were concentrated in the early 1950s. By 1960 progress had become slower—and more expensive. At the same time, certain types of affliction were increasing in scale—many of them arising directly or indirectly from social change. Vehicle accidents contributed an increased quota, as did certain chronic and degenerative diseases such as heart disease and diabetes. The number of diabetics in 1948 was some 100,000—today the figure is estimated at about one million, (Prof. W. J. H. Butterfield, "Changing medical needs," NHS *Twentieth anniversary conference report* p16) although better or more careful ascertainment—as well as a higher incidence—has probably contributed to this increase. Some forms of cancer and heart trouble appeared to be related to certain habits and life styles. Along with the ills of affluence, mental illness and mental handicap could also make insistent and plausible demands for more resources. Finally, community surveys showed that the prevalence rates of certain types of chronic ailment were much larger than the treatment rates. For example, the number of treated cases of rheumatoid arthritis among males over 45 was 230 per 1,000 in 1962; the total number of treated and untreated cases was estimated at 520 (Butterfield, *op cit*, p17).

What deductions for planning and policy follow from this heterogeneous evidence? First, the hope of advances in research and advanced technology remains, but the era of new discoveries achieved at a relatively low cost appeared to be over. The natural instinct of much of the medical profession was to concentrate resources on such research. One important job for a Labour minister was to make sure that some practical gains were being made for patients from the march of science. Secondly, there was clearly a need to develop research, treatment and rehabilitation for patients suffering from chronic physical diseases. Better physiotherapy for stroke patients might be less dramatic than a transplant unit—but both could do a great deal to save life and to raise its quality. Thirdly, it was not obvious why, in a supposedly civilised society, mental illness and mental handicap should command such low levels of resources, compared with physical illness. Here was one vital test for policy. Fourthly, evidence on the increasing scale of preventable disease suggested the need for much greater effort to be put into preventive health—including improvements in the environment and in opportunities for recreation. Finally, the evidence on latent and chronic illnesses both pointed to a need to strengthen community based care by the family doctor and the Local Authority Services. It suggested that the balance between care in and out of hospitals was a vital issue in health planning.

Against this background of changes in priorities we can define the tests of success for a Labour government and the time over which we could reasonably expect results. What could we expect from six years of Labour rule? Clearly, we could not expect long standing regional inequalities to be eliminated completely in that time—for there to be the same standard of medical care in Grimsby or Norwich as in Central London or Bristol. Nor could we expect standards in the care of the mentally ill and handicapped to reach those set in the care of the physically ill. But we could at a minimum expect that a Labour government would have the following five achievements to its credit.

1. The real resources available to the service should have shown a consistent and substantial increase over the Labour period in office..

2. Methods of planning and control should have been improved as to ensure that these scarce additional resources were put to most effective use.

3. Realistically funded and carefully worked out plans had been put in hand to raise standards of care where they were most deficient by region, type of hospital and social class.

4. Measures had been taken both to ensure standards of fairness in pay and conditions to staff working in the Service and to improve staffing structures and efficiency.

5. The voice of the consumer was more heard in the service. A proper complaints procedure had been introduced.

No overriding political obstacles stood between a Labour Government and these achievements. The NHS entered little into the general run of politics. Firm action carried few electoral hazards. Weightier political obstacles were perhaps to be found within the Service in the discontent of the medical profession. But as both the successful resolution of the conflict over the family doctor service in 1966 and the *annus mirabilis* of hectic activity at the end of the Government's period in office showed, the support of the professions could be won by a firm lead.

health service spending and financing

Since the 1890s, there have been three periods in which the share of social service spending in national income has risen significantly—1914-18, the 1940s and the 1960s. The pattern has been one of sudden displacements in spending levels rather than of steady growth. The NHS share in GNP at current prices rose from 3.86 per cent in 1964 to 4.70 per cent in 1969, showing a similar rise to that of education and of social security spending. These developments were a contrast to the position under the Conservative administration. Between 1950 and 1955 health spending as a proportion of GNP at current prices fell from 4.07 to 3.40 per cent. From then on it rose slowly but in 1964 at 3.86 per cent it was still below the share in 1950.

The test of aggregate spending was certainly one for which the Labour Government awarded itself very high marks indeed, at first sight with some justification. Mr Crossman, in the Commons on 1 July 1969, spoke of an "enormous expansion" in spending (*Hansard*, 1 July 1969, col 254). But the record in detail appears less impressive. The figures for current spending on staff and supplies, which amount to 90 per cent of total spending have weaknesses as measures of real inputs. They do not take account of improvements in technical efficiency or in the quality of labour. Nevertheless, they provide a rough guide to the levels of additional real resources becoming available to the Service.

These figures from *National Income and Expenditure* tell a clear story, of rapidly rising spending in the two years 1964 and 1965 and of quite moderate increases in other years both before and after. Thus, between 1963 and 1969 the increase in real current spending was £188 million (*National income and expenditure* 1970, table 4). But £90 million or about half of the increase came in the two years 1964 and 1965. Should these years be counted as Labour years or Conservative years? When the Government took office in October 1964, budgets for the financial year April 1965 would have been in an advanced state of preparation. It would have been very difficult, even if the Government had desired to do so, to change spending plans. Thus the real Labour years, the years over which the Government had a full measure of discretion, run from 1966 to 1969. Over this period, the additional real current resources available to the Service fell year by year. In 1966 the NHS had £38 million extra, in 1967 £32 million, in 1968 £21 million—and in 1969 £7 million. This record is hardly one of sustained "enormous expansion".

For the capital programme the pattern of increase was rather different and more sustained. The main reason why the health share of GNP was so small under the Conservatives was that little was being done to renew the capital stock. Before 1962 hardly one major building project was begun in any part of the NHS. Between July 1948 and December 1966 only 28 health centres were opened. In the following three years 98 were opened and at 31 December 1969 79 further centres were under construction and another 74 had been approved (DHSS, *Annual Report* 1969, p 193 HMSO Cmnd 4462). Before the 1962 Hospital Plan no new hospitals were under way. By 1963-1964 the Conservative Government had begun to repair this omission. The hospital building programme was not initiated by the Labour Government. But it became the major priority of the Labour years together with investment in new health centres. The rate of increase of real current spending on average under Conservative and Labour administrations was much the same. Current spending in real terms increased by 2.44 per cent a year on average between 1959 and 1964, and by 2.71 per cent a year between 1964 and 1969. The Labour Government did not raise equally all types of spending. It introduced a major capital programme, which was maintained until the end, while keeping a tight hold on current spending.

This pattern of spending in the late 1960s means considerable difficulties for the early 1970s. The capital programme is now running at 8 per cent of current spending compared to 5 per cent in 1961. In 1968 current spending in real terms rose by only 1.86 per cent but in 1969 this modest increase was reduced to a real increase of 0.6 per cent. Current spending in real terms was virtually static at a time when many new beds and much new equipment was being commissioned. As Mr Crossman rightly said before leaving office, one of the major problems was "how to ensure that we have enough revenue to operate the capital equipment that we have produced" (*Hansard* 1 July 1969, col 254). Some capital investment is labour saving but most is not. It creates a demand for more staff to man more complex equipment. The same pattern of heavy capital investment and relatively slow increase in current spending was found in the family doctor service. The increasing number of health centres built or projected during the Labour years has already been referred to. The number of GPs fell slightly between 1964 and 1969 and consequently the average list size rose by 4.9 per cent.

In the local authority sector NHS spending rose by 65 per cent from 1964-1969—much the same increase as in the hospital sector (*National income and expenditure* 1970, tables 41-42). But capital investment was cut back here after 1967. As part of the cuts in public expenditure in January 1968, there was in the words of the Ministry's annual report for 1967 a "reduction in the planned growth of health and welfare capital expenditure amounting in Great Britain as a whole to an average of £5 million a year over the three years 1968-69 to 1970-71 (Ministry of Health *Annual Report 1967* p17, HMSO, Cmnd 3702). The result was that loan sanctions (apart from spending on health centres) showed a fall for England in 1969-70 over 1968-69 as shown in the table on the next page. The local authority sector bore the brunt of the cuts.

Local authority provision was on a smaller scale than provision by the hospital service. In 1968 there were 8,140 places in hostels for the mentally ill or handicapped compared with 181, 187 occupied beds in these types of hospital (DHSS, *Digest of health statistics, 1970*, tables 10.7, 10.8 and 10.12).

LOAN SANCTIONS RECOMMENDED FOR ENGLISH LOCAL HEALTH AND WELFARE CAPITAL WORKS PROJECTS IN £ MILLIONS*

welfare	1967-68	1968-69	1969-70
residential accomodation under National Assistance Act	13.20	13.50	12.60
other National Assistance Act Services	0.84	0.98	0.96
health			
training centres for the mentally sub-normal	3.80	3.90	3.70
residential accommodation for the mentally disordered	1.80	1.50	1.60
ambulance stations and vehicles	1.10	0.87	0.90
clinics and health centres	2.80	3.80	5.30
nurses and midwives accommodation	0.33	0.27	0.20
other services	0.61	1.00	0.66
total	24.50	25.90	26.00

* the figures do not include the cost of capital works (for which the latest available estimates are about £7.2 million in 1967-68, £7.4 million in 1968-69 and £7.9 million in 1969-70) financed by means other than loan sanctions recommended by the Department or capital expenditure on health and welfare schemes approved under the Government's Urban Programme.
source: DHSS, *Annual report 1969*, table 32, HMSO, Cmnd 4462.

But at least provision of hostel places had doubled between 1964 and 1968. In other respects the improvements were less clear. Thus visits by district nurses to the under 65 age group hardly rose between 1964 and 1969 (*op cit*, table 6: 2). In general the bias in spending was towards the hospital service. The Labour Government left three major problems in expenditure and financing unresolved. It did not succeed in establishing criteria for setting the level of aggregate expenditure on health. The need for such criteria can best be seen by looking at the comparative rates of increase of health spending relative to education since 1950. In 1950 the Government spent £7.3 (at current prices) per capita on education in the UK and £9.4 per capita on health: by 1964 the priorities were reversed; per capita spending on education (again at current prices) was £29.1 and on health £20.9. By 1969 the figures were £41.9 per capita on education and £32.6 per capita on health (*National Income and Expenditure* 1970, table 49, and 1961, table 44, and Annual Abstracts of Statistics). Most of the increase in educational spending reflected improved provision rather than demographic factors. There is still a significant real increase when the figures are calculated for each head of the population under 21. Three main factors were responsible for this switch in priorities. First, demographic and political pressures operate much more strongly to push up spending on education and on social security than they do on health. Secondly, productivity gains have clearly been much greater in the NHS than in education. Thirdly, the overall spending decision in health does not emerge from any coherent framework of choice between competing projects nor is the output to be obtained from extra spending clearly measurable.

From one point of view, health is in competition with the economy as a whole for additional resources; from another it is in competition with the other social services. Certainly until 1964 it was seriously deprived even compared with the other social services. The balance here, which emerges from the overall balance of spending, has a wider significance for social justice. Spending on education, particularly spending on higher education, helps the young and mobile. There are powerful lobbies for it. Within the NHS some pressures operate to push up spending on the acutely ill. But spending on the chronic sick, the mentally ill and handicapped has few powerful advocates, while it benefits some weak groups in the community.

The aggregate spending decisions of the Labour Government appeared to reflect three sets of factors: the general rate of increase of social service spending, the exigencies of the hospital building programme and the influence of immediate crises such as the doctor shortage. Little attempt appeared to be made to weigh up at the margin the costs and benefits of various forms of additional spending. This represented a failure to introduce a more reasoned sense of priorities into health spending.

The Government left partially unsolved the financing problem of the Service. The balance in financing at the beginning and end of the Labour period is set out in the table below.

NHS SOURCES OF FINANCE AS PERCENTAGES OF TOTAL (GREAT BRITAIN)

	1964-65	1968-69
taxation	69.1	72.7
NHS contribution	13.0	10.1
charges (national)	4.4	2.6
rates (estimated)	5.6	5.5
rate subsidy (estimated)	5.8	6.9
charges (local authority)	1.8	1.9
miscellaneous	0.3	0.4

source: DHSS, *Digest of health statistics*, 1970, table 2.2 (adjusted).

Central government services are financed from taxation, NHS contributions and charges. Each has its particular difficulties. Finance from general taxation is progressive but involves fierce competition with the other social services. The NHS contribution is ear marked revenue, but on a flat rate basis is a highly regressive tax. Charges are also regressive as effective exemption arrangements are difficult and they also lead to distortions in the pattern of care. In general the balance in financing became much more progressive during the Labour years. This is to the credit of the Government. General taxation contributed a higher proportion of finance in 1969 than in 1964. But this change carried with it the difficulty that the NHS has less ear marked revenue available to it.

For the local authority services the balance in financing swung away from the rates towards central government support. Charges remained an important source of revenue—relatively much more important than for central government services—and particularly so on the welfare side.

Labour ministers attempted, particularly in a debate on NHS financing in July

1969 (*Hansard*, 1 July 1969), to define the main financing problem. The then Secretary of State for Social Services saw it basically as one of a lack of buoyancy in the revenue in face of the spending possibilities created by new technology and latent or induced demand. The remedy in the long term, Mr. Crossman suggested, might be a progressive NHS contribution partly financed by employers. But the new pensions scheme was thought to prevent implementation of this until the mid-1970s. Thus in the short term the NHS had no buoyant source of revenue available to it apart from general taxation.

It is hard to quarrel with this analysis—that the service was likely to become even more dependent on general taxation. But it is difficult to see why this should in itself be more of a problem for the NHS than for the other social services which were becoming similarly dependent. Over the two previous decades the NHS has made much smaller incremental claims than the other social services. Its productivity record was good. Yet an aura of crisis in finance seemed always to hang over the NHS and not over the other services. One possible reason for this has already been mentioned—that the overall expenditure was so loosely linked to measured outputs or any coherent framework of project choice. This gave ministers the feeling of being faced with huge bills for nebulous purposes. It might have been a better approach to state more clearly and adamantly the reasons why the Service would have to continue to be financed out of general taxation and to improve the planning framework so that expenditure could more clearly be seen to be related to specific improvements in care. By this approach the general financing problem becomes not one of lack of buoyancy in the revenue, but one of an inadequate budgetary system tending to produce high levels of anxiety among politicians, civil servants and voters.

The local authority services raised specific financing problems which were never fully faced. Between 1964 and 1969 the general rate subsidy element in local authority finance grew from 82 per cent of total rate revenue to 113 per cent (*National income and expenditure 1970*, table 41). Yet in spite of increased support from central government, local authorities were slow to develop their services. The issue of lack of buoyancy in revenue presented itself in a much more acute form here than in the hospital services. The local authority service had no national standards and was in part locally financed. Responsibility was diffused and the consequences of this for some people in need were very serious.

methods of planning and control

In administrative change the Labour Government's record can be summed up as one of little progress on fundamentals but some useful progress on secondary issues. Thus the Government left office without having unified the Service but having sponsored some useful changes in, for example, the way nursing work is organised, the role of the Health Education Council and the ways in which the central department deals with suppliers and with the drug companies. Administrative change is not a frill—it is an essential step towards improving the quality of care and planning for the future. It was a tragedy for the Service that reform was held up for so long, in waiting for local government reform particularly as there were few dissenting voices on the need for it. The main features of the administrative structure as set up by Aneurin Bevan, and as developed during the 1950s, were that separate authorities controlled the three branches of the service (the hospital, local authority and general practitioner services); that control of the Hospital Service was divided between the Ministry of Health, the over large Regional Hospital Boards and the over small Hospital Management Committees, and finally that the Ministry of Health was to be weak. The powers of the central department even within the Hospital Service were obscure. Even when asked, it was not in practice willing to give a strong lead, before the 1960s. One particular example of its style was over the minor, but, in practice naggingly controversial, question of the role of the Medical Superintendent in psychiatric hospitals. For a number of years in the 1950s, the Department was being pressed to give a ruling. In 1960 it finally produced one. The circular read: "As and when a Superintendent post becomes vacant, it will be for the Hospital Authorities to decide whether or not the Hospital should continue to be administered by a Superintendent, and if one is appointed what his precise duties should be." (Pauline Morris, *Put Away*, pp56-57).

By the middle 1960s issues were arising, such as the future role of the family doctor, which were very difficult to resolve within the old tripartite system. At the same time the scale of the hospital building programme was forcing the Department to adopt a more active role. By the end of the 1960s the unsatisfactory state of the local authority sector added powerfully to the case for reform. Local authorities have increasingly fallen down on their obligations towards old people. Between 1959 and 1969, the number of people over 65 in local authority residential accommodation in England and Wales rose 44 per cent from 71,412 to 102, 985 (DHSS *Digest of health statistics*, 1970, table 7.3). Between 1959 and 1969 the number of available and occupied beds in England and Wales in geriatric hospitals doubled. The average number occupied daily rose from 16,000 to 34,700. The numbers of cases treated more than doubled, from 65,800 to 143,600, as the average length of stay fell (DHSS *Digest of health statistics*, 1970, table 4.9). In many areas it was a matter of chance whether old people in need of help were put in local authority accommodation in a geriatric hospital or in a psychiatric hospital. But the chances of their being sent into the geriatric hospital rose overall.

The swing to the hospitals resulted in part from lack of planning in the local authority sector. The long term plan for this sector was simply a compilation of the plans of individual authorities. A revised edition of this was published in June 1966. Authorities started with widely differing levels of provision and had different plans for the future. The Ministry of Health's Annual Report for 1966 spoke only of exhortation as a means of dealing with these anomalies: "There were wide variations between the levels of services planned by different authorities and it was expected that in the light of these variations some authorities would think it necessary to revise their plans. . . . Where the provision of a service of particular authorities appeared to be substantially below an adequate level and likely to remain so over the whole period covered by their plans, the Minister subsequently drew this to the attention of the authorities concerned." (*Annual report of the Ministry of Health 1966*, pp19-20, HMSO, Cmnd 3326).

The effectiveness of these measures is not recorded. But certainly the lack of planning contributed to the limp pace of development. A change in methods of planning and financing local authority health and welfare was urgently needed. But none was forthcoming from the Labour Government. Instead there was the strange spectacle of two totally different plans for reorganisation following each other in quick succession.

The failure to set up a comprehensive NHS was crucial for the local authority services. It also implied that there was no major change in the powers of the central department. Such a change was an important recommendation of the second Green Paper. This gave important decisions that "Certain functions which are at present performed by Regional Hospital Boards will in future be performed by the central department—particularly the programming, planning and execution of major building schemes. . . . The central department will also play a more active role in manpower planning and training" (*The future structure of the National Health Service*, pp24-25 HMSO 1970). This desperately needed change was still in the air in June 1970. But while in office, the Government did adopt several piecemeal changes which strengthened the department's hand. It set up stronger central and regional organisations for bulk purchase of hospital supplies. As the Hunt Committee (NHS *Report of the committee on hospital supplies organisation*) had shown, hospital supply practice was oddly decentralised compared with that of the most efficient commercial organisations. Following the Sainsbury Report on the drug industry (*Report of the committee of enquiry into the relationship of the pharmaceutical industry with the NHS 1965-67*, HMSO, Cmnd 3410), the methods by which the department monitored costs, profits and the quality of drugs were re-organised, even though the committee's advice on how this should be done was largely ignored. The department itself was to negotiate with the manufacturers on cost, while an independent medicines commission was set up to monitor quality. The Sainsbury Report presented clear evidence to suggest that the voluntary price regulation schemes set up by Conservative governments had been failures. It concluded that the "figures suggest that the cost (of drugs) to the NHS has been inflated by excessive prices to the extent of several millions of pounds over this period of three years" (1963-65) (*op cit*, p38). The report also revealed deficiencies in the quality of drugs. Two separate expert panels of six members each classified 2,657 preparations. Of the 2,241 preparations on which the two panels were able to agree, 35 per cent were classified as undesirable preparations (*op cit*, pp208-9).

Another innovation which affected the central department was that of the Hospital Advisory Service set up after the Ely scandal in 1969. This was an organisation which sent teams of experts to visit hospitals and then reported directly to the Secretary of State. This service was designed to give policymakers a more realistic and detailed picture of what was going on than was available through normal channels. The need for such a parallel structure was in itself a worrying sign of inadequacy. Such a service could not be a substitute for more basic reform. But, immediately, it was a hopeful sign that the Department was willing to give a stronger lead.

As well as the general administrative structure a main area of change, or perhaps of talk about change, was in the internal administration of medical and nursing work. On the medical side little progress was made in implementing the "Cogwheel" Report (*First report of the joint working party on the organisation of medical work in hospitals*, HMSO 1967). But on the nursing side a more serious attempt was made to introduce the recommendations of the "Salmon" Report (*Report of the committee on senior nursing staff structure*, HMSO 1966). Under the old system there was no clear centre of responsibility for nursing at group level nor had nurse administrators above the ward sister level had clearly defined jobs. The Salmon Report provided for a clearer hierarchy and more definite roles for senior nurses.

The administrative work of the Labour Government can be faulted in three main ways. First, change came desperately slowly and the first four years in office were largely lost time. Secondly, there was a failure to give adequate support to the "Cogwheel" reforms. There was growing, if impressionistic, evidence of conflict between the doctor's role as a clinician taking personal responsibility for patients and his role as the initiator of action by large teams of people—nurses, laboratory technicians and the professionals supplementary to medicine. Without supplanting the ethic of personal responsibility, there appeared to be a good deal of room for improvement in how work was organised in hospitals. Even such simple matters as the legibility of prescriptions appeared to require some fresh thought. Many people in the medical profession were waiting for the department, and its professional advisers, to give a strong lead in these matters. It never came.

Finally the Government failed to rethink the role of lay participation in the running of the service. Nominally Regional Hospital Boards and Boards of Governors, with substantial lay representation, were the agents of the Secretary of State in the running of the Service. Hospital Management Committee members were selected by the Regional Hospital Boards. The Second Green Paper appeared to accept the criticism that these bodies were undemocratic and "that many hospital authorities are in practice controlled by self-perpetuating oligarchies" (*op cit*, p8). But it did not question their role. There was a clear need for some proper research into the role of these committees in the face of impressionistic evidence that it varied from the nebulous to the pernicious. They could have a pernicious effect in inhibiting the development of proper professional management or in interfering in clinical matters which were beyond their competence. More often, perhaps, their role was nebulous. Pauline Morris in *Put away* records of one Hospital Management Committee that it was "largely passive . . . Most members remained completely silent throughout the meetings attended by the research worker" (*op cit*, p213). The idea that lay members could play a directorial role was on the face of it an odd one. Nor could such committees be an adequate substitute for a proper complaints system both for patients and for staff. When Labour left office the ombudsman system for patients' complaints was on the way, rather belatedly, but had not yet arrived. A more hopeful role for such committees might have been as organisers of voluntary help and of community interest, leaving local control to the professionals and overall control to the normal processes of parliamentary democracy.

inequalities between types of hospital

Differences in cost per case or cost per week between hospitals can arise from a number of different causes: differences in the mix of cases treated, in the efficiency and suitability of buildings and fixed plant or in the level of resources and the quality of care. Over many years there have been two main types of cost difference which have caused concern—between different types of general hospital and between hospitals for the physically ill and those for the mentally ill or handicapped.

There are substantial differences in cost per case not only between teaching and non-teaching acute hospitals, but much more surprisingly between London and provincial teaching hospitals. Between teaching and non-teaching hospitals these differences reflect both the more complex types of cases treated by teaching hospitals and the additional costs involved in the teaching role. Between London and provincial teaching hospitals they would partly seem to reflect an extra degree of professional influence on the part of the London teaching hospitals. The comparative costs are shown in the table below.

COST PER CASE IN ACUTE HOSPITALS			
type of hospital	1960-61	1964-65	1968-69
London—teaching	£88.85	£103.49	£131.09
provincial—teaching	£61.28	£76.12	£96.83
non-teaching	£53.62	£61.15	£76.25
ratio London teaching to provincial	1.45	1.36	1.35
ratio London teaching to non-teaching	1.66	1.69	1.72

source: DHSS, *Digest of health statistics*, 1970, table 2.9.

The gap between the provincial and London teaching hospitals narrowed significantly, as a result of deliberate policy, during the last four years of Conservative rule, but did not further narrow under Labour, whereas the gap between London teaching hospitals and non-teaching acute hospitals has been widening throughout the decade. Of course, such simple figures only indicate a problem. Policies for re-allocation could only follow from a much deeper study of the reasons for cost differences and of a variety of different measures of cost difference. But it would be fair criticism that the Labour Government neither made such a study, nor began to develop such a policy.

The Labour Government's work for the mentally ill, the mentally handicapped and the chronic sick fell into two parts: five years of neglect followed by an *annus mirabilis* of hectic activity. Relative costs per week were unchanged up till 1968-69 as between these hospitals and hospitals for the physically ill. These figures are not available outside the acute hospitals on a per case basis but only on a per week basis.

Such figures are crude but telling indicators of whether the Government allocated relatively more resources to hospitals outside the acute sector. The pattern of care can be traced for each type of hospital. In hospitals for the mentally ill, the number of beds fell, between 1964 and 1968, from 168,000 to 155,000 (DHSS *Digest of health statistics* 1970, table 4.2). The occupancy rate fell from 81 to 79 per cent, with more rapid turnover the

COST PER IN-PATIENT PER WEEK

type of hospital	1960-61	% of acute	1964-65	% of acute	1968-69	% of acute
acute	£27.85		£35.72		£49.38	
chronic	£11.71	42	£15.47	43	£21.18	43
mental illness	£8.37	30	£11.30	32	£16.07	32
mental handicap	£7.48	27	£9.88	28	£13.49	27

source: DHSS, *Digest of health statistics 1970*, table 2.9.

number of cases treated rose by 13.3 per cent. Medical staffing per occupied bed improved. But the numbers of doctors in these hospitals grew rather more slowly than overall. Numbers of doctors (in WTE's) specialising in mental illness rose by 13.5 per cent, while in general they rose by 19.9 per cent, over the years 1964-68 (DHSS *Digest of health statistics* 1969, table 3.4). There was certainly a rise in the medical time available and improvements in drugs may also have improved the effectiveness of treatment. But it was still worrying that numbers of doctors grew less rapidly than overall, given the deficiencies at the beginning of the period. Not all the responsibility for this rests with the Government. If doctors by their choice of speciality have voted with their feet against certain types of hospital, it becomes extremely difficult to improve staffing in them.

The quality of nursing staff in hospitals for the mentally ill and handicapped can be assessed both in terms of the quality of initial recruits and of changes in the balance of the nursing force between trained, semi-trained and untrained grades. A minimum educational standard for entry was introduced only in 1966. In 1969-70 24.5 per cent of entrants to psychiatric nursing had some "O" levels compared to 58 per cent of entrants to general nursing (GNC, *Annual Report 1969-70*, p8). Between 1964 and 1969 staff with an SRN and a Registered Mental Nurse qualification fell from 40 to 37 per cent as a proportion of the nursing force in psychiatric hospitals (DHSS, *Digest of health statistics 1970*, table 3.13). This was when the job of nurses in these hospitals was changing rapidly. They were increasingly involved in active rehabilitation of patients, including such tasks as leading group therapy sessions. There were also major discrepancies in staffing levels between psychiatric hospitals in different regions.

In the care of the mentally ill there were, however, some hopeful developments. Some new units with higher staffing levels were opened within district general hospitals. In the last year of the Labour Government planning started for new pilot projects in community care in Worcester and in Sheffield. But the picture for the care of the chronic sick was one of almost unmitigated gloom, nor, until the last year in office, was the picture much brighter for the mentally handicapped. In 1963 there were 206 doctors (in whole time equivalents) working in hospitals for the handicapped and in 1969 there were 201. This was a ratio of about one doctor to 300 patients. Nor were nursing staff either abundant or in a good state of morale.

Poor living conditions, the lack of serious attempts at rehabilitation and the social isolation of patients are the three most important characteristics of hospitals for the mentally handicapped. The effect of life in these institutions is to reinforce handicap not to alleviate it. Pauline Morris has shown how many aspects of life in these hospitals contribute to the destruction of personal identity. Patients are herded in large and crowded wards. At the time of her survey in 1965-66, 69 per cent of patients were in dormitories with less than two feet between the beds (Pauline Morris, *Put Away*, p 86). Only 21 per cent of adults had personal shaving or washing kit (*op cit*, pp 43-4) and the majority of children had no toys of their own. 42.7 per cent of patients had not been visited in the past year (*op cit*, p 198).

During its first years in office the Labour Government showed little awareness of these problems. In the light of the need, it was a most odd decision to cut loan sanctions for building local authority training centres for the handicapped and residential accommodation for the mentally ill. Spending in 1968-69 was below its 1967-68 level, both for hostels and for training centres. After the Ely scandal, Regional Hospital Boards were persuaded to divert £2 million to long stay hospitals for 1969-70. But this simply went, in many cases, towards catching up on routine maintenance, providing temporary accommodation for the worst over crowding and to raising dietary standards. The Labour Government left office with its long term policy for the mentally handicapped still awaited.

inequalities between regions

In 1967—to take the extremes—a person needing hospital treatment had a much greater chance of getting it if he lived in the Liverpool Region than if he lived in the Sheffield Region. There were about 120 cases treated per 1,000 population in Liverpool compared with 80 in Sheffield (DHSS, *Digest of health statistics 1969*, table 4.7). There were disparities both within and between regions in the provision of hospital beds, of medical and nursing staff, and in the size of GP's lists. Regions that were weak in one type of care tended to be weak in all. How far did the disparities lessen during the Labour Government's period of office?

It is, first, hard to make a judgment on disparities within regions—those between towns and HMC areas. NHS planning has not developed to the stage that local black spots can be identified with any confidence. The NHS lacks any system for designating priority areas, such as has existed in the education service since the Plowden Report. But the levelling up of standards between regions has for many years been a proclaimed objective of policy.

Success in reaching this objective can best be tested by looking at three sets of figures—those for each region's percentage shares of total current and capital spending, and those for current spending on a per capita basis shown in the table below. The table shows a rather ambiguous picture. On a per capita basis current spending in the four less favoured regions showed a faster rate of increase than the avarage. But the differences were not great. For example spending in the most backward region—Sheffield—rose 46.6 per cent compared to a 47 per cent increase in the more highly favoured Metropolitan Board areas. The figures also suggest that there was some redistribution both of capital and of current spending. Three of the four poorest Boards gained in current spending. In capital spending the only apparent loser of the four—

REGIONAL HOSPITAL BOARD PERCENTAGE SHARES IN TOTAL
AND PER CAPITA SPENDING

	current %			capital %			per capita £		
region	1964 -65	1969 -70	% change	1963 -65	1968 -70	% change	1964 -65	1969 -70	% inc
Newcastle	5.85	5.69	−2.73	6.48	4.49	−30.71	10.65	15.44	44.9
Leeds	6.29	6.34	+0.79	9.82	5.71	−41.85	11.10	16.52	48.8
Sheffield*	7.2	7.23	+0.42	6.88	8.32	+20.93	8.92	13.08	46.6
East Anglia*	2.69	2.87	+6.69	3.26	5.22	+60.12	9.31	13.88	49.1
Metropolitan†	37.11	36.79	−2.32	32.18	32.19	+0.03	14.59	21.45	47.0
Oxford	3.41	3.62	+6.16	5.15	4.57	−11.26	10.85	15.70	44.7
South Western	6.40	6.25	−2.34	5.36	6.87	+28.17	11.98	16.84	40.6
Birmingham*	8.57	8.77	+2.33	10.19	8.11	−20.41	9.70	14.32	47.6
Manchester*	8.35	8.30	−0.60	6.63	8.32	+25.49	10.34	15.27	47.7
Liverpool	5.05	4.93	−2.38	3.67	5.35	+45.77	12.70	18.29	44.0
Wessex	3.47	3.53	+1.73	3.38	3.56	+5.32	10.46	14.94	42.8
Wales	5.60	5.68	+1.43	6.95	7.29	+4.89	11.67	17.50	50.0
total average	100	100	—	100	100	—	11.02	16.10	46.2

* worst off regions.
† London undergraduate and post graduate hospital expenditure is included
with these figures for the four metropolitan boards. Provincial teaching hospital expenditure has been included in appropriate regions.
sources: DHSS.

the Birmingham Region—had a 38.1 increase in share between 1960 and
1964. The figures suggest that the distribution of resources between Regions
showed a small improvement. It is not of course possible to say in the existing
state of knowledge, what distribution would be optimal.

Less sensible was the distribution of large new hospital building projects
towards the end of the Labour term of office. The last DHSS Annual Report
gives the location of large schemes in progress. The Report suggests that
about 40 per cent of the work was going on in the London area. Of work
to a total value of £247.2 million on large schemes, £90 million was being
carried out within a twenty minute journey of central London. The concentration of large new projects in the London area included the rebuilding of Guy's,
Charing Cross and St Thomas'—and new District General Hospitals at North-
wick Park and Greenwich. This method of presentation does exaggerate the
concentration on London, This is because most of the projects in London
are large and will stay on the books for a number of years while smaller
provincial projects will be finished and replaced by others. Nor is it easy
to say what extra amount of new building would be justified by the special
teaching responsibilities of hospitals in central London. But even with these
provisos, a difficult problem of staffing so many new hospitals in Central
London seemed likely to emerge in the early 1970s. The position—taken
together with the overall pattern of spending on the hospital as against the
GP and Local Authority services—seemed also to reflect a certain bias in
decision making within the NHS. Resources seemed to be more available for
the more advanced types of hospital based medicine for strengthening the
family doctor service. But the most immediate implications of the location

of large schemes were for the future regional pattern. Would the tendency to greater regional equality be reversed? Would there be a drift to the South East? These were unanswered questions when the Government left office.

inequalities between classes

Part of the punishment of being poor is to have on average poorer health and lower life expectancy. Class differences in opportunities for life and health start at the cradle and continue through the lifespan. In 1964-65 the incidence of infant deaths was more than half as high again in the two lowest social classes as in the two highest social classes (38.0 and 24.5 per 1000 respectively) (I. Gough, "Poverty and health a review article" *Social and Economic Administration*, vol 4, no 3, July 1970).

The rates for the upper classes have shown a steeper fall since 1949. Poor children have lower nutritional standards and a higher proportion are short for their age. When the children grow up and enter employment they have higher morbidity rates. In 1961-62 28 per cent of all men recorded at least one spell of sickness of four days or more. But for the highest social classes the proportion was 18 per cent and in the lowest 35 per cent. Men in this social class are, for example, more prone to bronchitis and have fewer and worse teeth than those in higher social classes. The incidence of mental illness is strikingly higher in the lower social groups. In retirement unskilled workers are more likely to be severely disabled (*op cit*, pp213-214).

Although the evidence on differing standards of health between social classes is quite clear, it is not so clear whether standards of health *care* differ so markedly. Poorer health reflects generally poorer living conditions as well as possibly poorer standards of medical care. Martin Rein has pointed out that patients in Classes IV and V do consult their doctors—according to surveys both in 1952 and in 1964—more frequently than those in the higher social classes (M. Rein, *Social Class and the Utilization of Medical Care in Hospitals*, JAHA, July 1 1969, p6). The evidence on inequalities in care in the maternity services is perhaps clearer than that for the family doctor service. Women in the lower social classes at the time of the last survey in the late 1950s were less likely to have had an early examination after becoming pregnant. M. Feldstein showed for 1961 that mothers with high risk in the lower social classes were often not being confined in hospital (M. Feldstein, *Economic analysis for health service efficiency*, chapter 8).

Certainly there was no easy solution to these problems. But the Labour Government seemed to show little awareness that there were problems at all—that at least constant vigilance was needed to ensure that the NHS was truly national. The only exception was the use made of money under the urban programme to start day nurseries in deprived areas. But there was a need to go beyond this and to find new ways of improving the health of the poor and of their children.

staff pay and conditions

The NHS has over many years imposed conditions and made demands on many of its staff which few commercial employers would ever have dared to make. It could be argued that this followed the logic of the market. But in most civilised communities considerations of equity count in setting public sector pay. One test for a Labour government was whether it managed to improve conditions, pay and career structures for staff.

The Government inherited a major crisis in medical manpower and in medical morale which affected both GPs and hospital doctors. The greatest success was recorded in dealing with the crisis in the family doctor services. By 1969 retention of UK born GPs had improved (*Review body on doctors' and dentists' remuneration, twelfth report*, p 17, HMSO, Cmnd 4352). Changes in the payment system and conditions of work of family doctors—the GPs Charter—had been effective. The picture in the hospital sector was less happy. The Government increased the intake to medical schools and in 1969 cut down on the intake of Commonwealth doctors. But the proportion of UK born doctors in the registrar grade still fell—from 55.1 to 44.5 per cent between 1964 and 1969 (DHSS, *Digest of health statistics 1970*, table 3.9). Nor was much progress made towards reforming the antiquated career structure in which young hospital doctors found themselves trapped. There was a clear shortage of senior posts and too many able doctors were spending too long in nominally training grades. More careers advice to young doctors was also needed. In general the period saw, for the medical profession, a change from open crisis to uneasy balance. The emigration rate, in relation to the numbers of doctors qualifying, appeared to be well down on the 1950s and early 1960s. The hospitals were still heavily dependent on immigrant doctors. Without access to third world labour markets, the NHS would have had to restrict its activities considerably. But a dangerous slide in manpower and morale had been arrested.

Some progress was also made in improving conditions for nursing staff particularly as a result of the NBPIs report on nurses' pay published in 1968 (*Pay of nurses and midwives in the* NHS, Report 60, HMSO, Cmnd 3585). This introduced a much more substantial pay lead for nurses in psychiatric and geriatric hospitals, and also for the first time premium rates for night and weekend work. But these rates, at time and a tenth for nights and at time and a quarter for weekends, were still much below those found elsewhere in the economy. Nurses still worked 42 hours a week *exclusive* of mealbreaks while the average hours of other women workers were about 42 *inclusive* of mealbreaks. Thus even in 1970 nurses were still working 47 hours a week, more than half a day longer than other women in the working population. Between 1965 and 1969 the rate of increase of nurses' pay fell far behind those prevailing in the rest of the economy. Parity in rates of increase was only restored by the catching up increase of 1970.

A high proportion both of manual and non-manual men in the NHS are low paid. At the time of the September 1968 earnings survey, 29.3 per cent of men covered by the NHS ancillary staffs council were earning less than £15 a week—a proportion exceeded only under two other collective agreements (*Department of Employment and Productivity Gazette*, June 1969, table 23). The NHS had the highest proportion of any industry of non-manual workers earning less than £15 a week—11.8 per cent. Some progress was made in raising the pay of manual workers through incentive schemes. Here again the NBPI was the catalyst of change. But in general the NHS maintained its reputation of being a notoriously low wage employer.

Much needed improvements were however made in the pay of the junior hospital doctors. Between 1959 and and 1970 while earnings levels of manual workers rose 75 per cent, the salaries of house officers more than trebled and those of registrars more than doubled. Most of the relative improvement—as for the nurses—came in the 1970 settlements.

A weakness in the Labour record was its lack of any policy for improving industrial relations in the NHS. In spite of the statutory obligation to consult jointly there was certainly room for improvement. There are no effective industrial relations—in the sense of joint discussion and regulation of the main issues affecting people's working lives—in most hospitals. The Whitley system and divisions between professional and non-professional groups both contributed to this position. Without abandoning the principle of central pay determination, there was, and is, a great need to develop effective local industrial relations and grievance procedures in the NHS.

Finally,—the fifth of the five tests for a Labour Government: little progress was made either towards giving the consumer more voice in the running of the service or towards an effective complaints system. The Government left office without having set up a hospital ombudsman nor had much been done to make the NHS more responsive to the needs of people in local communities.

conclusions—and a pattern for the future

How does the Labour record stand? The Labour Government was clearly more successful in dealing with the inherited problems than with meeting the changing demands. Its main achievement was to shore up the NHS against imminent collapse. It was willing to put more resources into the Service. It built some new hospitals and Health Centres and did something to improve staff conditions. But it did not manage to improve the way in which decisions are taken within the Service, nor the methods by which priorities are set. Thus the question of balance between community care including general practice and hospital provision was not fully faced. Nor were mental illness and mental handicap given a relatively greater share of the Service's growing resources. Nor were the services much improved for people suffering from chronic physical ailment or from the crippling aftermath of strokes, although for the old some progress was made in setting up geriatric day hospitals. Finally, it cannot be said that much progress was made in ensuring that decisions on research and on the distribution of specialist resources were more openly arrived at. In general, the Government did not score well on the five main tests set out earlier. The real resources available showed some increase—but not a sustained one over the Labour period in office. Work to improve planning methods only began at the end of the term in office. Some efforts were made to reduce inequalities in standards of care—but they amounted to no more than a very small beginning. Finally, the Government hardly got to grips with the manpower or consumer problems of the service.

For a future Labour government the main priority is already predictable: to set in motion consistent and realistic plans which over a period of a decade can put an end to the two standards of care within the NHS. It is often said that a larger private sector would introduce two standards of care within the

NHS but it would be more correct to say that it would introduce three. We already have two standards, in that the resources available for the mentally ill, the handicapped, the elderly, the chronic sick or even the temporarily disabled, are of quite a different order than those available for the physically ill. For some groups—autistic children—virtually no provision is made at all. It is greatly to the credit of the Labour Government or rather to that of its Secretary of State for Social Services and his junior ministers, that the issue was so sharply posed during the last year in office. But even in that year the size of the problem was not fully set out.

To provide a decent health service outside the field of physical illness, would take first of all substantial increases in expenditure. But in addition to money it would be necessary to plan imaginatively for changes in recruitment standards, training and staffing for people working in these fields. At present there is a desperate shortage of remedial staff of any kind in these hospitals.

Thus there are only 166 speech therapists in the entire Hospital Service, and in 1966 there were only about 60 social workers—nine of them trained—between the 60,000 patients in hospitals for the handicapped. Poor use is often made of such staff. Compared to physical medicine the work lacks a research base. There is little known about the relative value of different methods of care and treatment in bringing about recovery. Thus much more than money is needed to bring about an improvement in these services.

Following from the basic priority the first problem is that of finance. An earnings related contribution from employees would help here, together with a larger employer's contribution. But in general there is no option but to continue financing the service mainly out of general taxation.

The second problem is that of improving the planning and cost-effectiveness of the Service. At present the balance between Local Authority and hospital services is virtually unplanned. There is evidence that the hospitals have been doing jobs which the Local Authority services ought to be doing. There is also a need for long-term planning in the NHS to ensure that among other goals more progress is made towards reducing inequalities within and between regions. The DHSS could learn a great deal here from the Ministry of Defence. Part of the benefit of such planning is that it would force a clearer definition of objectives and of priorities in care.

Thirdly there is a great need to rethink both manpower planning and the relationship between different professional groups all of which are concerned with the patient. At present each group tends to work in its own small compartment, and its future is planned almost without reference to that of other groups, or to any standards for an overall balance of manpower. The Todd report on medical education was the classic example of such blinkered planning. There is a need for new initiatives at all levels—for more shared experiences in training, for better liaison and mutual understanding in work, and for better manpower planning at the centre. The NHS's greatest investment is not in bricks and mortar, but in the time and energy of people with many different skills. It needs to make much better use of this investment not least by rethinking the pattern of staff relations in the Health Service.

October 1964	Appointment of Kenneth Robinson as Minister of Health.
February 1965	Prescription charge of 2s per prescription abolished.
February 1965	Review Body on Doctors and Dentists Remuneration submits a report recommending an increase of 10 per cent for family doctors. This compares to the profession's claim for 30 per cent. Unrest among GPs. Doctor's organisations submit a *Charter for the family doctor service.* Collection begins of undated notices of resignation from the Health Service. Discussions follow on the new charter.
July 1965	Local Authorities asked to prepare revised plans for the long term development of their services.
February 1966	Government sets up a stronger Health Education Council.
May 1966	Government makes final proposals for changes in the conditions of service of doctors. The Review Body also publishes its pay proposals. In *June* these are provisionally accepted by the profession. The new terms are introduced from 1 October 1966 although the increase is staged.
May 1966	Revised hospital building programme published.
June 1966	Revised plan for local authority services published.
June 1967	NHS (Family Planning) Act receives the royal assent.
September 1967	The Sainsbury report on the drug industry published.
October 1967	Abortion Act 1967 reaches the statute book.
	General Practice Finance Corporation set up.
January 1968	Hospital building programme uncut.
April 1968	Report of the Royal Commission on Medical Education published.
June 1968	Prescription charges of 2s 6d an item introduced.
July 1968	First Green Paper introduced. It proposes a single tier system with 40 or 50 area authorities.
July 1968	Publication of the Seebohm Report.
July 1968	White Paper dealing with "Sans Everything" allegations published.
July 1968	Urban programme introduced to deal with areas of special social need.
October 1968	Appointment of R. H. S. Crossman as Secretary of State for a new Department of Health and Social Security, combining the functions of the former ministries.
March 1969	Ely Hospital Report published. Regional Hospital Boards asked to divert £2 million to long stay patients in 1969-70.
March 1969	Hospital Advisory Service established.
February 1970	Second Green Paper published. It proposes setting up smaller authorities based on populations of 200,000 to 1.3 million.
February 1970	Local Authority Social Service Bill introduced to implement main recommendations of the Seebohm Report.

5. inequality and the personal social services

Muriel Brown

The welfare or personal social services are not often or easily discussed in terms of their impact on inequality. This is primarily because they have been traditionally directed towards minority groups with special needs, such as the old, the disabled or deprived children. When social services such as education or health are considered we are conscious that they effect the whole population, directly or indirectly, and we can more readily acknowledge their potential for intensifying or reducing inequality. Personal welfare services have tended to be seen as an attempt to counteract the individual's 'natural' inequalities, for example the handicaps imposed by physical disabilities, rather than as a means of influencing socially determined inequalities. They have, therefore, been regarded to some extent as peripheral, affecting only minorities and politically non-controversial. It has been assumed that there is consensus that society should care for the neglected child, visit the lonely old person and rehabilitate the disabled since such compassion befits a sensitive and civilised society but does not threaten to change the ordering of it. There might be disagreements on the best methods employed but not on the underlying principle of help to those with special need.

It is arguable, however, that this approach is no longer valid: the personal social services are now as vital to the community as a whole as the basic social services and they effect the whole population not merely the more obviously handicapped groups within it. The personal social services are increasingly and rightly involved with the socially disadvantaged as well as with the emotionally or physically disabled. Indeed, it is now acknowledged that the extent to which a given disability actually handicaps a person is primarily socially determined. Moreover insofar as the services are increasingly concerned with the overall quality of life they have an obvious contribution to make to the entire population in, for example, improving social cohesion and promoting integrated and meaningful communities.

Our whole concept of personal welfare has in fact radically altered over the last twenty years. It has altered from a concept of several minority oriented, institution-based casualty services towards a concept of a unified, preventive, promotional, community-based service which must, logically, be as comprehensive in provision and universal in scope as, for example, the health service. This change is the direct outcome of the policy decisions implemented in the postwar reconstruction years and developed subsequently in the light of increasing awareness of social needs. Because an appreciation of this change is central to an understanding of the role of the personal social services in combating inequality it would be useful to look more closely at the development of social policy in this field over the whole post war period before turning to a more detailed examination of the record of the Labour government from 1964–1969.

Although there were many differences of detailed principle among the various post war acts which established the "welfare state" it is fair to say that there was one common implicit assumption: that the state should be concerned to provide a service for all who needed it regardless of the recipient's income level. This principle of universality, or selection only by category of need and not by class or income level, is fundamental to socialism. It was stated with clarity in the 1940 National Health Service Act and the 1945 Family Allowance Act, was present despite the distortion of the insurance principle in the 1946 National Insurance Act based on the Beveridge Plan, was barely noticeable in housing legislation and coexisted precariously with selective methods in other social service schemes. The belief that universal social services are a prerequisite of a more cohesive and egalitarian society has been argued elsewhere. It is only mentioned here because it is not often argued in the context of personal welfare services. But despite the initially attractive proposition that directing help to those who need it most would be the simplest way of combating inequalities, ultimately it is only possible to promote a meaningful equality in a society that does not categorise, and discriminate between, the rich and the poor in its social provision. Indeed, insofar as the personal social services are often directed towards groups who suffer some stigma from disabilities or deviance it is doubly important that the further stigma of means tested services should be avoided and the principle of general availability be emphasised. A universal approach carries with it the implication that concern will widen from narrowly defined minority groups to the general community and the emphasis shift from casualty and rescue work towards preventive and promotional welfare. Only in a climate in which such positive concepts thrive can one hope that society will learn to abandon discrimination and move on from mere compensatory welfare to a genuine commitment to the improvement of the quality of community life.

Because the principles underlying a social service will influence its development and objectives it is important to note that the personal welfare services created or redefined in 1948 alongside the basic provision contained some element of universality. The Children Act of 1948 made it clear that it was the duty of the local authority to receive into care any child who was without parents or whose parents could not for any reason care for him, if it was in the interest of the welfare of the child (The Children Act 1948, section 1). This contrasts sharply with the poor law principle that only the destitute should receive public care.

In the National Assistance Act of 1948 there was considerable confusion of principle and the main impetus of this legislative ragbag was the negative one of destroying the poor law. In part III of the Act, however, provision was made for several groups for whom public assistance committees had exercised responsibility or for whom little or no statutory provision had previously existed. In section 21 local authorities were given a duty to provide "residential accommodation for persons who by reason of age, infirmity or any other circumstances are in need of care and attention which is otherwise not available to them." Subsequent circulars were quite explicit in their insistence that such accommodation, to be provided in small informal homes more akin to private residential hotels than institutions, was to be available to all who needed care, regardless of income.

In section 29 of the National Assistance Act local authorities were given a power, to be converted to a duty at the discretion of the Minister of Health, to promote the welfare of the physically handicapped. In the setting out of the various powers and duties which would do this the emphasis was clearly on the needs of *all* disabled people to receive help and information.

Finally the social needs of the mentally handicapped were to be the responsibility of local authority mental health departments and these, being part of the National Health Service, were to direct their assistance to all the people who needed it without consideration of ability to pay.

This brief resumé of legislation concerned with personal welfare shows that the principle of universality was as implicit here as in the major social provisions of the post war reconstruction. The major developments in policy, in regard to children, the old and the handicapped which took place during the 1950s and 1960s were all concerned with a growing disillusionment with institutional provision, an emphasis on prevention and a gradual movement towards community care. The implications of these trends in all fields were a continuing demand for more and better trained staff, especially social workers; of growing confusion over the boundaries of administrative responsibility; and steadily increasing costs as the services reached more and more people. These trends and their implications are directly linked to the universality of the legislative framework, although naturally they reflect other influences, for example the views of professional social workers about the need for prevention or the practical problems of staffing institutions. A closer look at the development of services for one group, the aged, will make this clearer.

development of social welfare for the aged

In 1948 the legislation did not reflect any comprehensive consideration of the needs and problems of the elderly in our society. The financial problems of retirement were tackled in the social security reforms and the need for medical care was catered for by the creation of the National Health Service. But the general problems of ageing, such as growing physical and emotional dependence, were not widely acknowledged. The provisions of the National Assistance Act disregarded existing evidence of widespread neglect and loneliness amongst the elderly and merely gave local authorities a duty to provide residential accommodation for the minority in need of care and attention not otherwise available to them. It also empowered the authorities to grant aid voluntary bodies concerned with the provision of meals or recreation facilities. But in the event the general availability of residential care resulted in a growing demand for it. Local welfare departments were restricted in their building programmes and forced to make unhappy choices between the competing priorities of emptying the old institutions and coping with increasing waiting lists. Inevitably they turned towards the possibility of providing more help on a domiciliary basis to alleviate the needs of those awaiting admission to homes.

Gradually services for old people in their own homes were introduced and seen as a positive alternative to residential provision rather than as mere stop gap measures. At first welfare departments relied heavily on voluntary bodies, using the services of the Local Old Peoples' Welfare Committees to arrange friendly visiting and the Red Cross and WRVS for the provision of mobile meals. Another important source of domiciliary care, possibly the most important one, was the local health department providing the home help and home nursing service. Gradually the welfare departments acquired more social work staff to make contact with old people and assess their needs. The efforts of the welfare departments varied widely, but they achieved increasing recognition. Following the Younghusband Report of 1959 training courses for social workers in the health and welfare field were established, and in-service training encouraged. The 1962 Amendment Act gave local authorities the power to provide meals and recreational facilities directly and many took advantage of this to be more imaginative in the provision of such services. The 1963 "Community Care Plan." (*Health and welfare: the development of community care*, HMSO, cmnd 1973) gave official sanction to a policy in which the need for residential care was no longer to be considered the first priority: services that would enable old people to live independently in their own homes were now regarded as most vital. As a logical outcome of this approach subsequent revisions of the plans requested information on the provision of units of sheltered housing. By 1968 local authorities were given, largely as a result of their insistence, powers to "promote the welfare" of old people in order to allow them greater flexibility in the provision of services (Health Services and Public Health Act, 1968).

the implications of promoting welfare

As this policy of community care and promotional welfare was gradually accepted and put into effect some of its implications became clearer. A community care policy manifestly defied the narrow administrative boundaries that neatly defined the responsibilities of different agencies. It was slowly realised that no one department could be fully responsible for community care the way it could be for a minority and institution based service. For example, one of the major problems of the aged was that of housing. Many old people lived in conditions which made it almost impossible to retain their independence without suffering acute privation. It was clearly vital that the housing conditions of old people be improved and it was also apparent that, while building was a housing authority responsibility, in plans for the provision of sheltered housing the welfare authorities should play some part.

Community care also had major implications for staffing. There was a need for more staff, particularly social workers, but also a need for a change in the accepted pattern of social work and welfare administration. Social workers were required in growing numbers for the work of visiting old people and co-ordinating, for the individual, the increasingly bewildering range of statutory and voluntary services effecting his welfare. They were also needed, if community care was to become more than an empty phrase, as community workers to foster neighbourhood schemes, utilise and encourage volunteers and liaise with voluntary organisations. By the mid sixties it was possible for the welfare department to offer *all* old people, however varied their needs, some help in combating the problems of ageing, but it could only do so if it forgot the "department" in favour of the "service" and adopted the role of an enabler, not merely providing some residual services but also enabling people to benefit from the provisions of other services such as housing. To do this the administrators of welfare departments had to be alive to many problems which they did not face when residential accommodation was their primary concern. For example they had to consider the need for making services readily accessible to all the people who could make use of them. This meant and still means that services must be conveniently located, well publicised, and sufficiently attractive to advertise and sell themselves by recommendation. Promotional and preventive welfare provisions are little use if they are not both known about by those who need them and perceived in a favourable light. The department had also to consider the need to ensure that services be rapid in action: the old could not and cannot afford to wait months or even weeks for a particular service. Provisions had also to be imaginative, responding sensitively to people's need not just for help, but for help offered and provided in a thoroughly acceptable manner.

In order to become accessible, sensitive and rapid in action the welfare provision had to be completely flexible in operation and yet be meticulously planned well ahead. Welfare therefore needed staff, not just social workers but also administrators, who were capable of achieving this. Social workers were needed to ensure accessibility and sensitivity but they had to be used in a manner which would minimise any tendency towards inflexibility arising out of rigid professional attitudes. Moreover administrators were needed who were alive to the implications of promoting welfare especially those concerning the need for co-ordination and for a truly accessible service. They had to be aware of developments in social policy generally and to be able to reconcile a devotion to the concepts and techniques of co-ordinated social planning with the working context of a society increasingly concerned with consumer participation.

Finally, as the welfare service for old people moved out, beyond the minority provision epitomised by the solitary duty in the 1948 Act, towards a wider concept of welfare embracing prevention and community care, it had to reach out to more and more people until it offered a service, potentially, to all. It had, therefore, to anticipate, and argue for, a dramatic increase in the quantity of provision and, of course, in the overall costs. And just as the quantity had, logically, to increase, so also had the quality of provision since as services become universally available and generally used their standards should rise. This double increase in quantity and quality of provision should, therefore, be reflected in a really striking increase in spending.

the potential for reducing inequality through personal welfare

What has a change in emphasis within the welfare services to do with equality or inequality? It has been argued that equality can only thrive in a society that makes universal provision for social welfare, selecting and positively discriminating in favour of some categories of need or certain areas only on a basis of universal service. It has also been argued that this principle is no less valid for the personal welfare services. If they merely try to increase equality by compensating deprived or disabled persons they will tend to intensify segregation and stigmatization and this can never result in greater equality. What is required is the sort of community welfare service that can help those with special needs in a framework of provision designed to serve the community as a whole and enhance its general well-being.

One can reasonably ask "How far have the various personal social services moved towards the goal of comprehensive community welfare?" and this question, rather than the simpler one of "What have they done to help the handicapped?" is the real question to ask in considering the relationship between personal welfare services and inequality within our society. In considering the record of the recent Labour government, therefore, we need to assess what progress was made during its period of office towards the following closely related objectives:

1. Establishing a pattern of administration conducive to planning and co-ordination.

2. Improving the scope, quantity and quality of the services provided.

3. Re-defining the roles of social workers and administrators as well as increasing their numbers and training.

4. Reorientingg the objectives of the personal social services away from a concept of efficient social casualty work towards a concept of promoting a participating and integrated community welfare service.

administration and planning

The administration of services concerned with personal welfare has always been considerably fragmented and the post war legislation underlined the piecemeal and uneven development of provision. This confused pattern of administrative responsibility at local level was made more intricate by the substantial role of voluntary organisations in personal welfare provision. Moreover central government responsibility was no less complicated.

Dissatisfaction with confusing adminstrative boundaries has a lengthy history. In about one quarter of local authorities health departments actually administered the welfare service from 1948 and in many more they have argued a strong case for taking over the care of the aged and the physically handicapped. Welfare departments felt frustrated in making adequate provision for the domiciliary care of the aged when they were basically responsible for residential accommodation and lacked control over the home help service. Childrens departments complained that they were unable to make early contact with families at risk of break up while welfare departments were frequently at a loss with the homeless family problem. As concern to promote welfare developed, the administrative confusion inevitably increased. The problem was perceived most acutely in the growing attempt to prevent children from coming into care. At the same time mounting interest in the prevention and treatment of juvenile delinquency led to a growing awareness of the importance of the family and intensified concern over the lack of provision for its welfare. Action was in fact precipitated by the White Paper *The child, the family and the young offender* published in 1965. This led to the appointment of the Seebohm Committee in December 1965 "to review the organisation and responsibilities of the local authority personal social services in England and Wales, and to consider what changes are desirable to secure an effective family welfare service."

The Seebohm Committee did not restrict itself to a narrow interpretation of family welfare but looked widely at the problems of co-ordinating and strengthening all the personal social services for children, families, old people and the mentally and physically handicapped and at improving their relationships with other social services. The committee reported in July 1968 and recommended "a new local authority department providing a community based and family oriented service, which will be available to all. This new department will, we believe, reach far beyond the discovery and rescue of social casualties; it will enable the greatest possible number of individuals to act reciprocally, giving and receiving service for the well-being of the whole community."

Meanwhile widespread discussion of the 1965 White Paper on young offenders resulted in a modified set of proposals being issued in the 1968 White Paper *Children in trouble*. This proposed the retention of the existing juvenile court system but stated that where possible action to deal with young offenders should be on a voluntary basis. New forms of intermediate treatment were to be developed; and children in need of residential treatment would be placed in the care of local authorities who would operate a comprehensive system of community homes for both deprived and delinquent children.

These proposals for dealing with children in trouble were embodied in the 1969 Children and Young Persons Act. The recommendations of the Seebohm Report were enacted in 1970 in the Local Authority Social Services Act. (In Scotland, following the Kilbrandon Report *Children and young persons* (Cmnd 2306) and the White Paper *Social work and the community* (Cmnd 3067) the Social Work (Scotland) Act 1968 has already created local authority social work departments on roughly similar lines.) These measures were undoubtedly progressive and provided an improved administrative framework for the operation of personal welfare services. They are both to some extent the product of a growing awareness of the interdependence of the social services, of the importance of the family and indeed of the whole community in both the engendering of social problems and attempts at their solution. But they can only unify and streamline to a very limited extent: they cannot achieve comprehensive welfare provision because it is fundamental to personal welfare that basic needs for an adequate income, for decent accommodation, and for employment, education and medical care as required, be met fully, and no single local authority department can do this. The new Social Services Departments will bring together the social welfare provisions for children and families, the aged, and the mentally and physically handicapped. This will avoid some confusion to the public, provide staff with an improved career structure, facilitate early referral and better deployment of staff. It should give some opportunity to create a better image for welfare services and enable them to become more truly universal in their application. But fundamentally welfare depends on a high quality of basic provision and this the new departments, despite their ambitious titles, are not able to give. Moreover despite the implied acceptance of the interdependence of social provision and the opportunity which fairly radical reorganisation at local and central government level afforded, the need for comprehensive social planning was still ignored.

Planning in all its forms is still rudimentary in the welfare field. Simple planning can be regarded as an attempt to ensure the development of services in a rational manner in order that a recognised need can be met adequately. This involves some measurement of the need and the planned development of services to meet the need. Complex social planning is the more demanding task of taking into account the ways in which the different social services interlock and the ways in which social policy interrelates with economic policy and the whole social structure. As the example of policy for the aged has shown we have become more aware of the necessity for simple planning so that needs— for places in homes, mobile meals and so forth—can be met. We have also had to acknowledge that the welfare of the elderly must depend on broader social planning to ensure that policy in the health, housing and income maintenance fields is co-ordinated with the policy of the welfare departments and takes account of the realities of the economic and social structure. This is apparent in all the personal social services: the expressed community care policy of the 1959 Mental Health Act underlines the necessity of co-ordinating hospital and community services and seeing them in relation to education, social security and employment provisions; the growing and intractable problem of homelessness has classically demonstrated the interdependence of social services such as welfare and housing and the need to think of a detailed area of social policy in the context of wider issues such as the economic stagnation of certain parts of the country, the growing imbalance of population in the congested south east and the priorities of a transport policy.

In the issue of planning the record of the Labour government was, however, quite clearly appalling. Some planning initiative was taken under the Conservative administration in 1962 when local authorities were asked to state their proposed provision of staff, such as social workers and home helps, and facilities such as places in day and residential care units for a ten year period. The calculations related to provision by the health and welfare authorities only of services for four groups of the population: the elderly, the physically handicapped, the mentally disordered and mothers and young children, and were regarded as complementary to the Hospital Plan (*A hospital plan for England and Wales*, HMSO, 1962, Cmnd 1604). The resulting "plans" were published in *Health and welfare: the development of community care* (HMSO, 1963, Cmnd 1973) and they showed how vague was the relationship between need and provision in the areas touched on.

The community care plans were repeated in 1964 and 1966. Then the experiment was abandoned. While it is fair to say that this attempt at planning was open to many detailed criticisms about the scope of the enquiries and ambiguities in the data collection, and while the collective local proposals hardly constituted an overall plan in any real sense of the word, nevertheless it was a beginning. The community plans did do something to document and publicise geographical inequality and made a tentative start in laying down some common standards. But this valuable initiative was not followed up by the Labour government which initially took over existing procedures then let them drop. Provision has been allowed to continue to reflect what each individual local authority thinks it should afford rather than what is needed as assessed by any rational and reasonably objective process. This has meant the continuance and intensification of gross inequalities and inadequacy of provision which have been well documented. For example in her survey

Social welfare for the elderly published in 1968 Amelia Harris pointed out in a discussion of home helps: "In the area with the least unmet need, the service would still have to be expanded by about 40 per cent, while in the area with the most need unmet, the service would have to be almost quadrupled." In 1965-66 local authority registration of the physically handicapped ranged from over ten per 1,000 of the population to 0.7 per 1,000 while expenditure of welfare provisions ranged from an average of £53 per person registered to one of less than £2 (Sally Sainsbury *Registered as disabled*). By 1969-1970 the range of persons registered was from over twenty two per thousand to 1.5 per thousand. Expenditure varied from £73 per person to less than £1. The variation in provision has, therefore, worsened and still bears no valid relation to variations in local circumstances. Virtually nothing was done about this neglect of the disabled up until 1970 when the Private Member's Bill for Chronically Sick and Disabled Persons became law.

quality and quantity of service

The absence of planning even in a rudimentary form has resulted in the provision of personal social services remaining locally idiosyncratic and generally inadequate. The absence of an attempt at more comprehensive social planning has made primary prevention of social problems an empty phrase. This is not unrelated to the second question of the quality and quantity of the services provided. Here the evidence we have of both the current provision and the progress made during the late 1960s is remarkably depressing. In 1968 the Seebohm Report provided a lengthy catalogue of inadequacy: long waiting lists for various lands of residential day care for the aged, the mentally and physically handicapped; "*at least* one child in ten in the population will need special educational, psychiatric or social help before it reaches the age of 18 but at present *at most* one child in twenty-two is receiving such help;" services for the physically handicapped "are in urgent need of development," and so on.

The survey on the home help service carried out in 1967 for the Ministry of Health concluded that "in order to satisfy the unmet needs of present recipients and to provide home help for those who are eligible by present standards but are not currently receiving it the size of the home help service would need to be increased to between two and three times its present size" (Audrey Hunt *The home help service: England and Wales* HMSO, 1970). The failure of most local authorities to provide the range of community care facilities which would be necessary to achieve a substantial change of emphasis in the provision for the mentally subnormal from institutional to community care is well known. In 1965, 123 local authorities had no hostels for the mentally subnormal. In the plans published in 1966 40 authorities admitted that they had no plans to build any by 1976 (*Health and Welfare the development of community care* 1963, revised 1966).

Shortages or absences of staff and facilities are well known. There is also ample evidence of poor quality in existing provision. While many authorities can provide a showplace to demonstrate their high standards of residential accommodation or day care for the disabled much is still manifestly inadequate and fall far short of the expressed aims of policy. Ill adapted and converted premises in isolated areas are still in use as old people's homes.

In 1969 there were 4,415 old persons accommodated in joint-user establishments and another 4,980 in homes provided by the local authority with bed complements of over 150 (Department of Health and Social Security Annual Report 1969, HMSO, Cmnd 4462). In the same year, despite a steady reduction in such numbers there were still 7,428 children in the care of local authorities who were accommodated in larger homes rather than in family group homes or foster homes (Home Office, *Report on the work of the Children's Department*, 1967-1969, HMSO, 1970). Despite evidence of the rising demand for day care for children under five and exposure of the scandals of unregistered child-minding there has been no increase in the numbers of day nursery places provided. Moreover much of the criticism of existing provision cannot be put into figures but must remain impressionistic. Many occupation centres for the physically handicapped are ill-equipped and unimaginative in the work they offer. The standards of temporary accommodation for homeless families are usually low and frequently totally unsuitable for any effective rehabilitation and encouragement of pride in home management. All too often it can be fairly said that the impression gained of social care provisions —homes, luncheon clubs, day centres and the like—is one of meanness: makeshift premises, dreary decor and cut price equipment with staff working against the odds to create the necessary homely or stimulating environment. And this impression has not changed for the better in the years of Labour's administration.

Growth has of course taken place. From 1964-1969 spending rose and numbers of staff and places in homes, etc. increased. The point is that during the period when Labour was in office growth was remarkably slow and appallingly slight for a government that could reasonably have been expected to pay special attention to some of the most underprivileged groups within society. The accompanying table gives some indication of expenditure on some of the major items of personal social service. It can be seen that actual expenditure more than trebled in the decade 1959-1969. This could appear a very gratifying increase but several points must be noted. At constant prices the expenditure only doubled during the period, moreover the rate of increase was actually greater in the first five years than in the years of the Labour government's rule and since compared with health or education, for example, the national resources devoted to welfare are very small, the increase was from a very low base. During this period there was not only a general population increase but a greater increase in the proportion of dependent groups in the population, notably the very young and the very old which must certainly account for part of the increase in real expenditure. There was a deliberate attempt to improve the numbers of professional, and therefore more costly, staff within the services. There was a deliberate shift of emphasis for the care of the mentally disordered from the hospital services to the local authority health and welfare services and a declared policy of preventive family casework. With such points in mind one can hardly regard the increase in expenditure as indicative of the massive development of services both to reach more people in order to implement policies of community care and prevention and to improve the quality of provision. As a percentage of total social service expenditure the growth in personal welfare costs from 1964-1969 is pathetically small, from 2.21 per cent to 2.45 per cent. These increases made it impossible for local authorities even to meet the criticisms of inadequate

EXPENDITURE ON UK LOCAL AUTHORITY PERSONAL SOCIAL
SERVICES FOR 1959, 1964 AND 1969

year	1959	1964	1969
current and capital	£m	£m	£m
welfare	28	53	98
child care	25	39	65
domestic help and mental health*	17	33	61
total expenditure	70	125	224
total at constant prices (1963)	80	116	156
total as per cent of GNP	0.33	0.43	0.58
total at constant prices as per cent GNP at 1963 factor cost	0.34	0.41	0.49
increase, per cent, during five year periods at constant prices		45.00	34.50
total as per cent of expenditure on all social services†	1.89	2.21	2.45

*these are rough estimates only, including an allowance for administration.
the cost of junior training centres is included.
†social security, welfare, NHS, education and housing.
sources: *National Income and Expenditure, 1970, Annual Report of Ministry
Health and DHSS.*

services for which the government itself had produced repeated evidence.
They had no chance fully to implement a positive, preventive community
care service. But this check on expenditure was deliberately imposed by the
government when, in 1966, cuts in local health and welfare costs were
required as part of the general policy of stringent economic restraint. This
was surely not the proper area in which to impose economies dealing as it
does with the most vulnerable sections of the community. As a result, capital
spending declined. There were also unfortunate developments in current
services, for example, after rising steadily for many years the numbers of
local authority home helps in Britain as a whole actually *declined* between
1967 and 1969 despite the evidence of the need to redouble the rate of
expansion (Department of Health and Social Security, *Digest of health statistics 1970*, HMSO March 1971). The need for more resources to be directed to
welfare was apparent when Labour came to power and even in times of
economic difficulty it should have been possible for the government to afford
this social service a much higher financial priority than it did.

staffing

The staffing position in the personal social services remains a confused one.
Social workers have increased their numbers, their professionalism and the
range of their methods of intervention. Demand for social workers increases
sharply when personal welfare policy turns towards objectives of prevention
and community care. But although the output and recruitment of trained social
workers has been stepped up considerably, so has the recruitment of untrained
personnel. For example, of the 3,621 child care staff in posts in 1968, 46 per
cent were without social work qualifications as compared with 39 per cent
untrained workers out of a total of 1,434 staff in 1962. Of 5,334 serving staff
in health, mental health and welfare departments in 1968 it has been calculated

that one-fifth were fully qualified, two-fifths partially qualified and two-fifths unqualified. But training facilities, depending as they do on adequate field supervision during the professional courses can only be increased gradually. Progress is being made but there is still a shortage of social workerrs, particularly of trained workers, and the shortage is geographically very uneven. The training position remains highly complex with a bewildering range of courses at different levels and for specialisation with different groups. The output of non-graduate social workers with the certificate in social work and the certificate of recognition in child care has increased most rapidly during the 1960s, and the awards of the Home Office letter of recognition and the Council for Training in Social Work's declaration of recognition of experience have been increasingly made use of. There have also been increases in the output of the graduate professional social work courses. The creation of the Local Government Training Board has encouraged local authorities to second staff for training but in general the need for trained social work staff has been increasingly recognised at local level apart from any central initiative. The question of training residential workers was investigated by a committee set up by the National Council of Social Service under Professor Lady Williams' chairmanship. The report, *Caring for people*, which was published in 1967 indicated severe problems in the recruitment of staff for homes and recommended training courses to improve the quality of the service and to encourage recruitment of staff by adding the status and career prospects that qualifications in residential care might afford. More courses have subsequently been established but there is still little generic training and scepticism remains over the wisdom of this policy.

There is still much confusion over social work training and the specialist/generalist problem has not been resolved. The creation of unified social services departments should accelerate progress towards more generic training but the lengthy history of fragmentation and the continued development of separate courses and qualifications make change difficult. The creation of the British Association of Social Workers is a vital step towards professional unity and the establishment of a Central Council for Education and Training in Social Work, to take on the work of the previously separate training councils, is in line with the administrative changes brought about by the 1970 Social Services Act. But more could have been done to develop a concerted manpower policy and aim for a better balance between specialised and other staff and therefore between prolonged and short courses of training.

The demand for social workers has been fairly constant for many years but there is a growing criticism of the assumptions behind it. Apart from the issue of generic training and the concept of the general purpose social worker there is a mounting concern at the emphasis placed on casework training. In 1968 the report of a study group, under the chairmanship of Dame Eileen Younghusband, on training for community work was published entitled *Community work and social change*. This concluded both that there was a need for trained community workers and that the time—in the context of a proposed reorganisation of services based partly on a recognition of the interdependence of welfare policies and their importance to the whole community—was most opportune for their introduction. The report was generally well received but was not followed by the injection of resources that would have been necessary to ensure that training for community work could begin to provide a viable alternative to the existing social casework training. Most of the training developments that have occurred in this field have resulted from individual initiative and professional concern.

Interest in community work has, then, been a growing phenomenon observable in the personal social services scene during the late 1960s. It is one reflection of an ongoing and useful reappraisal of the objectives and values of social work training but it is not a development for which the government could claim credit. The relative newsworthiness of the social workers must not, however, be allowed to distort their importance in welfare provision. As the Seebohm Report recorded, of 90,000 staff working in personal social services in 1966 only 7,700 were social workers. The importance of home helps, residential care staff, workers in day centres for the mentally disordered and physically handicapped, nursery nurses, sheltered housing wardens, chiropodists and occupational therapists and a long list of other personnel is increasingly acknowledged. But little has been done systematically to improve the recruitment of auxiliary workers.

No less important is the need for administrative staff with good managerial skills, ability to promote and utilise research into social need, a grasp of the importance of co-ordinated planning and an awareness of the place of personal social services in the broader framework of social provision. The need for a body of genuine professional social administrators is emerging ever more strongly as concepts of community welfare development. Disastrously little has been done to provide such people, despite much discussion and awareness of this need in the early and mid-sixties. There should have been, by 1969, a reasonable body of trained and experienced administrative personnel to take over the new departments with confidence if courses for post experience staff had been vigorously developed. This again is a failure of central government initiative.

a new "community" service

We now come to the final question: "What progress has been made towards reorienting the objectives of the personal social services away from a concept of efficient social casualty work towards a participating and integrated community welfare service?" This is a difficult question to answer. It is not easy to assess what progress has been made in fulfilling new concepts, especially when they are vague and controversial in definition, and it is even less easy to ascribe any part of such progress to the credit of a particular administration. The creation of new, unified personal social services departments under the 1970 Act provides the necessary administrative framework for a more effective family service but it does not itself change the image or the objectives of the personal social services. More staff are needed but thought must be given to the type of staff best suited to the services. Standards of provision must be raised and facilities made more available but there is a danger in, for example, arguing straightforwardly for more places in homes or hostels because of high waiting lists if due regard is not paid to some alternative forms of social care provision that might be more acceptable, and more in line with long term objectives. This is why it is important to consider long term objectives and the wider aims of social policies even when the administrative and economic realities of the situation force a development that is opportunist and incrementalist.

Within the personal social services there are several dilemmas which are becoming more imperative. One is the momentum within policies of prevention and community care which brings the social worker and administrator face to face with his impotence in effecting dramatic social change. The other main dilemma is: how can the necessity to plan, to make provision for obvious needs and develop professional skills to respond to needs be reconciled with the demands of a community that is becoming tentatively conscious of its desire to participate more directly in the determination of social policies? In dealing with both these issues the question of leadership remains vital. The personal welfare services have much to contribute not only to those members of society who have special needs and are particularly vulnerable, but to a better understanding of the aims and objectives of a comprehensive social policy. The dilemmas presented by the problems of homelessness, mental subnormality, the alienation of old people and the break up of families illustrate vividly and urgently the need for a co-ordinated approach to social planning. A good social administrator should be prepared to tackle the immediate problems of the vulnerable groups within the community and also contribute forcefully to the formulation of policies which will more effectively promote welfare. A start can be made at local authority level where the initiative for co-ordinating housing, health and education policies with those of the personal social services departments should come from the directors of social services. But this comprehensive approach should clearly be regarded as fundamental by the central government also and efforts should be made to ensure co-ordination at central planning level.

One example from the personal social services field will suffice to illustrate this. There is a known shortage of day nursery facilities which contributes to the problems of unregistered child minding, the break up of families and the necessity for many unsupported mothers to rely on supplementary benefits and remain at a subsistence standard of living. Partly because of the recognition that day nurseries cater for social need responsibility for them has been transferred to the new social services departments. But if the departments increase provision in order to help only the most urgent priority cases in their immediate need this does little to move towards a universal and community based service. Perhaps day care should be provided on a more rational basis available to any mother who wishes, rather than is forced, to work, and offering a valuable and educative experience to the child? We have yet to decide whether such a policy would be desirable on medical and psychological grounds. We have yet to begin to find out whether it is what most people want. We do not know what would be the likely take-up of a truly universal day care service or what effect there would be on the economy of releasing a potential labour force or whether such a policy would be one sensible approach to the problem of family poverty. We do not know whether such a universal service could be staffed without depleting the ranks of recruits to other services, or whether we could, or should, afford it. In other words we need a policy. Viable policies in this and every other field can only be worked out if we have some democratically agreed and informed long term objectives in mind. Even as we act to deal with the emergency situations and to reduce the scandals of neglect we must be considering the long term aims otherwise we shall continue to respond erratically to presenting problems or merely perpetuate the mistakes of the past. In day nursery care we have responded in an erratic and unconvincing way, ambivalent about the desirability or feasibility of the provision and therefore trying to ignore the consequences of neglect. In our care of the mentally handicapped we have perpetuated the mistake of relying on institutional care and are overwhelmed by the efforts required to reverse a socially disastrous policy.

Central government has the responsibility for refining and defining long term objectives. It must make explicit, for example, a determination to implement community care for the elderly and the mentally handicapped and decide what policies are best for the care of children and families. Without this neither the simple nor the complex social planning can come into being. Local authorities are given catchwords like "prevention" but the prevention of social casualty situations like homelessness, child neglect, family break up and the massive institutionalisation and alienation of the handicapped can only come about by the development of long term policies that spell out the objectives of equality and universal provision as well as the details of progress. In coming to terms with the growing demand for participation by the consumer in social services the administrators of local social services departments need to drastically reorient traditional patterns of paternalistic care. When community action is viewed as a partnership between statutory and voluntary action there is considerable acceptance of the idea, although many of the field staff in social services departments are casework trained and have their own problems in experimenting with a community approach. But when there is a latent or apparent conflict situation there is a genuine confusion over the democratic rights and wrongs: local government in theory is democratic and local administrators are already constrained in their paternalistic and professional aspirations by the council members: why then should they submit to demands for further participation? This resentment is particularly acute when the demands are aggressive and disruptive on behalf of, for example, the homeless. At present little if any progress has been made by local welfare services to improve consumer participation or encourage community action. Some expansion has taken place in the numbers of community workers employed by social services departments, but these are mostly expected to involve themselves in the more traditional, and still very necessary, community organisation projects that maximise the use of volunteers and co-ordinate local activity. But few authorities would consider discussing their proposed policies on sheltered housing or day nurseries or foster homes with their potential consumers and many are alarmed by any signs of spontaneous community action being generated amongst clients. So there is a long way to go before this interest in community becomes more than a token acknowledgement of a fashionable word. Eventually the local social services departments will have to see that there is a logical, and potentially fruitful connection between their two main dilemmas: if they want to encourage the social change necessary to prevention they might proceed by enlisting the aid of the groups of people most affected by the inequalities and inadequacies of basic social provisions.

What has been the role of the Labour government in this? It made gestures and gave some encouragement to experiment but this was not enough. The Community Development Programme began to operate in four pilot areas from 1969, and was subsequently to extend to about a dozen more areas. This programme was designed to formulate and test new approaches to the problems presented by individuals, families and communities suffering from severe social deprivation. The object was to increase co-operation between social service agencies and between them and the consumers. There is an explicit commitment not only to improve social situations which "display many symptoms of individual, family and community malfunctioning" but to attempt to do so by methods which help people to increase control over their own lives and reduce dependence on the social services.

The programme is undoubtedly an important experiment but it has been strongly criticised as lacking any real interest in community action since it is essentially to be exercised through local authorities adopting a consensus approach. It can also be criticised, along with the Educational Priority Areas and the Urban Aid programme, for its selectivist implications. Positive discrimination is a basically sound approach but the idea should mean the direction of additional resources to groups or areas of special need on top of the basic provision of services. There is a danger with such programmes that they offer to selected areas only what should be the basic minimum for all areas and serve, therefore, as a means of stalling on the major objectives while appearing to do something active and interesting. The only true virtue of a community development programme, in the absence of a national onslaught on poverty and urban squalor, would be if it set out to achieve a high level of local self consciousness and to generate spontaneous community action. If it intends primarily to focus on experimenting, *via* central government co-ordination, with greater local inter-agency co-operation and improved public relations work it is only doing what should be fundamental to the central administration and to every area and social service department in the country. If the present community development programme is only doing the obvious, and doing it on a shoe-string budget, it will intensify cynicism rather than encourage communication. The reorientation needed is a subtle process that cannot easily be induced or accredited. The administrative reorganisations that the government achieved have laid some of the groundwork for change. The neglect of social planning has been detrimental to it. Much will depend on a change of attitude amongst all those concerned with the personal social services from the policy makers to the field staff. But the government failed to give a lead as it did not provide a consistent statement of policy objectives or establish a convincing moral commitment to universal welfare provision and consumer participation.

conclusion

The progress made towards establishing a truly universal comprehensive welfare service was not very great during the period of the Labour administration. It has been argued that only by emphasising the universality of provision will the aims of promoting greater social equality, to which a Labour government should be dedicated, be achieved. While the personal social services exist solely to help minorities they will remain of poor quality and they will tend to be paternalistic in their presentation and more interested in social control than social change. They must be seen to be a vital part of our social provision concerned with the well being of the whole community, preventing distress and deprivation where possible and helping those with special need to function within and contribute towards a more integrated and self-determining community. If these are to be the long term objectives when progress must be made towards making services more generally available, improving their quality, emphasising the importance of co-ordinated social planning and moving towards a more central and meaningful use of community participation.

Some credit can be claimed by the recent government for the administrative changes of the 1970 Social Services Act, for the initiation of the community development programme and for consistent encouragement of social work training. But the spending on the welfare services has been grossly inadequate despite the slight percentage increase between 1964-1969. It has been inadequate to maintain existing services let alone improve quality or extend scope. No attempt has been made to emphasise the universality of provision, indeed nothing has been done even to enforce minimum standards. The failure to embark on an attempt at more complex social planning in order to ensure that the provision of personal services is backed by satisfactory basic social services is damning. Continued inadequacies in housing, the increase in poverty and the lack of sufficient investment in health and education services have distorted the work of the personal social services, making the objectives of promotional welfare impossible to achieve. The welfare services have had to continue to operate as casualty departments with a consequent frustration for staff and a lowering of standards.

While the basic social services are starved of resources and even the standardisation of minimum social care provision is not enforced there is little hope of achieving a reorientation of objectives towards community welfare. Virtually no attempt has been made to educate the public to an understanding of the relevance of the personal social services to the achievement of a more integrated and caring community. The services continue to be regarded as welfare for the deprived and deviant and hence abysmally low standards of provision are tolerated, and community participation is generally discouraged. The Labour government has claimed that it achieved some important developments in its welfare legislation and argued that it had thereby created the groundwork for future changes in attitude and scope of provision. It can also argue that financially it did what it could in the face of harsh economic reality. But the fact remains that the general impression created in the late 1960s was one of an encouragement of empty phrases. Community care, prevention, co-ordination and participation were much discussed, but neither the money nor the planning were there to make them meaningful. Above all there was no commitment made to the services, no projection of a vision, of an ideal, that could inspire the necessary progress. The issue was never made politically important and the objectives of universal provision, equality and greater self-determination, were never powerfully articulated. In terms of future policy the implications of this for socialism are clear: personal welfare services must be given the priority they deserve. They must be given the resources, the staff, the planning machinery, the publicity and the *conviction* necessary to transform them into services with a positive, integrative and universally beneficial role to play in our society.

6. education and inequality

Howard Glennerster

The concept of equality in education has always been a rather confusing one. During the 1960s the concensus of opinion, reflected in official reports at least changed somewhat. This chapter therefore begins by tracing the shift of emphasis from "parity of esteem" to "positive discrimination." The main part of the chapter analyses the nature of the expansion in education expenditure that took place in the 1960s and in particular during Labour's period in office and asks the question—who benefited? The paper ends by pointing some lessons for the seventies.

Politicians and educationalists usually refer to equality of opportunity not to equality. Yet the two are in practice indistinguishable. Writing in *Encounter* (July 1961) Anthony Crosland distinguished a weak from a strong version of the concept. The weak version assumed: "that access to élite education is based not on birth or wealth, but solely on intelligence as measured by IQ tests, and hence that all children of the same measured intelligence at the appropriate age have completely equal access."

But, as Crosland went on to argue, measured intelligence was not a purely innate characteristic. It was partly acquired and the child's environment, the education his parents had received, the level of poverty in which he was brought up, all affected the result. "The strong definition is therefore that, granted the differences in heredity and infantile experience, every child should have the same opportunity for *acquiring* measured intelligence, so far as this can be controlled by social action."

He concluded that equality of opportunity entailed equality. No child could truly be said to have had an equal chance educationally without equality of social conditions, income, housing and the rest. Hence for those committed to a free enterprise society equality of opportunity becomes both impracticable and undesirable as the more honest exponents of that ideal argue (E. G. West, *Education and the state*).

Closely linked to the weak version of the concept was the assumption that a child had an equal chance if the facilities offered it in different schools were all equally good. This proposition underlay the case for the tripartite system in 1945. Secondary modern schools were to be given equal resources though "parity of esteem they must earn by their own efforts." Moreover, at the end of the 1950s much of the case against the selective system was that it did not in practice produce this equality of provision or esteem. Even Crosland's article only argued for an end to selection at eleven and "an immensely high standard of *universal* provision" (my italics).

By implication Crosland did not envisage that those from poor homes should receive more education to compensate for other deficiencies but merely that society should attempt to remove social barriers to educational achievement. In a footnote, however, he went on to suggest that "the strongest of all definitions of equal opportunity would be that every child had an equal chance of developing its interests and personality regardless of measured intelligence and this might mean giving more education to the less intelligent child than the brilliant." Here the objective was not the more efficient recruitment of an able élite but the pursuit of a more equal society in which individuals had a more equal capacity to enjoy the experience of life.

Julia Evetts in a recent article in the *British Journal of Sociology* (December 1970) suggests that while equality of opportunity used to imply equal provision the current concern was to achieve more equal attainment and this implied unequal provision since children required different amounts of education to achieve a given standard than others. A careful consideration of the education reports in the 1960s suggests that no such clear shift in outlook occurred. The concept of positive discrimination took shape gradually but the logic behind it remained somewhat obscure.

Both the Crowther and Robbins reports work on what Crosland called the weak definition of equal opportunity. Their motives for stressing the unequal access of different social groups to further education varied. Crowther made the case for raising the school leaving age and emphasised the needs of the economy: "The growth in the proportion of highly skilled jobs and the decline in the proportion of unskilled jobs imply a reassessment of what must be attempted by people of only average intelligence" (para 190).

The Report concluded: "(a) The country is a long way from tapping all the available supply of talent by present methods, half the National Service recruits to the Army who were rated in the two highest ability groups had left school at 15. (b) It is most unlikely that this waste of talent can be remedied within a reasonable period without compulsion, because leaving at 15 is so deeply embedded in certain parts of the social structure" (para 202).

The Robbins committee used the same inequalities to strengthen their case for a more rapid expansion of higher education. They were ammunition against the "more means worse" school of thought (paras 137-146). The Report showed that even amongst the most successful candidates at the 11 plus examination the proportion of children from professional homes gaining two "A" levels was three times as great as those from semi-skilled manual homes. Overall the proportion of young people entering full time higher education from the "higher professional" groups was 45 per cent and only 2 per cent from the semi-skilled manual group.

The committee made no reference to ways in which the community might tap these particular "reserves of ability" more effectively, although it pointed out that past expansion had favoured children of professional parents as much as the rest of the population.

The Newsom report, which came out a fortnight before Robbins had already begun to point in a different direction. Asked "to consider the education between the ages of 13 and 16 of pupils of average or less than average ability," it had commissioned a special study of secondary modern schools in slum areas and described in vivid terms the environment in which they had to work. They concluded that, "schools in slums do require special consideration . . . They seem to us, for example, to need a specially favourable staffing ratio." How this was to be achieved was far from clear. The committee suggested, in a half hearted way, "Perhaps this can be secured simply by making it clear that professionally it is an asset to have served successfully in a difficult area." Clearly unconvinced itself about this proposition it went on to say "But perhaps more tangible inducements may be needed," and referred readers to an appendix in which two people giving evidence has suggested a form of differential salary.

Despite its inconclusive recommendations Newsom suggested a different approach. In his foreword, Sir Edward Boyle used exactly the same phrase as Crosland had two years earlier: "The essential point is that all children should have an equal opportunity of acquiring intelligence."

In 1964 Alan Little and John Westergaard (*British Journal of Sociology*, December 1964) reviewed our lack of progress in reducing the differences in social class access to education and concluded: "The point is crucial, though obvious, the widening of educational provisions does not by itself reduce social inequalities in educational opportunity; it does so only if the expanded facilities are made proportionately more accessible to those children previously least able to take advantage of them."

The Plowden Committee, appointed by Boyle and reporting to Crosland, felt able to propose not equal provision but more resources for schools working in deprived areas. "We ask for 'positive discrimination' in favour of such schools and the children in them, going well beyond an attempt to equalise resources. Schools in deprived areas should be given priority in many respects. The first step must be to raise the schools with low standards to the national average; the second quite deliberately to make them better. The justification is that the homes and neighbourhoods from which many of their children come provide little support and stimulus for learning. The schools must supply a compensating environment."

Plowden's major contribution was to suggest criteria by which such areas could be defined and the specific policies to be pursued in them—more capital expenditure, higher salaries for the teachers and so on. The Labour government accepted the principle and permitted extra building allocations to some authorities for 1968-69. This was repeated in subsequent years. The Burnham committee agreed that nearly £$\frac{1}{2}$ million should be set aside to pay teachers in priority schools (£75 extra a year not £120 as Plowden had suggested). In 1968 the Urban Aid Programme was launched to give extra help to areas with a high concentration of immigrants and general overcrowding. The concept of positive discrimination was taken up explicitly in other services, for example, it was recommended by the Seebohm committee. I shall be discussing the adequacy of the Government's response later. Here the relevant point to notice is that in theory public policy had moved from the weak to the strong concept of equality of opportunity.

My basic theme in this chapter is that in practice education policy did not succeed in discriminating in favour of the deprived in the 1960s. If it is to do so it requires a firm commitment to the principle at each level of education. Since the concept is central it may be worth pausing to look rather more carefully at chapter 5 of the Plowden Report in which positive discrimination was first advanced in administrative terms.

The first strand of thought derives from the social ecology school who have talked about social or neighbourhood "disorganisation." Plowden says "From some neighbourhoods, urban and rural, there has been a continuing outflow of the more successful young people. The loss of enterprise and skill makes things worse for those left behind." This was part of a vicious circle that caused "cumulative deprivation." The conclusion was that teachers were more difficult to recruit to such areas, partly because they did not want to live there and partly because the job itself was much more difficult.

This reasoning was sufficient to justify higher salaries for those in "deprived areas." It did not on its own justify more teachers. Simply to attract the same number of teachers as a similar school in another area will require extra inducements—higher salaries, better equipment, a house.

Plowden also complained that because nearly all new school building had been concentrated in areas of population growth, central city areas and many rural areas had had very few new schools. This was not so much a reason for "discrimination" in favour of central areas so much as a plea for the DES and Treasury to take account of replacement needs as well as "roofs over heads." A third strand in the argument was an echo of Crowther. There was, the committee said "a great reservoir of unrealised potential" amongst children of poor families. The implication is that these reservoirs lie underneath certain geographical areas. To pursue this oil drilling metaphor further, there would be a high return on investing extra sums of money in extracting this valuable substance. Logically, however, this does not follow. The return on investment depends on the cost of drilling. The greater the difficulties of extraction the higher the cost, and it is certainly plausible that the greatest increase in measured ability per pound spent can be gained by investing in middle class suburban areas where both home and school are working together. There is indeed some small evidence for this. So far then the interesting thing to emerge is that some of the justifications for spending extra, for example, on teachers' salaries could be seen merely as ways of equalising provision while the application of pool of talent analogies are not necessarily valid.

The fourth strand in the committee's thinking, however, appears more egalitarian. It draws upon the international mathematics survey which had shown a wider spread of attainment in England than in many other countries and the committee concluded that "steps should be taken to improve the educational chances and the attainments of the least well placed, and to bring them up to the levels that prevail generally" (para 146). The justification is argued on general economic grounds—that the kind of jobs the children would be required to do and the changes they would have to adapt to, required a higher minimum standard of achievement.

These grounds are not as convincing as they might be since we know very little about the future manpower needs of the economy. The basic approach is important though. The model is drawn from social insurance. The assumption is that the spread of achievement is wider than the spread of inherited ability and that by concentrating resources where the effects of environment are greatest it will be possible to raise the achievements of many of the children nearer to the average. Quite apart from any economic criteria this has a social rational.

True democracy is incompatible with wide extremes of wealth or attainment. We are at present making our society unnecessarily bureaucratic and complex for those with least capacity to cope, but even if we can check this process any attempts to establish basic rights for the individual demand a fairly high level of education. David Donnison recently used the phrase "Liberty therefore equality" (*Three Banks Review,* December 1970). This applies with particular force to education.

Nor must the case rest on attainment alone. Education is itself a thing to be enjoyed and holds the key to the quality of future experience. In many areas the range of experiences enjoyed by children are so limited that their capacity for enjoyment and development is stunted. This deprivation is even greater than might be supposed by considering income or housing conditions. In classes of teenage girls who live only a 10p ride from central London it is not uncommon to find that they have never been to central London let alone the countryside. The school can help to widen these horizons and to give children a greater awareness of their own community and environment. Yet as Plowden recognised the school can achieve little if it works alone. "We delude ourselves if we think that we can equalise the social distribution of life chances by expanding educational opportunities while millions of children live in slums without baths, decent lavatories, leisure facilities, room to explore and space to dream." (R. M. Titmuss' introduction to Tawney's *Equality*.)

The case against positive discrimination has been argued on social and on administrative grounds. Some critics have concentrated on the element of stigma that may be involved. A school, it is argued, may be stigmatised by being classed an EPA school. Yet, for all practical purposes, such schools carry their stigmata too clearly for any EPA allowance to make much difference. The allowance does at least show that someone in authority cares a little.

A much more fundamental point has been made by Basil Bernstein who has criticised the concept of "compensatory education." This he argues has detracted attention from the deficiencies of the school and concentrated them on the community and the family. "The concept 'compensatory education' serves to direct attention away from the internal organisation and the educational context of the school, and focus our attention upon the families and children. The concept 'compensatory education' implies that something is lacking in the family, and so in the child. As a result the children are unable to benefit from schools. It follows then that the school has to compensate for something which is missing in the family, and the children are looked at as deficit systems. If only the parents were interested in the goodies we offer, if only they were like middle-class parents, then we could do our job. Once the problem is seen even implicitly in this way, then it becomes appropriate to coin the terms 'cultural deprivation,' 'linguistic deprivation,' and so on. And then these labels do their own sad work." (Basil Bernstein in Rubinstein and Stoneman, eds, *Education and democracy*.) The same point has been made by Rosenthal and Jacobson in their study *Pygmalion in the classroom*. The very designation of schools as having "deprived children" could lead teachers to expect less of their pupils who would in consequence achieve less.

This is salutary. What it does is to make the case for different teaching and different attitudes. It does carry the danger, however, that society may use this kind of argument as an excuse for sitting back and doing nothing about resources. If the reading ages of children in slum area schools are much lower than in other schools it is partly society's fault. It will take more resources to put it right. Others have criticised positive discrimination on administrative grounds. These critics have concentrated on the quite distinct idea of priority *areas*. The area concept has been criticised on a number of counts but it is not a necessary consequence of adopting positive discrimination and I shall leave the discussion of these areas until later.

THE OUTCOME OF THE 1960s

This section is concerned first to answer the question: is there now greater equality of access to different levels of education. Here it is appropriate to see just how far the "pools" or "reservoirs" have indeed been tapped. Has there been more equality of opportunity using the weak definition?

The second objective is to see how the extra public funds that have been devoted to education in the last decade have been distributed. Who has benefited most—those whose homes and surroundings have offered them least? Has there been more equality of opportunity using the strong definition?

The third objective is to look at education as a redistributive system on its own. Has it contributed to greater equality in the "command over resources."

more equal access

The sixties saw a sharp increase in the proportion of young people staying on at school beyond the statutory leaving age. It outpaced what either Crowther or Robbins had predicted and it coincided with the birth rate bulge which increased the 18 year old age group by one-quarter in 1965. The Robbins committee's recommendation for an emergency expansion was accepted by the Conservative government in 1963 but the expansion itself had to be financed during the Labour period. What was more Robbins had underestimated the numbers gaining "A" levels by over 20 per cent. The Labour Government expanded higher education faster than the Robbins targets and as a result there are over 430,000 places in full time higher education in 1971 compared with the figure Robbins recommended of 305,000 in England and Wales (DES, *Planning Paper*, no 2). The expansion was undertaken without any reduction in the student staff ratio. Taken on its own merits this whole operation was a substantial achievement.

The tragedy has been that provision for the school leaver has failed to match that for the child who stayed at school. While the numbers in the sixth forms of maintained schools increased by nearly 50 per cent between 1963 and 1969 and the proportion of the age group staying on also increased by about half, the number of young people granted day release by their employers rose hardly at all during the same period. In 1961 250,000 youngsters under 18 were released. In 1969 the figure was 255,000. The chance of a girl being released was still a quarter of that for a boy. In 1969 only 10 per cent of girls and 39 per cent of boys under 18 were allowed time off from work to pursue their education—a right that the 1944 Act envisaged 27 years ago. The inequality between those in full time and those in part time education, and the inequalities between those in apprenticeships and those who are not, those with relatively generous employers (mainly in the public service) and those without, these remain the deepest divisions in our education system. It is clear, then, that the working class gained little from the expansion of day release which mainly caters for them despite both the Crowther and Henneker Heaton Reports.

How far did they gain from the expansion of sixth forms and full time higher education? This is not an easy question to answer. There is no one systematic study. There are merely an assortment of different surveys. However, by piecing these together a fairly clear picture emerges.

The Crowther report gives us an indication of the social composition of sixth forms in the mid 1950s. A national survey of sixth formers for the Schools Council published in 1970 but referring to sixth forms in 1968 enables us to make a comparison over the ten year period. What it shows, in brief, is that despite the fact that numbers in sixth forms have increased by 50 per cent in the period the social class composition has changed hardly at all. In 1957, of the army recruits who had been in a sixth form, 70 per cent came from non-manual class homes. In 1968 the figure was 67 per cent. This is not a significant difference taking account of the nature of the surveys.

If the social composition of sixth forms has changed little it is to be expected that the same will be true of higher education overall, though the experience of different sectors may vary. The Robbins survey of training colleges in 1961 showed that more working class children reached these institutions than the universities. 42 per cent of the students in that survey came from manual class homes. No later national survey has been conducted, but a survey of one large college of education in the north reported by D. Lomax in *Dear Lord James* (T. Burgess, *et al*) showed that 40 per cent of the students fell into the same categories and this is broadly consistent with a survey of two other colleges made by S. Hatch.

The colleges of education were expanded by the Labour Government faster than any other part of the education system but the balance between children from manual and non-manual backgrounds appears not to have changed greatly. There is less evidence still about the polytechnic and advanced further education sector though what there is suggests little change here either (S. Hatch, *op cit*).

It is only for the universities that any recent information on a national scale exists. Even here there are difficulties. The UCCA reports for 1967-68 and 1968-69 give a break down of entrants to universities by parental occupation. The analyses refer to students entering in the autumn of 1968 and 1969. Unfortunately the analysis is not in terms of social class as the Robbins surveys are but merely of occupational group. By using the detailed categories a reasonably accurate translation can be made. (The 25 basic occupational categories are given in the UCCA's statistical supplement and categories XIV and XXV are divided into 37 sub-groups. But for most of the manual groups there is no distinction between skilled and non-skilled status and in three groups there are probably a significant proportion of higher status jobs like foremen. It was assumed that the occupation-status breakdown was the same as in the 1961 Census [Occupation tables]. This enabled the occupational groups to be allocated between social class groups in the same ratios. This probably over states the size of the manual grouping slightly and the semi-skilled. It seems very unlikely that the end result could be more than 2 per cent out in either case.)

Bearing in mind this qualification, it would seem that a significant increase has taken place in the share of places filled by children from the clerical group. There has been a fall in the share taken by the intermediate group—teachers, social workers, and so on. On the other hand while young people from the manual groups are better represented the improvement is only a slight one— from 27 per cent in 1961 to 30 per cent in 1969. These groups are still substantially under represented. In 1966 they formed 63 per cent of all parents in the relevant age band.

THE SOCIAL CLASS COMPOSITION OF UNDERGRADUATES IN GREAT BRITAIN 1961, 1968 AND 1969 (PER CENT)

social class (Registrar General's categories)	1961 Under-graduates	1968 Entrants	1969 Entrants	married male working population aged 45–54	
				1961	1966
I professional, managerial	19	19	19	3	4
II intermediate	42	32	33	19	20
IIIa clerical	12	18	18	12	12
IIIb skilled manual	20	19	18	38	38
IV semi-skilled manual	6	10	10	21	20
V unskilled	1	2	2	7	6
all categories	100	100	100	100	100

sources: Robbins Report, appendix 2B. UCCA Sixth and seventh reports, statistical supplements. *1961 Census for England and Wales and Scotland.* Occupational tables. *1966 Sample Census for England and Wales and Scotland.* Economic activity tables.

Another way of looking at the same information is to consider how many young people from each social class enter university and how the relative chances of entry have varied in the sixties.

The Robbins committee showed that between the 1930s and 1940s and the early 1960s the proportion of boys going on to university had risen by about half, but it rose at the same rate for boys from non-manual as well as manual homes. The ratio between them, or the degree of inequality remained unchanged. In attempting to bring these figures up to date it has been necessary to estimate the number of 18 year olds in each social group. This was done by adjusting figures for the social class distribution of married heads of household of the appropriate age in the 1966 Census to take account of the differences in completed family size.

The results are interesting for they show that there has been a narrowing in the class differential in the 1960s. The percentage of boys from non-manual homes going to university rose from 16.8 per cent to 20.2 per cent. The percentage of manual boys rose from 2.6 to 4.8 per cent. The boys from non-manual class backgrounds had four times the chance of going to university in 1968 but the comparable figure in 1960 had been over six times—see table below. This is an important conclusion for it does mean that at least on one interpretation there has been a move to more equal opportunity. How is this shift compatible with an apparently small change in the composition of the university population?

The answer is that the increase in the percentage of manual class entrants coincided with a drop in the percentage of the age group having fathers in these occupations. The increase in the number of professional and intermediate class parents has not led to an increase but a decrease in their representation at universities.

PERCENTAGE OF BOYS AGED 18 ENTERING UNIVERSITY BY SOCIAL CLASS*

social class	1928–47	1960	1968
A non-manual	8.9	16.8	20.2
B manual	1.4	2.6	4.8
C all boys	3.7	5.8	10.0
A divided by B	6.4	6.5	4.3

* as in Robbins the number of initial entrants in each social class was expressed as a percentage of the 18 year olds in the previous June.
sources: 1928-47 and 1960: Robbins appendix one, part II, table 15. 1968: UCCA sixth report Statistical Supplement (Numbers from N. Ireland included). 1966 Sample Census for England and Wales and Scotland. Economic Activity Tables and Fertility Tables. Registrar General's Statistical Review, 1968 (England and Wales and Scotland).

The same picture holds good for girls, where the biggest inequalities of all exist. Middle class girls used to have thirteen times as much chance of getting to university. Now they have only ten times as much chance—see table p92. Girls overall still have half the chance of a university place as against boys. The other table overleaf shows the range of opportunity that still exists. The proportions entering university range from 35 per cent of children with professional parents to 2 per cent of those with unskilled manual workers as fathers.

Before concluding this catalogue of inequality it is worth recalling that Britain

PERCENTAGE OF GIRLS AGED 18 ENTERING UNIVERSITY BY
SOCIAL CLASS, 1960 AND 1968

social class	girls aged 18 in	
	1959	1968
A non-manual	9.4	11.2
B manual	0.7	1.1
C all girls	3.0	4.5
A divided by B	13.4	10.1

source: Robbins appendix one, p39, survey of 21 year olds born 1940-41, and
UCCA, *op cit*.

is not alone in this respect. Indeed it has been suggested that more places in
universities in this country are taken by working class children than is the
case in many other Western or indeed Eastern European countries. However,
the numbers staying on from all classes are much lower in this country (see
the Donnison report).

In short then, the past decade has seen a narrowing in the extent of inequality
in access to universities but substantial differences still persist. In further
education, advanced courses expanded faster than university courses and since

PERCENTAGE OF 18 YEAR OLDS ENTERING UNIVERSITY BY
SOCIAL CLASS, 1959 AND 1968

social class	1959	1968
I professional, managerial	33	35
II intermediate	11	12
IIIa clerical	6	13
IIIb skilled manual	2	4
IV semi-skilled manual	1	3
V unskilled		2
all 18 year olds	4	7

sources: Robbins, appendix one. 1959 figures refer to 21 year olds in 1940-41
entering full time degree level courses which will have included a few non-
university courses. 1968 figures, *op cit*.

at the beginning of the period these courses had more working class students
than the universities had, working class access to higher education overall may
have moved even further. There are no comparable later figures for the further
education sector however.

who benefited most?

Another way of viewing the experiences of the 1960s is to ask what social
groups benefited most from the really substantial increase in expenditure that
took place. In this context some social classes got more out of education than
others for a number of different reasons. The most important factor is the
differential access to each *level* of education discussed earlier which is com-
pounded by the fact that as fewer working class children participate in any
level of type of education, so the resources devoted to it increase. Secondly,
there are differences in expenditure between *local authority areas* that may be
linked to their social class composition. Thirdly, there are variations in

PUBLIC EXPENDITURE ON EDUCATIONAL INSTITUTIONS ENGLAND AND WALES 1962-63 AND 1968-69

	£ millions	
	1962-63	1968-69
nursery and primary maintained	281	492
secondary maintained		
below school leaving age:		
grammar	93	92
secondary modern	183	211
comprehensive	23	89
other	23	30
above school leaving age	30	140
special schools	23	45
direct grant grammar	10	15
independent	6	11
further education (non advanced)	89	191
higher education		
colleges of education	35	73
advanced further education	22	68
universities including CATS	105	218
non classifiable	37	68
total	960	1,743

standards between *schools* at any level which are related to the social composition of the schools and their neighbourhoods. Fourthly, there are differences that arise *within schools* as a result of streaming, setting and other groupings.

PUBLIC EXPENDITURE ON MAINTENANCE GRANTS, ENGLAND AND WALES 1962-63 AND 1968-69

	£ millions	
	1963-64	1968-69
university	19.5	38.0
further education degree level	3.0	15.0
other further education	4.8	10.0
colleges of education	4.5	20.7
schools	0.9	2.3
total	32.7	86.0

sources: 1962-63: Peacock, Glennerster, Lavers, *Educational finance.* 1968-69: *Statistics of education 1969*, vol 5. Allocations to different types of secondary and further education are estimates derived from pupil numbers and unit costs either published by the DES or calculated for the Public Schools Commission.

Below, I discuss first the effects of expanding different levels of education at different rates and local variations and inequalities between schools.

from nursery schools to universities

The decade began with the Conservative government issuing a circular (8/60) forbidding the expansion of nursery education as part of an economy drive. This restriction was relaxed marginally just before the election (July 1964) when authorities were allowed to provide places where this would enable married women to return to teaching. Very few authorities took any action and the Labour Government followed this up in 1965 with a further relaxation allowing authorities to expand so long as they provided some extra places for teachers to whom priority was to be given. The number of children under five in maintained nursery, primary and special schools in 1965 was 222,000. In 1969 the figure was 239,000. The proportion of the age group in schools had increased only fractionally from 9.3 per cent to 9.5 per cent. (The neglect of nursery provision is discussed in detail in *A fair start* by Tessa Blackstone.) Demographic pressures existed at both the top and the bottom end of the system. The effects of the "bulge" and the trend on the older age groups have already been referred to. In addition the effect of the second post war "baby boom" were felt in the primary schools especially after 1964. The number of primary school children in England and Wales was 4.2 million in 1964, and 4.9 million in 1970. The check and subsequent fall in the birth rate that began at the end of 1964 did not bring any relief to the schools until 1970. The result was that both current and capital expenditure on primary schools had to rise between 1962-63 and 1968-69. Primary school building expenditure rose from £28 million to £82 million and despite the larger number of pupils the pupil teacher ratio fell in the decade from 29.0 to one in 1960 (28.7 in 1964) to 27.7 to one in 1969. These factors and price increases largely explain the 75 per cent increase in public expenditure on primary schools.

There was only a 2.4 per cent increase in *real* terms expenditure per pupil over the period 1962-63 to 1967-68. Whereas in the universities the expansion of numbers was carried out with a 16 per cent improvement in "real" expenditure per student—on resources, not grants (*Social trends*, table 88).

The secondary level saw the upheaval of secondary reorganisation. Dennis Marsden's chapter covers this and I shall only make two financial points. First, a decision was made right at the beginning of the Labour Government's term that no extra resources were to be devoted to going comprehensive. That decision explains a great many of the difficulties that ensued. Change involves costs, whether they appear in a budget or not. Second, the changes that have taken place should give children who used to be in secondary modern schools access to slightly more resources, more graduate staff and smaller classes. The change will, however, be small even in theory. Research undertaken for the Public Schools Commission indicated that current expenditure on an average grammar school child was nearly 30 per cent higher than on an average secondary modern child, but most of this was accounted for by the high sixth form costs. On average the 11-15 year old in a grammar school probably costs 10 per cent more than a child in a secondary modern. The better staffing in comprehensive schools means that a child of that age in those schools has about 6 per cent more spent on him than a secondary modern child and a bit less than the grammar child. The really big differences come at sixth form level in any type of school. It now costs 80 per cent more to teach at that level than below the age of 16 mainly because teaching groups are so much smaller.

In 1968 the Labour Government put off the date at which the school leaving age was to be raised. This was scarcely a disaster but it did cause needless confusion and again the money was "saved" at the expense mainly of working class children. During the sixties increasing numbers of teenagers took their "O" and "A" level courses full time in further education colleges, along with others taking pre-apprenticeship, pre-nursing and other courses. Full time students at "local techs" are more working class than the average sixth former but it is in the part time day release and evening courses where working class children predominate (nearly 80 per cent). This was the sector of post school education that has expanded least in the sixties.

The Labour Government accepted the Conservative Government's chosen instrument—the Industrial Training Boards, set up by the 1964 Act that were financed and dominated by industry.

In contrast the Labour Government expanded advanced level courses in further education much faster than the previous government or the Robbins committee had envisaged. Crosland sought to keep the rapidly growing state sector including the colleges of education separate from the universities. The characteristics of the state sector were to continue to be greater flexibility, more direct concern with the manpower needs of industry and greater accessibility to working class children. In practice, though, access is more affected by the nature of student finance than by institutional distinctions and this was not changed.

The sector of tertiary or post-school education that expanded fastest up to 1968 was the colleges of education. When Crosland was Secretary of State he insisted that the colleges take 20 per cent more students without expanding their physical capacity. This was on top of an already expanding programme of teacher training. The effects are now being felt. The pupil teacher ratio is now dropping significantly year by year. The danger is that restrictions on public expenditure under the Conservatives may make it difficult to employ these teachers.

The other initiative in higher education was the Open University. This has been subject to a lot of rather silly criticisms but the fact remains that with 80 per cent of its first intake of students coming from non-manual homes it is more middle class than the average university. It was a pity that it was not more firmly based in further education but it is helping to increase the opportunities of the adult population.

State support for the private sector is relevant too. Here the Labour Government had come to power committed in its election manifesto to "set up an educational trust to advise on the best way of integrating the public schools into the state system of education." The Public Schools Commission was the result. That Commission confirmed what we knew about the social segregation and the inequalities which these schools reinforce. Their recommendations for the integration of public and direct grant schools were not acted upon though proposals were apparently contained in the abortive green paper, *Education for a new generation*, that was to have been the basis for a new education act if Labour had returned to power. The document was never published. But the Government did act in one important area. Research for the Commission had shown that even on a moderate income parents could make various covenants and insurance arrangements for paying school fees that would give them tax remissions of at least £100 a year for each child. Rich parents could gain even more. (This was quite apart from the various tax benefits the schools themselves enjoyed.) Successive Finance Acts removed a good many of these personal tax benefits (H. Glennerster and G. Wilson, *Paying for private schools*). At the end of the 1960s the lower reaches of the private sector were contracting quite fast, but there was little sign of the peak of the system undergoing any major setback.

The Conservatives stated their intention to reverse all the relevant provisions in Labour's Finance Acts and they began in their first budget by repealing the provisions which amalgamated children's and parents' incomes for tax purposes, thus restoring the covenant to its original importance.

The overall picture is therefore a complex one. The expansion of primary school spending to cope with rising numbers, comprehensive reorganisation and the expansion of advanced further education were all factors balanced in favour of more resources for working class children. The rapid expansion of sixth forms without any major change in the maintenance grant system, the similar expansion of universities, all this meant more for middle class children. It is only by taking each level of education and assigning the expenditure on it to the social class groups using it that any overall conclusion can be reached. The results are summarised in the table below. It cannot be claimed that this is more than a general indication. We do not possess information on the class composition of pupils and students at each level and in each type of school at precisely the same points in time. We do, however, possess this information for at least one point in time for almost every level and type of institution and time series for the crucial sectors—sixth form and universities. Moreover, we know from earlier studies that the social composition of other institutions, like the grammar schools, have changed hardly at all over long periods. By piecing together results of surveys undertaken for Crowther, Robbins, Plowden, the Public Schools Commission, the Schools Council, NFER and a number of others, a reasonably accurate picture can be gained.

In all an extra £808 millions of public money were spent in 1968-69 compared

INCREASED EDUCATION EXPENDITURE BETWEEN 1962-63 AND 1968-69 ALLOCATED BY SOCIAL CLASS

social class	% of married males in 1961	1966	£	additional expenditure % of total increase	% increase 1962–68
I professional, managerial	4	5	64	7.9	136
II intermediate	17	17	180	22.2	106
IIIa clerical	13	13	112	13.9	93
IIIb skilled manual	38	37	298	37.0	72
IV semi-skilled manual	20	20	110	13.6	80
V unskilled	8	8	44	5.4	77
all classes	100	100	808	100.0	85

source: see text. Columns 2 and 3 derive from the 1961 and 1966 sample census.

to 1962-63 (excluding a small item unclassifiable by level). This constituted about 500 millions in 1963 prices. The highest social class, professionals and senior managers, constituted 5 per cent of all married couples in 1966 but 8 per cent of the extra expenditure benefited them. The other non-manual groups received more than their share of the extra resources denoted to education. Skilled manual workers families benefited in direct proportion to their numbers, but semi-skilled and unskilled families received a significantly smaller share than their numbers would lead one to expect. They constituted 28 per cent of the married population in 1966 but received only 19 per cent of the additional expenditure on education. Put another way all the non-manual groups enjoyed a greater improvement in their educational standards than the average improvement for the whole population. In brief then the expenditure on higher and sixth form education which largely benefited middle class children effectively outweighed the other attempts that were made to spend more on those types of education that primarily benefited the less fortunate. In this sense society did not "positively discriminate" in the sixties, it did the reverse. So far the calculations have ignored variations in expenditure between areas and schools. The next task, therefore, is to see whether this overall picture is modified when such variations are taken into account.

variations between local authorities

The inequalities between regions and local authorities to some extent reflect the different social composition of the areas but for the most part these variations are much more complex and subtle than that. At school level the actual variations in expenditure between authorities are reasonably small. This is particularly true of primary schools. In 1968-69 the average primary school child in a county borough in England and Wales cost £80.5 per annum. If we take a band 10 per cent above and below that point (£72.5-£88.5) we find it includes all except seven of the county boroughs, of which there are 83. Only four fall more than 10 per cent *below* the average. The English counties are even more homogenius. Only three of these fall outside the 10 per cent band. The Welsh counties are the exceptions to this rule. The picture at secondary level is complicated by the differing staying on rates but when these are taken into account a similar picture emerges.

The reasons for this uniformity are twofold. First the DES have applied a quota arrangement under which each local authority has been given a maximum figure for the number of full time teachers it could employ. The aim was to bring all authorities close to the average pupil teacher ratio by forcing the more mobile teachers to the less favoured areas. Though the system has been criticised it has worked reasonably well. The variation in teachers' salary costs per pupil are very much less than for other forms of expenditure and this item constitutes two-thirds of total current expenditure. The second factor is that central government grants to local authorities both in the form of the old rate deficiency grant and the resources element in the new rate support grant have evened out disparities between rich and poor authorities. There is scarcely any tendency for authorities with a large middle class population to spend more on their primary schoolchildren. Therefore, to return to the strong and weak definitions of equality, it is fair to say that on a weak definition and working on averages for whole authorities there is already a substantial degree of equality. This is particularly true of expenditure on teachers. When it comes to equipment and even more to school buildings the picture is rather different. Areas of declining population have faired very badly since the war in the school building allocations made by the central government. The West Midlands and the South East have done well for school building, the North West very poorly. (The best account of regional and local variations in education and their relation to environment is to be found in G. Taylor and N. Ayres, *Born and bred unequal*).

Nevertheless on a strong definition of equality one would expect areas with a poor home environment need rather *more* resources. Certainly the outcome of the education process varies sharply from one area to another. For example, the percentage of school children who stay on into the sixth form varies from 9 per cent in Bootle, Salford and Warrington to 25 per cent in Surrey. In the whole of the northern region only 13 per cent stay on until they are seventeen compared with 19 per cent in the South East. However, this is not a wholly North South divide since some of the highest staying on rates are in Wales and Westmorland while East Anglia has an even lower rates than the North. Moreover, the Midlands, despite the relative prosperity do poorly. This is yet another illustration of the fact than equal resources produce unequal results.

During the period of the Labour Government three changes occurred which operated in opposite directions. One relates to the effectiveness of the teachers' quota, another to aid for priority areas and the third to the grant arrangements. Simply because the supply of teachers improved, especially at the end of the sixties so the quota restrictions began to bite. In areas in the South East authorities found themselves turning away full time teachers. Moreover, the administration of the quota was adapted so that areas with a high concentration of immigrants and with education priority areas were given higher quotas.

The general grant that the Conservative Government introduced in 1959 replaced the old specific percentage grant for education. Instead local authorities received an exchequer grant which covered health, welfare, children's, and fire services as well as a number of other more minor functions. The sum total to be distributed between authorities was decided after negotiations with the local authority organisations and was based on estimates of future spending at national level. Once the global sum had been determined it was allocated between authorities on the basis of their populations, which were weighted to give what the original white paper called "a fair and reasonable measure of the relative needs of each local authority". One of these weights related to education. If an authority had more than a certain proportion of its population at school it received a supplementary grant for each pupil in a local authority school.

The 1966 rate support grant maintained the basic arrangements of the general grant but the formula by which the grant was distributed became more sophisticated. The "needs" element in the grant combined a portion for education as before. This was quite large and depended upon the number of "education units" for which the authority was financially responsible. However instead of being undifferentiated by age as in the previous system a primary school child was to count for one, a secondary school child under 16 for 1.9 and a child in the sixth form for 3.05. In one sense this is entirely reasonable. Large sixth form population costs more, but what it actually means is that areas where the home environments are most advantageous receive more central government aid. "Needs" have been interpreted as rate payers needs, rather than children's needs. What could happen instead is that authorities whose schools face much more difficult teaching tasks would be seen to have greater educational needs than other areas.

Thus the teachers' quota and the EPA policy worked in favour of the least fortunate authorities. The new grant structure worked in the opposite direction.

In an attempt to measure the effect of these different factors the table below shows the extent to which variations between authorities have diminished over time. The coefficient of variation is a measure of inequality. The larger the coefficient the greater the variation. The variations between standards in other local services is already much greater than in education. For example, in the health and welfare services in 1964 the coefficients of variation were well over 20 and that for home helps per 1,000 population was 35.4. Even in 1961 the variation in total cost per primary pupil was only 8.9. Since then the variation has been reduced still further. This was true for total cost, teachers' salary costs and the pupil teacher ratio.

The variation in secondary costs per pupil in contrast scarcely reduced at all (7.4 in 1961, 7.3 in 1969). This is consistent with the previous analysis of the effects of the Rate Support Grant. However, the greater equality in standards in primary schools was achieved between 1961 and 1968-69, despite the lack of any improvement between 1958 and 1961. In 1968-69 there was virtually no correlation at all between the social class composition of authorities and their expenditure per pupil (using the percentage of the population in the first seven socio-economic groups as an indicator, 1966 Census).

In comparison with the United States this is an important step towards equality, but it also shows that we are a long way as a nation from positively

VARIATIONS IN EXPENDITURE ON PRIMARY SCHOOLS BETWEEN LOCAL AUTHORITY AREAS*

year	total cost per pupil	teachers salaries per pupil	pupil teacher ratio
1950-51	10.6	9.9	—
1958-59	8.8	7.9	—
1961-62	8.9	7.2	5.6
1968-69	6.4	5.1	4.7

* as measured by the coefficient of variation.
source: B. Davies, "Social needs and resources in local services", IMTA, *Education Statistics*, for 1968-69.

discriminating in favour of areas with the highest incidence of educational need.

standards between schools

The comparatively even distribution of current expenditure between local authority areas, of course, hides the differences within them. It is clear to any interested observer, teacher or parent, that there is a great deal of variation between schools in terms of quantity of staff, quality of staff, staff turnover, the social background of the pupils and the standard of buildings.

There is, however, very little hard evidence. Various reports contain evidence of schools struggling with inadequate resources. The Newsom report, for example, undertook a small survey of inner city schools. It found substantially higher turnover of staff and much poorer premises. The reading age of the children was *17 months* lower than in the average secondary modern school. Illness and absence from school were much more common. Plowden's priority areas were the administrative response. To its credit the Labour Government acted upon that committee's advice. In July, 1967, six months after the report was published, the government announced that it was making £16 millions more authorisations for school building. Authorities had to show that the schools to be replaced fitted Plowden type criteria. Between 1968 and 1970 150 new schools were built under this programme.

The Burnham committee approved the allocation of £440,000 from that salary award which was to go teachers in "schools of exceptional difficulty". This amounted to £75 a year. Teachers in 570 schools chosen by the DES received this addition to their salary. In October 1968 as a response to Enoch Powell's "rivers of blood" speech amongst other things, £20-25 millions were made available for 75 per cent grants in support of local projects for immigrant areas. Of this over £2 million was devoted to providing nursery schools and classes.

Finally, action research in five education priority areas was sponsored by the DES. All this was on a national level. Local authorities themselves gave such things as extra equipment allowances to such schools. Indeed some had been doing so on an informal basis already.

As will already be clear the amount of money devoted to "positive discrimination policies" was very tiny. Psychologically its impact may well have been greater. For a short period the publicity the £75 and the novelty of the idea may have helped. Yet in the long term it will be the resources, the human resources attracted to these areas that will count.

The priority area concept has inevitably come under criticism. Some have argued that the choice of particular schools as ones facing "exceptional difficulty" merely stigmatised them in the local community and amongst local teachers thus adding to their problems. The choice of particular schools was criticised as arbitrary. On similar though more technical grounds Bleddyn Davies has criticised the idea of taking 10 per cent of all areas with the greatest needs. Concentrations of need do not cluster in neat

10 per cent groupings. There is a spectrum of differing needs, and resources should be matched to needs across that whole spectrum.

Towards the end of the sixties there was therefore some attempt to even up and then eventually give superior facilities to schools in otherwise deprived areas. Just how effective this was or will prove to be is not clear. There may well be strong forces pulling in the opposite direction. The policy of building very small primary schools together with rehousing policy may have produced more single class schools than ever before. The growing awareness of education (by middle class parents), their exercise of choice and their increasingly aggressive manipulation of the system may have achieved the same results even in moderately mixed neighbourhoods. Once deserted by aspiring parents a school can rapidly enter on a downward spiral of lower morale, increased difficulty for teachers, and more rapid turnover of staff.

internal school organisation

The final sphere in which inequalities arise is within the school. There is no space to go into detail but there is now a well established relationship between social class and the stream a child is in. "A" streams have a relatively high proportion of middle class children, "C" streams a relatively low proportion.

Streaming might in theory have been used to concentrate resources on the least "able," in practice this has never been its purpose. It appears that though the lowest streams are sometimes taught in smaller classes their teachers are less experienced (see for example J. Barker Lunn, *Streaming in the primary school*, the NFER study). The NFER's research for Plowden showed that the majority of children in junior schools were still streamed but that there had been a move away from it. More young teachers favoured unstreaming. Just which groups are benefiting in the new unstreamed classes, within which there are still "ability groupings," is very difficult to say. The preference given to the more literate or more well behaved child may be just as great.

But it has become more common, as the supply of teachers has eased, for part-time teachers to take small groups of "slow readers" in infant and junior schools, for more intensive coaching. Similarly in comprehensive secondary schools there has been a gradual trend away from streaming (see C. Benn and B. Simon, *Half way there*). If we know little about the distribution of resources between schools we know even less about the distribution within them. This has always been considered a "professional" matter, but it is crucial to the issue of equality.

summary

In brief, the main beneficiaries of the education explosion of the 1960s have been the middle class since the fastest expansion took place in that sector which was and remains predominantly theirs—higher education. This major trend has been countered in part by a greater uniformity in local expenditure —and a slight narrowing in the differential between "slum area" schools and the rest but none of these factors are sufficient to outweigh the first. Even so in absolute terms the increase in education benefits received by families from all classes have been substantial. In real terms even families of semi-skilled workers enjoyed significantly more education in 1968 than in 1962. The importance of this can be seen in the next section.

education and redistribution

So far education has been viewed merely as a benefit, but it is also part of the general revenue benefit system constituted by taxation and social service provision. Other contributors have discussed and drawn varying conclusions from the Central Statistical Office studies. These attempt to show how much various types of family in different income bands pay in tax and receive from the state by way of cash benefits and services in kind. In the latest study (*Economic trends*, February 1971) the type of benefits are distinguished and one of these is education. Each family with a child at a state school has assigned to it a benefit valued according to the average expenditure on children of that age. The results show that unlike most other benefits, the value of education benefits rises with income. Even so, the extent to which this is so is obscured by the fact that children are defined as being under 16.

Perhaps the main contribution that the Central Statistical Office study makes in regard to education is to show how large the total education benefit is in relation to income and the value of other benefits. The family with two children under 16, having a median income of £1,600 in 1969, received about £125 of education benefit (this figure is an average including families with children below 5 receiving no benefit). The total value of all other benefits, health, family allowances, national insurance, welfare foods, and so on come to £175. The case of the family with four children is even more striking. Their medium income is similar, about £1,600, but their education benefit amounts to £364 a year. This compares with £325 from all other state benefits.

In this sense education between the ages of 5 and 16 is a major redistributive factor. The incomes of the poorest families, after taxation has been subtracted and benefits added, is much higher than the original cash income of those families. The largest single element in the difference is the education benefit. Education at these ages is therefore a means of redistribution both vertically between income groups and horizontally between the family and the rest of society. The extent of this redistribution increased between 1962 and 1969. But provision after that age, especially higher education, is a different proposition. It is sometimes claimed that the greater use made of higher education by the higher income groups presents no redistributive problems since these groups pay higher taxes. By matching the Central Statistical Office data very roughly with earnings by occupation it is possible to test this proposition. Our tax structure is unprogressive in its total incidence. In the following calculations national insurance contributions were excluded as a specific tax not related to higher education. Column 3 of the table below shows the approximate average value of taxes, direct and indirect, paid by average male earners in the appropriate social class categories. These are it must be stressed only rough estimates based on the sources shown in the table but the orders of magnitude are consistent with other sources. Column 4 expresses this tax yield as a ratio of the tax paid by the lowest social group. Column 1 shows the proportion of children from each group that benefit from university education and column 2 relates these percentages to that of the lowest social group. Thus while the highest social group benefit *seventeen* times as much as the

TAX REVENUE BY SOCIAL CLASS COMPARED WITH ACCESS TO UNIVERSITY

social class	% of age group entering university 1968	ratio of entrants class V=1	average taxes paid per annum 1969	ratio of taxes class V=1
I professional, managerial	35	17.0	1,700	5.2
II intermediate	12	6.0	860	2.6
IIIa clerical	13	6.5		
IIIb skilled, manual	4	2.0	545	1.7
IV semi-skilled, manual	3	1.5	455	1.4
V unskilled	2	1.0	327	1.0

source: *Economic trends*, February 1971, UCCA, 1967-68 Report: Statistical Supplement. Department of employment, *Survey of earnings*.

lowest group from the expenditure on universities, they only contribute *five* times as much revenue. (This argument assumes that each type of non-specific revenue contributes equally to all government expenditure. There are difficulties in this assumption but it has often been made, as for example in A. Peacock, *Income distribution and social policy*.)

So long as entry remains, as it must do for a long period, so closely tied to class background the case for financing higher education differently is doubly strong. Not only do graduates earn more—so did their parents. The most probable alternative to the present system is to impose a higher rate of tax on those who have received higher education.

WHERE NOW?

The theme of this chapter has been that greater equality of opportunity entails unequal provision. It was this interpretation of the concept that came to be accepted as a principle of administration during the late sixties following the Plowden Report. It was unfortunately a superficial acceptance. The priority area programmes were small. On the other hand a great deal of expenditure was devoted to meeting the "social" demand for higher education of the traditional kind. In fact the demand for full time higher education is in no sense a pure measure of demand for post school education. It is the demand that survives a complex series of rationing devises and hidden costs—the lack of adequate financial support for those who stay at school or for those who wish to follow courses other than degree courses or for those who wish to follow part time courses at any level, the refusal of employers to release young workers.

The impetus to comprehensive reorganisation, the improvements in teacher supply and the school building programme were significant achievements. It is, however, fair to point to three major gaps:

1. The failure to extend day release, despite a promise given in the manifesto;

2. The failure to improve or replace school maintenance grants, despite a promise in the manifesto;

3. The failure to radically change the local authority grant structure.

To take positive discrimination seriously means adopting it as a total strategy, adopting it at every level of education, in every area, *in* schools as well as *between* schools, out of school as much as in school. It merges into and is an inseparable part of community development. What does this mean in specific terms?

a programme

1. A major investment in pre-school facilities, nursery classes, play centres and play groups. These should include the mothers in the organisation and provision as far as possible for pre-school education has social as well as narrowly educational goals. Provision should be made first and most intensively in areas with inadequate and overcrowded housing, inadequate open space and where most families that are too poor to provide the elaborate educational toys that litter the middle-class home.

2. Primary and secondary schools must be staffed and teachers rewarded in relation to the educational needs of the neighbourhood. Teaching in an area where parents' support has to be *won*, requires a degree of skill and effort of a different order than a post in a suburban grammar school. To be a form teacher in a class, half of whom have only one parent, who miss school regularly and who not infrequently land in court, involves more dedication and more sheer administration than "A" level work in the largest sixth form. Teaching in a school where violence is barely submerged, and sullen resentment of society is the dominant attitude demands complete mastery of the art of teaching as well as a level of understanding that most social workers rarely achieve. At the moment, for the most part, the criteria on which we distribute special allowances and determine headmasters' salaries, such as the size of sixth form and size of school, are based on an irrelevant set of values.

3. Primary schools in poor areas need more adults in the class room—teachers and others helping with reading, helping with talking. Many of the commonly used methods such as project work often tend to rely too much for their success on the parent to sustain the child's interest and inspiration. Parents with a very poor education themselves are unlikely to be able to do this unaided.

4. Schools of this kind need more equipment, more books. Books will get lost, be treated more roughly. If the homes have few books the school must have more. Public libraries instead of operating on the criteria "they don't use books in that area" should go out of their way to co-operate with the school. Reading out aloud at the end of the day is a successful way of encouraging the child to go on and read more of the book but if interest is expressed it must be followed up immediately with the book to take home. There must be enough. Reminding mum to ask teacher for the one copy next week will not do. All of this means grading allowances to schools for staff and equipment according to the school's needs in relation to its environment. It should preferably not mean picking just a few schools out but grading throughout the authority's area. This is all far from simple, and it raises the whole principle of national criteria and how far central control is required.

5. To enable authorities with a high incidence of social need to undertake this positive discrimination within their area they need a disproportionate amount of assistance from the central government. "Needs" as defined formally in the Rate Support Grant formula and informally in the criteria for building allocations, should include a significant element for counter balancing social deprivation.

6. Perhaps most important of all positive discrimination means investing more time and thought on the way children from deprived environments are taught. So much of the energy that has gone into new curricula has been directed at the most able. To use some of the new maths text books on which so much outstanding mathematical talent has been lavished with a class in an ordinary comprehensive school can mean devoting half the lesson to English not maths. The children have just not met the words. Teachers in these schools need to devote more time and resources to the way they present material and to what they teach just because few if any of them will have come from such areas themselves and they have fewer good books and aids to help them. The Schools Council has made a beginning here, but so much remains to be done. The curriculum needs developing in ways that are relevant. Eric Midwinter has argued from his experience in Liverpool: "We are convinced that the social rather than the austerely academic element in education must be stressed; in order to give the child a chance to break through the oppressive cycle of social breakdown. There is an urgent need to familiarise children with their environment, so that they might come to criticise it articulately and raise creative responses to the problems it presents them. Community schools need a community curriculum" (*Where*, February 1971). That statement raises some fundamental issues of practical politics but it does illustrate the need to give priority to curriculum development in these areas and the Liverpool project is only one example.

7. Priority in resource allocation and the concept of the community school of course presuppose the elimination of secondary selection. If the able children with enthusiastic parents are withdrawn at eleven these schools are crippled at the outset.

8. In some cases weekly boarding may provide an appropriate solution for one or more members of a family under stress.

9. At present the grant system for those over 15 discriminates heavily in favour of the middle-class child, and the industrial training and apprenticeship system discriminates in favour of the minority of potential craftsmen and against girls. The whole structure of further education for the teenager needs a major overhaul especially its financial aspect. The major responsibility should not be with industry but with the education authority. The reformers who pressed for the 1944 Act wanted young people to be released *for* work between 16 and 18. A whole range of possibilities are open involving different mixes of full and part time training and education paid for partly by the state and partly by industry not only for those under 18 but adults as well. The essential point is that the state's financial support for education should not be limited as closely as it now is to the full-time academic course entered upon at 18 plus. Concentrating support upon the young school leaver or the mature

working-class mother is as much "positive discrimination" as the more narrowly conceived notion.

10. The expenditure on such a programme would seriously conflict with the major sums that will be needed to finance an expansion of traditional higher education on demand. In the Fabian pamphlet *Planning education in 1980* a number of us tried to face this issue of priorities and suggested not only a faster rate of overall expansion in the education budget but savings in the cost of full-time higher education as a way of paying for these developments (see also Layard and Williams in G. Brosan, *et al, Patterns and policies in higher education*). A differential tax on those who benefit most from the system is still the fairest way to even out the financial results of unequal access.

If we try to respond to the demand for more full time higher education on the scale that seems likely without taking steps to alter access or to alter the nature and cost of higher education we shall commit the same strategic mistake that we made in the sixties. Only this time we shall commit it knowingly.

chronology

October 1964	Michael Stewart becomes Secretary of State for Education and Science. Decisions taken *not* to legislate for comprehensive reorganisation nor to provide extra finance for it.
January 1965	Mr. Crosland becomes Secretary of State.
March 1965	Drive to recruit more married women back into teaching begun.
April 1965	Crosland announced 14 point emergency plan for expanding teacher supply including more intensive use of College of Education premises.
April 1965	Crosland's Woolwich speech outlining the "binary philosophy"—the strengthening of the state sector of higher education.
June 1965	Publication of *The ninth report of the National Advisory Council on the Training and Supply of Teachers*. Recommended speed up in Robbins' targets for teacher training.
July 1965	Crosland told colleges of education they must expand places by 20 per cent without extra accommodation.
July 1965	Circular 10/65 issued calling on local authorities to submit plans for comprehensive reorganisation within twelve months. (Now withdrawn by Mrs Thatcher.)
October 1965	National Plan contained new commitment to expand advanced courses in further education faster than Robbins proposed—up to 70,000 places in 1970.
December 1965	Public Schools Commission set up to recommend ways of integrating public schools into the state system of education.
December 1965	Addendum 2 to circular 8/60—a slight relaxation of the ban on nursery provision.
February 1966	Publication of the White Paper—*A university of the air*, Cmnd 2922.
May 1966	Publication of the White Paper—*A plan for polytechnics and the colleges*, Cmnd 3006. This proposed the designa-

tion of a small number of polytechnics in which advanced work would be concentrated.

June 1966	Circular 10/66 linked approval for capital expenditure on secondary schools to comprehensive reorganisation. (Now withdrawn by Mrs. Thatcher).
January 1967	Plowden committee reported—major proposals: priority areas (EPAS) and universal part time nursery education.
April 1967	Plans announced to establish 30 Polytechnics.
July 1967	£16 million additional approvals for school building in EPAS areas announced.
July 1967	Comptroller and Auditor General given access to UGC and Universities' accounts.
September 1967	Patrick Gordon-Walker becomes Secretary of State.
November 1967	All registered independant boarding schools had to seek "efficient" status or be closed. (Now reversed by Mrs. Thatcher).
January 1968	As part of general economy cuts the raising of the school leaving age postponed two years to 1972-73.
March 1968	Budget announced end to separate taxation of children and other measures affecting support for private education.
April 1968	School meal charges raised from 1s to 1s 6d. Edward Short becomes Secretary of State.
July 1968	Education Act 1968 becomes law. Under it colleges of education have to have separate governing bodies. Public Schools Commission produced first report recommending creation of a Boarding Schools Corporation to supervise integration of public schools.
August 1968	Central Government Capitation grant to Direct Grant Schools reduced from £52 to £32 a year.
October 1968	Urban aid programme announced in a joint circular—some money for pre-school facilities. Total programme including other services £20-25 million over four years 1968-72.
January 1969	School building programme for raising school leaving age announced—£105 million.
February 1969	About £2.4 million allocated to education mainly nursery provision under the first two phases of the Urban Aid Programme.
August 1969	The regulation setting 40 as a maximum class size in primary schools and 30 in Secondary schools cancelled. Emphasis laid on reducing class sizes in primary schools.
November 1969	Queen's Speech announced intention to introduce a bill requiring LEA's to prepare comprehensive plans.
March 1970	Public Schools Commission second report recommended an end to direct grant status and fee paying.
June 1970	Proposals for a major New Education Act ready for publication.

7. politicians, equality and comprehensives

Dennis Marsden

Only ten per cent of secondary school children were in *fully* comprehensive schools in 1970 when Labour went out of office (C. Benn and B. Simon, *Half way there: a report on the British comprehensive school reform*, p57, McGraw Hill, 1970) and it had long been apparent that a new Education Act would be necessary to carry through the reorganisation of education on comprehensive lines. Yet we should welcome Labour's failure to pass an education act in 1965. The educational policy record of Labour's leading politicians shows that any legislation would have been a partial, half-baked and confused measure which could have set back the cause of educational reform for another 20 years. And indeed the first socialist education act still seems a long way off.

In the field of comprehensive reorganisation Labour's politicians have had the worst of both worlds: they have achieved no changes in the educational system, yet they have been successfully branded as trying to "interfere politically" with education. The truth is, of course, that educational policy is inevitably political and a matter of controversy, since it deals with the distribution of life chances, resources and power in society. That is why Conservatives try to present education as an area which should be the exclusive province of the professional. But unfortunately Labour has gone along with this view. Within rather broad and confused egalitarian and democratic intentions, no detailed educational policy has been worked out. As a result, the policies pursued when Labour has been in office appear to have been largely dictated by the "permanent politicians" of the Ministry of Education (now the Department of Education and Science). And these civil servants have been far from radical in their conception and execution of educational policy.

Thus, Labour's basic strategy in 1965 was to present comprehensive reorganisation as a response to overwhelming technological and popular demands, backed by increasing research evidence of waste and social divisiveness in the bipartite system. Politicians, Labour suggested, had merely to ride and guide the swell of economic and social change. Comprehensive schools were allowed to appear as machines to engineer equality without the redistribution of resources in the educational system or the rest of society. Crucially, Labour politicians failed to embrace what should be the Party's historic role. The Labour Party's task has always been not merely to articulate and guide but actually to arouse and lead a popular demand for equality in education, a demand which has been perpetually damped down and distorted by the overshadowing images of the public and grammar schools. Without such a lead during the last Labour Government's spell in office little progress was made towards the reduction of educational inequality.

Failure to move towards equality in education thus raises as many questions about the nature of the Labour Party and its leadership and ideological base as about any supposed "conservatism" and rigidity in the educational structure itself. Only a section of the Labour Party, not the leadership, has ever contemplated radical changes in education, but the Party has been ineffectual because of internal arguments at cross purposes and a lack of decision coupled with a failure to learn from experience.

Fortunately, if the Party is now prepared to learn, a start has already been made upon the essential historical, political, sociological and administrative analysis of educational changes (O. Banks, *Parity and prestige in English secondary education*, Routledge, 1955; P. W. Musgrave, *Society and education in England since 1800*, Methuen, 1959; D. V. Glass, "Education and social change in modern England" in M. Ginsberg (ed) *Law and opinion in England in the twentieth century*, Stevens, 1959; B. Simon, *Education and the Labour movement*, Lawrence and Wishart, 1965, and *The common secondary school*, Lawrence and Wishart, 1955, and the Labour Party's educational policies). Throughout this chapter I have drawn heavily on M. Parkinson's *The Labour Party and the organisation of secondary education, 1918-1965*, Routledge, 1970, (see also O. Banks, *op cit*), and we can also draw on a number of detailed discussions of comprehensive reorganisation and the workings of comprehensive schools (C. Benn and B. Simon, *op cit*; R. Pedley, *The comprehensive school*, Penguin (revised edition), 1969; D. Rubinstein and B. Simon, *The evolution of the comprehensive school*, Routledge, 1969; T. G. Monks, *Comprehensive education in England and Wales*, National Foundation for Educational Research, 1968; and see also articles in *Comprehensive education*, and *Where?*).

What is most needed is to close the disastrous gap between the "political" and the "educational" elements of the comprehensive debate; the gap which has been Labour's achilles heel and which the Conservatives try so assiduously to maintain. Labour and the egalitarians must think much more strenuously about what political definitions of equality mean in terms of the everyday workings of the comprehensive school. And at the same time educationists and educators need to be much more aware of the implications of particular school structures for the wider society. Closing the gap thus involves an exploration of the various "political" aims for the comprehensive school, to see how far they match up with the internal dynamics of existing comprehensive schools.

We will find that different sections of the Labour Party and the educationists who support comprehensive schools have never agreed upon how great a social change can be expected from secondary reorganisation alone. Nor has there been adequate discussion of the alternative strategies and possible contradictions contained in an educational policy which is variously described as aiming for a meritocracy, for engineered social equality, or towards the wider goal of helping to create a community. The debate inside the Labour Party obscurely mirrors the political disagreements among the left as to whether we are content with a society stratified on intellectual criteria, where control is in the hands of a small number of the most able, or whether we want a wider diffusion of control in society to create local democracy.

When we turn to research on the schools we find that research projects themselves embody or conceal a confusion of values. As a result it becomes difficult to decide how "successfully" existing comprehensive schools embody the various political goals which have been set for them by politicians. We can, however, use recent educational research to challenge the Labour politicians' lack of interest in the educational process. For legislation about the framework of education is vital but not sufficient, and ultimately the achievement of the comprehensive *principle* and equality in education will be dependent on the teaching profession. Research also questions the Fabian Society's faith in achieving societal change through bringing influence to bear on only a small legislative elite.

LABOUR'S EDUCATIONAL POLICIES UP TO 1964

Labour has never passed any major piece of educational legislation, but has worked within the blueprints provided by other governments. This is unfortunate because education acts passed by other governments have been complex compromises, notably between the central government and the secondary school teachers, the private schools and the church interests; but also between different sections of the political parties, between the Minister and his civil servants, and between the central and local administrations. As a result the major education acts (for example 1870, 1902, and 1944) have all appeared late on the scene to legitimate changes which were already substantially under way and to shore up the existing creaking and out of date structures, but scarcely to promote change. Moreover, the rather loose compromises provided by the acts have been over-ridden both by pressures inside the schools and by the external demands made upon the educational system (see O. Banks, *op cit,* for a discussion of parental and teacher influence on the grammar school curriculum, and P. W. Musgrove, *op cit,* on the role of Education Acts in educational policy).

Most importantly, the public schools with their high prestige and elite academic curriculum have distorted our state educational system, in spite of politicians' hopes to the contrary. Under competition from the public schools and hypnotised by their example, the grammar schools have retained a curriculum which is predominantly non-vocational and largely non-technical academic.

And the emerging parental and pupil demand for education has consistently been geared to this academic curriculum, because it obviously gave access to the more prestigious local jobs and to the higher reaches of the national educational system (see G. Lacey, *Hightown grammar,* Manchester University Press, 1970, for an analysis on the use of a grammar school by its local population). But worse, the Conservative influence of this elite image on Labour's own politicians and policies is the most striking feature of the period both before and during Labour's post-war spells in office. Labour's obsession with the public schools and with gaining access to the grammar school has prevented adequate discussion of the education of the bulk of the population.

Thus before the Second World War Labour was preoccupied with opening up the grammar schools to the highly achieving working class child, and now the Party's official policy is comprehensive reorganisation. But the shift in emphasis is, for the majority of the Party, merely from unequal educational provision in different schools to the provision of different and unequal education within the same school.

Radicals in the Labour Party have been worried that official policies were doing too little to promote equality and democracy through education. They have argued that if we want children to have more equal chances in later life, then education is one very obvious area where the legislature possesses influence, and at the very least an equally good education should be provided for all children. More recently it has been suggested that for the lower achiever education ought in some ways to be superior, in order to "compensate" for the initial unequal distribution of life chances.

The urge of the radicals has been, therefore, to push selection out of the schools altogether, or at least to delay differentiation in education and to foster qualities of citizenship by the provision of a schooling which would be common to all children. An associated change towards more democratic ethos in the schools has also been sought. For example the 1925 Labour Party Conference was urged to seek: "the creation of a specifically working-class education which would develop socialist values, substituting co-operation for competition among children and other qualities and outlooks essential to a citizen of a co-operative Commonwealth." (M. Parkinson, *op cit*, p21). Such calls echo an earlier, pre-urban English radical ideal of the "common school." But to suggest any very strong direct link with the past would exaggerate the degree of support for such schools. There has been no movement in England of comparable strength to that which powered and shaped the expansion and achievements of the American comprehensive high school.

In America, because the aim of the common school was to break away from hierarchical and stultifying societal patterns and to found a new, more democratic society, the common school became associated with the "progressive" movements in education which have tried to emphasise looser organisational structures and more child-centred learning, with less emphasis on set curricula and hence on formal examination passing techniques. In England, however, the most conspicuous, and even notorious, experiments in progressive secondary education have remained cloistered retreats for the children of rich deviants, and their influence on state secondary education has remained, by reason of their vastly superior resources, peripheral and irrelevant (M. Punch, Ph D thesis, Essex University, 1971).

Since the 1920s, however, and more successfully since the last war, supporters of the common school among teachers in England have begun to work out innovations in forms of school organisation and the curriculum which will be appropriate in mass education. For example the National Association of Labour Teachers early pressed for a school with a variety of courses around a common base, and more recently there has been a movement towards non-streaming and open plan schools, especially in the primary school (see various issues of *Forum*).

The study of Labour's educational policy thus becomes a twofold analysis: of an internal debate about three or even four possible working definitions of "equality," which takes the form of a slow, partial and often acrimonious transition from one definition to the next more radical policy; and of an external and uneasy debate with educationists who have tended to become impatient with the Party for its lack of application to the practical details of teaching.

the 1944 education act—an opportunity missed

Seen from this perspective the 1944 Education Act was a great opportunity missed. Both the grammar schools and the public schools were at a low ebb of popularity. The country was ready for change—but the Labour Party was not. The public schools were feeling the financial draught and in those egalitarian times had made overtures to the state concerning some form of "integration" (M. Parkinson, *op cit*, p98). Also it can be argued that because the working class had never been admitted to the grammar schools in any numbers, only a minority of the electorate would have regretted the absorption of the schools into a "multilateral" system of streamed "comprehensive" schools such as we are getting in many areas today. There was not then the determined public and professional support of the grammar school which we have seen develop more recently. For in the 1920s and 1930s the grammar school had obstinately remained, to the despair of its teachers and more elitist supporters, largely "a social factory for turning the sons of clerks and shopkeepers into clerks and shopkeepers" (Lord Eustace Percy in 1933, quoted in O. Banks, *op cit*, p124). Its curriculum was forced to make some concessions to the duller fee-paying pupils who formed part of its intellectually more "comprehensive" intake. "Multilateral" schools (which preserved a grammar stream within a larger school) had won some support from the selective and fee-paying schools' Assistant Masters Association. And the NUT was more wholeheartedly in favour of multilateral schools because the union had always recognised that the different function of the elementary schools in which its members taught had influenced their inferior rewards and working conditions (Rubinstein and Simon, *op cit*, pp15-16).

The LCC had already during the 1930s announced its intention of reorganising its secondary education on multilateral lines—although Sir Graham Savage, the Chief Education Officer, intended that within these schools the teachers should "stream like mad" (R. Pedley, *op cit*, p98). And in 1942 the Labour Party as a whole had advocated selective development of multilateral schools. Rubinstein and Simon, *op cit*, p24). Politically, then, a much stronger bid to curb the public schools and the establishment of a system of multilaterals would have been feasible in 1945.

But the Labour Party as a whole was not committed to changing the structure of education, and the moment passed. There were even influential voices among the Party's educational policy makers who feared that the LCC's multilaterals might be "sacrificing educational for social considerations" (M. Parkinson, *op cit*, p33). A coalition government had drafted and passed the 1944 Education Act only a year before, and rather than reopen the whole field Labour submerged its disagreements and implemented some of the Act's provisions. This Act accepted much of the existing structure. The public schools remained unscathed, protected by the smallest token of integration in the Fleming proposals (see J. Hipkin, "Integration: the Fleming response",

New wine in old bottles? Bell, 1968). Once again the shaky church schools were propped up with state cash. The Act's main achievement was probably to whip into line the majority of backward authorities who had not yet followed the Hadow and Spens recommendations for the reorganisation of elementary education on primary and secondary lines. True, grammar school fees were abolished. But, thanks to Labour's earlier efforts to expand the free place system, equality of opportunity (in terms of equal access to grammar schools for children of equal measured intelligence) had arrived in some areas as long ago as the 1920s, and it was within the power of all local authorities under the previous educational structure. The 1929-31 Labour Government had raised the number of free places an LEA could offer to 50 per cent and the middle class, by and large, did not compete for these (see J. Floud, *et al, Social class and educational opportunity*, Portway, 1966, and M. Parkinson, *op cit*, p27).

The left wing of the Labour Party can be seen to have won a small victory by insisting that the 1944 Education Act should not actually specify tripartitism, thus permitting some experiments on comprehensive lines (see O. Banks, *op cit*, p133). But this action tempered the restrictiveness of the selective system and relieved the 1964 Labour Government of the absolute necessity of passing new legislation. Thus it can be seen to have helped the 1944 Education Act to postpone by 20 or 30 years the major reform of the structure of education which was then due.

There were, in fact, to be rather few major schemes for comprehensive schools. The exceptions were London and Coventry, after extensive bomb damage, the West Riding and Leicestershire with enlightened education officers, the New Towns where there were no entrenched grammar schools, and a few rural areas like Anglesey where the comprehensive school made economic sense. Most authorities proceeded to reorganise on bipartite lines (the third element of tripartitism, the secondary technical school, was killed by the grammar school). And indeed many solidly Labour local authorities failed to plan comprehensives at any time in the later years when comprehensive reorganisation became Labour's national policy.

By and large the teaching profession accepted the offer of parity of conditions between different types of secondary school (which however has never been honoured because of the extra resources allocated to schools for sixth formers). Meanwhile the grammar school teachers began to swing away from support for multilateral schools as they sensed the vulnerability of the separatist grammar school culture which they were, at that time, trying to maintain.

After the nation's education had been reconstructed on bipartite lines it became less likely that authorities could be persuaded to go comprehensive: the very buildings and educational capital became a conservative influence, not altogether precluding reorganisation but restricting it to schemes using the existing bipartite schools. Yet this factor was as nothing compared with the post-war rise of the grammar school. Once the grammar school was opened to a slightly wider and larger population and the teachers achieved their ambition of making it a preparatory school for the universities, the political problems of reorganising secondary education increased (see C. Lacey, *op cit*.) Public support for the schools grew. And following on the Hadow, Spens and Norwood Reports a whole rationale of intelligence testing and psychological typing was elaborated to bolster up the academic curriculum and cognitive style of learning. To do the psychologists justice many would have little part in this, and to some extent we have to distinguish between the use for which psychological testing was devised by psychologists and the use to which it has been put by educational administrators in rationing resources. But not until the late 1950s were psychologists able to mount any kind of counter attack on the predictive validity of the tests in education, and even today supporters of the tests are strongly entrenched (see A. Jensen, "How much can we boost IQ and scholastic achievement," *Harvard educational review*, Winter 1969, and replies, Summer 1969). Now as a final defence against reorganisation the grammar schools have claimed a monopoly of elite culture and have begun to assert a "centuries old tradition" of training leaders and transmitting the national heritage, a "tradition" which has reached its apotheosis in the *Black papers*.

Comprehensives made a little headway before 1964. Saddled with a large number of grammar schools over which it had no control, London succeeded in getting 45 per cent of secondary school children in new comprehensive schools by 1964, although many of the schools were heavily creamed (A. Corbett, "Far from comprehensive," *New Society*, 11 July 1968). In Leicestershire a very influential scheme showed how comprehensive reorganisation could be carried out within the limits of buildings designed for bipartitism, by tiering lower and upper schools. Together with the West Riding schools these schemes went some way to confound continuing fears about the "lowering of standards."

They confirmed what was already being learned from the secondary modern schools where the attempted official embargo on examinations had been broken, that many pupils rejected by the grammar schools could succeed in national examinations (Rubinstein and Simon, *op cit*, pp55-57).

Unfortunately this very slow and unco-ordinated build-up of comprehensive education got the worst of both worlds. There was relatively little chance for educational innovation where schools still deprived of the top ability range of pupils had to struggle to justify their existence in terms of examination results. And the schools were permanently in a politically delicate situation, newsworthy only if there was some catastrophe or hooliganism. Because the schools were largely replacements for secondary modern rather than grammar schools, there was little education of the public as to what they were intended to be. London's new comprehensives had to be single sex rather than coeducational to convince the public they had academic pretensions. And the fate of Risinghill tells us much about the political climate in which comprehensive schools had to struggle to "coexist" with the old attitudes (Leila Berg, *Risinghill, the death of a comprehensive school*, Penguin, 1968).

At this time, then, the aims of the common school advocates, to introduce new methods of teaching or to work out a new educational ethic, could gain their opportunity only in the *primary schools*. In these schools, for example in Leicestershire under the Leicestershire plan, the removal of the 11 plus strait-jacket released a "creative explosion."

Labour's internal disagreements

Labour's period of power after the war brought into the open the very deep cleavages of educational opinion within the Party, both at national and local level. Because the public schools remained intact, Labour Ministers of education were the more reluctant to touch the grammar schools for fear of weakening their competitive position. Above all the Ministers believed in the grammar schools, and it became clear that their views were those of the civil servants at the Ministry of Education.

The civil servants, in official ministry pamphlets, had tried to ensure only a limited role for the comprehensive school, and they continued to press (as in pre-war days) for a reduction of grammar school places on the grounds that there were too few able pupils to fill the places already available. After the war the Ministry tried to prevent secondary modern pupils from entering for external examinations, on the unrealistic grounds that the schools were supposed to be catering for a different kind of child and should therefore develop a different curriculum.

An acrimonious running battle between the Minister and the Labour left continued throughout the post-war government's spell in office, crystallising in the refusal of the Minister to withdraw the civil servants' pamphlet and refusal to permit the absorption of grammar schools into comprehensive schemes (see R. Pedley, *op cit*, pp37-42, M. Parkinson, *op cit*, chap 3). To do the Ministry of Education justice there was as yet no research evidence that the abolition of grammar school fees had failed to open up the grammar school to working class children, nor was there any working experience of English comprehensives which would point to new directions.

Towards the end of Labour's first spell in office the left won the Party's nominal acceptance of a comprehensives policy, the official commitment being made in 1951. The process had been gradual with the National Executive Committee swinging against the Minister in the later stages of the battle. Thereafter the comprehensive issue dropped temporarily out of sight. There was no controversy visible within or between the parties, for little was happening (M. Parkinson, *op cit*, pp71-72).

Disagreement reappeared, however, a year or two later when the Party tried to decide what sort of comprehensive schools should be established. Finally a commitment was made to the 11-18 school, with the possibility of a minor role for a sort of senior or sixth form college system, but the latter was much mistrusted by the left at that time (M. Parkinson, *op cit*, pp73-75). The remaining period up to 1964 was marked by considerable confusion about what comprehensive schools were to be like, what was their purpose, how they were to be presented to the public and how local authorities were to be persuaded to reorganise. In fact the debate had to be damped down to avoid tearing the defeated Party to pieces. Lack of detailed working evidence from comprehensive schools and the difficulty of discussing the subject without causing rifts were to cost the Party dear when a firmer, clearer policy was needed in 1964. Considerable energy was still being diverted into discussing the issue of the public schools.

the changing image of the comprehensive school

In different ways support for the comprehensive school in the early 1950s was couched in social terms. The National Association of Labour Teachers (NALT) stressed the common school concept. But some of the major theorists of the left saw only a limited role for the comprehensive school, and there was in their thinking a limitation on changing the actual education the schools offered. G. D. H. Cole, for instance, wrote that the schools should be "designed so as to give every child a chance, but at the same time to avoid the creation of a new class structure based on differences of ability." In his ideal school *"differences of curriculum and standard in the classroom are combined with equal participation in mixed activities on the playgrounds, in clubs and societies and in any sort of out-of-school activity"* (my italics). ("Education, a socialist view," *Year book of education 1952*.) It seems significant that Cole, at that time, did not foresee the present day developments in non-streaming, mixed ability teaching, and integrated curricula. Later in Labour's approach to educational policies there were the same blind spots: change was to be achieved by "social engineering" *around* the existing curriculum, rather than, as NALT wanted, through a change in the structure and ethos of education itself: merely easing the friction of inequality was not a function of the comprehensive school which would content "common school" supporters.

These more detailed disagreements about internal structuring of the schools went largely unrecognised, subsumed under the common if vague aim of a more equal society. They were to be totally submerged by a complete switch of the image of the comprehensive school away from explicitly social aims to a stress on its "efficiency" in the provision of educational "opportunities." This came about through the difficulty of selling egalitarianism to an electorate which was now shown to be largely indifferent to the social divisiveness of the educational system. The Labour policy makers were thrown into temporary disarray by the severe shock of a private poll in 1957 which revealed that the general public were almost totally ignorant on the comprehensive issue, and that only ten per cent felt that segregated education was socially undesirable (M. Parkinson, *op cit,* p81). On this basis the comprehensive programme looked a non-starter. And worse, the programme had become politicised as the Conservatives, the grammar schools and the press managed to create the persuasive and not altogether artificial distinction between policies which were "educational" in aim and those which were "politically motivated."

Yet whatever the degree of uninformed support for the existing inegalitarian structure of education the public's dislike of the 11 plus was at its height, for the 11 plus was in its crudest "stand and deliver" form during the 1950s. Any programme which planned the abolition of the 11 plus was therefore a potential winner. This public dislike of an important examination at the early age of eleven was sufficient to push the Conservatives in 1958 into a grudging admission that new comprehensive schemes would be permitted provided that the proposals were genuinely "educational"; that is, if they did not involve interference with existing inequalities of education provision, a policy which restricted new schools to working class estates or New Towns.

The political problem of comprehensive reorganisation was (and to some extent remains) that large numbers of people, including MPs of both parties, apparently cannot be made to connect the continued existence of the grammar school with the injustices of the 11 plus and inferior secondary modern schools. As a Labour Party study group put it in 1957, in advocating comprehensive reorganisation, "a policy argued around conventional educational opportunities is bound to have considerable popularity. One which argues on manifestly doctrinal or egalitarian grounds would prove unpopular even among our own supporters" (M. Parkinson, *op cit*, p82). The acceptance here by the Labour Party of the language of Conservative propaganda is startling.

The solution to the problem of selling the comprehensive school to the electorate was sought by the Labour politicians in a change of image for the programme. They exhibited a growing squeamishness in relation to the issues of educational and societal inequality. And in this switch of emphasis they were helped by the accumulation of evidence about the "wastefulness" of the bipartite system and the "inefficiency" of the 11 plus. Educationists who supported the comprehensive school were also forced to concentrate on more expressly (but for the public more obscurely) educational arguments. The shift in tone is well caught by this passage: "Some educationists still held, as had long been argued, that the move to comprehensive secondary education was inspired by a wish to promote social equality—a 'sentimental egalitarianism'—rather than representing a positive educational policy. In response the general move in the direction of unifying secondary education in many European countries was pointed to and the fact that the technological revolution created new educational needs and opportunities" (Rubinstein and Simon, *op cit*, p96). Politicians too now began to bracket the notion of educational equality with technological and economic efficiency. The arguments for comprehensive became more "meritocratic" and less concerned with the possible divisiveness of a society stratified by intellectual attainment: comprehensive schools, it was said, would make better use of the nation's brain-power but just in case they didn't, influential figures like Roy Jenkins argued that established grammar schools should be preserved with "comprehensives as a bridge between them and the secondary moderns" (M. Parkinson, *op cit*, pp80-87). As in the nineteenth century, "school power" seemed likely to prove a handier political slogan than a mere call for social justice. Such a programme fitted all too well Harold Wilson's new technology and science image of 1964.

It is not being argued here that the community school cannot be "efficient" *and* egalitarian. And at that stage supporters of the community school might expect to move forward towards their aims within the overall strategy of comprehensive reorganisation. But it became apparent once more that the Labour Party leadership had no wish to change education but merely wanted to enclose the grammar school ethos within a more accessible framework. Anthony Crosland, who would be the man in charge of implementing comprehensive reorganisation, had tended to accept the feeling of the 1950s that economic differentials had been narrowed, and from this he drew the conclusion that the comprehensive school must replace the grammar school only to remove the status or life style distinctions created by education (C. A. R. Crosland, *The future of socialism*, Jonathan Cape, 1956). This over-simplified the problems faced by schools in a society which, we have learned since, is still heavily unequal in its distribution of economic life chances. Harold Wilson, for his part, in the nervy period immediately before the 1964 election, assured the teachers that the grammar school would be abolished "only over his dead body," and as late as 1970 in a TV appearance he was still presenting the comprehensive school (in Gaitskell's earlier phrase) as a "grammar school for all." This was hardly the leadership to carry through a major restructuring of education.

the persistence of educational inequality in 1964

The dimensions of educational inequality in the twentieth century, against which we may measure the achievements and problems of the Labour Party up to 1964, may be summarised as follows. After the 1902 Education Act had officially permitted state secondary education but of a grammar school type only, with a subsequent backing of scholarships and free places, the flow of working class boys receiving secondary education increased from virtually 0 to 10 per cent before World War Two: at that time almost 15 per cent of all boys of secondary school age went to grammar or independent schools, but only 40 per cent of the boys' grammar school intake was working class (see J. Floud, "Social class factors in educational achievement," in A. H. Halsey (ed) *Ability and educational opportunity*, pp34-37 and 91-109, OECD, 1961). Only 1.7 per cent of manual workers sons reached university. The situation of working class girls was even poorer educationally.

After the 1944 Education Act, abolition of grammar school fees and an overall expansion of selective school places resulted in about 15 per cent of working class boys attending grammar schools: there were now about 23 per cent of the secondary school population in grammar and independent school places, and the proportion of the grammar school intake which was working class had risen to 56 per cent. Yet now only 1.6 per cent of manual workers' sons reached university. Meanwhile almost half of all middle class boys went to independent or grammar schools, and almost a quarter went to university. The post-war attempts to open up education tended to bring into the grammar schools and the few technical schools only the *most able* sons of the *skilled* workers, and by no means all the working class children whose measured ability should have entitled them to a place. And having entered grammar school many children still left at or before the sixth form threshold, which now replaced the 11 plus as a barrier to highly achieving working class children. Altogether, as has been demonstrated by the *Crowther Report*, half the nation's top ability boys had left school at the age of 16 or younger, and this huge wastage occurred mainly in the working class (*15-18*, HMSO, 1959). Could we but develop working class potential to the same degree as that of the middle class child we would need to double and treble the provision of university places. It has been said that there is enough talent here to provide top staff for another Britain.

One cause of these inequalities of educational opportunity was the large regional variation in selective and other school provision. The policy of "roofs over heads" (that is concentrating on building new schools for the expanding and migrating population rather than renovating old schools) had led to growing inequality between north and south, city centre areas and the new surburbia. A NUT survey published in 1962 had shown that a quarter of all primary schools and a sixth of all secondary schools should be rebuilt (*The state of our schools*, NUT, 1962). The *Newsom Report* in 1963 found only 21 per cent of secondary modern schools "generally up to present standards," and as many as 41 per cent of schools "seriously deficient in many respects" (*Half our future*, p258, HMSO, 1963). Schools on council estates or in new towns were considerably better than those in mining areas, one-third of the former achieving an excellent score and only one in ten a very poor score, compared with the mining area schools where none were rated excellent and one in six scored very badly. Some areas were so bad that the Report made the hitherto novel suggestion that they should be made priorities for spending, a recommendation which was later strongly reinforced by the Plowden Committee's report on primary education. The *Plowden Report* confirmed the NUT Survey's findings and made the staggering estimate that to bring all primary schools up to an acceptable standard £588 million would need to be spent: almost three-quarters of a million primary school children were in school buildings put up before 1875 (*Children and their primary schools*, p389 and 391, HMSO, 1967). We can see what good use the Conservatives and Mrs Thatcher have made of this particular inequality in de-fusing the comprehensive debate. Associated all too closely with these inequalities of building provision were the inequalities in staffing, since poor schools in poor areas have what the Newsom Report described as "poor holding power." Conditions of educational deprivation substantially mirrored conditions in the surrounding catchment areas.

Overall, Brian Simon calculated one indicator of educational inequality, by region, sex and school provision, showing that a middle class Cardiganshire boy had 180 times as much chance of reaching university as the daughter of a West Ham unskilled labourer (*Inequalities in education*, CASE, 1965).

Such inequalities cannot, however, be entirely attributed to unequal provision of educational resources. Early in the 1960s evidence was mounting to show the very early influence of social class and inequality on a child's *educability*—that is, on the child's acquisition of those skills and abilities which enable him to do well in school. The complex influence of such environmental factors on the child's skills and motivation and disposition handicaps him in school.

The two major areas of loss to the educational system could thus be identified in the early 1960s as the early years before five, when most children are not provided with schooling, and the threshold of the sixth form, where some schools lose almost two thirds of their pupils. Evidently secondary school reorganisation without expenditure in other areas of policy would not solve all these problems of educational inequality.

Patently, when Labour came into office in 1964, almost 60 years of the Party's struggle for educational equality had achieved virtually no reduction in educational differentials. Nevertheless, in view of what we are now learning about inbuilt trends in our society towards greater inequality, it may even be a matter for congratulating the Labour Party that the working class share in the expansion of educational expenditure did not actually decline over this period. For the discovery of continuing and possibly growing inequality in education was paralleled by the rediscovery of inequalities in other areas of the social services, for example, housing, the health service, and the social security system.

COMPREHENSIVE REORGANISATION IN 1964

By 1964 Labour should have been prepared for the Party's first major piece of educational legislation, and should also have been preparing to deal with inequality in other areas of policy. The failure of the 1944 Education Act to achieve greater equality, even on a narrow definition, had been repeatedly demonstrated. The distorting influence of private and grammar school education was manifest, and indeed struck at the base of egalitarianism. The form of common secondary education had been debated since the 'twenties, and working comprehensive schools—albeit struggling to "coexist" with grammar schools—had been in operation for a decade. Comprehensive reorganisation had been the official policy for 13 years. But again, as in 1945, the Party was unprepared with its own legislation (with less excuse this time), and existing patterns and trends in education were accepted.

It is true that there were more formidable political and practical obstacles than in 1945, largely through Labour's failure to seize the earlier opportunities, and also at first there was only a small political majority. But it might be argued that a really imaginative educational programme could have won support (and the same might be said of the 1970 election). This would have required careful handling, of course, for unfortunately the new educational needs and opportunities which, it had been asserted, were created by social and technological change did not emerge in demands either by parents or industrialists for a switch to comprehensives. Rather the public looked to a slight improvement of the schools they knew: as late as 1967 a much quoted *New Society* poll which ostensibly gave 52 per cent of the population in favour of "comprehensive" schooling also revealed in two other questions that only 16 per cent would choose comprehensive school for their own child, and 76 per cent wanted to retain the grammar schools ("Education and opinion," *New Society,* 26 October 1967). As David Donnison rightly observed in his commentary on these figures, this was not a vote for comprehensive education so much as a vote against the secondary modern schools. Moreover a poll of this kind does not indicate the strength of the choices. Pro-grammar school marches of local citizens, teachers and pupils, were the only marks of political agitation about the comprehensive school, and it seems very likely that the support for the grammar school was far more vehement and practical than any wishy-washy poll preference. A further problem, indicated by the poll, was that the educational debate was still obscure so that its details might play little part in the electorate's calculations. Claims of a mandate for comprehensives were therefore so much eyewash. Nevertheless a determined campaign to abolish 11 plus and the secondary modern school would have made sound electoral sense and is indeed proving effective in shifting reluctant Conservative councils today, in

Richmond and Bedford (see *Times educational supplement*, 25, 1970, *Comprehensive education* 10, 1968). Moreover at this time the public schools, although never stronger, were again growing uncomfortable about their social elitism and were once again flirting with the idea of some deal with the state.

The Labour Party also inherited a large balance of payments deficit in 1964, but lack of cash was not the main obstacle to comprehensive reorganisation. Educational expenditure expanded more rapidly than any sector of the economy apart from natural gas, and money could have been found for comprehensive reorganisation had the Labour Party been prepared to take the step of choosing priorities—which might, for example, have meant holding back the decision just taken by the Conservatives to expand a largely middle class higher education sector (*Planning for education in 1980*, Fabian research series 282). The major influence of the cash shortage should have been only to cause more serious thought to be given about tailoring reorganisation to the use of existing buildings in tiering schemes such as that of Leicestershire. The further problems created by the lateness of the Plowden Committee's recommendation for the age of transfer from primary schools, the single sex schools and church education, also indicated complex local tailoring, but not a major barrier to progress.

It was characteristic of Labour's remoteness from education that a problem which did not receive sufficient attention was that the attempt to combine secondary education under one roof involved the fusion of two sets of teachers who had maintained a careful social distance from one another for the last 100 years. Teachers resented the demonstration of the state's power over their working conditions, and there were genuine worries over the assimilation of career structures and the disappearance or raising of qualification standards for jobs. Extensive and public information services at both national and local level, and consultations with teachers, were therefore essential. The same was true for parents, and especially for local Labour councillors who could have controlled the details of many comprehensive schemes. In the event an understaffed and under-budgetted Transport House did not even know who represented Labour on the local education committees.

Legislation was all the more necessary because although the Minister of Education's powers had grown large (in spite of attempts to build in countervailing mechanisms), they were unspecific in key respects. In line with comfortable Conservative consensus philosophies, the powers were extensively delegated to local power groups; and, most important, the Minister could not directly specify the form of secondary education and had only the weapon of power to approve new schools. (We can see a notable example of this decentralised rule in Mrs. Thatcher, who not only withdrew Circular 10/65 but has said that she will not approve local schemes as a whole but only plans for individual schools.) A clear national statement of goals in legislation was evidently needed before any substantial educational change could be brought about.

Labour's failure to legislate had its roots in the failures of perception and will described earlier: the leadership was still quite prepared to live with the grammar and the public schools. And there is evidence of a lack of commitment to the ideal of reducing inequality in society. There was a failure to appreciate that economic and structural changes left to themselves will not reduce and may increase inequality. Labour politicians had apparently developed an overpowering coyness about taking any action which would curb or interfere with the existing maldistribution of power or resources.

As a result the direct grant schools have continued to receive state support and to create problems for local comprehensive schemes into the 1970s, although here was an area easily within the Labour Government's control. And yet again the issue of the public schools was fluffed. A policy of integration was available but instead there was a Commission because the Party could not resolve its own internal difficulties. This was revealed as a sham when the advice of its research workers, to the effect that the schools could not and would not in any meaningful sense be "integrated", was ignored in producing the final recommendations for integration (Royston Lambert and his research team felt impelled to put out to the press a note disowning the Report). There was some interference with the tax evasion whereby parents paid children's fees, but other forms of support from the government have been untouched and Eton is, ludicrously, still a charity.

the ineffectuality of circular 10/65

Labour's lack of commitment to equality and manifest unpreparedness in educational policy emerges most clearly from a study of the strategy adopted in comprehensive reorganisation. The new Labour Government chose unconvincingly to define itself as responding to an overwhelming spontaneous "grass roots" movement, which merely required to be regulated in the interests of coherence, much as the 1944 Act had regulated secondary reorganisation, but which needed little central guidance. The assistance of such a "grass roots" movement was indeed necessary, but to pretend that it was actually there was either a gross misreading or misrepresentation of the actual facts.

Whatever else Labour learned from the first post-war spell in office, it should have been manifest that controversial change could not be entrusted to the DES to accomplish. Yet this is substantially what happened. Lacking a policy, Labour may have adopted suggestions from the civil servants, and the device of Circular 10/65 was used to request, but not to require, local authorities to prepare plans for the reorganisation of secondary education on comprehensive lines. A year later Circular 10/66 also made it clear that funds would not be provided for reorganisation, but added teeth to the earlier Circular by refusing to sanction building on bipartite line. Above all, in January 1968 the postponement of the raising of the school leaving age struck a major blow against reorganisation, since the measure would have brought much-needed funds for building new schools on comprehensive lines. In 1970 a bill to outlaw the 11 plus was defeated by Labour's negligence and by the running out of time.

A lack of central guidance and definition appears clearly from the form of circular 10/65 itself. No commitment was made to comprehensive reorganisation, the Circular merely commenting on six schemes which had been tried out by local authorities. Some of the schemes were not even comprehensive in that they retained parental "choice" of transfer into an academic sector, a choice exercised mainly by middle class parents. Middle schools, the one scheme which was feasible without rebuilding, were at first explicitly discouraged (although this injunction was later withdrawn). Throughout, the civil servants behaved as if there were no controversy. It has been pointed out that certain actions of the new Department of Education and Science seemed to assume the permanent co-existence of comprehensives with the bipartite structure: for example, no ongoing research to evaluate the comprehensive school has been undertaken, and research projects on timetabling and allocation procedures have continued to deal only with the selective system, as though comprehensives will always be peripheral (Benn and Simon, *op cit*, pp40-41).

Anthony Crosland may have hoped that slow changes at local level would provoke less hostility and permit time for the education of the public. Comprehensive schemes are proving difficult to reverse (although not to subvert). It is arguable that, with another spell in office and reorganisation plans for most of the country secure, Labour could have isolated a few recalcitrant authorities and used all available sanctions to bring them into line. But the issue was already hotly controversial, and no programme of public education was undertaken—indeed the only successful one seems to be the establishment of comprehensive schools. Moreover time was not on Labour's side in that public pressures against the 11 plus were on the whole diminishing: secondary selection was shifting away from the 11 plus single shot examination and becoming more secret and more unfair, *but less disliked*. It was the *exam* rather than selection itself which people disliked (see D. Marsden, *Where*? no 9). Authorities such as Essex have now switched to verbal reasoning tests, and teachers' judgements which are biassed against the working class (see P. E. Vernon (ed) *Secondary school selection*, NFER, 1957).

Thus the expectation that handing over the problem of redistribution to local authorities would damp down opposition seems naive. In the event there has been a long drawn-out quarrel, rather than a short sharp one.

For all its shortcomings, this comprehensives policy had some results. There are now more comprehensive schools, including more fully comprehensive ones, than there would have been without a Labour government in office. Authorities who were cautiously moving towards the change were encouraged to produce plans, and with some reluctant authorities the small weight of the Circular's request may have tipped the balance or bluffed them into reorganising. The discussion of comprehensive education and the establishment of more schools has also apparently won some support: current figures in a poll which correctly asks the question of whether the respondent prefers the comprehensive system to the continuation of grammar *and* secondary modern schools shows 46 per cent for comprehensives as opposed to 37 per cent in favour of bipartitism, with 17 per cent "don't knows," the bulk of support being in areas where schools have been established (*Comprehensive education*, no 14, Spring 1978). From the new schools we are gaining more valuable experience of the practical working out of the comprehensive principle, information which has been badly needed and which no amount of discussion could have afforded.

But now that the dust has settled, the dimensions of the changes can be seen to be disappointing when compared with the expectations aroused by Harold Wilson's hundred days. The Circular was unsuccessfully challenged in the courts (R. Batley, *et al*, *Going comprehensive*, pp11-14, Routledge, 1970), but reluctant authorities found that they need not openly oppose the Department; they had merely to engage in endless "consultations" or to submit a scheme which moved towards comprehensive education at a vanishingly slow pace. So pathetically eager, or incompetent, was the DES that the official statistics relating to the speed of reorganisation were worthless: they included such items as plans for which no date of completion was ever fixed, partial plans, and plans which were selective in principle but which were never required to become comprehensive (C. Benn, *Comprehensive reorgansisation survey* 1968-69, CSC). The rate of change was artificially inflated by counting authorities rather than the proportion of school pupils involved in schemes. As a result, for accurate information the public had to turn to the Comprehensive Schools Committee, the major private pressure group campaigning for reorganisation. Much of the behaviour of officials in inflating the figures and accepting non-comprehensive schemes is, however, explicable in a less than Machiavellian way, by the fact that sheer pressure of work on the DES necessitated the extensive delegation of the vetting of plans to officials who neither understood the aims of comprehensive education nor perceived when these were in fact being flouted in particular schemes.

For a while after Labour came to office the number of comprehensive schools expanded at a faster rate, from 262 in 1965, to 387 in 1966, 507 in 1967, 745 in 1968, 960 in 1969, 1,150 in 1970 and a projection of 1,275 for 1971 (Benn and Simon, *op cit*, p58). Nevertheless, by 1970 when Labour went out of office and Circular 10/65 was immediately withdrawn by Mrs. Thatcher, only 10 per cent of all secondary school children were in schools with an unselective intake. One third of secondary school pupils were in schools called "comprehensive" but these were still skimmed, sometimes by as much as the top 20 per cent of their ability range: they should not be permitted the description "comprehensive" in some instances. The comprehensives are still missing on average the top 5 per cent of the ability range, and at the moment despite rising numbers of schools this proportion is not changing (Benn and Simon, *op cit*, p301). By the end of Labour's spell in office it was clear that a number of large and very influential authorities like Birmingham were determined not to reorganise, and that a new Act would be necessary to compel genuine planning for comprehensives. In fact over the years 1961 to 1969 the percentage of the secondary age populations in grammar schools dropped hardly at all (see *Social trends*, HMSO, p124). Thus far comprehensives had merely upgraded secondary modern schools.

equality and the neighbourhood school

Circular 10/65 had failed because it ignored the obstacles created for the redistribution of educational resources by the existing unequal distribution of resources and power at the local level. In the debates of 1964 Labour ducked the issue of redistribution most obviously in relation to the neigh-bourhood school concept. In fact the issue of redistribution of educational and other resources crystallizes in the neighbourhood school. As Benn and Simon have pointed out, the bulk of the population have always gone—and will continue to go in the foreseeable future—to "neighbourhood" schools, the old elementary schools, and the sometimes not so new secondary modern schools, and often the grammar schools. The "community school" ideal comes up against its severest political obstacle in the inequality and class segrega-tion of large urban areas, for here there is no balanced community mix, and the populations of such areas suffer not merely from educational deprivations but from a shortage of many other types of resources. Comprehensive schools alone could not hope, and should never has been asked, to solve such prob-lems alone.

The effect of the debate about neigbourhood comprehensives was to focus attention on the fact that if schools were zoned to neighbourhoods and parental choice was restricted to those zones, some pupils who had formerly gone to grammar schools would have to share the comparative deprivations of the secondary modern schools: the few bright working class children whom the state now "rescues" from such conditions would be "contaminated" by the education it provides for the residue. Meanwhile, the superior resources of the former selective and new suburban schools would often be even more overtly devoted to a predominately middle class population. Yet instead of seeing the moral that the comprehensive school must be part of a wider attack on inequality, the debate turned to give the impression that the comprehensive school would *create* inequality. Both the Labour and Conser-vative Parties evaded the issue, but it was the Conservatives who were able to exploit inequality to defeat the neighbourhood school concept.

Thereafter there was a switch in the DES's presentation of the comprehensive school from that of a school serving the population of a neighbourhood to a school which, Labour allowed it to appear, would engineer equality by containing within its walls a balanced social mix of children. The ideology of this alternative definition of comprehensive education is that where "social engineering" schemes operate the catchment areas are drawn and the intakes of the school adjusted in other ways (by bussing, by allocation according to bands of ability, and so on) to form as representative a social cross section as possible, the schools thus being required to undertake the social mixing which radicals desire but which market forces inhibit. Students of the new towns policy will see a close parallel in the ideology here (see B. Heraud, "New Towns: the end of a dream," *New Society,* no 302, 1968). In fact, of course, as Benn and Simon have shown, in the large majority of cases the dilemma is not acute and carefully drawn boundaries do not flout local communities, claims for whose existence can in any case be sometimes over optimistic. The problem remains, significantly, a feature of our larger cities like London, which almost alone has tried to operate a banding scheme.

It is important to note that it was at this point that community school and social engineering definitions of the comprehensive officially diverge. All earlier Ministry documents had defined a comprehensive school as a school providing secondary education for all the pupils in a given area. But after 1965 the definition frequently put forward by the DES was merely a a school in which pupils of all abilities and social classes are represented. As Caroline Benn has pointed out, even the official research commissoned by the DES could not decide by what criteria to define comprehensiveness (C. Benn, reviewing Monk's survey, *op cit, Comprehensive education*, no 10).

equality and the local power struggle

Having evaded the issue of redistribution at national level the Labour Party then proceeded to evade it at local level. Without any guidance they handed over to local councils and local education authorities the hot potatoes of drawing the catchment areas of the schools and determining by how much parental choice should be restricted. In these two issues lie the bases of redistribution, which is undoubtedly why they generate so much noise and why, with the abrogation of central authority, there were such unequal local struggles.

We are only just beginning to piece together reports of the mess. There were wide variations in willingness to reorganise, and splits opened up not only between the opposing local political parties but within the Labour Party itself, the unconvinced older members clinging to "their" grammar schools. To a striking degree some Labour councillors are out of key with even the limited advances of central policy, a phenomenon only partly explained by the lack of information and coordination within the Party, and more expressive of the peculiar propensity of some natural conservatives to operate under a Labour banner.

Depending on the quality and commitment of the local councillors and particularly upon the persuasion and experience of the Local Education Officer, the participants in the debate might be more or less well briefed. Some councils gathered a great deal of evidence and visited widely to look at existing schemes; but others were merely fed by the Education Officer with all the most negative evidence on reorganisation. In the absence of evidence the argument could not but be "doctrinaire" on both sides. On the other hand, as examples of what a good Education Officer can do with councils which are not markedly radical we have only to look at Sir Alec Clegg in the West Riding, and the Mason Plan in Leicestershire.

Without clear central guidance the councils also varied in the extent to which they consulted local teachers and parents. One study indicates that the teachers' unions voted in different ways in different areas, to some extent depending on the branch members' ages, for the younger NUT teachers backed "egalitarian" aims while the older teachers were more concerned with the possible disruption of career lines. However in none of the four areas studied did the teachers' opinions materially alter the final plans (P. E. Peterson, "The politics of comprehensive education in British cities," paper given to American Political Science Association).

The greatest mockery was in the pretence of parental "consultation." Minority groups of middle class grammar school supporters and teachers were much more active and articulate, and they were better served by the press. The behaviour of middle class parents appears sometimes to have been very much affected by the proportion of grammar school places in the area: for instance a shortage of grammar schools in Richmond meant that 25 per cent of children were in fee paying schools, a fact which evidently helped to power local middle class resentment of the state selective system (see *Comprehensive education*, nos 10 and 13). But in the majority of areas the middle class were well served by the grammar schools and were reluctant to relinquish segregated education for their children.

The verdict of a comparative study of the two areas, Gateshead and Darlington, is worth quoting in detail (R. Batley, *et al, op cit*). The authors conclude that in Darlington the grammar school supporters were able to influence the form of the plans to some extent, while the hardest battle for the comprehensive principle was fought between different members of the Labour Party, the final plan being the work of the Chief Education Officer. In Gateshead, without a middle class, where a Labour council had long been in favour of comprehensives, the constraint was the problem created by the early reorganisation of education on bipartite lines. Councillors and the Education Officer worked together, and the final plan appears to have been influenced more by the configuration of school buildings and the geography of Gateshead than by pressure groups. It may be that only where power is evenly balanced can external groups influence the decisions. The authors of the study conclude that "consultation" functioned mainly as a valuable pill sweetener. The truth is, of course, that it is difficult for "consultation" or "participation" to take place where bodies of teachers and parents are radically split in their opinions and differ very greatly in local power. What was needed here was a strong central definition within which these local discussions could have been educative.

The resulting local comprehensive schemes display a range of aims lying between a "meritocratic" concern to preserve the grammar school ethos and more explicit social engineering or neighbourhood school schemes. For example, different schemes can be seen to be more or less concerned with speed, with the retention of selectivity at sixth form level, with the sometimes conflicting aims of providing all schools with sixth form work yet conserving scarce sixth form staff (a problem with a thoroughgoing set of 11-18 schools), and with opening up the schools to the community.

Almost three fifths of the schools have an age range from 11 or 12 to 18. years, a small proportion of these schools taking pupils at sixth form level from other schools (Benn and Simon, *op cit*, p72). Another fifth have an age range of 11 or 12 to 16 years, and these are more typically old secondary modern schools. One in fourteen schools is an upper school, from 13 or 14 years, or a sixth form college. There are two types of sixth form college, with selective or non-selective entry, and there are now interesting proposals for linking the sixth form with the local College of Technology, a development which is frustrated by the separate administrative structure of the schools. One in seven schools, approximately, is a lower school, taking pupils from 11 to 13, 14 or 15 years only. Only 27 per cent have been purpose-built, and 23 per cent of schools occupy more than one site. Most interest is now being shown in the sixth form college, and plans submitted by 1968 indicated that in future only 38 per cent would be all through schools, 25 per cent would be tiered, and 32 per cent would have separate sixth forms (Benn and Simon, *op cit*).

But the overall design of the schemes tells us nothing of the inbuilt dynamic of change in the comprehensive ethos, and the social and intellectual achievements of the schools. Are we yet in a position to say that the schools are "successful" in achieving anyone's goals? To answer this question we must take a rather more strenuous and sceptical look at the aims and the evidence than has yet been attempted by the bulk of political supporters of the comprehensive school.

EVALUATING THE COMPREHENSIVE SCHOOL

A rational model of planning in the social services, such as is Labour's aim, would seem to require that change should follow careful research and prediction. But an examination of the development of comprehensive policies in education has revealed a different pattern. Research has followed changes which have been initiated on the grounds of ideological criticism of the existing order. And so far, research has served primarily to legitimate and perhaps accelerate such changes. Disturbingly, with the comprehensive programme nominally one third to a half implemented, many of the findings of educational research are still proving of little help to those concerned in the formulation of the next stages of policy.

The problem lies at a number of levels. Above all there has been considerable confusion and lack of finer educational detail at the level of formal statements of the aims of the comprehensive school, and correspondingly about the criteria which must be used in its evaluation. But even if we could agree on a number of alternative aims which could be tested against one another, there would still remain very formidable methodological and value difficulties in the educational research. In view of the increasingly technical tone of the educational debate—including in the *Black papers* —some of these problems must be briefly discussed here.

meritocracy, equality machine, or community?

One way of describing, if not resolving, the confusion about the goals of the comprehensive school is to abstract from the debate three sets of criteria—the "meritocratic", the "social egineering," and the "community" aims for the schools which have been underlined in the previous discussion as they appeared. It must be stressed, however, that this is chiefly a comment on the public political *debate,* on the stated intentions for the schools, and only in an indirect way relates to the workings of the schools themselves (see Marsden, "Which comprehensive principle," *Comprehensive education* no 13, 1969 and replies in two following issues). These aims express sets of political beliefs and in some sense derive from and possibly influence existing schools, particularly if we are dealing with teachers' statements about their goals. But we have enough studies of organisations to know that the form which they take is a result not merely of their stated goals but also of the sometimes conflicting aims of their many members or participants, and of internal and external pressures.

The difficulty in specifying the exact relationship between the ideal types of schools described in the debate and the actual schools symbolises the gap between politicians' simplified aims for education, and the practical dynamic embodied in the comprehensive school as a complex working structure. The lesson is that we must look more closely at what education is doing, not what politicians and teachers (and writers of pamphlets) hope or intend it to achieve. Real schools will exhibit trends in one or another of the following directions, but cannot, as we shall see later, be as dissimilar as the many participants involved in the debate about comprehensives might wish them to be.

The "meritocratic" view of the comprehensive school may have few or indeed no overt strictly social aims: the comprehensive school must stand or fall on its development and maximisation of the child's qualifications at whatever consequences to social and societal relationships and, some opponents would add, to education (see R. Boyson, "Threat to tradition," in N. Smart (ed), *Crisis in the classroom*). Such a view of the schools is as far as the present nervous flirtation has taken some Conservatives, and it avoids all discussion of the undoubted social influence of present educational arrangements.

The "social engineering" approach has looked for both the development of talent *and* for improved qualities of citizenship, but has not contemplated any radical change in the education offered in the schools: change is to come about by manipulation of social relationships, but around and not through the curriculum and the educational process. Thus, to take another quote from Anthony Crosland, "Both common sense and American experience suggest that (unstreaming) would lead to a really serious levelling down of standards and a quite excessive handicap to the clever child. Division into streams remains essential" (*The future of socialism*, p202, Cape, 1963). Such a view is undismayed by the prospect of societal divisions based on intellect, which are in fact one democratic justification for rule by a small number of individuals.

The supporters of the "community school" would subscribe to the aims of academic excellence and improved social relationships, but would stress that these cannot be achieved without a change in the educational ethos and the structure of the learning process itself: accordingly the true community school must exhibit a whole range of educational innovation and openness in the curriculum and teaching methods and relationships with the outside world which will bring about a new ethos and a new view of the child. Only in a cooperative framework which sees children as of equal worth will equality eventually be achieved.

It will be seen that these prescriptions represent distinctly different educational systems. The variety of goals and orientations of the supporters of comprehensive schools would lead in evaluation to a differing stress on, for example, examination results, rates of stopping on after the school leaving age, the children's qualities of citizenship and social horizons, aspects of the school's internal structure, of rewards and punishments, of decision taking, of learning, and the overall integration of the school with the surrounding community. As yet the relative importance and inter-relationships of changes in these areas, as an indication of the attainments of the comprehensive principle, have scarcely been spelled out.

The major points to look for in evaluating the comprehensive school would be: how nearly do the existing schools approximate to any of the above models; and do the schools bear out what would be the community school criticism of Labour's "social engineering" approach, that Labour has wanted talent development and citizenship but has not been sufficiently aware of the need to change the ethos of the schools towards greater internal democracy. It is interesting to look at Julienne Ford's attempt to construct Labour's ideal type of comprehensive and then to evaluate an existing comprehensive school against a grammar and a secondary modern school to see which system best fulfils Labour's goals (J. Ford, *Social class and the comprehensive school*, chap 1, Routledge, 1969). Unfortunately Dr Ford's survey, which is meant to be a systematic evaluation of use to socialists, seems seriously misleading both in its design and in its conclusions. She has not indicated that the ideal type of comprehensive she constructs is drawn mainly from the social engineering approach of Labour's leading politicians rather than, say, community school writers. And she does not sufficiently stress that the school against which she tests her ideal type is apparently of the more crudely "meritocratic" kind, with scarcely any of the attempts even at social engineering which may be found in other schools. A further serious defect in the research design itself (discussed later) vitiates her findings, which seem to support the *Daily Telegraph* thesis that the introduction of comprehensives will reduce opportunity even for the bright working class child. In any case, no London school can be fully comprehensive.

From other surveys, on more narrowly meritocratic criteria there appears as yet to be fairly little to choose between the comprehensive schools and the bipartite system. Obviously from any standpoint examination results are of some interest, and significantly one of the original comprehensive bogies of size was laid for the meritocrats (see R. Boyson, *op cit*) chiefly because of the range of opportunities and specialist teaching which could be offered in the larger school. Benn and Simon (*op cit*, pp81-82) and Pedley (*op cit*, 105-113) in their surveys of comprehensive school "O" level results were able to conclude that there was no evidence that the schools have "lowered standards". The "O" level results from some of the new comprehensive schools which do not gain their full quota of the top ability groups are actually up to and slightly above the corresponding results for the bipartite system. The interpretation of "A" level results is still premature because of the lack of top ability students and the newness of the schools. The proportions of pupils in all through schools who stop on after the minimum school leaving age is above the national bipartite average (Benn and Simon, *op cit*, pp72-73). But the stopping on rate for schools which are not providing education up to eighteen, and where a transfer to another school is involved, is very poor, as indeed was feared by the left in the early 1950s when the schemes were first suggested (M. Parkinson, *op cit*, pp72-73), and a tendency for more able pupils to leave early from "comprehensive" systems has been noted (J. W. B. Douglas, *All our future*, pp62-63, Peter Davies). The situation is that such schools are usually older secondary moderns, and the transfer is to what used to be the grammar school—in other words these are scarcely comprehensive systems (Benn and Simon, *op cit*, p124).

I have not quoted the comprehensives' figures here in detail because it seems to me that while they may already be a little better than the bipartite performance in some respects, neither supporters nor opponents of the comprehensives would claim that they are as yet *sufficiently* different in either direction to constitute meritocratic arguments for or against the comprehensive school at the present time. And in that case the burden of proof of the superiority of the comprehensive system must depend on future firmer evidence or must shift to social criteria.

However, the evaluation of the new order in the comprehensive school cannot yet take place because the educational ethos appears to have changed only slowly under the impact of comprehensive reorganization. For those who had hoped for a new educational and social order to be bred in the comprehensive schools, initial reports of the internal organisation of the new schools were disappointing. Virtually all the schools were streamed, some of them very intensively; and some research by Douglas Young has suggested that certain kinds of streaming in large schools create serious problems of morale and social control, not only for the schools but later for society. Thus, if pupils are streamed by IQ but are frequently moved according to their attainment, there accumulate at the bottom of the school pupils who have low attainments and/or low motivation, and the larger the school the more disastrous the sieving (D. Young and W. Brandis, "Two types of streaming and their probable application in comprehensive schools," *Bulletin*, XI, pp13-16, University of London Institute of Education, 1967).

We do not know how often this situation occurs, but it has been suggested that the phase of competition with the grammar schools and direct grant schools which lies, perhaps, at the root of such anti-educational practices will be only temporary. When the comprehensive schools have been established longer and the comprehensive system becomes more widespread, new patterns will appear (Benn and Simon, *op cit*, chaps 9 and 14, R. Pedley, *op cit*). And already there is evidence of a trend away from streaming and the competitive atmosphere. Up to 1963, according to Benn and Simon (*op cit*, p151), there was rather little movement, but the National Federation for Educational Research (NFER) in 1965 indicated that four per cent of comprehensive schools were using complete non-streaming, and only three years later Benn and Simon found 22 per cent of schools using predominantly mixed ability types of organisation (*op cit*, p151). A greater proportion would be experimenting with non-streaming in non-academic subjects. Robin Pedley from a survey of long-established comprehensive schools had found that in 1968 38 per cent "were operating in unstreamed situations to a greater or lesser extent" (*op cit*, p101). There remains the question of how far this swing will go. Have we here the beginnings of a "grass-roots" movement among teachers? Will it fizzle out, or can it be assisted by the national policy makers?

Another, cruder indication that the schools are shaking off tradition and adopting new initiatives is in the abandonment of organisation into houses.

The NFER survey found that in 1965 as many as 90 per cent of schools in their survey had house systems of organisation. (T. J. Monks, *op cit*, p41.) By 1968, however, according to Benn and Simon a pure house system with no other form of organisation was used in only 17 per cent of the comprehensives and was combined with other divisions in only a further 20 per cent. Robin Pedley has some suggestive data on the move away from "competitiveness." In 1961 nine-tenths of his sample of comprehensive schools gave their children ranking orders in class. In 1968 the proportion had dropped to just above a half (R. Pedley, *op cit*, p131). On the other hand he found that the award of trophies and prizes for academic or sporting achievements had remained constant involving around four-fifths of the schools.

One straw in the wind might be taken as an indication of curriculum changes. Only three-fifths of the comprehensive schools with sixth forms were offering Latin, and the proportion for all comprehensives was only 43 per cent (Benn and Simon, *op cit*, pp145-146). Benn and Simon comment on the relationship between Latin and streaming: where Latin is taught there is invariably division of the curriculum since it is never taught to all ability groups. This stresses the social divisiveness inherent in some of the academic curriculum's specialisms. And the way in which such control of knowledge through the curriculum determines children's life chances is further underlined when we note that many universities still cling to Latin as a requirement in language subjects: until the universities relax this requirement, pupils in comprehensives not teaching Latin will be disadvantaged (Benn and Simon, *op cit*, p354). Finally, 44 schools more intensively surveyed by Benn and Simon were fulfilling the function of community schools to some extent (Benn and Simon, *op cit*, 34). Only two schools, both in country areas, were not open after hours. 33 were open after school for two or three hours, and more important 31 were open in the evenings. Half the schools had evening classes, and half let the schools be used by local groups for meetings. Only four schools had sports facilities in use all the year round by the community. These, however, are only very crude and superficial indicators of the relationship between education and the community. Very few schools would yet fit many of the criteria of the local community school.

the best comprehensives we have—the primary schools

For the most useful and suggestive research on attempts to create a new educational order in the schools we must turn to an area of education usually neglected by politicians, for the primary schools are the best comprehensives we have. They are the only uncreamed schools where non-streaming is practised to any great extent, now that examination pressures are being reduced in a way that the comprehensives cannot expect to happen for some time.

NFER research on *Streaming in primary schools* by J. Barker Lunn stands out head and shoulders above research on comprehensive schools, and it is worth quoting here not only for its implication for the future of comprehensive reforms but also as an indication of the sorts of methodological difficulties which must be overcome if we are to compare fully the success of two educational systems embodying different sets of values.

The survey attempts with some success to evaluate streaming and non-streaming as alternative forms of organisation in primary schools. Its greatest contribution is to focus our attention on the teachers and the teaching process, rather than the organisational framework. Non-streaming and a changed ethos in a school appear to be as much a result or expression of teachers' (or the head teacher's) values as an influence upon them. Thus, the survey notes, "any effect which may be shown to be associated with streaming or non-streaming is unlikely to be purely and simply due to the form of organisation used. Teaching methods, the ideas which underlie disciplinary systems, the views teachers hold about their children, in short the whole climate of relationships built up by what teachers say and do and what they appear to their pupils to imply may be well be the critical factors." As a result, *"It is clear that a mere change in organisation, such as the abandonment of streaming, unaccompanied by a serious attempt to change teachers' attitudes, beliefs and methods of teaching is unlikely to make much difference*; in fact it is likely to result in a change from streaming between classes to streaming within classes" (my italics). It was found that "teachers believing in streaming in non-streamed schools treated their class as a streamed one. Their teaching methods, their lessons and their attitudes tended to reflect the pattern found in streamed schools. They even streamed their children into geographically located ability groups."

What may yet prove to be the key finding of the research was that teachers on the whole consistently over-estimated the ability of middle class children and under-estimated that of working class children. Research is now demonstrating the effects of teachers' expectations upon children's school performance, and here may lie a major barrier to the achievement of equality in education (R. Rosenthal and L. Jacobson, *Pygmalion in the classroom*, Holt, Reinhart and Winston, 1968).

Thus, in this research on the primary school, we are brought suddenly face to face with the classic problem of those who seek radical reforms in society: when the formal revolution has been won there remains the "cultural revolution." The behaviour of the "streaming" teacher in a non-streamed school appears a microcosm of the comprehensive *non*-reorganisation previously described.

Because of the problem of "streamers" in the non-streamed school, the full effects of non-streaming could not be effectively tested. But the research concluded that academically (or meritocratically) there was nothing to choose between the two systems in terms of performance on attainment tests. Socially, however, there were advantages to be gained in an improvement in the atmosphere of the school.

Lest we be tempted to try to legislate for non-streaming (a step not, in any case, possible under the existing structure of control in education which gives individual head teachers large powers), the research found that the worst possible teaching situation for the below average child is in a non-streamed school with a streaming teacher: such teachers manage to make below average children isolated within the class. Incidentally, one controversy about streaming which was convincingly resolved was its effect on the child's self-image. A below average child was found to be likely *himself* to feel duller in a non-streamed class in comparison with his brighter class-mates, yet a similar child in a low stream was likely to feel that *other people* would think him duller although he himself might have a better opinion of his own abilities.

The survey may provide an important result for socialists, the first indication we have from research about the influences of separatism in education upon parental attitudes. It was found that in streamed schools the children's parents were also "streamed" by aspirations, whereas in unstreamed schools the parents' aspirations were higher. "It seems that the mere fact of a child being in anything but the top stream has the effect of lowering parental expectations and aspirations for a grammar school place." However, as we shall see, such results must be treated with caution: it seems likely that schools where unstreaming was possible (against parental and local authority pressures) would already be in areas where the class composition of the neigbourhood was of a different kind, more homogeneous in other respects apart from the parents' educational aspirations.

This research seems to confirm the tentative findings of research on comprehensives, that there is no evidence as yet that without a change of school ethos a comprehensive framework will make better use of reserves of talent. Moreover a comprehensive school which (like the school in Dr. Ford's research) makes no serious attempt to organise pupils' relationship across social and intellectual difference will achieve nothing in the way of class mixing. In any case a rigidly hierarchical school structure would appear to be an outward expression of a hierarchical view of intellect and society. Across attempts to move away from a rigid structure at primary or secondary level falls the pressure of examinations, at 11- or 18-plus. And the key to the achievement of the comprehensive principle must therefore lie in central administrative action which will combine with and foster a "cultural revolution" among the teaching profession.

research and values in the comprehensive debate

The delicate political situation of the comprehensive school has demanded quick proofs of success. However, the implications of this attempt to clarify aims and evaluate research have been that research alone cannot help us to choose between systems which ideally at least represent different educational orders. Indeed inadequate research and the premature or illegitimate use of research findings have only tended to obscure the debate over values. The NFER streaming research stands almost alone in its achievements; and I have therefore not quoted in detail from any other research on values in the comprehensive school, all of which inevitably suffers from methodological defects which render it insufficiently rigorous for use in an essentially political, rather than educational, argument. To make matters worse some highly influential research has been formulated in such a way as to ignore or distort the influence of inequality on parents' values and children's educational performance.

Consider first the methodological problems facing educational research workers who attempt to compare the results of bipartite and comprehensive schools (see H. Passow, "The maze of research on ability grouping," in A. Yates (ed), *Grouping in education*, pp161-169, UNESCO, 1966). The researchers must gain adequate responses from comprehensive schools which are flooded with questionnaires. They must in addition match a sample of bipartite and comprehensive schools for age of buildings and level of amenities, age of staff and their experience and qualifications, types of comprehensive scheme, staffing ratios, social origins and intelligence of pupils, curricula, teaching methods, and for geographical region (since the occupational structure and educational traditions outside the schools will influence stopping-on rates and performance in school). There are also factors which are more difficult to measure and control, such as the degree of commitment and enthusiasm of the staff at a time when comprehensives are in a minority and also in a delicate political position, when they may be recruiting staff who on the whole are more committed to the comprehensive ideal and more determined to prove that it works. Other imponderables are the school ethos, the mark-hungriness and test-sophistication of the pupils, the schools' commitment to examinations, their policy of entering pupils, and the difficulties of comparing "O" level standards across subjects like woodwork and Latin, and across Examination Boards. If opponents of the comprehensive schools insist that we must check pupil performance at all levels of intelligence, we find that we are as yet unable to make accurate reports on the high intelligence groups who, because of the continuation of selection, are under-represented in comprehensive schools.

It must be confessed that comparisons involving foreign countries such as Sweden and America, where comprehensive schools have been longer established, involve even more imponderables. It is for this reason that no parallels are here drawn between England's progress towards comprehensives and movements in other countries, because the underlying assumption of such comparisons is that change takes place through a sort of technological determinism and cultural borrowing. Such comparisons can therefore be seriously misleading, and they have been, indeed, a major weakness underlying Labour's official policy approach.

Thus, cross-nationally we have difficulty in comparing the different cultural traditions, of individualism in America and social engineering in Sweden. There are differing degrees of inequality in these other societies, and neither country suffers to the same degree as England from an entrenched private classical sector of education (see R. Bendix and S. M. Lipsett (eds), *Class, status and power*, pp437-472, Routledge, 1967). The administrative structure of education is centralised in Sweden, but decentralised in America. In Sweden teaching is anomalously traditional, whereas America pioneered "child centred" education on a mass scale. We might summarise the American problem by saying that the country possesses an overtly egalitarian ideology of education, but paradoxically anti-collectivism sets its face against willing the means for an egalitarian school structure. The comprehensive community school, in these circumstances, has met serious problems with the development and decay of the large American city and the residential segregation of the ethnic and income groups. Sweden, on the other hand, has a remarkably egalitarian philosophy which includes a redefinition of the masculine and feminine roles such as England has scarcely begun to consider in education, and there is a tradition of collectivism and social engineering to back it, but the teaching profession has not as yet lived up to the needs of the new structure. Sweden thus exhibits the paradox of formal teaching in a progressive and egalitarian structure. America, on the other hand, has covert differentiation in what is formally an open and egilitarian system. English comprehensives must try to avoid both these pitfalls. These difficulties of comparative research do not mean that we can learn nothing from cross-national studies; only that we must be more cautious in drawing inferences good or bad.

But in the context of political controversy methodological difficulties take on a new role. For a while sociological investigations, which have been character-istically sceptical and innovatory in the field of English education, were on the side of comprehensive advocates (although unfortunately they were negative in a society where only change needs positive justification). But then the oppon-ents of the comprehensive school began to play the researchers at their own game, and the previous discussion of research problems will have indicated why there is always some objection, major or nit-picking, which can be advanced against "proofs" of the comprehensives' superiority.

At the present time educational controversy has thus become erudite but obscure to the layman, who will feel justified in dismissing all research or alternatively may select from the flying references those which best suit his beliefs. Either way he can remain in invincible ignorance of research findings.

Turning now to research which is possibly misleading in relation to the influence of inequality and a divided educational system upon parental values, the failures here arise in the inadequacies of perception of social attitudes rather than from the inherent difficulties of research. The problem is that we wish to know whether a particular kind of school creates greater social mixing and a change of social attitude towards a feeling of community. Also we wish to compare performances. The difficulty is that research workers neglect to view and measure parental background with sufficient sublety means that we have a number of confusing results. For example, there are findings which seem to indicate that if we take two working class children of comparable measured ability and send one to a "good" primary or secondary modern school (as indicated by past 11 plus or "O" level figures, teacher qualifications and so on), which will invariably have a higher middle class intake, the working class child at the "good" school achieves a better academic performance (see J. W. B. Douglas, *op cit*, pp37-38). The same has been noted of working class children attending grammar school as compared with comprehensive schools (see J. Ford, *op cit*, p40). The superficial conclu-sion is that the school *moulds* the child to a measurable degree, independently of his class background, and in particular "rescues" working class children from a fate of manual work. Such an interpretation can be used for arguments for putting cash into schools rather than households, in favour of the retention of grammar schools and against comprehensives, and so on.

It is not denied here that schools may have *some* effect in changing the child's values and educability, but what needs challenging is the assumption that the observed effects are entirely due to the schools and are not in some way a further expression of the influences of home background and hence of eco-nomic inequality. All these pieces of research suffer from what might be called "background fallacies." Thus, for example, the kinds of children who get into grammar schools or who live in the catchment areas of "good" primary and

Parental attitude ways to determine
by economic status

secondary modern schools are the offspring of working class parents with relatively middle class attitudes, aspirations and styles of life. These aspects of the child's environment are seldom imaginatively explored by research. Similarly, we know that the kinds of children who go to grammar schools from working class homes are unusual in many ways. It is not surprising, therefore, that these upwardly-aspiring children should mix more readily with other children of the social class they are destined to join. But we cannot attribute this to the school's influence. The much-quoted finding from Ford's research that social mixing occurs to a greater degree in the grammar school than in the comprehensive *may* be entirely accounted for by differences in the social origins of the two sets of pupils, the bulk of that particular comprehensive's working class intake being drawn from a largely working class estate where children might be expected to come from families with different social horizons.

With the kind of patterns of residential segregation and the sorts of schools we have now, we should still probably picture schools less as moulders of social attitudes and performances and more as sieves or selectors of children with backgrounds and potentials favourable for high educational attainment. Although we cannot claim to understand why nominally working class parents should show middle class aspirations and behaviour, there is some evidence that the key may still lie in these parents' economic and social position in life, rather than being evidences of personality quirks or some cultural pattern which persists or develops independently of the structure of economic inequality (see D. Swift, "Social class, mobility ideology and 11-plus success," *British Journal of Sociology* XVIII, vol 2, 1967). Yet socialists have been side tracked by recent influential research, by Dr Douglas (*op cit*) and the Plowden Committee, which has appeared to demonstrate that economic inequality is of relatively less importance than parental attitudes in children's educational performance. The policy implications of such findings would be that a programme of parental stimulation and enlightenment, rather than one of economic redistribution, should be embarked upon. However, it is arguable that what Dr Douglas loosely calls an "interest in education" might more appropriately be described as an interest in the middle class pretensions of the grammar school and in upward mobility. And conversely a "lack of interest in education" is attributable to the class segregated nature of our educational system which has hitherto always excluded the bulk of the working class. Similarly the "attitudes to education" identified by the Plowden Report are arguably indicators of social class and are dependent on the parents' economic position, which in any case the research scarcely attempted to explore (see B. Bernstein and B. Davies, "Some sociological comments on Plowden" in R. S. Peters (ed), *Perspectives on Plowden*, Routledge, 1969).

The policies indicated by this alternative analysis would be the redistribution of educational and economic resources and rewards, since parents' attitudes could not be manipulated otherwise.

These seemingly dry and esoteric academic points must be stressed, for not only is educational research failing to formulate questions about the influence of the economy and educational system upon parental attitudes and children's performances in a sufficiently subtle and perceptive way, but the trend of influential research is actually misleading us. The problems of reducing inequality in and through education are being minimised, no doubt unintentionally, to fit all too closely the facile optimism of Labour's educational policies.

A SUMMARY OF LABOUR'S RECORD

This chapter has been primarily an attempt to clarify some of the confusion surrounding political aims for the comprehensive school, and to indicate why comprehensive education has been a key Radical issue in various guises for over a century and a half. Supporters of the schools have hoped that comprehensives would tackle the question of inequality and forge new societal bonds. We discover in the comprehensive philosophy a tradition of thought stretching back to some idealised pre-industrial and pre-urban community, alongside a half hearted and unpractical attempt at rational planning. In neither area has the Labour Party achieved much advance on the nineteenth century. The Party has always suffered from a confusion of aims, the leadership apparently being content with relatively minor adjustments to the educational system and accepting the view that education was responding to social and technological change rather than being a force in its own right. The left has taken the different view, sometimes too naively, that education can be a power for social good, and has pressed for more far-reaching reforms, although perforce working within a framework of changes acceptable to the leadership. In both post-war spells of Labour government the Party's arrival in office gave evidence of the lack of an original policy: 1945 saw the acceptance of the coalition's Education Act, 1964 the acceptance of the Robbins expansion of higher education partly at the expense of secondary reorganisation. In spite of much huffing and puffing the direct grant and public schools have remained unscathed. Only a small pressure group on the left has had a coherent educational policy which the leadership seems barely to have understood but which is at long last emerging as a possible challenge to the present structure. To do the Party leaders justice, the issues have been complex. The influence of inequality and our divided educational system in stimulating inegalitarian demands has a parallel in the field of wages, where the increasing rewards for the higher salaried classes and the manifest inequality in rewards generally is provoking wage demands from the workers and frustrating any development of a wages ethic which is in the national interest. In formulating demands for educational equality the Labour Party has had to persuade those of its own supporters who were not interested in grammar schools to see the value of extended education. The establishment of comprehensive schools has shown that public demand will follow rather than lead educational changes. Research has proved no substitute for commitment in pointing the way to new educational policies.

The absence of a clear perception of inequality and a commitment to its reduction appeared in the 1964 Labour government's behaviour chiefly in the handing over of redistribution to the local authorities and in shying away from the issues of poverty which the debate on neighbourhood schools had crystallised. The solution of turning the comprehensive school into an equality machine was both transparently evasive and abhorrent to the strongest advocates of comprehensive education and to much educational opinion.

The major lesson of the historical review of Labour's performance is that we cannot talk about Labour's educational policies because the Party is not unified and has never had an agreed policy. When in office the politicians' actions show too much evidence of the hand of the civil service, being concerned with the administration and the framework of schooling, and giving relatively little thought to education proper. Crucially there has been an artificial separation between political aims for education and the thoughts of professional educationists and teachers, between hopes and claims for the schools and the schools' actual achievements. This has not been for lack of educationists within the Party, but chiefly for lack of an adequate hearing. What is needed is to close the gap between politics and education, to persuade egalitarians and the Labour Party as a whole to work out the finer details of an egalitarian policy.

GETTING THE EDUCATION WE WANT

Would the Labour Party's having a policy have made any difference? How much truth is there in the Conservative position that education responds only to broad societal change? Paradoxically, although the rigidity of the school curriculum derives from its relationship, via examinations and qualifications, with the occupational structure, it is far from true to say that the schools "fit" society. The reason is that qualifications are given by educational institutions and recognised as valuable by parents, students and employers, but the teaching and learning behind the qualification may bear little relationship to the job for which it forms the credential. Indeed the tradition of the English "amateur" has been founded on education being completely *un*related to subsequent employment, except in a few professions.

The link between education and society therefore depends on confidence in educational qualifications. On the one hand, in the schools and universities there are professionals determined to teach what they know but what the country may not need economically, what may be of little interest and use to the student, and what, as Margaret Mead has observed, it may not be agreed that anyone has any desire to learn. This relationship is of course a good thing in some ways, certainly for the functioning of academic freedom and probably for the education of the child. The average child "needs" rather little education for the sort of work the economy affords: it is no accident that intelligence declines in adult life.

But what is being stressed here is that the proposition that we as a society somehow automatically get the sort of educational system that we want and deserve will not hold water. If we want an adequate educational system we'll have to fight for it. The schools are quite a long way out of line with society in terms of the curriculum, values and life style they aim to transmit. And such a marked lack of fit between education and society at least suggests that the educational system could, in some sectors and to some extent, lead society towards a more egalitarian ethos, could we but encourage teachers to share this view and behave in accord with it. Putting aside this not unpractical vision, the immediate problem remains the much more limited and obviously more feasible objective of bringing the social ethos and curriculum of our schools out of the nineteenth century.

The political goal of equality in and through education is still valid. But comprehensive reorganisation makes sense only in the context of a total educational programme where the policies are dictated not by largely middle class pressures to preserve the existing structure but by a rational application of planning to the needs of pupils, students and teachers. The present distribution and trends of growth of resources as between sectors of education, types of school, regions, and children of different abilities and sexes, is neither rational nor socialist. This is not merely an argument for more money to remove inequality. The necessity of an expansion of the education budget, in view of the birth bulge and the trend in stopping on, must be argued against the needs of services for the poor, the aged, the subnormal and other disadvantaged groups. It may indeed prove that education (or some sectors) have too great resources in view of the needs of other groups. In that case there would be all the more need for Labour and the DES to choose priorities in education in a way which has hitherto been avoided.

At present there is scarcely a procedure for deciding priorities within education, but we have the odd spectacle of a Conservative Secretary for Education and Science looking more determinedly egalitarian than Labour in her urge to balance up inequalities between the different sectors of education. As the writers of the Fabian pamphlet *Planning for education in 1980* (*op cit*) have pointed out, there is even less machinery for deciding priorities between education and other social services.

Fully comprehensive reorganisation with an egalitarian aim also makes sense only within the context of a redistributive programme of income and social capital between individuals, families and areas. The educational arguments for neighbourhood schools are strong, not the weakest argument being that we will get such schools under any system we can devise. Thus, as Professor Titmuss has written: "The real challenge resides in the question: what particular infrastructure of universalist services is needed in order to promote a framework of values and opportunity bases within and around which can be developed socially acceptable selective services aiming to discriminate positively, with the minimum risk of stigma, in favour of those whose needs are greatest?" (*Commitment to welfare*, p122, Allen and Unwin, 1968).

Since the Plowden Report and the Urban Aid Programme the idea of positive discrimination has gained some ground, but is still far from a practical achievement. However within a general programme of redistribution, positive discrimination around and through the neighbourhood school seems to be the policy which makes most educational and social sense. It might be argued that positive discrimination in buildings, teaching staff, amenities and play space would provoke a suburban backlash, but the fact is that a neighbourhood school and urban area programme would have to go a long way before resources were evened up. Another danger is that we must avoid priority schemes which become a substitute for other kinds of distribution, for the family remains the main transmitter of inequality in society and inequality is not confined to a few pockets of slum dwellings.

To carry through such a strategy against inequality, future Labour Secretaries of State cannot afford to adopt a Conservative supine posture. Yet how far does the Secretary of State have control over education proper? Evidently the existing decentralisation of the Labour Party and the educational administration, and backgrounds of the local councillors and various administrative officials pose obstacles to the co-ordination and execution of plans. But what the Secretary can supply is a strong central lead by a commitment to comprehensive reorganisation defined in the context of an imaginative Education Act. This above all was lacking in 1964. Comprehensive reorganisation is the policy *within* which, rather than about which, discussion should take place.

Beyond this Labour must start working out the crucial areas of control in education where a future Secretary might hope to prevent subversion of plans for equality by the permanent officials or pressures at local authority level. Some areas of Secretarial powers seem to be ambiguous or at least open to definition by the Secretary himself if he takes a firm line, as for instance in the recent attempt to overhaul the examination structure. A further new aspect of the Secretary's role must be that of an educator. The role of the DES must be oriented towards an extensive information programme.

A positive definition of the Secretary's role cannot mean authoritarian direction, for as we have seen, the organisation and attitudes embodied in education are as much or more expressions of teachers' values as influences upon these values. It thus becomes not only desirable but indispensable for success that there should be a movement among teachers to achieve the comprehensive principle within the comprehensive framework provided by the central decision to reorganise. This implies that apart from its function in disseminating information about comprehensives, the DES must look to the recruitment and training of teachers, the facilities which they are given, and the influence of the organisation of curriculum subjects and examinations upon teachers' behaviour. One of the consistently disappointing findings of educational research is that teachers leave the training colleges expressing the progressive philosophies which these colleges espoused long ago, but these same teachers very rapidly lose their idealism and progressiveness when faced with the exigency of a real-life teaching situation. This failure may be the responsibility of central government, in the sense that teachers' behaviour may be a response to scarce resources and large classes. For years a squeeze on resources in the secondary school sector in the face of rising demand has distorted the behaviour of primary school teachers, and we may still be seeing the after effects of this primary school 11 plus culture in the behaviour of teachers today. The same is obviously now true of distortions in teaching caused by the 18 plus. Again this underlines the necessity of awkward and complicated decisions about the setting of priorities for allocating resources. The next Education Act must have sufficient breadth of vision to inter-relate the effects of policies in one part of the educational system upon other parts. But all this discussion is still concerned with handing education out to the people. As Sir Fred Clarke has written: "Schools have always been provided for (the mass of the English people) from above, in a form and with a content of studies that suited the ruling interests. Hitherto there has appeared no sure sign of the growth of a genuine popular philosophy of education which would seize upon the elementary school and make it the instrument of its own clearly conceived social and cultural purpose" (*Education and social change*, pp30-31, Sheldon, 1940). Truly "democratic" community schools will need a different administrative structure and philosophy to bring into the educational process parents as well as children. Here, as with other talk of participation these days, there is lots of woolly thinking: English school teachers stoutly resist any threats of the dilution or control of education by parents, and if we are not careful the parents who do the "seizing" will be the middle class. How education might become less isolated and more internally democratic are matters which have not yet been sufficiently explored: somehow this should be in and through the learning process rather than around but in isolation from it. An Education Act which neglected this issue would be out of date. A resume of the areas of comprehensive reorganisation for immediate concern is therefore as follows The next Education Act must contain a clear definition of and commitment to a *fully* comprehensive system of secondary education. Recognising regional and individual inequalities, this commitment must be in the context of a wider priority area and redistributive policy. The issues of parental choice and school boundaries for a neighbourhood system must be faced for what they are, redistribution of life chances, and they must be rendered as open and democratic as possible. And within the national strategy for equality the crucial role of the teaching profession must be fostered. In the past Labour has given the appearance of wanting to "interfere" too much and yet has not taken a sufficiently strong line over those provinces where control and leadership should have been exercised. In the future there should be no doubt about the value of a positive central statement of what the structure of education and distribution of resources is going to be; but equally the ultimate dependence of any educational policy upon the teachers must be recognised. Towards the end of Labour's spell in office a new Education Act was being prepared. The indications are that at long last something will be done about the direct grant and public schools, the provision of nursery education, the integration of further education and higher education, the structure of control of the schools (with parental and teacher representation on the governing bodies), and the issue of parental choice of school. But of the nine issues discussed by Mr. Short in a *Where?* article comprehensive education and equality received no explicit mention (*Where?*, no 56, 1970). Perhaps Labour still believes a separate short bill outlawing the 11 plus will do the trick?

Mr. Short called for a great national debate. Such a debate has already started. The *Black papers'* dishonest attempts to blame the failures of the secondary modern school on a progressive education which is only just becoming established in the primary school, and discussions of the grammar school and examinations, mean that we are now talking about whether we like what has been taught and the way it is taught. Is separatist education really our cultural heritage, and are examinations natural ways of keeping up standards and preparing a pupil for life? Is the choice really between meritocratic and egalitarian ideals, or between meritocratic ideals well or badly carried out?

We must recognise that we can never hope to settle the definition of educational equality for good. The price of equality will be eternal debate and research: debate to provide a rolling, detailed *educational* definition of equality; and an ongoing programme of relevant and carefully designed research to inform the debate. Only in this way will Labour's educational policies ever catch up with the apparently infinite regress of educational inequality. Fortunately, the debate has started now, and not, as in the past, when the Party has found itself in office without an educational policy.

8. financing of social services

Peter Kaim-Caudle

In a study prepared by the Fabian Society in the late 1940s, W. Arthur Lewis wrote—"Socialism is about equality. A passion for equality is the one thing that links all socialists; on all others they are divided" (*The principles of economic planning*, p10, Allen and Unwin, 1950). To the term "equality" many different meanings can be attached, the one relevant to socialists is well expressed by Tawney—"while they (men) differ profoundly as individuals in capacity and character, they are equally entitled as human beings to consideration and respect, and the well-being of a society is likely to be increased if it so plans its organisation that, whether their powers are great or small, all its members may be equally enabled to make the best of such powers as they possess" (*Equality*, p 46, Unwin Books, Allen and Unwin, 1964). For Tawney the main endeavour is "seeking to establish the largest possible measure of equality of environment, and circumstances and opportunity."

Tawney, writing some 40 years ago, expressed convincingly and clearly the views to which most Fabians today would subscribe: "It is true, indeed, that even such equality, though the conditions on which it depends are largely, within human control, will continue to elude us. The important thing, however, is not that it should be completely attained, but that it should be sincerely sought. What matters to the health of society is the objective towards which its face is set, and to suggest that it is immaterial in which direction it moves, because, whatever the direction, the goal must always elude it, is not scientific but irrational. It is like using the impossibility of absolute cleanliness as a pretext for rolling in a manure heap, or denying the importance of honesty because no one can be wholly honest" (*op cit*, p56).

Socialism, a passion for equality, is in its very nature a minority creed. Most of those who consider that the pursuit of equality would harm their interest adhere to the traditional selfish maxim of "what we have we hold." Most parents want to give their children "the best start in life" rather than advocating equality of opportunity for all children. Trade unionists in the NUM and the AUEW quite as much as professional men in the BMA and the NUT believe in differentials rather than in equality, in looking after their own interests rather than that of the community. Any fair examination of the Labour government's record between 1964-70 in bringing about an increasing degree of equality ought to take account of the temper and attitude of the electorate and especially allow for the views of its own supporters.

The degree of equality can be increased by a variety of means. In an advanced industrial society the four most important are: the public ownership of some industries, an incomes and prices policy, fiscal measures and the collective provision of services. These four are by no means independent of each other but this chapter is primarily concerned with the third and fourth. Before examining the Labour Government's record three points ought to be made. At present (March 1971) it is only possible to make a preliminary assessment as some of the statistical material covering the latter years of the period under review has not yet been published. A detailed comparison with what happened in Europe during the same period will have to wait even longer. The International Labour Office report on *The cost of social security 1964-66* is due in 1971 so that the report for 1967-69 might be expected in 1974. The most recent report on the social situation in the countries of the EEC published in 1970, covers the year 1967 so that the report covering 1969 will only be available in 1973. Some more general figures contained in the national accounts statistics of the UN and the OEDC are more up to date but even these for 1969 will only be published about July 1971.

In modern conditions there is a considerable and possibly increasing time lag between deciding on a plan of action and the results materialising. The 1964 Labour manifesto stated "Labour will cut down our overcrowded classes in both primary and secondary schools"; and "Labour will get rid of the segregation of children into separate schools caused by eleven plus selection: secondary education will be reorganised on comprehensive lines"; and in the section on health—" . . . every woman who wishes to, or needs to, have her baby in hospital shall be able to do so," and "Labour will greatly increase the number of qualified medical staff. We shall train more doctors and dentists." All these four pledges were implemented to a considerable extent but the results cannot be seen by looking at statistics for 1965, 1966 and even 1967. Teachers take at least three years to qualify, comprehensive schools take many years to build, and the training of doctors and the building of hospitals takes even more years. Much of what Labour did in this and many other respects will materialise post 1970 under a Conservative government. Even administrative measures like major changes in the tax system or in pension provisions cannot be implemented immediately. Labour's fiscal policy was certainly much influenced by the inability of the Inland Revenue to cope with new legislation requiring several fundamental changes in a short space of time. The Assessment of a government's record by what actually happened during the period it was in office is therefore subject to many pitfalls. The number of additional college of education places made available is a more meaningful figure than statistics of overcrowded classes. Allocation of funds for the hospital building programme are more significant than the proportion of children delivered in hospital. Unfortunately it is the less meaningful figures which are more readily comprehended and therefore are more likely to have a greater popular appeal. Lastly, the freedom of action of any government is often exaggerated. This six years of the Labour government were overshadowed by concern with the balance of payment. The policy judged necessary to put our external accounts in order, greatly interfered with the economic growth which it will be argued later was essential to the implementation of Labour's election pledges. The sentence of the 1966 election manifesto—"In the next five years living standards for the individual and for the whole community will rise by 25 per cent, as we increase our production of goods and services,"—in its bold and unqualified assertion, reads rather odd in 1971. Yet, it was a perfectly reasonable statement to make in 1966. If the seamen had not gone on strike, if Nasser had not threatened to invade Israel, if George Brown had been the General Secretary of the TGWU—matters might have been different.

The expenditure on social services, excluding housing, between 1964-69 increased by 65 per cent while the GNP increased by only 37 per cent (see

National income and expenditure 1970, HMSO). In this five year period there was thus a substantial relative increase in expenditure on these services—from 14.6 per cent to 17.6 per cent, a proportionate increase of nearly one fifth. In the previous five years, 1959-64, social services had increased from 13.4 per cent to 14.6, a proportionate increase of less than one tenth. Expenditure for all the six types of social services distinguished in the national accounts statistics increased at a faster rate than the GNP though the rates of increase differed. Amongst the three major services, the increase was largest for income maintenance (73 per cent), about average for education (64 per cent) and least for NHS (60 per cent). Expenditure on capital, up by 47 per cent, lagged well behind that on current services. The cost of supplementary benefits and family allowances more than doubled in the five year period. Prima facie, it thus appears that in this period there was quite a substantial move towards equality, in the sense of an expansion in the provision of collective services. This first impression however is misleading.

R. H. S. Crossman attributes the increased expenditure on social services to three factors: the pressure of demography, the pressure of technology and the pressure of democratic equalisation (*Paying for the social services*, p5, Fabian tract 399). The first refers to the increased population of retirement pensioners at one end and of school children at the other; the second to science, technology and medical skill creating new and ever more expensive services (like kidney machines) which themselves then generate automatically even more expensive demand. By democratic equalisation Crossman means the demand for health, education and security in old age which were previously the perquisite of wealth and position becoming the right of every citizen. The first factor is clearly of great importance but the second and the third are of lesser importance and possibly overshadowed by others.

The increase in the money cost of social services and also that in real terms (money cost adjusted for price changes) requires little comment. It is only reasonable and should be expected that expenditure will move more or less proportionally to earnings. It is the increased expenditure as a proportion to GNP which requires an explanation. The causes of this change can be classified into four broad categories: automatic, semi-automatic, price rises and improvements. These groupings are of analytical interest but are neither exhaustive nor are the borders between them necessarily precise. Automatic causes are those requiring higher expenditure to maintain the present level (quality) of services. An increase in population requires an increased proportion of GNP to be spent on social services only if the dependent age groups increase proportionally to the total population. Between 1964-69 population between 15 years and the minimum pensionable age remained stationary, while the number of children of compulsory school age increased by nearly 11 per cent and that of persons above the minimum pensionable age by almost 9 per cent. These were exceptionally large changes for a short spell of five years. Other automatic causes are of many different varieties. Some are the consequence of people availing themselves of services to which they had been entitled but which they did not previously take up. Thus during these years the number of children attending independent schools dropped by some 55,000 and a corresponding number of places had to be found in maintained schools, the cost of pensions increased because of a decline in the proportion of men and women delaying retirement beyond the minimum pensionable age. The proportion of men retiring at age 65 was 57 per cent in 1964 and had increased to 70 per cent by 1968. This meant that the proportion of men aged 65-69 who were retired increased from 73 per cent to 80 per cent. Projecting the trend of these four years into 1969 the proportion retired would have increased to 82 per cent. This factor by itself, in the five year period, increased the cost of pensions for this age group by at least one eighth (see *Report of the Government Actuary on the financial provisions of the National Superannuation and Social Insurance Bill* 1969, p21, HMSO, Cmmd 4223). Another automatic cause is a higher incidence of the contingencies that lead to interruptions or cessations of earnings. The average number of unemployed rose from 380,000 in 1964 to 559,000 in 1969. In the latter year claims for sickness benefit also reached an all time high. In the main this was due to two separate epidemics of influenza, one at the beginning of the year and another one in December.

Causes are classified as semi-automatic when the increased expenditure is due to a higher uptake of a well established service to which there is no legal entitlement. Thus the trend for staying in school beyond the minimum school leaving age increased the number of pupils aged 15 and over by 36 per cent during the period; the number of university students increased even more rapidly. The rise in the proportion of children taking school meals from 44 per cent to 53 per cent is a change of a similar character. The 26 per cent increase in the number of prescriptions dispensed is a rather special and complex case. Part of the reason is due to two factors to which reference has already been made—the changed age composition and the higher incidence of illness and part is due to the abolition of the prescription charges in 1965. There may also have been other reasons making for increased prescribing. All these developments could have been prevented by a refusal to make available the funds required to expand these services. This would have resulted in either restricting uptake by charging (or increasing) fees (or prices) or by introducing (or extending) some form of rationing, for example, raising effective university entrance requirements, limiting school meals to children of a particular age group or restricting a doctor's freedom to prescribe.

An increase in the unit cost of a social service by the same proportion as the rise of other goods and services does not require higher expenditure relative to GNP but if teachers', doctors' and nurses' remunerations rise faster than other salaries a higher proportion of GNP is required to meet them. In this case the cost rises but the quality and quantity of the services remain the same. Some may argue that a teacher's productivity increases if he receives a status increase in salary, but this assertion is difficult to substantiate. The more reasonable assumption is that above average salary increases to suppliers of social services require increased expenditure in relation to the GNP without improving the quality of the service.

Improvements can be of three types: extending the number of people entitled to a service, rendering services of a higher quality and setting up new services. Here too the classification is meaningful but particular improvements may result in changes of more than one type. Thus the extension of the earnings limit for pensioners and its abolition for widows both increased the number of beneficiaries and improved the quality of the service for some of them—their standard of living went up. The introduction of short term earnings related benefits did not affect the number of beneficiaries but much improved the quality of the service received by some. It is incidentally interesting to note that both the extension of earnings limits and the setting up of short term earnings related benefits contained an element of selectivity in favour of the relatively well off. They benefited the school teacher widow and the unemployed who had been earning a substantial wage but did not help in any way the widowed mother of young children who stayed at home or the unemployed women who previously had earned £9 or less per week.

A rise in pensions which exceeds increases in earnings in an improvement in social services of the higher quality type. If Labour's national superannuation scheme had been implemented this would have happened to persons retiring after 1973. Family allowances which had not been adjusted since 1952, more than doubled during the period under review, and therefore increased expenditure relative to GNP. However, the device of the "claw-back" reduced this cost appreciably. A reduction in children's allowances for income tax led to an increase in tax receipts.

There can be very little doubt that the increased expenditure on social services in terms of GNP was largely due to those causes which here are classified as "automatic." These by definition were not the result of either an extension of eligibility or of an improvement in the quality of the service. The "semi-automatic" factors also contributed substantially to greater cost. The higher uptake of well established services contains some element of improvement but this is not likely to be acknowledged by the people affected; they more probably feel that they receive what was in any case their due.

It is not the purpose of this chapter to assess in detail the extent to which social services contributed to a reduction of inequality in the 1964-69 period. Anybody making this attempt would do well to remember Tawney's warning: "A man deprived of one eye and one leg is not 50 per cent as well off as one with two of each. Arithmetic has its uses, but neither the injuries inflicted by inequality nor the benefits conferred by diminishing it can be reliably ascertained by sums in long division. In reality, the consequences of social expenditure depend, not merely on its amount, but on the character of the evils removed and opportunities opened by it" (*op cit*, p 219).

The aggregate increase in social service expenditure in the period—£3,172 million—was equal to more than a quarter of the growth of GNP at market prices (£12,357 million) and to just over one third of GNP valued at factor cost (£9,282 million). The financing of this substantial sum clearly required a major adjustment in taxation. In the five year period tax receipts including national insurance contributions and local rates increased by as much as three quarters; the sum required to finance higher current expenditure on social services was equal to about 41 per cent of this increase. Receipts from all the nine groups of taxes enumerated increased but they did so at different rates.

Income tax on wages and salaries more than doubled. At first sight this appears rather remarkable especially as the total number of employees in

ANALYSIS OF GENERAL GOVERNMENT TAXATION

taxes	1964 £m	1964 %	1969 £m	1969 %	increase £m	increase %
income tax*	1,648	17	3,439	20	1,791	109
surtax	179	2	240	1	61	34
rent, interest, etc†	1,701	17	2,657	16	956	56
death duties	307	3	372	2	65	21
other taxes on capital	1	—	259	2	258	—
national insurance —employees	699	7	1,006	6	307	44
national insurance—employers and self employed	745	8	1,237	7	492	66
tax on consumers' expenditure‡	3,713	38	6,152	36	2,439	66
other taxes on expenditure§	745	8	1,716	10	971	130
total	9,738	100	17,078	100	7,340	76
total as proportion of GNP— at market prices%		29		37		8
at factor cost%		33		44		11

* on wages and salaries—includes taxes on pay of HM Forces and current grants from public authorities.
† includes taxes on dividends, trading incomes and profits.
‡ includes local rates, SET, tax on oil paid by business.
§ includes tax on public authorities current expenditure, on exports and on gross capital formation.
source: *National income and expenditure, 1970,* tables 43, 46 and 47.

employment declined slightly and the payments of wages and salaries increased by only just over a third. Between 1964-65 and 1969-70 the standard rate of income tax increased from 38¾ per cent to 41¼ per cent, that means by less than 7 per cent, the net effect of other changes was to reduce rather than increase tax rates (*Annual abstract of statistics 1970,* table 330). The reasons for the doubling of receipts was the impact of rises in money wages on a progressive tax structure. In a system where tax absorbs a larger proportion of high than of low incomes, tax receipts are bound to rise much faster than incomes. This can easily be illustrated by example. At 1969-70 tax rates a person having an annual income of £325 was not liable to pay any tax, if his income rose to £337 his tax liability was £2.10 and at £346 it was £4.20. In this example his tax liability doubled for a rise in income of a mere 2.7 per cent. If the proportion of income to be paid in tax by the taxpayer with an average or median income is to be kept constant, then personal, child and other allowances have to be increased proportionally to average earnings and the band to which reduced tax rates apply has to be raised correspondingly. This was not done except in the case of the earned income allowance which remained at the rate of two ninths throughout this period.

The combined effect of changes in tax rates, national insurance contributions and wages on adult male manual workers in manufacturing industries whose earnings were 75 per cent, 100 per cent and 150 per cent of the average are shown in the table below. Figures are shown for the tax years 1964-65, 1969-

EFFECT OF CHANGES IN EARNINGS, NATIONAL INSURANCE
CONTRIBUTIONS AND INCOME TAX ON A MARRIED COUPLE
WITH ONE CHILD, 1964-65—1970-71

	75% of average			average			150% of average		
	64-65	69-70	70-71	64-65	69-70	70-71	64-65	69-70	70-71
earnings	£	£	£	£	£	£	£	£	£
gross	702	956	1,055	936	1,278	1,406	1,404	1,912	2,109
index*	100	136	150	100	136	150	100	136	150
national insurance									
flat rate	29	44	44	29	44	44	29	44	44
graduated	11	24	28	19	34	40	19	41	41
index*	100	160	180	100	162	175	100	177	177
% of earnings	5.7	7.1	6.9	5.1	6.1	6.0	3.4	4.5	4.0
income tax									
tax	23	76	99	78	180	212	218	382	439
index*	100	330	430	100	231	272	100	159	201
% of earnings	3.3	7.9	9.3	8.3	14.1	15.1	15.5	20.0	20.8
all deductions									
total	63	144	171	126	258	296	266	467	524
index*	100	228	272	100	204	235	100	176	197
% of earnings	9.0	15.0	16.2	13.4	20.2	21.0	18.9	24.5	24.8

* 1964=100

source: author's calculations—income tax—rates and allowances, *Annual abstract of statistics*, table 330; national insurance contributions, DHSS, *Annual report 1969*, tables 139, 140 and 142; earnings—average weekly earnings of men manual workers aged 21 and over in manufacturing industries in October 1964 and 1969 multiplied by 50, earnings for 1970 as for 1969 plus 10 per cent, *Annual abstract of statistics 1970*, table 153.

70 and 1970-71, though the earnings for the last year had to be estimated, for married couples with one child under eleven.

During these years earnings of this group of workers increased by 36 per cent between 1964 and 1969, and an estimated 50 per cent between 1964 and 1970. For all three reference groups the marginal increase in taxation was greater for high than for low incomes as shown in the table below.

MARRIED MAN WITH ONE CHILD			tax as %
	increase in		of increased
	earnings	tax	earnings
reference group	1964-65—69-70	1964-65—69-70	1964-65—69-70
75% of average	254	53	21
average	342	102	30
150% of average	508	164	32

However the tax liability for the married man with one child increased proportionally most for the low wage earners and income tax as a proportion of income increased for all three reference groups but decidedly more for the lowest income groups as shown in the various tables.

MARRIED MAN WITH ONE CHILD, PERCENTAGE INCREASE IN INCOME TAX

reference group	1964-65—69-70	1964-65—70-71
75% of average	230	330
average	131	172
150% of average	59	101

Therefore this tax in 1969 was decidedly less progressive than it had been five years earlier. The combined effect of the Budget in 1970 and the rise in incomes further accentuated that trend. In October 1970 the low paid married worker with one child earning 75 per cent of the average paid more than 9 per cent of his gross income in tax while six years previously his tax liability had been just over 3 per cent. The corresponding proportions for the average worker were 15 per cent and 8 per cent.

These figures are based on workers claiming only personal and children's allowances. Other possible claims in respect of dependents, life insurance premiums and mortgage interest are not taken into account. These claims almost certainly are made more frequently and for larger amounts by people having relatively high incomes. To this extent the tax liability of workers having 150 per cent of average earnings is overstated. It also seems probable that the amount of these claims during the period under review increased

MARRIED MAN WITH ONE CHILD, INCOME TAX AS A PERCENTAGE OF INCOME

reference group	1964-65	1969-70	1970-71
75% of average	3.3	7.9	9.3
average	8.3	14.1	15.1
150% of average	15.5	20.0	20.8

more rapidly for higher wage earners. If this supposition is correct it would have presented a move towards greater inequality in the incidence of taxation.

At present (March 1971) a single man with average earnings pays £315 in tax, a married man whose wife is at home looking after one young child receives no family allowance and pays £212 in tax. This appears to bear only minimal relation to taxable capacity—a net income difference of a mere £2 per week to support a wife and child.

Aggregate receipts from national insurance and similar contributions increased by much less than income tax on wages and salaries. Between 1964 and 1969 receipts from employees rose by 44 per cent and from employers and the self employed by 66 per cent. The combined ordinary flat rate of national insurance, industrial injury insurance and NHS contribution payable by employees was 11s 8d per week for an adult man in 1964 and went up to 17s 8d in November 1969, an increase of 52 per cent; the corresponding increase for adult women was 55 per cent. The rates payable by employers for adult men increased from 9s 8d to 16s 8d per week—72 per cent. The flat rate national insurance contribution paid by employees is a regressive tax—it absorbs a smaller proportion of high than of low incomes. In 1969 it took 4.6 per cent of the income of the man who earned 75 per cent of the average wage and 2.3 per cent of the man who earned twice as much. Over the period of 1964 to 1970 the increase in flat rate contributions paid by employees was approximately the same as the estimated increase in earnings.

By 1964 employees not contracted out of the graduated pension scheme paid a contribution of $4\frac{1}{4}$ per cent on weekly earnings for incomes between £9 and £18. By November 1969 this had increased to $4\frac{3}{4}$ per cent and in addition employees had to pay a contribution of $3\frac{1}{4}$ per cent on earnings between £18 and £30 per week. These contributions have much in common with income tax. The first £9 of weekly earnings on which no contributions are paid have the same effect as the personal allowances in income tax, they make a tax progressive which otherwise would be proportionate. The graduated contributions however differ from income tax in three respects. First, the contribution is not levied on incomes in excess of £30 per week and on incomes above this limit becomes regressive while income tax is paid on all incomes and in effect, at a higher rate on incomes above £4,005 per annum. Second, income tax is meant to take into account taxable capacity and does so by allowances in respect of a wife, children, dependent relatives and certain other commitments, while contributions are paid by people in all conditions at the same rate. This distinction, however, is becoming increasingly less important as allowances for dependent relatives have not been increased since 1960 and those for children not since 1963, their relative importance has thus declined. The latter allowances were actually reduced by £42 for second and subsequent children to offset the increase in family allowances. Third, income tax payments give no entitlement to specific benefits while graduated contributions are the basis for claiming both graduated pensions after retirement and short-term earnings related benefits in unemployment, sickness and widowhood. These pensions and benefits are proportionate to contributions paid, but the contributions are also the source of a substantial proportion of the finance of flat rate pensions.

The monthly average general index of retail prices increased by 23 per cent between 1964 and 1969 (*Employment and productivity gazette,* November 1970, table 132). The married man with one child whose earnings were average experienced during these years an increase in gross wages of £342 of which £174 was absorbed in price increases, £102 went in higher income tax and £30 in higher national insurance contributions. This left him with increased net earnings of £36 over the five year period, equivalent to 4.5 per cent of his gross earnings less deductions in 1964-65. Not all workers' wages increased at the average rate, some rose by more others by less. It is thus quite probable some groups of workers who experienced less than average increases had no rise in net earnings at all.

There was last year some controversy whether the level of retirement pensions under the Labour Government had increased proportionally to earnings. The results of such a statistical comparison depend partly on the dates chosen. If the dates selected are March 1965 when the Labour Government had increased pensions to £6 10s for a married couple and November 1969 when the pension was raised to £8 2s it appears that pensions went up by 25 per cent while industrial earnings increased by about 33 per cent. This would be a fair comparison if the proportion of deductions from industrial earnings had remained the same. However, for the man earning 75 per cent of the average wage, deductions were about 20 per cent in March 1965 and 25 per cent in 1969 so that his net earnings increased by only 25 per cent. (Retirement pensioners pay no national insurance contributions. Their pensions are subject to income tax. However if a retired couple has an aggregate income of less than 160 per cent of their pension, they are exempt from tax.) On this basis retirement pensions have increased in line with the earnings of lower paid workers. For obvious reasons this is not a point which government spokesmen would have wanted to stress.

The incidence of national insurance and other contributions paid by employers is a disputed topic. The conventions used in national income accounting up till 1969 assume that they are part of the employee's income as well as a tax on his income. The underlying assumption, based on the theory that wages are determined by marginal productivity, is that, but for these contributions, wages would be higher. Alternatively it may be argued that these contributions are paid by employers for the benefit of employees and as such are similar to wages in kind. The selective employment tax which from the employer's viewpoint is very similar to the national insurance contribution has *ab initio* been treated in national accounts as a tax on expenditure. This appears to be more in accordance with reality. In the present economic climate taxes on wages are not likely to reduce either wages or profits but are virtually certain to be passed on to the consumer. For this reason the Central Statistical Office in estimating the incidence of taxes and benefits will, as from 1969, treat national insurance contributions as an indirect tax included in the prices of all goods and services produced in the UK.

The taxes mainly paid by the well off sections of the population—surtax, death duties and other capital taxes—have increased relatively slowly. The reasons for this are complex and outside the scope of this chapter. Soaking the rich, experience shows, is in a democratic society operating in a mixed economy, quite as difficult as it is popular. The Labour Party has always been conscious of the importance of these issues and referred to them in the 1970 Election Manifesto under the heading social equality. "Until Labour came to power those living off capital gains or land profits were allowed to substantially escape the net of taxation. We have dealt with this, and similar problems, through the capital gains tax, land levy and by removing some loopholes in covenants and in estate duty. We shall continue to close loopholes." Some of the measures introduced will take effect only in the years to come, others which would have been effective—the Land Commission, the combining of children's unearned income with those of their parents—have been repealed by the Conservative Government.

Receipts from taxes on consumers' expenditure have risen by £2,439 million, equal to 66 per cent. This represented an average increase in tax on expenditure from 15.2 per cent in 1964 to 19.2 per cent in 1969. Between these years prices increased by 23 per cent, approximately 8.4 per cent of that increase was due to higher taxes on expenditure which thus accounted for more than a third of the increase in prices; the remainder was due to rises in factor cost including prices of goods imported. The level of tax on consumer goods differs widely. It is heaviest on tobacco, alcoholic drinks and the purchase and running of motor cars. These types of expenditure also account for more than £1,000 million of the increased tax receipts during the period under review. Taxes on food, fuel and light, books and newspapers are comparatively light. It appears, therefore, that the increases were least burdensome for the less well off section of the population. They may drink beer and smoke tobacco but will not have paid much towards the £138 million increase on wines and spirits or the £496 million increase in taxes born by private motorists.

The Central Statistical Office publishes annually estimates of the incidence of all benefits received from public authorities and of all taxes paid which can be allocated to individual families. The purpose of these estimates is to ascertain how much families in different circumstances gain or lose on balance. These estimates are discussed in other chapters of this book. Here it is only relevant to note that the official estimate gives tentative support to the general impression that taxation has not become more regressive in the 1960s and possibly has become marginally more progressive.

In these years indirect taxes were only slightly regressive and for the great majority of all incomes the burden of all taxes, direct and indirect, was and is virtually the same. The level of taxation has increased by approximately 5 per cent but the relative tax burden between different income groups has remained unaltered. Amongst direct taxes the progressive characteristics of income and surtax are partly offset by the regressive characteristics of national insurance contributions.

An analysis of general government finance as shown in the earlier table does not support the popular view that during the years of the Labour government there was a marked shift to indirect taxation. For the five year period for which figures are available at the time of writing (1964-69) all taxes on consumption remained constant at 46 per cent. Taxes on consumers' expenditure actually declined as a proportion of all taxes but this was offset by an increase in taxes on other expenditure.

The NHS is financed by four sources—general taxation, local rates, charges to users and NHS contributions paid by employers and insured persons. The contributions from these sources in 1964-65 and 1969-70 are shown in the table below. Payments out of general taxation and local rates both increased by about 70 per cent and accounted for the major share of expenditure in both years. The table suggests two comments. Receipts from NHS contributions increased by only 8 per cent over the five year period. These flat rate contributions since May 1968 have been 3s 2d per week for a male employee and 8d for his employer. A further increase in these regressive taxes would have had little to recommend it. They differ from the equally regressive national insurance contributions in two respects. Claims for national insurance benefits' depend on the contribution record while NHS benefits are an entitlement of all residents irrespective of contribution conditions. Total NHS expenditure is unrelated to NHS contributions while national insurance contributions are related to benefit levels.

The Labour government had intended to replace the flat rate NHS contributions in 1972 by the imposition of a charge of 0.3 per cent on earnings up to

£1,900 (one and a half times the earnings of a male adult industrial worker) payable by the employee and 0.6 per cent on earnings, without an upper limit, payable by the employer. These charges were estimated to yield approximately £200 million in 1973-74 at 1969 earnings levels. The aggregate contribution for a man with average earnings would have been slightly higher than at present but the employer's share of the total would have increased from one eighth (8d out of 3s 10d.) to two thirds. The employer's contribution would have been passed on to the consumer in higher prices and thus have been in essence a tax on expenditure. The proposed arrangement, by substituting a

FINANCING OF HEALTH SERVICES

	1964-65	1969-70	increase	
*expenditure**	£m	£m	£m	%
central government	1,027	1,591	564	55
local authorities	104	179	75	72
total	1,131	1,770	639	57
source of finance				
hospital, specialist service charges	9	13	4	31
pharmaceutical services charges	25	18	—7	—
general dental services charges	13	18	5	38
opthalmic services charges	8	10	2	25
NHS contributions†	166	180	14	8
local rates‡	104	179	75	72
miscellaneous§	65	87	22	34
general taxation	741	1,265	524	71
total	1,131	1,770	639	57

* excluding capital expenditure.
† paid by employers and insured persons.
‡ including consolidated fund grants to local authorities.
§ receipts from hospital endowment fund and superannuation contributions.
source: *Annual abstract of statistics 1970,* tables 42, 43 and 52.

small proportionate charge on employees for a larger regressive one, would certainly have been a marked improvement. All the same it is by no means obvious why part of the NHS should be financed by contributions. Even under the proposed scheme the main justification for the contribution-link with total expenditure and basis for entitlement—would still have been absent.

The second comment relates to expenditure by persons on pharmaceutical services. These "prescription charges" yielded a mere £18 millions without allowing for the cost of administration and the additional payments to pharmacists (*Economic Trends,* February 1970, p xviii). A 10 per cent increase in NHS contributions—4½d per week for adult men—would have yielded the same amount without any administrative cost at all. Whatever may have been the reasons for introducing these charges it is difficult to believe that it was the desire to find a new source of revenue for the NHS. From the point of view of equity a flat rate regressive NHS contribution is almost certainly preferable to a "tax on the sick." In any case the complete clinical freedom of doctors to prescribe may well require some modification. It is not easy to understand why unfettered prescribing deserves a higher priority than other desirable health measures which are restricted by the availability of resources —by what the country can afford. The scheme introduced last year in Ontario which encourages, but does not compel, the dispensing of less expensive preparations, may be a model worth careful study.

The British system of financing health services is distinctly different from that employed by other European countries. It is less complex, more unified and a larger proportion of total expenditure is financed by general taxation.

Germany has no general health service, but some 87 per cent of the population are covered by statutory health insurance schemes; these are, with few exceptions, financed solely by the contributions of their members without financial aid from either central or local government funds. Contributions are proportionate and average about 10 per cent of earnings. For those who are compulsorily insured half the contribution is paid by the employer while those who are voluntarily insured have to pay the whole contribution themselves. Approximately a fifth of the expenditure of the schemes is on cash benefits the remainder is on health services. The method of financing the services has a marked element of redistribution. As contributions are proportionate to income and benefits in kind (health services) independent of income, low wage earners pay less for identical health services than those with higher incomes. As all dependents are covered by the contribution of the wage or salary earners, larger families receive more benefits than single persons or small families. The contributions are also fixed in such a way that those at work subsidse the cost of health services for the old, the disabled and the survivors of deceased contributors. Cost sharing by beneficiaries is on a very moderate scale and applies to much the same services as in Britain. In recent years the extent of cost sharing, especially for medicines, has increased.

In the four Scandinavian countries health insurance covers virtually the entire population; in all hospitals care is free of charge to patients, but for other health care there is some cost sharing. A general impression of the

FINANCING OF PUBLIC NET EXPENDITURE ON HEALTH CARE, 1966

	public authorities %	employers %	insured persons %	cash benefit as proportion of all benefits %
Denmark	78	2	20	4
Norway	49	18	33	12
Sweden	73	11	16	19
UK (1969)	89	1	10	Nil
Germany	5	39	56	22
France	16	57	27	*
Italy	26	67	7	*

*figures not available
source: Scandinavian countries— *Social security in the Nordic countries*, report 16, table 10, Copenhagen, 1970; U.K.—*Annual abstract of statistics 1970*, tables 42, 43 and 52; EEC countries—*Bericht de Entwicklung der sozialen Lage in der Gemeinschaft in 1968*, Brusells, 1969.

financing of net public expenditure of health services in Europe can be gained by examining the table above.

The extent of cost sharing is difficult to assess and even more difficult to interpret. It may operate as a condition to obtain basic services such as the $12\frac{1}{2}$p prescription charge in Britain or the payment of £2.30 to obtain a pair of spectacles. Alternatively it may be a charge for obtaining service such as a payment for amenity beds, for more fashionable spectacle frames or for more elaborate dental treatment. Charges may vary according to the cost of the service, as in Germany for medicines or as in Denmark where charges for medicines are based not only on the cost, but also depend partly on the nature of the illness and the type of drug prescribed. In some countries health insurance funds reimburse to (some or all) members a fixed amount for a service they have required but the cost of the service normally exceeds the sum received.

The experience of foreign countries in financing their health services may be relevant in considering new ways of financing ours but it must always be borne in mind that techniques of finance are frequently based not only on ideology but also on the historical development of a service and its present structure and organisation.

Statistics for the financing of income maintenance are, at the time of writing, only available up to the year 1968-69. In this four year period total expenditure increased by 61 per cent, that on services entirely financed by the Exchequer out of general taxation rose as much as 78 per cent. It represented

FINANCING OF INCOME MAINTENANCE

	1964-65	1968-69	increase	
flat rate contribution	£m	£m	£m	%
national insurance	929	1,415	486	52
NI (industrial injuries)	68	84	16	24
graduated contributions				
national insurance	270	429	159	59
income from investment				
national insurance	36	54	18	50
NI (industrial injuries)	14	16	2	14
payments from balances				
national insurance	21	72	51	242
NI (industrial injuries)*	—10	—3	7	—
exchequer contributions				
national insurance	219	342	123	56
NI (industrial injuries)	14	17	3	21
exchequer financed services†	502	896	394	78
total	2,063	3,322	1,259	61

* credit balance

† including, supplementary pensions and benefits, family allowances, war pensions and the cost of administering these schemes.

source: DHSS, *Annual Report*, 1969, tables 123, 130, 131.

in 1968-69 about 27 per cent of all income maintenance expenditure compared with 24 per cent four years previously. The Exchequer contribution to national insurance increased by about the same proportion as contributions from employers and insured persons. In 1968-69 payments out of the national insurance fund exceeded receipts by £72 million. Increases in contribution by the Exchequer, employers and insured persons to the national injury fund were less than a quarter, while payments into the national insurance fund were well over half of what they had been four years previously. The increase in wages since 1968 will have meant, for reasons discussed earlier, that receipts from graduated contributions will have risen sharply during the last two years.

In Europe income maintenance services like health services are financed in a variety of different ways as shown in the table below.

FINANCING OF OLD AGE, SURVIVORS AND INVALIDITY PENSIONS, 1966

	public authorities %	employers %	insured persons %
Denmark	77	5	18
Norway	24	42	34
Sweden	47	35	18
UK (1969)	32*	36	32
Germany	31	33	36
France	22	49	29
Italy	31	42	27

* includes 3 per cent interest on investment funds
source: for Scandinavian countries and EEC as in above table, for UK estimated by aggregating national insurance receipts and supplementary commission payments.

The widely different proportions of total expenditure levied on the three types of contributors do not elucidate the underlying differences in the systems of the seven countries. Some pensions are demogrants, others are social assistance, subject to a means test of varying severity, still others are social insurance benefits payable as of right subject to contribution conditions. There are different ages of retirement and different conditions in which invalidity pensions become payable.

The one point all the schemes have in common is a transfer of income by people at work to the pensioners. The incidence of the burden is very difficult to ascertain. It is quite possible that an increase, say, in employer's contributions will have different effects in 1971 as a similar increase had in the same country in 1967 or that an identical change will have different effects in one country than in another.

The average German worker pays some 14 per cent of his gross earnings in social insurance contributions while his British counterpart pays 6 per cent. Such differences are the results of historic developments and are a fact of life which can only be modified gradually. In any case deductions from workers' earnings must be considered comprehensively, for example insurance contributions and taxes on income ought to be co-ordinated.

Expenditure on public education is almost entirely met from two sources of revenue: taxation and receipts from local government rates. There are no specially designated taxes or rates for education. Income from fees is small absolutely and insignificant proportionally. However fees in some types of further and adult education are sufficiently high to discourage demand which socially deserves to be encouraged. This is also the case for University tuition fees for overseas students from the developing countries.

The record of the Labour government between 1964-70 must, for reasons discussed in an earlier section, not solely be judged by what happened during these years but also by the measures taken which had not fructified. One of the most important of these was the still born National Superannuation and Social Insurance Bill (1969) which was to be implemented in April, 1972. The proposed superannuation scheme is discussed in a Fabian pamphlet by Tony Lynes with whose general conclusions I am in complete agreement. "The bias in favour of the lower paid in the pension formula goes as far as could reasonably be expected, and probably much further than some of the Government's advisers (especially those concerned with the impact on holders of sterling) would have wished. To give over twice as much pension for every pound of contribution on earnings below, half the national average as on earnings above that level is, if anything, to invite the charge of 'soaking the rich' " and in the final passage "On balance, the scheme cannot be described as radically redistributive. Compared with the present situation, however, it has a distinct bias in favour of the lower paid worker." (*Labour's pension plan*, Fabian tract 398, p31). The scheme was a move away from inequality but its provisions would not have been fully operative before the death of all pensioners who had retired prior to 1992, say about the year 2015. The pension levels of those retiring between 1973 and 1991 would have been partly determined by the new scheme but the present seven million retirement pensioners would not have been directly affected. Their pensions were to be reviewed in 1972. It is of course not possible to know what would have been the result of this review. Presumably this would have mainly depended on the state of the economy at that time.

The proposed earings related short term supplements to sickness, unemployment and industrial injury flat rate benefits also would have had a marked redistributive element, especially for a man with adult or child dependents. The aggregate benefit was similar to the present scheme. It would have been for the first one third of average earnings, 60 per cent for the single and 97 per cent for the married man. For earnings between one third and one and a half of the average it was to be 33 per cent irrespective of family circumstances. Earnings above one and a half times the average would not have given entitlement to higher benefit. For the same proportionate contribution the single man earning three quarters of the average wage would have received an aggregate benefit of 48 per cent of his earnings while the man receiving twice as much would have received 40 per cent of his earnings. The corresponding proportions for a married man would have been 67 per cent and 48 per cent. During the first two weeks of interruption of employment only flat rate benefits were to be payable, but as entitlement to these was based on contributions related to earnings they also contained a marked element of redistribution.

The broad strategy of the Labour government in the collective provision of services seems to have been right. But measures like the decision to abolish the scheme of giving free school meals to large families irrespective of means and the reintroduction of prescription charges were not quantatively of great importance but appear to have been steps in the wrong direction. A more serious criticism can be levied against the Budget of 1970. This increased the personal allowance for single persons and the married woman's earned income allowance by £70 and the personal allowance for married couple by £90. Simultaneously it abolished the reduced rate of tax on the first £260 of taxable income. The benefit of these reliefs accrued mainly to single people and married women earning less than £700 per year and to married couples earning up to £800. It also reduced by £8 per year the tax liability of all couples with an income of more than £800.

Amongst the two million main beneficiaries of these tax reductions of £139 million there were some 700,000 single persons, 800,000 married women at work but only 400,000 married men (*The Economist,* 18 April 1970, p69). None of these had high incomes but the married women belonged to households where there will have been normally two income earners and a large proportion of the single persons benefiting will have been teenagers. There can be little doubt that equity would have been better served if the Chancellor had taken the advice of the Child Poverty Action Group and instead of reducing personal taxes had increased family allowances subject to the "claw-back," by reducing income tax childrens allowances by such an amount as to concentrate the benefit of the higher family allowances on those people with incomes too low to pay tax. Alternatively tax concessions to the low paid married man (though they can not help the poorest who pay no tax) would have been preferable to concessions to single people, who in Britain are relatively lightly taxed compared with other European countries.

One measure which would have involved only minor expense might have led to a considerable reduction in poverty. The Labour government gave encouragement to local authorities to subsidise and provide family planning clinics, but all the same this important service continued to be under financed. The people most in need of advice are the least likely to visit the clinics. Family planning can be an inexpensive measure of preventing poverty but it ought not be provided on a take it or leave it basis but should be promoted with drive and determination possibly largely as a domicillary service. The problem of overpopulation in Britain is as yet not properly appreciated. A social historian looking, in the year 2000, at what happened under a Labour government may well consider the reduction in the number of births during this period (1.02 million in 1964 to .92 million in 1969) as the most important social happening.

During the six years of Labour government expenditure on social services increased very rapidly and much faster than real personal incomes which, allowing for price rises and higher tax and national insurance deductions, increased only marginally. Most of the increased social service expenditure was not incurred to finance improved services but was caused by factors which were classified as automatic and semi-automatic, like the increase in the proportion of the dependent age groups, a larger up take of services and so on. It seems unlikely that in the present climate of opinion people will be prepared to contribute more in taxes to finance social services while their own incomes fail to rise. The further extension of social services of all kinds will have to depend on either a growth of the economy and an increase in real wages and salaries or on a fairly radical change in public attitudes. The Labour government presumably extended social services expenditure to the limit which was tolerable in a stagnating economy. Some might argue that given public attitudes they went beyond the limit and thereby lost the General Election.

The "revolution of rising expectations" is a grim reality in Britain even more so than in the rest of Western Europe. The willingness of all organised groups of "workers" to "hold the community to ransom" is one of the manifestations of this revolution. In my view the failure of the Labour government to move away faster from inequality was not due to a disregard of the importance of collectively provided services or an unwillingness to improve the standards of the least well off, nor to a misjudgment of the best time for devaluation or to lack of economic know how, but to more fundamental causes. The government failed to persuade the country and especially the trade union leaders of the overwhelming need for a prices and incomes policy and even more important failed to persuade all "workers" that rising standards of living are not the result of "fighting" but of producing more goods and services. It was not reasonable to expect that Zurich bankers, the Association of Life Insurance Offices and the Confederation of British Industries would support a Labour government but support from men and women on the shop floor, in the offices, the classrooms and the hospitals, as well as from their trade unions was a not unreasonable expectation. From the failure to gain this support much of the rest followed. In my view no different policy in the financing of social services, indeed no measures in the social policy field could have made a significant contribution to winning the confidence on which this support could have been built.

A future Labour government will have to start by "putting the economy right." A progressive social policy is hardly possible with a huge deficit in the balance of payments or a stagnating economy slipping into unemployment. The reasons for this can not be blamed on the bankers or the Treasury Knights but is caused by the unwillingness of doctors and dockers, of dustbinmen and teachers, or printers and seamen to pay more taxes, whether directly or indirectly, out of incomes which do not rise sufficiently fast to give them the higher standards of living to which they consider themselves entitled. The "passion for equality" is a minority creed.

A rising GNP however is not sufficient by itself, it has to be accompanied by a general change in attitudes. The guide lines for a progressive social policy moving towards greater equality are quite easy to outline. Any prices and incomes policy which restrains rises in incomes can be the basis of economic growth but only a policy which favours the least well off and aims at reducing earnings differentials will lead to greater equality. Similarly the expansion and improvement in collectively provided services should be concentrated on those in greatest need. This should be done not by setting up a means test state or by introducing such schemes as negative income tax but by giving priority to groups whose needs can be demonstrated and whose limits can be easily defined. This might include the introduction of disability pensions, improvements in psychiatric services and in mental subnormality hospitals and greatly increased expenditure on the education of young children who live in areas where social conditions are inferior. There is also for a variety of reasons a strong case for raising family allowances and recovering part of the cost by a further extension of the "claw-back." An alternative to the claw-back is a family allowance tax which is levied at different rates depending on the size of the aggregate income of the parents and the number of children in the family. This is a type of selectivity which does not require a personal means test and is a flexible device of concentrating Family Allowances on those whose need is greatest. Such a tax would, like the "claw-back," have the political disadvantage of reducing for all but the poorest families the father's income while simultaneously increasing that of the mother. Social services should be financed by levies, contributions and taxes which are progressive that means take a greater proportion of high than of low income.

The acceptance of a social planning programme based on these guide lines will present great difficulties. The people who have to concede reduced earnings differentials and provide the resources for financing the expansion of social services will have to be persuaded that these measures are desirable in spite of the fact that they do not further their own interest immediately and directly.

In my view any fiscal measures which reduce the standard of living of large sections of the population in order to expand social services will be very difficult to implement in the immediate future. I view with concern proposals for modifying the rule that mortgage interest is a charge and not a disbursement of income. This would detrimentally affect about a quarter of all households and be most unpopular with many people whose demands and views influence those who make policy.

The next move towards greater social equality through the provision of collective services will have to rely on three factors: A growth in GNP which will make it possible to allocate some of the increased wealth for an expansion and improvement of social services. A determined public education campaign to win support for the spirit of Tawney expressed in the quotation at the beginning of this chapter. Last, but not least, the attainment of the highest possible levels of efficiency within the social services.

In a pressure group society it is eminently desirable that the few who speak for the poor shall continue to press hard on behalf of that fifth of the population who are least able to care for themselves. Unless that happens this group might become relatively poorer at an ever accelerating rate. Present economic and social trends appear to lead to greater inequality. To prevent this must clearly be the first objective of socialist policy for communal services.

9. the low paid

John Hughes

"The Government's economic objective is to achieve and maintain a rapid increase in output and real incomes combined with full employment. Their social objective is to ensure that the benefits of faster growth are distributed in a way that satisfies the claims of social need and justice" (*Joint statement of intent on productivity, prices and incomes*, 16 December 1964).

The Labour Government faced acute dilemmas in its incomes policies from the very beginning. It is important to recognise what these were and how they affected the general growth of real incomes, and more particularly the position of low paid workers.

In 1965 when the incomes policy was being launched there was very little that could be given away in terms of higher real wages and salaries. The economy was fully stretched, and there was limited scope for short run increases in real output. The improvement in the balance of payments account was being accorded priority, and therefore operated as a claim on available output. Productive investment was increasing and acting as a further claim on additional resources. The finances of the whole public sector were in deficit while, particularly as a result of a disproportionate increase in the dependent population, real public expenditure was rising.

It was therefore a difficult problem, whether thought of in money or in real terms, to handle incomes in the middle 1960s. If there were any serious aspirations about income re-distribution (the lack of re-distributive emphasis in fiscal policy hardly suggests it), they were obviously curtailed within a policy framework that put emphasis on money wage restraint and could not offer any general advance in real wages. One sign of this is that all the official "norms" of pay increase throughout the whole period represented in *real* terms a reduction in pay.

The initial basis of "consent" that was forthcoming for the Labour Government's incomes policy could not but break down if the promised advance in real pay and conditions was continually deferred. But that was its fate. In retrospect what is surprising is that the trade unions co-operated for as long as they did, and tried for as long as they did to develop a constructive dialogue with the Government about both growth and income distribution. Granted that the *initial* period of economic management and incomes policy presented such difficulties, why did the subsequent handling of policy also dissipate the hopes for a progressive incomes policy?

We may note four distinct phases in all. Phase one was the initial period in which "the inheritance" so clearly limited the scope for action. Phase two was marked by the plunge into a deflationary policy with the July 1966 measures, on the incomes side backed by a statutory freeze followed by "severe restraint." As this sharply curtailed the growth of the economy it represented the choice of under-employed and unemployed resources instead of growth in output and real income. It will be argued, subsequently, that the doubling of male unemployment that was the persistently maintained consequence within the labour market represented a sharp setback for many lower paid workers. In phase three there was for just over twelve months a sharp rise in real output—but this was largely directed to the swing of the payments balance from heavy deficit to surplus. I say "largely directed" because in the latter half of 1967 an attempt was made to prevent the recession in activity going too far (by then manufacturing investment was declining). The technique chosen was a stimulus to consumer durable spending through an easing of credit—thus offsetting what would have been a winter rise in unemployment. One senses here the unplanned nature of the devaluation decision. Phases two and three together produced a period of nearly three years during which advances in real pay were sharply circumscribed. Devaluation, instead of deflation, in 1966 might have foreshortened this period of further deferment of earned income improvements. (This is not being wise after the event. George Brown evidently would have preferred devaluation then. I advocated it, myself, early in 1966 in *Tribune*—against editorial protest and a disclaimer.)

Phase four, roughly the last year of life of the Labour Government, was the most extraordinary phase of all. By then every single one of the constraints on a planned growth of real earned income that had existed in 1965 had been removed. The economy was working well below capacity, with a rising trend of unemployment. The payments balance had swung to surplus and its further improvement was not a necessary or desirable policy object. New capital formation was falling sharply in the public sector, and barely rising in the private one. The finances of the public sector had swung to massive surplus, and real spending in that sector was falling. Now, when a planned expansion of real wages with an emphasis on social priorities, would have met the needs of economic management, now the Government appeared trapped in its old ideology of "restraint" and the Treasury pursued even more rigorously its deflationary policies. Seasonally adjusted unemployment rose continuously in the last 15 months of the Government's life. Instead of a dialogue with the trade unions on a new growth strategy with priority to real wage advance, we had the massive diversion of discussion to *In place of strife*. Incomes policy disintegrated, with its final White Paper still repeating but at even greater length the old platitudes, and with a "norm" which if anyone had followed it would have again been a cut in real pay. This would not primarily have been because of the money wage push. In 1968-69 increases in indirect and labour taxes and post-devaluation import price increases together accounted for a 7 per cent retail price increase (out of a total rise of $11\frac{1}{2}$ per cent), while Treasury deflation of the economy slowed the productivity growth to well below its normal level and thereby reduced the offset it could have provided to rising business costs.

Against this sombre background of the frustration of the hopes placed upon an incomes policy, and of an unprecedentedly slow rate of real pay advance (by post-war standards), we have to assess the position of the lower paid. The rise in "constant price" earnings of the average adult male manual worker in the four years from 1965 to 1969 was only 7 per cent. But this overstates the improvement since the burden of direct taxation increased by over 2 per cent of the original income of working class households. Thus disposable real earnings were on average rising only about 1 per cent per annum over this period.

The Declaration of Intent declared its interest in "social justice" and the April 1965 White Paper on Incomes Policy more specifically set out low pay as one of the four headings justifying "exceptional" pay advance: "Exceptional pay increases should be confined to the following circumstances . . . where there is general recognition that existing wage and salary levels are too low to maintain a reasonable standard of living."

Even at this stage incomes policy was already confusing the issue, however, for in earlier paragraphs of the White Paper we had been told that "less weight than hitherto will have to be given" to factors traditionally used in wage and salary determination including "changes in the cost of living." Thus an undefined concern about low pay and living standards had to be matched with a diminished weight to be given to cost of living—and therefore real wage—arguments.

failure to follow up concern for low paid

In any case, the approach to low pay was characterised by a failure to follow up—either at all, or except with major delays—the expressed concern for the low paid. This showed in a number of ways:

1. On investigation the problem of low pay turns out to be extremely complex. It connects with the problems of groups disadvantaged in the labour market, through the areas they live in, through lack of relevant skills, through discrimination (women; immigrants), through age and disability, through greater job insecurity and unemployment, through defects in work organisation and wage structures, and through weak or non-existent trade union organisation. These forces may operate cumulatively, even if they can be analysed separately. Any genuine concern for the low paid has to be based on continuing, and continually more comprehensive, analysis of the complex of factors generating low and insecure pay, and this has to lead on into an increasingly comprehensive planned response. No such effort was made by the Government. It was, though belatedly, the TUC that established a working party and published a comprehensive analysis, and used this to shape its subsequent policies (*Low pay:* TUC *General Council dicussion document,* February 1970). The final irony here was that at the end of 1969 the Government, lacking both adequate analysis and adequate policies, was nevertheless ready to pontificate about the inability of collective bargaining to tackle low pay. It said: "One of the weaknesses of the system of free collective bargaining has been its inability to solve the problems of the low paid" (*Productivity, prices and incomes policy after 1969,* Cmnd 4237, p21, HMSO). This was at the very moment when the trade unions breaking clear of the restraints of incomes policy were making the most distinctive effort that we have yet seen to give priority through pay settlements to the lower paid. So far as analysis went the Labour Government made one stab at the problem, but tackled it the wrong way round. Instead of an attempt at analysing the total situation of the low paid, and an exploration of the range of policies that would be needed, it set up at the end of 1967 an inter-departmental working party on a national minimum wage. This report, not published till 1969, viewed in isolation an

approach which could only be significant as part of a wider strategy (DEP *National minimum wage, an enquiry*). It also produced completely misleading and exaggerated estimates of the "cost" of a statutory minimum; a dismal exhibition of the low quality of civil service work in such a field.

2.   To analyse low pay and judge with discrimination the effects of particular developments or policies there have to be more adequate statistics. It was a long while before the decision was made to carry through a major sample study of pay dispersion covering the whole field of wages and salaries. From April 1969 this material, based on a September 1968 survey, began to be published and to provide a comprehensive statistical account. (It was immediately put to use by the TUC in its *Low pay* study, but no governmental inquiries were set on foot.) The subsequent survey, taken in April 1970, began to be published in November 1970, and affords us a picture of pay dispersion at the end of the Labour Government's life. Thus, the right step was taken, but three years late, and in consequence the knowledge obtained was not transformed into a new impetus in Labour Government policy, though it did contribute to the new emphasis in trade union bargaining strategy in 1970. Finally, it was only in 1970 as part of a group of references to the NBPI dealing more particularly with low pay that an organised social survey was carried out into the actual circumstances of low paid workers in three industries (see *General problems of low pay,"* NPBI Report 169, appendix A, April 1971).

3.   Similarly, there was a considerable delay before the NBPI was given references which dealt with any sizeable numbers of low paid workers. Late in 1966 there were references on agricultural workers, retail drapery, and on manual workers in local government, the health service, and other public utilities. This led to very little either by way of the direct impact of the reports or by way of a broader understanding of the features and needs of the low paid. The first report covering agricultural workers led only to a munificent 6s increase! This was followed in February 1969 by government acceptance of an "above the ceiling" increase for farmworkers. Even so, between 1964 and 1969, the increase in weekly pay of the average farmworker was slightly less in percentage terms than the "all industries" average, and only 70 per cent of the "all industries" increase in money terms. By 1969 the hourly earnings of the average adult male farmworker were only three-fifths those of the average man working in manufacturing. It is true that on a limited scale the NBPI reports encouraged incentive payments schemes to be developed in local government and elsewhere. But it was a strange "solution "to develop fragmented schemes that not only were very patchy in their coverage, but were not even standardised in their measurement of work and effort. A sad feature of the NBPI's interest in low pay is that it led them into the surprisingly narrow and inadequate conclusion that "so far as improving the position of the low paid" was concerned "the main remedy is to be found in the improvement of efficiency . . the improvement of the position of the low paid can be subsumed in the general problem of improving efficiency." (NBPI *Fourth General Report*, Cmnd 4130, July 1969). It is hardly the language of sympathetic understanding —although the handling of individual references (such as that on clothing manufacture) was at variance with this gradgrind philosophy. A full five

years after the incomes policy was launched, the government (in March 1970), referred to the NBPI a group of three industries—laundry, contract cleaning, and health service ancillary workers—for reports which were to pay particular attention to aspects of low pay. In the event, these were published in April 1971 together with what was called a "general" report but which was in fact little more than some general observations on the three specific references. By then the NBPI was being wound up, and this may account for the sketchy and inconclusive nature of the general report. Its methodology and range of inquiry were alike inadequate. Thus, it chose to concentrate on only the bottom 10 per cent of both men and women's pay dispersion, an approach which could not but be defective when applied to the connection between low pay and women workers. It concentrated on comparisons of weekly earnings, although notoriously there are major industries where low hourly rates are associated with excessively long weekly hours, like road haulage. And it avoided the acute problem created by high effective rates of taxation on marginal income across income ranges that embrace the low paid workers. Its cautiously expressed "conclusions" broke no new ground, and its appeal for further studies looked like falling on deaf ears.

4.　Since the norm played such an important role in the handling of incomes policy, it might have been thought that the government would use it to signal their concern about the social priority represented by low pay. It is at least surprising, therefore, that throughout the norm continued to be expressed in percentage terms. It was not that this was sheer absence of mind either. From 1968 onwards, the TUC which had then developed its own independent analysis of the situation of the economy and its own declaration of income priorities expressed for the trade unions a rival norm which at all times was put in flat rate monetary terms. There was no initiative on the part of the government to explore this re-casting of income priorities. In the end it has been the greater egalitarianism of TUC wages policy that has shown through at least within the major bargaining units and settlements of 1970—with a very wide adoption of flat rate increases.

5.　It was at all times open to the Labour Government to exert a more positive influence in improving the position of low paid workers since the public sector itself happens to be on a large scale an employer of low paid workers. Besides, it could have redirected the criteria used by wages councils in pay determination, and used the existence of statutorily enforced pay minima to advance pay levels for the least protected. It did neither. Instead of any major review of wages councils and their actual operation, this matter was only looked at peripherally by the Donovan Commission whose level of interest in wages councils was so low that they did not commission any

PERCENTAGE OF MEN MANUAL WORKERS EARNING UNDER £15 A WEEK GROSS IN SEPTEMBER 1968 AND £17 IN APRIL 1970

	1968	1970
national agreements, private sector	5.2	4.9
national agreements, public sector	11.5	11.5
wages board/council orders	22.6	22.8

source: *Employment and productivity gazette*, November 1970.

research work in that field. As the table above shows the proportion of low wage earners in different sectors hardly changed between 1968 and 1970 —a clear indication of the inertia of public policy. There were about 250,000 men in public sector employment under £17 in April 1970, and about 135,000 manual men in wages council industries, compared with only about 100,000 under £17 in private sector collective bargaining—although the last named sector embraces more manual employees than both the other two sectors combined.

6. The most positive achievement of the Labour Government in the field of low pay only scraped home on to the statute book on the eve of the 1970 electoral defeat. Legislation for equal pay for men and women for "the same or broadly similar" work, by 1975, was only beginning to be reflected in collective bargaining terms on any substantial scale in the last year of life of the Labour Government. Between September 1968 and April 1970 median hourly earnings of full time women employees had risen $17\frac{1}{2}$ per cent compared with a 15 per cent increase for men. A number of settlements by 1970 were giving large money increases to women than to men (notably in distribution), and greater proportionate increases in minimum rates for women than for men were a feature of the majority of agreements. Since the majority of women workers are low paid (median weekly earnings in April 1970 for full time women workers were only £14.60), the shift in pay distribution as a result of the transition to equal pay for men and women has major importance. The statutory commitment might well be viewed as the one distinct achievement of the Labour Government in the approach to low pay. Of course, this was a necessary commitment if the British economy was to be brought into line with Common Market requirements. Women's pay in Britain as a proportion of men's pay is considerably lower than in other West European countries; thus for manual workers the proportion in Britain is in round terms 50 per cent compared with a range of 60 per cent to 65 per cent in other European countries (UN, *Incomes in post-war Europe*, chap 5, table 5.14).

who are the low paid?

In view of this long catalogue of ways in which the intervention of the Labour Government in the interests of the lower paid was lacking, or was too little and too late, it does not come as a surprise to find negligible improvements in the relative position of lower paid workers—so far as available statistics can serve as a guide. It is nevertheless useful to make a statistical survey, since

THE FULL TIME ADULT LABOUR FORCE, 1970

	number (millions)	% of total	average weekly earnings	% of total earnings
manual men	8.3	46.3	£26.20	48.3
non-manual men	4.1	22.9	£35.70	32.4
manual women	2.1	11.7	£12.90	6.0
non-manual women	3.4	19.0	£17.60	13.3

source: *Employment and productivity gazette*, November 1970. The earnings' basis taken for this table is basis C, which includes workers whose pay was affected by absence but who were paid in the pay period covered by the survey, but the numbers represent the entire full time labour force (basis A).

this can help to chart the recent or current situation of the more disadvantaged workers in the British labour market.

We can start with a general view of the composition of the full time labour force in 1970, simply classified into manual and non-manual, men and women, as shown in the table on the previous page.

The degree of inequality involved in the range of employee income may be indicated by comparing for each of these broad groups the *lowest decile* and the *highest decile* earnings.

WEEKLY EARNINGS: COMPARISON OF LOWEST DECILE (LD) AND HIGHEST DECILE (HD) (ALL INDUSTRIES AND SERVICES)

	lowest decile	highest decile	HD as % of LD	LD as % of manual women's LD	HD as % of manual women's LD
manual men	£17.20	£37.70	219	196	429
non-manual men	£19.40	£55.00	283	221	625
manual women	£8.80	£18.50	210	100	210
non-manual women	£10.20	£27.60	271	116	314

source: *op cit*. This material on dispersion of earnings is based only on the sample that did not lose pay due to absence (basis D).

The inequality in the spread of earnings so far as manual workers are concerned looks less extreme when hourly instead of weekly earnings are compared, since men manual workers work for longer hours than women workers. (Thus on an hourly earnings basis the highest decile earnings of manual men are 3.3 times as high as the lowest decile earnings of manual women workers, whereas on a weekly basis the highest decile earnings of manual men are over four times as high as the lowest decile of manual women.)

Comparisons of average earnings of manual workers over most of the life of the Labour Government show little movement in their ranking. Between October 1964 and October 1969 average weekly earnings of manual men rose by 37 per cent. Within manufacturing, the industry with lowest average earnings (clothing) increased its average earnings by 36 per cent, the one with highest earnings (paper, printing, and publishing) increased its average earnings by 37½ per cent. There were thus a slight widening in the inter industry spread of earnings. (In 1964 weekly earnings in paper, printing, and so on had been 134 per cent of those in clothing, for men manual workers; in 1969 they were 136 per cent.) The lowest paid industry of all, agriculture, did not improve its relative position.

Over the same period (October 1964 to October 1969) the weekly earnings both of manual women and of girls rose only 35 per cent compared with the 37 per cent increase for men. (The more recent earnings survey, it has already been noted, suggested however that there was some relative catching up in women's pay between 1968 and 1970.) The only category that showed a distinct relative advance was that of "youths under 21" whose weekly pay rose 43 per cent. This reflects the result of collective bargaining in many industries which has reduced the age at which the adult rate is paid. It is worthy of note in any study of low pay, since contrary to popular belief younger male workers have had relatively low earnings and for many of these relatively poor earnings extend into early adult life. The September 1968 Earnings Survey is revealing. 7.9 per cent of all full time men then earned under £15 gross per week. But *almost twice that proportion* (14.9 per cent) of men aged 21-24 earned under £15, and so did *nearly two-thirds* (63.7 per cent) of youths aged 18-20. The problem here is partly one of low starting salaries in the non-manual field and over-long incremental scales; TUC collective bargaining policies singled this out for attention as deserving disproportionate pay advance. In 1968 32 per cent of men clerical workers aged 21 to 24 years had gross weekly earnings under £15. This must seriously affect the financial position of many young married couples, whose low pay while juvenile workers must have largely prevented any accumulation of personal capital. So the more rapid increase in pay of "youths" deserves a modest cheer.

When we turn to regional differences in earnings levels it is once again difficult to see any tendency for those characterised by relatively low earnings to improve significantly—or at all. The September 1968 Earnings Survey and the annual figures of regional earnings dispersion given in the family expenditure surveys offer some guidance. The regions with a high proportion of low paid men employees are, apart from Northern Ireland, East Anglia, the South Western Region, and Scotland. In these regions of Great Britain in 1968, lower quartile earnings for men were around £17 10s some 30s below the lower quartile figures for Great Britain as a whole, and £2 10s a week below the figure for the South East and the West Midlands (the regions with highest earnings). The series of data available for manual earnings show average earnings in East Anglia and the South West rising more slowly than the national average in the years 1967-69 (changes in regional boundaries prevent any complete analysis for earlier years) while earnings in the South East and West Midlands grew slightly faster than the national average. The figure for average (mean) earnings of manual workers in Scotland has shown some relative advance, but the available data on the dispersion of Scottish earnings suggests that this is due to an advance among higher paid workers and that the relative improvement has not extended to the lower paid. Male earnings show a wider dispersion in Scotland than in other regions; thus upper quartile earnings in Scotland were in 1968 higher than in the East Midlands, Yorkshire and Humberside and Northern regions, but the lower quartile earnings in Scotland were lower than in these other regions. So far as low pay among women workers is concerned, Wales, Yorkshire and Humberside, and the Northern Region join these other regions of low pay in the common misery of lower quartile earnings for full time women workers of £9 10s (September 1968). With the exception of East Anglia (where low pay connects with the importance of agricultural and associated employment) these regions with high proportions of low paid workers all had unemployment rates higher than the national average, and in some cases the unemployment situation had deteriorated considerably during the later years of Labour's period of office. It is important to recognise, particularly so far as men are concerned, the linkages between high rates of unemployment and low pay. To take some obvious examples.

1. *Older manual workers.* The September 1968 Earnings Survey found 9.4 per cent of men manual workers earning less than £15 a week gross; when earnings are analysed by age group we find 6.5 per cent under £15 in the 40 to 49 age group, 10.9 per cent in the 50 to 59 age group, and 18.2 per cent in the 60-64 age group. These figures relate to those who work a full week. There is a similar progression in the rate of unemployment experienced, by age group. When Labour left office, male unemployment had reached the peak seasonally adjusted rate of $3\frac{1}{2}$ per cent, the rate for men aged 60-64 was about $8\frac{1}{2}$ per cent.

2. *The unskilled.* The earnings survey in1968 placed about one fifth of the manual men it identified as unskilled as having less than £15 earnings for a full week's work. There would be between $1\frac{1}{2}$ and $1\frac{3}{4}$ million male manual workers that might be classified as unskilled. But the occupational analysis of unemployed men in mid 1970 showed as many as 232,000 listed as labourers out of a total of 437,000.

3. *The disabled.* Unfortunately the earnings surveys have not separated out this category, but it may be assumed that a considerable proportion would be low paid. The "low pay" reports of the NBPI published in 1971 revealed a high proportion of disabled workers in the low-wage industries of laundries and "ancillary" workers in the Health Service, and that the pay of these disabled tended to be lower than other workers. The unemployment statistics showed 60,000 registered disabled who were unemployed in July 1970 although "suitable for ordinary employment" (the 10,000 severely disabled unemployed are not included in the published figures); the percentage of unemployment of those on the disabled persons register was about 10 per cent.

For all three categories, the background level of unemployment had worsened considerably during Labour's last four years in office. Thus, the number of unemployed men aged 60-64 had doubled from mid 1966 to mid 1970 (to reach over 93,000). The number of unemployed labourers had risen from 105,000 to over 232,000, that is to 2.2 times the 1966 level. And the number of unemployed on the disabled register "suitable for ordinary employment" rose from 35,000 in mid 1966 to the 60,000 of mid 1970.

Thus, for these and doubtless for other groups of disadvantaged workers, the much higher unemployment rate among men that followed the July 1966 measures (and has persisted since) represented a major deterioration in their labour market position. This is partly a matter of the income loss involved in spells of unemployment—this net loss of income in 1970 must have been at least £100 million more than it was before the unemployment rate rose (that is as compared with the early years of the Labour Government), and this loss occurred in about $1\frac{1}{2}$ million more spells of unemployment than in, say, 1965. But there is also the downward push on pay exerted by unemployment as the ominous alternative to working for low pay. The doubling of the rate of male unemployment was the greatest dis-service that the Labour Government did to the low paid. It is astonishing in retrospect how little criticism the Labour

Government were subjected to on this score, partly because of the smoke-screen of soothing statements that attempted to show that unemployment now was in some way different to what it had been in the past. It is worth saying that in no respect, in fact, was unemployment, its incidence or its characteristics, different to that experienced in earlier post-war cyclical peaks—except, alas, in the deliberate official persistence in maintaining it at such levels after 1966.

The same sorry picture of increasingly severe unemployment marks several of the regions with a high proportion of lower paid employees. For Great Britain as a whole the unemployment rate (for both male and female employees) rose from 1.3 per cent in 1965 (just over 300,000) to 2.6 per cent by July 1970 (nearly 600,000) by which time the Labour Government had fallen. (The figures are seasonally adjusted estimates). To take some regions characterised by a high proportion of low paid workers: in the South Western region, the unemployment rate rose from 1.5 per cent in 1965 to 2.9 per cent by July 1970; in Yorkshire and Humberside the unemployment rate rose from 1.0 per cent to 2.9 per cent in the same period; in Scotland the unemployment rate was 2.8 per cent in 1965, and although it rose subsequently the deterioration was relatively less severe than elsewhere until 1969; but from mid-1969 unemployment grew faster in Scotland than in any other region and by July 1970 the rate was 4.2 per cent and in the Northern region the unemployment rate rose from 2.4 per cent in 1965 to 4.6 per cent by July 1970.

These four regions alone contained (on a seasonally adjusted basis) 115,000 more unemployed when Labour left office than during Labour's first year. Moreover, as had been experienced before when economic recessions produced a high rate of post-war unemployment, there was a disproportionate increase in longer period unemployment. In mid-1966 there were 107,000 who had been unemployed for over 8 weeks; in mid-1970 there were over 300,000. These are not figures that any study of poverty and inequality among workers during Labour's term of office can neglect. In 1968 (*Poverty*, September 1968) I estimated that the workers currently on the unemployment register had then "represented approximately 10,000,000 weeks of unemployment". The calculation would be broadly true of unemployment examined at any time between 1967 and today.

To summarise the evidence of the statistics. We cannot find any important example of relative improvement in the lot of the low paid worker during the years of Labour Government, up to 1969. But many lower paid workers must have experienced greater job and income insecurity, and a more severe incidence of unemployment, during the last four years of Labour Government. This experience, which has particularly struck at the most disadvantaged groups in the labour market cannot be left out of the reckoning. In retrospect they may have been the innocent victims of the Treasury's pursuit of that shadow of an economic theory that argued that a sufficiently high rate of unemployment (and $2\frac{1}{2}$ per cent was a figure frequently advanced in statistical "correlations") would of itself moderate the pace of pay increases. As to the "absolute", as against the merely relative, condition of the low paid, the slow pace of "real" wage advance has already been noted. What should be said, besides, is that on the evidence of that very imperfect price index, the "Pensioners" index, it is likely that the "cost of living" of the lower paid may have risen slightly faster than the measure indicated by the official index. This was not compensated for by any lightening of the tax burden on lower income households. If we take households of two adults and one child, the lower quartile of such households bore direct taxes representing 13 per cent of original income in 1964, and 15 per cent in 1968. Income after all taxes and benefits as a percentage of the original household income had fallen from 84 per cent in 1964 to 82 per cent in 1968.

At the pace at which their real disposable income was increasing from the mid 1960s, it would have taken the lowest decile of manual workers over 30 years to reach the present standard of living of today's "median" manual worker.

In the end, it remains an arbitrary matter where one cuts into the range of earnings to identify the low paid workers. But we should at least take some arbitrary yardstick and measure the massed battalions of the low paid still there after five and a half years of Labour Government. In April 1970 there were nearly two-thirds of a million men whose actual weekly earnings were under £15 gross (this excludes those who received nil in the survey week). This was about 5 per cent of the total number of men employees. (One perhaps ought here to remember as an addition the $3\frac{1}{2}$ per cent of the male employees of the country who were unemployed). There were approximately 3,000,000 women whose actual earnings in the survey week were below £15 gross, or about 55 per cent of the total. If we shift our arbitrary yardstick to under £17 gross weekly earnings for men, we have about $1\frac{1}{4}$ million men whose actual pay fell below that (or near 10 per cent of the total of men employees).

The analysis of earnings as they were revealed by the survey of April 1970 is not, however, the end of the story of low pay and the Labour government. The trade unions were writing their own ironic post-script. For 1970 was the year in which the incomes policy was swept aside; at this point, instead of there being a "free for all" there was a marked emphasis on improving the position of the lowest paid within a very wide range of different bargaining units. The TUC surveyed over 200 major agreements made since September 1969 (it was after then that the incomes policy was increasingly repudiated in the actual practice of collective bargaining). They found:

1. Nearly three-quarters of settlements gave larger increases in percentage terms in women's minimum rates than those for men. A number gave larger increases to women in money terms. (Major settlements in distribution advanced women's pay rates by a quarter or more).

2. Over 60 cases were identified where equal money increases were obtained for all grades; many of these were groups which had previously settled in equal percentage terms.

3. Many settlements, including white collar settlements, tapered the percentage increase given.

4. An increasing number of groups were negotiating reductions in the age at

which workers receive the adult rate. Other agreements have eliminated the lowest rates or scales, or negotiated changes which improved the job content and therefore earnings potential of lower paid grades.

This view that, *within* bargaining units, the lower paid have been accorded more priority since the collapse of incomes policy than they had during it appears to conflict with findings of the NBPI's report *General problems of low pay*. There it is argued that during the first four years of incomes policy pay rates in the lower paid industries and services increased slightly faster than average, but that the reverse was the case in the twelve months to April 1970 (NBPI report no 109, p14). The explanation is a straightforward one; April 1970 was still quite early in the 1970 "wage round" and many lower paid industries and groups including Wages Councils and bargining units catering for large numbers of women had not yet settled. A study of the wage indices makes it quite clear that it was mainly groups of male manual workers that made the initial break through into higher rates of pay settlement. But the egalitarian emphasis in the agreements struck and the eventual universality of major pay increases led through to very dramatic increases in pay for a wide range of low paid workers. The wage indices bear this out.

Thus in April 1970 the index of basic hourly wage rates had risen by an identical amount (since the base date in 1956) for men and for women. From then till March 1971, manual men's hourly rates rose by 11.6 per cent but women's rates rose by 14.6 per cent. Juveniles' rates rose even faster, by 14.9 per cent. Nor is it true that the workers in the least protected industries have been left behind. In the fifteen months from January 1970, pay settlements for workers in Wages Council industries through statutory wage regulation orders accounted for 14 per cent of the money total of increases in manual workers' wage rates. The proportion in the previous three years had averaged 11 per cent. The money increase in Wages Council pay rates in 1970 was as large as in the preceeding three years put together.

This is not the place to argue the social costs as against the benefits of the rapid pay advance of 1970. Clearly, the consequential more rapid rise in retail prices had at least short run adverse effects on many households dependent on benefits, since these were only tardily adjusted. It is true also that the regressive bite of Conservative fiscal policies counteracted the benefits that the collective bargaining process brought to lower paid workers. But there is, nevertheless, something positive for the Labour movement to consider. Once a general incomes policy breaks down, it is only through particular bargaining units that wage priorities can be expressed. But the wage push in 1970 expressed more clearly a degree of priority for the lower paid within many of these settlements than the official incomes policy had ever managed to do. It suggests that an incomes policy with emphasis on social justice and on the needs of low paid workers would evoke a response within the trade union movement. By contrast, the realities of real wage and employment deflation that emerged from all the confusion of the Labour Government's incomes policy could lead only to a massive repudiation of the whole economic strategy involved and repudiation of pay "moderation" with it.

10. inequality at work

Dorothy Wedderburn

Socialists have always been concerned with the many facets of inequality—of income and wealth, of status and prestige and of power. But when discussing or assessing political programmes attention is often heavily focussed upon what government can do either as a provider of collective social services or as a taxing authority to reduce, maintain or to increase inequality. There is interest, however, in beginning our examination of inequality at the other end, that is at the point of production and in considering the different ways in which inequality is generated through the employment relationship. For by using this approach even economic inequality has to be considered in a context wider than simply the distribution of wealth or money income. Moreover, we are brought face to face with some important aspects of power relationships. In this chapter I shall first summarise some of the more obvious inequalities in the employment situation as they exist today; second, I shall discuss some of the dynamics producing and maintaining such inequalities; third, I shall consider what contribution to the reduction of these inequalities was made by the Labour Government of 1964-70: finally, I shall discuss some of the implications for the future policy of the Labour movement.

inequalities in the work place today

It would not be possible in the space available to document the full nature and extent of inequalities which spring directly from the employment relationship today. But there are some new sources of data which provide a fuller picture than hitherto, and which highlight some aspects of inequality which have received all too little attention.

Much of this data still has to be presented as a simple dichotomy between groups which are described as "manual" and "non manual" or "blue collar" and "white collar." Yet at the outset we should recognise that this begs some of the most important political questions which a full study of inequality at work would investigate. There has been a continuing debate about the political significance of the rapid growth of non-manual occupations in the economy. Using one of the broadest definitions of "non-manual" occupations G. S. Bain has shown that the proportion of workers in these occupations in the total labour force in Great Britain has increased from 19 per cent to 36 per cent in 50 years (*Trade Union growth and recognition*, Royal Commission research, paper 6, table 1, HMSO, London, 1967). Some occupations like clerks have even increased nearly three fold over the same period. Is this a situation where the employment conditions of non-manual workers are converging with those of manual workers? (See John Goldthorpe, *et al*, *The affluent worker in the class structure*, CUP, 1969.) Or are there now emerging important differentiated strata within the non-manual group? R. Dahrendorf, for instance, has suggested that the critical distinction is where people stand in the power structure of their occupational context ("Recent changes in the class structure of European Societies," *Daedalus*, vol 93, no 464).

I shall return to this point later in the discussion but first let us examine some of the data about inequalities arising from the employment relationship under three headings:

1. Inequalities in total economic return over the life cycle.

2. Inequalities in physical conditions of work.

3. Inequalities in the intrinsic nature of work and in the experience of power relationships.

Inequalities in the earnings of different occupational groups are well documented and it seems that, at least over the long period, the idea that there has been a narrowing of differentials is false. Non-manual earnings still show a considerable lead over manual earnings. It is worth noting however, that non-manual earnings are far more heterogeneous than those of manual workers, although this does not appear to hold for other aspects of the market situation of the two groups. For instance, the 1968 Department of Employment and Productivity new earnings' survey showed only a difference of £5 a week between the median earnings of unskilled and skilled manual workers, but of £26 a week between the routine clerk and the marketing or sales manager, two occupations both classified as non-manual. (DEP, "A new survey of earnings in September 1968," *Employment and productivity gazette.*) What is less well recognised, however, is that lifetime earnings may be even more unequally distributed between the manual and non-manual groups. The Department of Employment's data show that average earnings within age groups tend to increase to a peak, and then to decline before retirement for all occupational groups. But the increase for manual workers is much less, and the decline more rapid and marked than for non-manual workers.

Indeed, one curiosity of these figures, which are of course cross-sectional, is that there should be any *decline* at all in the income of non-manual workers as they get older. There may be two separate factors influencing these cross-sectional figures. On the one hand, institutional factors like incremental scales would lead to, if not a continuing rise in income level with age, at least a plateau (although it has been put to me that demotion of older white collar workers particularly in large institutions affected by technical change such as computerisation, is more common than is supposed). On the other hand, there is the economic factor that younger non-manual workers have higher general and specific educational levels and may therefore command relatively higher real salary levels than their older counterparts.

Many non-manual workers have quite a high chance of being promoted to a higher grade of employment and a recent survey showed that in manufacturing industry, at least, 80-90 per cent of non-manual grades also had a reasonable expectation of an annual pay increase compared with only 20 per cent of manual workers. (Dorothy Wedderburn, "Workplace inequality," *New Society*, 9 April 1970, and Christine Craig, *Men in manufacturing industry*, Department of Applied Economics, Cambridge, 1969.) It has sometimes been argued that this annual increase (which may be at the discretion of management and subject to satisfactory performance by the worker) is the non-manual worker's equivalent of the manual worker's increase obtained through collective bargaining. But there is evidence that where both types of worker are employed within the same enterprise, non-manual pay scales are often increased voluntarily by employers when manual increases are granted, with the specific objective of maintaining differentials. There is, however, a qualitative difference between a pay increase obtained only as the result of collective struggle and dependent upon the current balance of economic power and one which may be granted as a result of custom or as part of the terms of the contract like incremental pay scales. Custom and contract combined with promotion prospects mean that most white collar workers know that they have an expectation of rising incomes over their working life. This is not the case for most manual workers.

Expectation of a rising life time income is also combined with greater security of income for non-manual workers in two senses. First, there is greater security of employment. Although it is almost certainly true that non-manual workers now experience dismissal more frequently than in the past (as for instance in the aircraft industry, or because British industry is engaging in a cost "shake out,") the only recent comprehensive survey of labour mobility to be carried out in this country shows a big difference between the proportions of non-manual and manual workers changing their jobs involuntarily (Amelia I. Harris, *Labour mobility in Great Britain 1953-63*, Social survey, March 1966). Another smaller but fascinating piece of evidence about security of income comes again from the Department of Employment and Productivity's earnings survey. Over 90 per cent of non-manual workers' earnings are derived from their basic pay. That means the bulk of their income is known and predictable. But only just over two-thirds of non-manual workers' pay is their basic pay and no less than 16 per cent is obtained by overtime and 9 per cent from payment by results. These are two unpredictable elements in the pay packet. Moreover, in the week of the Department's survey only 2 per cent of non-manual workers had lost pay for any reason at all, whereas no less than 15 per cent of manual workers suffered some loss of pay.

Other important differences in the predictability and security of life time income have been revealed by official reports on occupational pension schemes and sick pay schemes (*Occupational pension schemes*, Third survey, by the Government Actuary, HMSO, 1968; MPNI *Report of an inquiry into the incidence of incapacity for work*, HMSO, 1964). Although there has been a considerable growth in the coverage of manual workers by employers' schemes of these kinds, there remain wide differences between occupational groups. Moreover, the mere existence of schemes often conceals wide variations in the type and quality of benefits offered. A recent survey showed that half of the employers' occupational pension schemes for manual workers in the manufacturing sector provided a pension calculated as a fixed sum per year of membership. In contrast three quarters of the non-manual schemes provided pensions based on final salary or on salary in the last years of service. Similar differences can be found in sick pay provisions (Wedderburn, *op cit*). The extraordinary aspect of this type of inequality is that it represents inequality in the basis of treatment. If pensions or sick pay were simply earnings related there would still be inequality because of earnings differentials. But superimposed upon this are more or less generous bases for the calculation of benefit for different groups. This brief review of what can be called the "totality" of the market situation facing different classes of workers shows the importance of looking beyond income differentials alone as indicators of economic inequality. But another area of inequality at work to which too little attention is paid is that of working conditions. This is a shorthand phrase to cover aspects such as numbers of hours of work, discretion about hours at work, length of holidays, shift working, as well as the straightforward consideration of physical working conditions. It also covers last, but by no means least, risk of accident at work. It is fascinating to find in the enquiry previously quoted, that not only were manual workers' holidays shorter, but only 35 per cent of them had any choice about when they took their holidays, compared with over three quarters of most non-manual grades. Only 2 per cent of manual workers did not have to "clock on," and 90 per cent would lose pay if they were late. The corresponding percentage for non-manual grades are shown in the table below (Wedderburn and Craig, *op cit*).

TERMS AND CONDITIONS OF EMPLOYMENT—PER CENT OF ESTABLISHMENTS IN WHICH DIFFERENT CONDITIONS APPLY

	operatives	foremen	clerical workers	technicians	middle managers	senior managers
holidays: 15 days+	38	72	74	77	84	88
choice of holiday time	35	54	76	76	84	88
normal working 40+ hours per week	97	94	9	23	27	22
sick pay—employers' scheme	57	94	98	97	98	98
pension—employers' scheme	67	94	90	94	96	96
time off with pay for personal reasons	29	84	83	86	91	93
pay deductions for any lateness	90	20	8	11	1	0
warning followed by dismissal for persistent lateness	84	66	78	71	48	41
no clocking on or booking in	2	46	48	45	81	94

Shift working is increasing. The recent report of the NBPI estimates "the underlying trend in the percentage of the manual labour force on shifts in manufacturing has been about 1 per cent per annum." Whilst this report refers to growing numbers of non-manual workers being on shift work as a result, for instance, of the introduction of computers, it gives no estimate of the proportion affected (NPBI, *Hours of work, overtime and shift working*, Cmnd 4554, pp64-65, HMSO, 1970). Reference back to the Department of Employment's new earnings survey showed, however, that in 1968 only 2.7 per cent of non-manual male workers were receiving a shift premium compared with 19.3 per cent of manual male workers. This gives a rough indication of the marked difference between the two groups (*Employment and productivity gazette*, August 1969). The physical and social disadvantages of shift work have been the subject of much study (see for instance P. E. Mott, *et al, Shift work: the social, psychological and physical consequences of shift working*). The NBPI report is, in fact, more sanguine than many, implying that a process of self-selection goes on where the advantages of shift work, like higher pay and free time during the day, are balanced against its disadvantages. "Our studies of the impact of shift working on the individual worker lead us to conclude that workers will, when they have balanced the level of earnings against the changes in their way of life which a job involving shift work may demand, tend to seek out a job where the pattern and length of hours most nearly meet their needs" (Cmnd 4554, *op cit,* p93).

First of all, this assumes that workers have some choice, which is certainly not always the case. More importantly, however, for our discussion of inequality, this is not the kind of off setting of advantages and disadvantages which most non-manual workers are required to engage in.

It is less easy to give statistics about physical working conditions, but it does not require much documentation to establish that many more manual workers are exposed to worse noise levels, extremes of temperature, unpleasant smell as well as lower standard amenities, such as lavatories, canteens, etc. than their non-manual counterparts. Industrial accidents are a matter of great concern. They are showing a steady rate of increase and occur principally to manual workers. The total of reported accidents under the Factories Act increased in 1969 for the seventh year in succession. As the TUC comment: "On these figures every worker can expect on average to be the victim of at least two disabling accidents during his working life. In some industries the chance is considerably greater" (*Trades Union Congress General Council Report* 1970, p260). Not only does such a difference in the risk of accident have its economic aspects in terms of earning power, but it also results in differences in terms of physical and psychological suffering.

Finally, there are inequalities in the experience of power relationships and in the general quality of social relationships in the workplace. One attempt has been made to quantify some of these differences by selecting particular situations, which might be regarded as typical of employment rules and regulations, and exploring whether such rules and their interpretation differ for different occupational groups. Some examples are shown in the table above. They include the granting of time off with pay for personal reasons, disciplinary procedures for bad time keeping, loss of pay for lateness, etc. These data all suggest that there is a marked variation in the ways in which different occupational groups are treated. On the one hand, the manual worker is subjected to bureaucratic rules, while on the other hand, non-manual workers, in varying degrees, are treated with discretion, apparently on the assumption that they will "behave responsibly" or "not abuse privileges."

The type of work which a man performs may also be regarded as a source of, or experience of, power. One sociologist has spoken of alienation at work as a "sense of powerlessness" and has said "the industrial system distributes alienation unevenly among its blue collar labour force, just as our economic system distributes income unevenly" (R. Blauner, *Alienation and freedom,* The University of Chicago Press, Chicago, 1964). Clearly, in a short chapter we cannot enter into the now extensive discussion about the meaning to be attached to "alienation" and in particular, the important comment from Goldthorpe and his colleagues, that "A real difficulty in trying to explore the neo-Marxian theory of alienation, by means of empirical research, is in fact that of knowing exactly what connection is being presumed between the nature of the work tasks and roles on the one hand and the bases of industrial authority on the other" (Goldthorpe, *op cit,* p182). The important point for our discussion of inequality, however, is that both in terms of the type of work done, and of the possibilities of participation in any decision making processes, there is considerable inequality between different occupational groups.

Some interesting points emerge from this discussion. Whilst, as we pointed out earlier, the disparity between manual and non-manual earnings remains, there is so much heterogeneity within the non-manual group, that it is perfectly possible for certain non-manual occupations to have lower earnings than some manual occupations (*Employment and Productivity Gazette,* May 1969). But in the broader aspects of economic inequality or market position it does appear that the sharp divide falls between manual occupations on the one hand and non-manual on the other. In the survey results quoted in the table above, there is generally a much greater uniformity of conditions between foremen, clerical workers, technicians and middle managers on the one hand, than there is between these somewhat disparate groups and manual workers. As for the very rough indicators of authority relationships in the table (the treatment of persistent lateness, the recording of presence at work), there is a suggestion that there may be important stratifications within the non-manual group. And if the material were available to enable us to extend the analysis more systematically to the actual exercise of authority and the intrinsic interest of the work done we would expect such stratification within the non-manual group to be further underlined.

the dynamics of such inequalities

In answer to the question what produces such unequal distribution of life chances, one simple answer offers itself. It is the capitalist system itself. As Robin Blackburn has said: "From the employer's side the labour contract is open-ended. In principle the nature of the exact tasks the worker has undertaken to perform becomes the province of management. The work shop or office operates on a command structure in which the powers of decision rest with the owners chosen representative, the manager" ("The unequal society" in *The incompatibles,* Penguin, 1967). But here we have been concerned with a distribution of inequality in the work situation which exists within the employees' group itself and which then raises the interesting question "who are the owners 'chosen representatives' "? The development of technology has changed the position of the non-manual worker. Although, as we said earlier, the sharp divide often falls between manual and non-manual occupations there is an indication that gradations within the non-manual group are of immense importance.

It is easy to see historically how the non-manual worker as the "employer's substitute" or "l'homme de confiance" came to have privileged employment conditions extended to him. In any case they were partly modelled on the standardised regular employment conditions developing for the growing numbers of "bureaucrats" or servants of the state in the 19th century (M Weber, *The theory of social and economic organisation,* p332, The Free Press, 1964). It is clear that in addition to the development of differentiation within the non-manual group, however, there has been a narrowing of the gap between manual and non-manual workers in certain important respects, such as occupational pension and sick pay provision. There is also a great deal of discussion about the importance of extending "staff status" to manual workers (advocates range from the Duke of Edinburgh through the Donovan Commission to Barbara Castle). Nonetheless, the evidence suggests that the objective changes in the last few years have on balance been small and that the experience of these inequalities at work has great significance for workers' well being, quality of life and perceptions of the world.

The first point which has to be made is that the workplace, as a social system in capitalist society is co-ordinated through a hierarchy of authority. Such a hierarchy needs its own outward and visible signs of status differentiation to support that exercise of authority. In parenthesis it might be added that for socialists a crucial question becomes whether such a system of status differentiation becomes important for *any* industrial society.

A second very important factor is the operation of the competition between "collective provision" and the private market. In so many areas which impinge upon aspects of the employment relationship—sick pay provision, pensions and, now also, periods of notice and redundancy payments—the state has attempted to make minimum provision for all on a uniform basis, irrespective of occupational or social grouping. But because there has been no decisive ideological break with the theory of the superiority of the market (indeed in some cases the state itself has flirted with such a market ideology as the basis of its own provision), the natural development has been competition from the private sector (D. Wedderburn, *Facts and theories of the welfare state,* Socialist register, 1965). Hence the growth of private occupational pension schemes (on top of state provision) aided and abetted by government tax concessions. Almost automatically these "market" provisions have adopted the principal of a "better" basis of treatment for the non-manual than manual worker.

In addition, however, it must be recognised that in contrast to the position of many manual worker unions, some non-manual unions have used the minimum guarantee of the state as a jumping off ground for the negotiation of improved conditions over and above the state provided minimum (like redundancy, periods of notice, pension provision). Thus inequalities will become perpetuated until the manual worker unions become alerted to their own potentialities.

It could be argued that there is a straightforward economic explanation of the phenomenon we have been discussing. If companies invest more in training particular groups of workers they will wish to attach these workers more securely to their employment. One way of doing this might be to offer more attractive fringe benefits. One would then expect levels of fringe benefits to be broadly related to levels of skill and training specific to the employer. Two factors seem to weaken this argument, however. The first is that one would not then expect to find the relative homogeneity among the non-manual group which seems to exist in respect of fringe benefits. The amount of company investment in different occupations will vary considerably and not always in the same direction and across the manual/non-manual line. For instance, it will probably take less investment on the part of a chemical company to train a routine clerk than a chemical process operator. Secondly, this argument does not explain why there should be differences in the quality of social relationships for different groups. It almost seems that the "non-manual" worker becomes "doubly blessed." He receives company training which enables him to perform a more interesting job, to exercise authority and gives him expectations of promotion. On top of this he is also treated with more consideration as an individual and given better market conditions.

the record of the Labour Government

The discussion of the dynamics of inequalities in the work situation only serves to show that these inequalities derive from basic features of the capitalist or industrial system itself. It is not perhaps surprising, therefore, that the Labour Government of 1964-70 had no very coherent policy towards the elimination of such inequalities, for in a sense to tackle this source of inequality is to tackle the very core of power in industrial society itself. A number of measures are of interest, however, first because in some areas, they represent the first legislative attempt in Britain at intervention in aspects of the contract of employment. Second, because in that legislation was enshrined the principles of equality of treatment for all occupational groups.

One important statute, however, ante dates the Labour Government—namely the Contracts of Employment Act, 1963. The Act was one of the first examples of legislative attempts to enforce certain conditions in the contract of employment between worker and employer. It requires among other things that every employer shall give the employee "written particulars" of the terms of his employment, and particularly important, it lays down minimum periods of notice. The interest, for us, of the latter provision is that the notice is the same for all occupational groups and varies only according to length of service with the employer. Thus the employee who has been employed for 26 weeks or more is required to give to his employer a week's notice of his intention to leave. All employees with a minimum period of service are entitled to notice of dismissal, varying from one week for continuous service up to two years, to four weeks for service of over five years.

The Wedderburn/Craig (op cit) survey showed some interesting developments after this legislation. First, there has been an attempt by employers to enforce longer periods of notice for employees. Thirty per cent of the establishments in the survey stipulated that an employee of five years' service or more, should give four weeks' notice (there was no evidence, however, to show how many of these employers would have taken legal steps to enforce this requirement had it been ignored). Second, a large number of employers were already making more generous provision to their non-manual employees in respect of notice than was required by the Act. Well over a half would expect to give more than the legislatively required notice to managerial grades, a quarter to clerical, technical and foreman grades, but only 13 per cent to manual grades.

Thus legislation appeared to be providing a floor upon which differentiation was reasserting itself.

But the 1963 Contracts of Employment Act was followed by a major piece of Labour legislation, the Redundancy Payments Act of 1965. This imposed upon management the obligation to make compensatory payments to those workers dismissed by reason of redundancy after two years' continuous service. Again the principle is established that all employees are treated alike, irrespective of occupation (except of those occupations specifically excluded from coverage by the Act). The amount of compensation varies according to pay, because the unit of calculation is "a week's pay," and according to length of service, between different ages. For workers with a minimum of two years' service who are over 18 but below 22 the payment is one half a week's pay for each year of service; between 22 but below the age of 41 it is one week's pay and between 41 and 65 it is one and a half weeks' pay (with a tapering for those approaching retirement age). Such legislation was a welcome move away from the situation where "golden handshakes" existed for the executives, or even where compensation was provided by the employer voluntarily but on a very different basis according to whether or not the employee was a manual or non-manual worker (D. Wedderburn, *White collar redundancy*, CUP, 1963). No consistent evidence is available about how far this uniformity of treatment has been preserved but there are three interesting indicators that already non-manual workers are receiving rather better treatment. First, some white collar unions, as we suggested above, have already negotiated substantially improved terms for their members over and above the basic legal amount. Second, there is some suggestion that industrial tribunals, which are responsible for adjudging disputes which arise under the Act, have interpreted such phrases as "suitable alternative employment" rather more leniently for non-manual than for manual workers (D. Wedderburn, "Redundancy," in D. Pym (ed) *Industrial society,* Pelican books, 1968). Third, what constitutes a "normal week's pay" is often in dispute for manual workers where overtime and bonus payments may or may not be regarded as "normal."

The next important piece of Labour legislation relating to the inequalities which we have been discussing was the introduction, in 1966, of earnings related supplements to the flat rate national insurance benefits for sickness and unemployment. The first of these certainly went some way to compensate for the differences in the basis of treatment of manual and non-manual workers under private employers' schemes. The second helped in part to compensate for the greater risk of economic insecurity from loss of job to which manual workers were exposed. Whilst there is no doubt that these measures represented a considerable advance on the earlier situation, a number of aspects of the legislation still operate to the disadvantage of manual workers. First, earnings related supplements become payable only after a waiting period of twelve days and cease after six months with a maximum benefit of 85 per cent of average earnings. Coverage by a private employers' scheme remains valuable therefore. Second, because such benefits are tax free, in real terms they are worth relatively far more to the higher tax payers, that is more to the non-manual workers than to manual workers. On the other hand, it is interesting to note that "average weekly earnings" are taken as one fiftieth of gross earnings in the preceding year, so that manual workers with large fluctuations in weekly earnings because of overtime or piece rate payments should not be penalised.

Perhaps one of the most ambitious legislative proposals of the Labour Government in the area which we have been discussing, was one which never found its way to the statute book. That was the proposal for earnings-related pensions. Of crucial importance for our argument once again is that under these proposals all occupational groups were to be treated similarly, for example the basis of the pension scheme was to apply to manual and non-manual workers alike. This is not the place to discuss in detail the likely effects of the scheme, had they been legislated. Judged solely from the view-point of its long term effect upon the differentiation between manual and non-manual workers it seemed that it would go a long way towards narrowing the gap. But an important caveat has to be entered because in part the eventual outcome would have turned upon the treatment of private occupa-tional schemes. There appeared to be a marked unwillingness on the part of the Labour Government to engage in a head-on collision with the insurance companies. The White Paper on National Superannuation and Social Insur-ance offered, as Tony Lynes described it, "an ingenuous solution which it describes as 'partial contracting out'." He went on to say "Contracting out, therefore, should not be seen as a way of raising standards of retirement provision but simply as a way of ensuring that most private schemes remain in existence albeit on a reduced scale in some cases." (*Labour's pension plan*, p25 and 28, Fabian tract 396, 1969). On the face of it, therefore, where private schemes remained in existence there might have been a lessened tendency for more generous or favourable terms to develop for manual workers.

In the area of industrial health and accidents the Labour Government made some tentative moves. Mr. Gunter, as Minister of Labour, issued a consulta-tive document which would have had the effect of extending the legislation at present enforced by the Factories Act to all places of employment. But in 1970 the Employed Persons (Health and Safety) Bill was introduced which would have given trade unions (recognised for negotiating purposes) the right to appoint safety representatives from among their workers. Once again the Bill never reached the statute book before the General Election of 1970. One by-product however was the setting-up of a committee to inquire into occupa-tional safety and health, under the chairmanship of Lord Robens, which has so far not reported.

This brief review of the Labour Government's record should not end without some reference to the report of the Royal Commission on Trade Unions and Employers' Associations. The Commission was set up under Lord Donovan in 1965: "to consider relations between management and employees and the role of trade unions and employers' associations in promoting the interests of their members and in accelerating the social and economic advance of the nation, with particular reference to the law affecting the activities of these bodies." These terms of reference might be said to cover the whole question of inequality at work, but the approach adopted by the Commission was to concentrate primarily upon the institutional framework of industrial relations both formal and informal. In consequence their recommendations were directed towards changes in this framework which would promote "effective and orderly collective bargaining" over a wide range of job regulation. In the long run had their recommendations been followed they would obviously not have been without consequence for the issues we have been discussing. But the Commission touched specifically on the manual and non-manual division at three points.

As we have already noted, it referred, almost in passing, to what it termed "invidious" manual non-manual distinctions in industry and suggested that when, for instance, productivity bargains were used as an opportunity to eliminate or reduce these distinctions they helped to create an atmosphere more conducive to good industrial relations (*Royal Commission on Trade Unions and Employers' Associations*, 1965-68, Cmnd 3623, p83, HMSO, 1968). This conclusion seems somewhat naive, because there is little evidence that different strata in industry use each other as reference groups. To the extent that they do, non-manual workers are more often to be found using the pay levels of manual workers as an argument for pressing for increases for themselves (Dorothy Wedderburn and Christine Craig, "Relative deprivation in work," *British Association for the Advancement of Science paper*, 1969).

The Commission did, however, argue clearly against the view that there was any "special" relationship between employers and white collar workers which made trade union organisation inappropriate for the latter (Cmnd 3623, *op cit*, p56). Finally, three and a half pages of the three hundred page report were devoted to an inconclusive discussion of workers' participation in management (Cmnd 3623, *op cit*, pp257-260). This laid the basis for the Government's own weak references to the problem in its policy document *In place of strife*. First there was a declaration of the Government's intention to legislate to enable trade unions to obtain from employers "certain sorts of information that are needed for negotiations." Further there is a reference to "other forms of participation for example through the appointment of workers' representatives to the boards of undertakings. The Government favours experiments in this method and will have consultation on how they may best be facilitated" (*In place of strife*, Cmnd 3888, pp16-17, HMSO, 1969).

We might summarise the record of the Labour Government in this way. Where it legislated it recognised no distinction between occupational groups, and in this sense initially probably contributed to a narrowing of some inequalities arising out of the work situation. On the other hand it did nothing to interfere with those fundamental ideological and market mechanisms which serve to perpetuate such inequalities. There was every probability therefore that inequalities would re-emerge, even if in new forms.

It might be objected that the whole of this discussion of inequality has ignored the question of the inequality of women. This is because I do not see it as arising only from the employment relationship, although it is of course a fact that inequalities in employment conditions between different male occupations are often insignificant compared with those between men and women. It is therefore worth nothing that greater progress towards equal pay and working conditions for women has been made in the professions and in non-manual occupations than in manual occupations. However, we should also record that the Labour Government did introduce the Equal Pay Bill (with all its limitations) which received Royal assent on 29 May 1970 and will become operative at the end of 1975.

implications for policy

This brings us to the present day, for the argument of this chapter leads logically to a close consideration of the connection between "inequality at work" and the meaning which can be attached to the concept of "workers control." We are really concerned with the central issue of distribution of power within the industrial enterprise. This major problem is outside the scope of the discussion in this volume. But I hope that by linking the question of inequality at work, with a discussion of inequality in a more controversial context, I have succeeded in underlining the close inter-connection of all these issues. As for a more immediate impact upon policy for a labour movement, the following issues can be singled out for attention:

1. The importance that attaches to the fact that government regulation of employment conditions (dismissal procedures, redundancy pay and so on) must be designed in such a way (or provided at such a level) that the possibility of competition from the private employer is limited. Provisions for the manual worker must be set at such a level that it becomes unattractive to offer better conditions to other occupational groups.

2. The need for the development of a more coherent and united labour movement strategy. Initiations have been taken by the TUC on some issues, like safety at work (although the campaign which they started requires to be pursued with much greater militancy). But unless the manual unions turn their attention increasingly to the issues raised in this essay the growing organisation and militancy of white collar unions may serve only to maintain or increase differentials rather than to narrow them. One of the important problems here is that manual worker unions—both leadership and membership alike—appear to have such low expectations about the way in which they should be treated at work. To reduce inequality in the work situation requires moving from a defensive to an offensive position on a much wider range of issues than have traditionally formed part of the collective bargaining stance of manual worker unions in this country.

chronology

August 1965	Redundancy Payments Act, 1965 passed
April 1965	The Royal Commission on Trade Unions and Employers Associations (Donovan Commission) established.
March 1966	National Insurance Act 1966 passed. Earnings related supplementation of national insurance benefits for sickness and unemployment.
January 1969	*In place of strife.*
December 1969	National Superannuation and Social Insurance Bill published.
February 1970	Employed Persons (Health and Safety) Bill published. Proposed legislation requiring the appointment of workers safety representatives and joint safety committees.
March 1970	Committee on Safety and Health at Work (Roben's enquiry) established.

11. wealth: Labour's achilles heel

Michael Meacher

For democratic socialist movements in the West, the extreme concentration of wealth in a few hands represents the crux of the dilemma between economic efficiency and distributional justice. How is it possible to reduce the unacceptable inequalities in personal power and opportunities which this concentration creates without impugning investment levels and hence the wider prospects of growth for all? Conversely, how is it possible to expand that privilege of security and immunity from immediate economic pressures which only capital resources can supply, when a persistingly huge inequality in the distribution of incomes makes capital accumulation an unrealistic goal except at high salary levels—or through large inheritances? And how is it possible to tax wealth efficiently without undermining the system of incentives to which the economy is geared? In short, how to break the cloying association between growth and inequality?

For Labour the problem was perhaps more acute that that facing similar movements in other Western countries. The concentration of personal wealth in Britain is clearly much greater than in the United States (for example, H. Lydall and J. B. Lansing, "A comparison of the distribution of personal income and wealth in the United States and Great Britain," *American Economic Review*, 1959, 49). On some estimates the concentration in the hands of the richest one per cent of the respective populations is actually almost twice as great in this country as in the US (R. J. Lapman, "Changes in the share of wealth held by top wealth holders," *Revenue Economic Statistics*, 1959, 41).

An examination of the Labour record therefore clearly first requires an assessment of the extent of inequality in wealth ownership at the outset of Government in 1964, from which basic changes can then be measured. This will be followed by an examination of the main Labour measures influencing the pattern of capital inequality. Then the wider secular trends affecting the distribution of wealth, including various longer term relevant on-going processes, will be briefly discussed. Finally, a number of recommendations designed to secure a more equitable distribution of capital power will be made, before a short chronology is appended at the end.

ESTIMATES OF WEALTH DISTRIBUTION

It is part of the conventional wisdom that the richest 1 per cent of the population owns about a quarter of the wealth of Britain, that 5 per cent owns roughly half and that 20 per cent own virtually three-quarters. It is equally widely believed that this intense degree of inequality is on the decline. Both assumptions are open to extreme doubt.

It is perfectly true, of course, that the Inland Revenue tables, which offer annual estimates from 1960-61 onwards of the total net wealth of individuals in Britain over the age of 15, do purport to substantiate these commonly held presumptions. It is true also that the Inland Revenue statistics are much the more reliable source of the two main techniques used for calculating the distribution of personal wealth. Yet they are subject to some extremely serious methodological limitations which must be very carefully assessed before any attempt can be made to judge the accuracy of the published figures or to determine how far any discoverable distortions in their validity can be allowed for.

methods of calculation

The other main source of information is unofficial surveys covering either a representative sample of the whole population or a selected group within it. Two such national sample surveys have been recently conducted into savings, in 1953 and 1954, both of which were designed to be representative of the personal population of Britain, excluding institutions. Inevitably, however, unofficial surveys can never guarantee either a complete or an accurate response, and these defects are very likely to be exaggerated where comprehensive honesty may involve substantial tax implications. The 1954 savings survey, which provided the fuller picture of the two, obtained a response rate of only 67 per cent amongst "income units" approached, while even those who completed the interview almost certainly substantially understated their ownership of assets. Indeed, it has been estimated, somewhat dubiously, that the total amount of personal capital revealed constituted only some two thirds of the true sum (T. P. Hill, "Income, savings and net worth —the savings survey of 1952-54", *Bulletin of the Oxford University Institute of Statistics*, 17 May 1955). Savings surveys cannot therefore be accepted

ESTIMATED OWNERSHIP OF TOTAL NET WEALTH IN GREAT BRITAIN, 1960-1968, BY VARIOUS PERCENTILE GROUPINGS

percentile group	1960	1961	1962	1963	1964	1965	1966	1967	1968
largest 1%	27	28	26	26	25	24	22	23	24
largest 5%	51	50	49	50	48	46	43	43	46
smallest 80%	26	26	27	25	27	28	29	31	29
smallest 50%	4	4	5	5	8	9	11	11	10
total number of holders ('000s)	17,927	18,257	18,448	18,497	19,483	18,560	17,921	17,300	17,255
total amount (£000m)	51.6	54.9	58.3	63.7	71.8	74.3	76.8	83.6	88.0
gini coefficient of concentration (%)	76	72	72	73	72	70	67	67	68

source: extrapolated from 104th-111th *Reports of the Commissioners of HM Inland Revenue*, 1960-61 to 1967-68, plus *Inland revenue statistics*, HMSO, 1970, table 123. It should be noted, however, that certain discrepancies occur between table 139 of the last report (Cmnd 3879) and tables 135 and 166 of the 108th and 109th Reports respectively (Cmnd 2876 and 3200). The later figures are quoted since they are based on the 1961 census of population, while earlier estimates were based on the 1951 census. But they do create an unrealistic lacuna between the figures for 1963 and beforehand and those for 1964 and thereafter.

as supplying accurate data where total personal holdings exceed perhaps £10,000.

The Inland Revenue tabulations, which consist of numbers of persons and total capital values by ranges of net wealth, are derived, since the estate duty returns are listed for each age sex group separately, by multiplying each sample by the reciprocal of the mortality rate for that group. A further refinement is possible, since taxable estates are mainly the perquisites of members of the "higher" occupational classes, by inflating the reciprocals of the estimated specific (age sex) mortality rates of persons in the Registrar General's classes one and two exclusively, as defined in the latest census.

limitations of the data

The Inland Revenue reports do themselves recognise defects in their tabulations and list such items of greatly varying significance. The most important of these acknowledgements, paragraph 27 (c) of appendix VII on death duties in the 111th Report, reads as follows: "Certain elements are omitted because no duty is payable on them, either because of special exemptions or because they fall outside the scope of estate duty law. Examples are: settlement property (like property held in trust for certain individuals) passing when a surviving spouse dies who had no power to dispose of the capital, property held under discretionary trusts and benefits under certain pension schemes. Certain other items are treated as estates by themselves and therefore may not appear in the statistics if by themselves they do not exceed the exemption limit. Examples are certain life policies, and property settled otherwise than by the deceased when the rest of the property passing does not exceed £10,000. Other assets such as annuities may disappear altogether at death." (Cmnd 3879, p212).

Crucially important though some of these caveats are, and the more disturbing since they are essentially unquantifiable, they are unfortunately far from being exhaustive.

The only attempt so far to examine comprehensively the deficiencies in the published data, both academic and official, has been undertaken by Richard Titmuss in his book *Income distribution and social change*, published in 1962, possibly the single most important contribution to the study of social policy since the War, and certainly so in its analysis of power within this field. A whole series of methodological questions are systematically raised which must be briefly reviewed here in order that existing information on wealth distribution can be more fully brought into perspective.

Firstly, it is of fundamental importance that the official statistics do not "marry up" data concerning different individuals in families. This means that capital, at one stage held by a single individual, may be split up and spread within the family, whether the immediate household or the wider marital community extending perhaps over several generations, and since at least a prime purpose is the mitigation of estate duty liability, it is hardly surprising that such manoeuvres do not show up in the Board's tabulations. Capital power has been retained within the family, at the same time as the statistics offer a conveniently more egalitarian camouflage. Some evidence to substantiate these conjectures is provided by the finding, in an analysis of the estate duty returns for 1951-56, that wealth is most unequally concentrated among the 20-24 age group (H. F. Lydall, and D. G. Tipping, "The distribution of personal wealth in Britain," *Bulletin of the Oxford University Institue of Statistics*, 23 (1), 1961). Another pointer is that the number of estates in Britain of net capital value in excess of £50,000 which were owned by women stood at fully 40 per cent in 1967-68 *(111th report of the Board of Inland Revenue*, tables 135a and b), which itself was a marked increase on the proportion of 35 per cent in 1958-59 (102nd report, tables 106-8). It may also be of significance here that a survey of registered holders of quoted ordinary shares on the Stock Exchange in 1963 discovered that women were almost as equally represented as men, 33.4 per cent of a total market value of £14,848 millions being held by women and 35.2 per cent by men, the remainder being held by trustees and nominee companies (R. Stone, J. Revell, and J. Moyle, *The owners of quoted ordinary shares*, p39, table IV.2, Chapman and Hall, 1966).

Secondly, UK estate duty law offers singularly generous opportunities for avoidance through the device of family settlements or trusts which have been adapted from a corresponding function in feudal times. The family settlement of former times, based upon the tenure of freehold land, has in the past half century given place to a different kind of family settlement in which the principal assets are stocks and shares and in which one of the main objects of the settlor is to diminish the incidence of taxation both upon the income of the beneficiaries and also upon the estate as a whole or its transmission on the death of the settlor (Keeton, *The law of trusts*, p343, Pitman, 9th edition, 1967).

As a means of alienating property to avoid both surtax and estate duty whilst nevertheless retaining an influence over its future management and devolution, nothing has proved as effective as a discretionary trust coupled with a direction to accumulate income. Discretionary trusts involve the making of a covenant with trustees carefully selected for the purpose, whose duty is to distribute the annual payments they receive among any one or more of a group of named beneficiaries in such shares as they may decide. Up to 1969 no estate duty was payable on the death of a beneficiary under a continuing discretionary trust provided there was at least one surviving beneficiary, even though the deceased beneficiary may have been receiving the whole of the trust income. Despite important attempts by Labour in 1969-70 to block the use of these trusts for duty avoidance, as will be more fully discussed later, they still offer substantial scope in this direction. Otherwise the main limitation on the indefinite exclusion of such settlements from liability to estate duty arises only from the generous maximum perpetuity period laid down by the Perpetuities and Accumulations Act 1964, which finally terminates non-charitable trusts. Almost certainly, however, the capital would have been long since distributed and subject only to the seven year rule risk, thus able to embark on a fresh lease of life entirely free of death duty.

As an aid to the disappearance of huge amounts of capital for literally centuries from the attentions of Estate Duty Office, the courts have been equally obliging. Where a settlement has been imprudently drafted or where its tax saving clauses have been overtaken by subsequent anti-avoidance legislation, steps can be taken to vary the trust deed.

In the case of trusts where there are infant or unascertained beneficiaries, applications must be made to the courts, usually under the Variation of Trusts Act 1958. Undoubtedly the main purpose to which this Act has been put is tax avoidance. For apart from the decision in *Re Weston's Settlements* (1969 1, ch 223), there has been virtually no decision where approval of an arrangement was refused on the grounds that its object was tax avoidance. This is, of course, hardly surprising when the duty imposed on the courts is to protect the interests of infant and unborn beneficiaries, and any arrangement which avoids large payments of duty can hardly fail to benefit such potential beneficiaries.

The problem facing the courts in *Re Weston's Settlements* was whether to sanction the removal to Jersey of an English settlement by which a liability to capital gains tax of some £163,000 would be avoided. So tenuous were the links of the settlor and the beneficiaries with Jersey that the court had little difficulty in refusing the application. However, applications have since been made for the removal of English settlements outside the UK, and indeed the practice is even recognised by Parliament in the estate duty legislation (Finance Act 1969, schedule 17, para 4) as a means of avoiding the duty. No figures are available showing the loss of revenue from this type of application or those which do not embrace a foreign element, but the size of many of the estates involved indicates it must be considerable. A fortiori, where all the beneficiaries are known and of full age so that no application to the court is required, very large amounts of capital can elude public notice and entirely escape duty liabilities.

Furthermore, many foreign settlements should involve the settlor or the beneficiaries in a liability to tax in this country, but nothing is paid for the simple reason that the Revenue cannot enforce payment of the tax due. Subject to the exchange control regulations, a trust can be established in Liechtenstein with its very favourable trust laws and protection from investigation by the Revenue secured by the appointment of a Swiss bank as trustees, thus taking full advantage of the Swiss banking secrecy laws. Already the US and West German Governments have been considering steps to overcome this protection, but so far this flagrant form of tax evasion continues to survive. The number of discretionary trusts at present in existence, the distribution of their beneficiaries and the total sum of capital involved remains unknown (*Hansard*, 11 February 1971, written answers col 241). Revell, however, has ingeniously tried to establish their magnitude by his calculation of the aggregate market value of personal trusts administered by corporate trustees in 1961 at around £1,700 million (J. Revell, G. Hockley, and J. Moyle, *The wealth of the nation*, pp169-70, Cambridge University 1967), which alone would represent $3\frac{1}{2}$ per cent of the Inland Revenue's valuation of total net personal wealth in that year. His researches into both dutiable and exempt settled property at that time suggested that about 10 per cent of all personal wealth was then held in trust, though he concluded that discretionary trusts accounted only for some £200 million.

A third large caveat in the estate duty statistics derives from avoidance via gifts inter vivos. Gifts forming part of the "normal expenditure" of the estate owner and gifts in consideration of marriage (subject to certain limits, especially after section 53 of the Finance Act 1963) achieve an immediate saving in duty, while gifts to a charity are subject only to the donor's surviving by one year. The value of such gifts which were caught for duty as part of estates over £5,000 net capital value rose to £41,532,000 in 1967-68 (*111th Report of the Board of Inland Revenue*, table 133), and this compares with an annual average of £6 million between 1946-47 and 1958-59 (*Hansard*, 16 February 1960, col 105). This indicates that the use of gifts is considerably increasing and, provided they are made at least seven years (five till 1969) before the death of the donor, all liability for estate duty is avoided. The significance of this increase must be seen in perspective against the dual facts, firstly that the Finance Act 1960 substantially reduced liability to estate duty where death occurred in the third, fourth or fifth year of the relevant period (then five years) after the gift, and secondly that the decline in mortality rates since 1946, when the five year rule was established, should have meant an increasingly declining number of gifts being caught at all.

Fourthly, the scope for duty avoidance through life assurance, despite repeated checks by successive Finance Acts, is still such that brokers can proclaim their successful circumvention of the will of Parliament in the most flagrant manner: "Solve your estate duty problem overnight. You can achieve an instant solution to your estate duty problem without any seven year waiting period. What's more, you can add to your tax free income right away." So runs an advertisement by Towry Law, the insurance brokers. The extent of duty avoidance through this loophole can be partly gauged by the massive discrepancy between estate duty and life office statistics. Lydall and Tipping, for example, noted that the published total of sums assured in 1954, nearly £8,000 millions, corresponded with an amount of less than £900 millions estimated from the estate duty returns to be the value of life insurance policies held by persons with more than £2,000 net capital in the same year ("The distribution of personal wealth in Great Britain," *Bulletin of Oxford University Institute of Statistics,* 1961). Revell has shown that in 1960 the estate duty statistics accounted for only 41.3 per cent of the sums assured and less than one twelfth of the number of policies. His grossed-up estimate from the Inland Revenue tables of the value of policies in the hands of living persons is, at £6,579 millions, more than £7,900 millions short of the total reported by British Life Assurance 1957-61. This is explained, apart from death claims on small estates not requiring the production of probate, by discretionary trusts, the netting out of loans (especially house mortgages) secured by policies, non-aggregable policies, life of another policies (within partnerships and private companies often involving large sums), and such miscellaneous other policies as those for the protection of liability to duty on gifts inter vivos (J. Revell, *The wealth of the nation,* p 170-4, 1967). It is worth noting here that about two-fifths of ordinary branch business, amounting even in 1960 to £3,049 millions in sums assured, is concerned with occupational pension schemes and that in most cases the death benefit lies at the discretion of trustees and is therefore not dutiable.

A fifth loophole in the estate duty figures concerns the purchase or indirect investment in foreign land and immovable property. Clearly the purchase of real estate in countries abroad with either low death duties or none at all, like Bermuda or the Bahamas, offers many allurements. Nor is it likely that the Finance Act 1962, in bringing immovable property outside Great Britain within the duty net, has been as effective as it might seem prima facie. For property still secures exemption where the deceased was domiciled abroad, and given the increasing rapidity of travel and communications today, a foreign domicile is not incompatible with wide business and social interests in this country. The actual extent of acquisition of immovable property abroad, however, is not known, though net investment abroad 1948-63 has been computed at £1,593 millions (*National income and expenditure*, 1970, p 10-11, table 7).

the extent of personal wealth in Britain today

The accumulation of these deficiencies in the estate duty figures renders the calculations derived from them, frankly, sheer mathematical artefacts increasingly remote from reality. Indeed, in reviewing the ingenuities of the income statisticians which seem to grow inversely to the reliability of the data, one is struck by the subtlety of their statistical sophistications erected with such tantalising spuriousness on premises of factual sand. Attempts have been made, nevertheless, to find order in uncertainty. It has been suggested, for instance, that even if the shape of income or wealth distributions were amended by greater knowledge, it does not follow that the *trend of changes* would be discredited since a consistently defined aggregate is available through the years (R. J. Nicholson, "The distribution of personal income," *Lloyds bank review*, January 1967). But even this argument fails since the collective size of the various distorting factors remains unknown and hence a fortiori not necessarily in any consistent relationship with the known material.

Is therefore any realistic evaluation of current net wealth impracticable? A third and perhaps more reliable method lies in capitalising investment income. Unofficial estimates made by *The Economist* using this technique established the sum of total personal wealth, including owner occupied houses, at about £54,100 millions in 1959-60, which was about a tenth higher than estimates made at that time from the death duty statistics. More significantly, the degree of concentration in ownership which these calculations revealed was substantially greater even than that demonstrated by the Inland Revenue. The richest

ESTIMATES OF PERSONAL WEALTH BASED ON OFFICIAL FIGURES OF INVESTMENT INCOME, 1959-60.

range of wealth £	tax payers %	total wealth %	average wealth £
below 3,000	87.9	3.7	107
3,000–10,000	5.1	12.0	6,000
10,000–25,000	4.9	29.0	15,200
25,000–50,000	1.2	16.6	36,250
50,000–100,000	0.6	15.1	68,250
100,000–200,000	0.2	10.6	136,400
over 200,000	0.1	13.0	334,100
all ranges*	100.0	100.0	2,576

*21,000,000 persons, £54,100 millions
source: *Economist*, 15 January 1966.

one per cent of tax payers emerged as owning 40 per cent of total wealth, 2 per cent as owning 55 per cent and 7 per cent as owning 84 per cent. Indeed, the richest tenth of 1 per cent was actually found to own 13 per cent of total wealth, a sum of £7,033 millions, representing an average fortune of rather over one third of a million each.

As a further methodological check, another tactic is explored here which seeks to circumvent the inherent untrustworthiness of the estate duty tables. It can be seen from the next table that, both as a proportion of total central government revenue from taxation and in relation to net national income, a smooth progression occurred in the increase of estate duty yield between 1858 and 1915. Thereafter in comparative terms the yield dropped sharply despite the remarkable fact that the rate of levy on estates of a net capital value of at least £1,000,000 rose (and proportionately at lower values) from 8 per cent to 11 per cent in 1907, and then to 15 per cent in 1909, to 20 per cent in 1914 and to 30 per cent in 1919—a four-fold increase in twelve years. The most likely explanation for this paradox is that, in the face of what would then have seemed very sharp increases in the estate duty impost, avoidance began to be adopted on a significant scale. For the purposes of this argument, however, the point being made here is simply that the years 1908-15 would appear to be the latest period at which, in the absence of major avoidance practices, the estate duty statistics may be accepted as offering a reasonably reliable guide for the estimation of total wealth holdings.

Now several calculations were made of total net wealth at this time. One study reached a figure of £10,900 millions as capital wealth in private hands in the United Kingdom (including then Southern Ireland) about 1910 (B. Mallet and H. C. Strutt, "The multiplier and capital wealth," *Journal Royal Statistical Society*, 1915). Another survey, based on applying general mortality rates to the relevant estate duty data, produced an estimated range for total wealth in 1911-13 in Great Britain of £8,800-9,900 millions, while the use of differential social class mortality rates raised the total to £9,300-10,500 millions (H. Campion, *Public and private property*, p 24, Oxford University Press, 1939). The same author also employed an income method of calculation, based on deducing the value of capital assets held from the investment returns yielded, and this method, regarded as rather sounder, provided a range of total wealth in Britain of £11,100-12,900 millions. A further corroboration is obtained from a third independent study which, again using the investment income method, computed that in the UK in 1914 total wealth lay within the range of £12,400-16,200 millions (J. C. Stamp, *British incomes and property*, King, 1916). Bearing in mind the different territorial coverage of these studies, a remarkable degree of consensus between them seems to crystallise around the approximate total of £12,000 millions for Great Britain in the period of 1911-14. This would mean an estate duty yield of about 0.19 per cent of total net wealth at this time, when we also know it represented some 1.1 per cent of net national income.

Now by 1969 net national income (GNP less capital consumption) had risen 1590 per cent over its mean level at 1911-14. If therefore the estate duty yield had maintained a constant relationship with net national income, it would have stood by 1969 at about £366 millions. Two qualifications, however,

THE RELATION OF ESTATE DUTY YIELD TO CENTRAL GOVERNMENT REVENUE FROM TAXATION AND TOTAL NET NATIONAL INCOME IN BRITAIN, 1858-1969

years ending 31 March (inclusive)*	duty rate on estates valued at £1,000,000	mean total estate duty per annum £m	mean proportion of net estate duties to central government revenue from taxation %	mean proportion per annum of net estate duties to net national income at current prices
1858-67	—	3	5.8	0.4
1868-77	—	5	7.9	0.5
1878-87	—	6	9.6	0.5
1888-97	8	10	12.6	0.7
1898-1907	8	17	14.4	1.0
1908-15	11 then 15	23	16.1	1.1
1916-19	20	30	6.4	0.7
1920-22	30	46	5.0	1.0
1923-32	30	69	9.8	1.8
1933-38	40	84	11.3	2.0
1939-42	44 then 48	82	6.7	1.3
1943-46	52	106	3.7	1.3
1947-48	70	160	4.9	1.7
1949-58	80	175	4.2	1.2
1959-64	80	249	4.1	1.1
1965-69	80	320	3.5	1.0

*groups of years have been taken together since estate duty yield in single years fluctuates widely. Changes in duty rates do not, however, entirely coincide with the years selected to illustrate the progression in duty yield.

sources: C. T. Sandford, *Taxing inheritance and capital gains*, p17, Institute of Economic Affairs, 1965. Net national income estimates from C. H. Feinstein, "Income and investment in the UK, 1856-1914," *Economic Journal*, June 1961, A. R. Prest, "National income of the UK, 1870-1946," *Economic Journal* 1948 and National income and expenditure tables.

are required. One is that continuous growth in the productivity of capital should yield increasingly greater income flows for any given quantity of capital. Now the best available evidence of capital productivity throughout this period is as follows: the depreciated value at current prices of the total capital stock (defined as the value of assets at current prices less an amount for accumulated depreciation of older assets) has been estimated in 1920 at £13,552 million (B. R. Mitchell and P. Deane (eds), *Abstract of historical statistics*, p377, Cambridge University Press, 1962), while net capital stock at current replacement cost in 1969 has been valued at £102,500 million (*National income and expenditure blue book*, table 61, 1970, HMSO). Of course these two concepts of the total capital stock are not precisely identical, but they are certainly similar enough to serve as a broad basis for comparison. If therefore it is accepted that the capital stock has grown some 7.6 times in the last 50 years, then assuming a similar rate of increase also during the ten years preceding 1920, it will have grown 9.1 times over the last 60 years. Given the 15.9 times increase in net national income, capital productivity can be assessed as the order of 75 per cent. It may thus be reasonably argued on this premise that the increase in estate duty yield throughout this period might be expected, relative to the increase in net national income, to be reduced in the ratio 4:7. Now a caveat to this argument is that real national capital, which is what relates to output and the growth of productivity, is by no means identical with total *personal* wealth. But the latter, seeking out the highest rate of return and the highest rate of appreciation irrespective of type of investment and of territorial constraints, is unlikely to have grown less fast and may very well have increased faster. A reduction of the suggested rise in the expected degree of increase in the estate duty yield is therefore quite likely to overstate the qualification necessary.

The other proviso is that since 1909-14 the duty rate on estates of £50,000 value has increased five times and on estates of £1 million value by six times. This should mean that, subject to the maintenance during the ensuing 60 year period of the same ratio between the number of estates at different capital ranges (and the actual very marked shift in the balance of the proportion of recorded estates of different sizes revealed by the table below is of course only to be expected, given the hypothesis of widespread tax avoidance at the higher ranges), then the duty yield should have increased between five and six fold.

NUMBERS OF ESTATES BY RANGES OF NET CAPITAL VALUE,

net capital value £†	1908-09*		1967-68*	
	number	%	number	%
not over 3,000	6,422	17	146,373	55
3,000– 6,000	10,729	28	58,944	22
6,000– 60,000	17,266	45	58,902	22
60,000–150,000	2,328	6	2,615	1
150,000–450,000	1,215	3	521	$> \frac{1}{2}$
450,000 and over	443	1	74	$> \frac{1}{2}$
total	38,403	100	267,429	100

* the figures for 1909 relate to the United Kingdom and those for 1968 relate to Great Britain only.
† since £1 in 1870 was worth £1.20 in 1909 and only £0.20 by 1967-68, the capital ranges for 1908-09 have been multiplied six times in value to produce comparability with the later figures.
sources: *Annual report of Commissioners of Inland Revenue for 1909*, Cd 4868, and *Annual Report of Commissioners of Inland Revenue for 1968*, p194, table 129, Cmnd 3879.

Taking both these reservations into account, estate duty might have been expected to yield some £1,200 million by 1969, whereas the actual yield was £381.9 million (Inland revenue statistics, table 1, HMSO, 1970), a short fall of about £820 million. Since this actual yield has been officially calculated to derive from a total of net wealth estimated at £88,000 million (*op cit*, table 123), a projected yield of £1,200 million should pari passu indicate a total holding of personal wealth at the present time of some £276,000 million. The fact that this conclusion is necessarily a tentative and hypothetical approximation subject to a wide margin of error does not, however, detract from its startling implications. It means, first, that the real tax potential of estate duty is actually less than one-third realised, and that a huge gap equal in amount to the annual cost of an extra £2.30 weekly for every retirement pensioner is annually punched in the revenue net by the combined contrivances of evasion (illegal) and avoidance (anti-social though legal). Secondly, it suggests that the application of such statistical subtleties as the Gini coefficient of concentration to known wealth, which purport to reveal a degree of redistribution (albeit chiefly from the very rich to the rich (A. B. Atkinson, *Political Quarterly*, January 1971), is wholly illusory. Since undetected wealth is likely to be disproportionately crystallised among the very rich, in view of both their greater incentive and greater capacity to employ the whole armoury of tax planners, such tabular deductions as the share of wealth confined to the richest 1 per cent or 10 per cent are little more than ingenuous fictions. Thirdly, it implies that the 23 fold increase in total net wealth in Britain above the 1911-14 level of £12,000 million exceeds by some 45 per cent the total increase in net national income.

evidence of tax avoidance

It is possible, however, that an alternative theory might be posited to explain the current low yield of estate duty. This is that the reason for the shortfall of the estate duty yield below the level projected for the present time is quite simply that wealth has been so eaten away by taxation that it isn't there to tax at levels at all comparable with the past. Any hypothesis of sizeable avoidance or evasion, it may be argued, is therefore superfluous. Convenient though such an explanation doubtless is to many powerful interests and more in accord with prevailing tax orthodoxies, it fails to elucidate many highly revealing tell-tale signs.

One pointer is the finding, already referred to, that wealth is most extremely concentrated among the youngest adults aged 20-24. This suggests that any observed apparent deconcentration of wealth is really only a generational switch from the elderly to younger persons, largely in the same family. A similar relevant factor, to which Revell has drawn attention, is the increasing

SETTLED PROPERTY PASSING FOR ESTATE DUTY AS A PROPORTION OF TOTAL GROSS CAPITAL VALUE OF ESTATES OVER £5,000 NET CAPITAL VALUE, GREAT BRITAIN, 1960-61 TO 1967-68

| year | property settled by deceased or others | | | total gross capital value | settled property % of gross capital |
	personalty £m	realty £m	total £m	£m	value
1960–61	64.1	10.2	74.3	1,074.3	6.9
1961–62	74.6	10.4	85.0	1,165.8	7.3
1962–63	83.7	15.3	99.0	1,168.0	8.5
1963–64	75.5	13.7	89.2	1,205.4	7.4
1964–65	66.0	14.3	80.3	1,233.0	6.5
1965–66	60.9	9.9	70.8	1,278.1	5.5
1966–67	63.8	6.6	70.4	1,344.7	5.2
1967–68	58.3	9.7	68.0	1,431.9	4.7

source: Annual reports of the Commissioners of Inland Revenue.

longevity of women relative to men, and he has documented the significant rise between 1927 and 1954 in the proportion of medium sized estates held by widows (J. Revell, "Changes in the social distribution of property in Britain during the twentieth century," *Actes du troisième Congrès International d'Histoire Economique*, vol 1, p 383, table 8, Munich, 1965).

Secondly, there has been a suspiciously large drop in the proportion of property subject to estate duty which passes by means of settlements. The Colwyn Committee in 1927 reported the Inland Revenue estimate that under a capital levy about one sixth of total property liable would be settled property (*Report on national debt and taxation*, p 248, HMSO, Cmd 2800, 1927). In actual fact the proportion has fallen from 14.9 per cent in 1948-49 to 4.7 per cent in 1967-68, as shown in the table. Certainly other factors have been influential here, particularly a decreased reliance on the trust as a normal means of property holding, which it certainly was in the nineteenth century, and also the change in prices of the types of property which feature extensively in trusts (J. R. S. Revell, "Settled property and death duties," *British tax review*, May-June 1961). Nevertheless, a significant part of the explanation must lie in the development of tax avoidance by the use of discretionary trusts. Professor Revell believes that "it seems reasonable to assume, although there is no firm evidence to support this, that discretionary trusts were formed in large numbers and for large amounts as a result of the post-war increases in the rates of death duty." Certainly one tax authority, Professor Wheatcroft, has recently estimated that 95 per cent of all discretionary and accumulation trusts are created solely for tax saving reasons (*Estate and gift taxation*, p136, Sweet and Maxwell, 1965).

RELATIONSHIP BETWEEN GIFTS INTER VIVOS CHARGED TO ESTATE DUTY WHERE ESTATES EXCEEDED STATUTORY EXEMPTION WITH VALUATIONS FOR STAMP DUTY OF PROPERTY TRANSFERRED BY VOLUNTARY DISPOSITIONS INTER VIVOS (AS CERTIFIED BY THE VALUATION OFFICE), GREAT BRITAIN, 1959-60 TO 1968-69

	gifts valued for stamp duty			gifts charged to estate duty		
year	number	value £m	rate of increase in value	number	value £m	rate of increase in duty
1959–60	4,638	22.0	100	—	—	—
1960–61	5,081	29.0	132	6,775	25.2	100
1961–62	5,915	37.0	168	6,498	31.1	123
1962–63	6,685	38.7	176	7,931	31.4	124
1963–64	6,889	54.9	250	7,400	31.4	124
1964–65	8,341	73.3	333	6,976	34.5	137
1965–66	10,357	119.8	544	6,592	35.6	141
1966–67	12,784	124.0	564	7,632	40.0	159
1967–68	12,031	115.3	524	7,220	41.5	164
1968–69	10,809	135.3	615	7,016	45.3	180

sources: *112th Report of Commissioners of Inland Revenue for 1969*, p 67, table 51, HMSO, Cmnd 4262; and 103rd-112th Reports for years 1960 to 1969 for gifts subject to duty annually.

Thirdly, a pointer to the extent of inter vivos gifts escaping duty is provided by the wide and increasing discrepancy between gifts actually charged to estate duty during the 1960s and the gifts that were valued for stamp duty in the same period. The table below reveals that whilst the latter have risen in value more than six times during the last decade, the former have less than doubled in value. Similarly, the assumption of a massive transfer of property by gifts inter vivos was invoked by the *Economist* (14 January 1961, p 112) as the only explanation for the apparent relative drop in the investment income of the rich during the 1950s in comparison with the 1930s.

Fourthly, the irrelevance of the over taxation view is glaringly exposed by the assessment in 1954 by the Minority Report on the Taxation of Profits and Income of the long-term rate of capital appreciation in all forms, even before the huge Stock Exchange booms of 1959-61 and 1967-68, at a minimum of £600-1,000 million per year (p 381, para 80, Cmnd 9474, HMSO). On this basis the annual death duty yield of around £175 million at that time represented the taxing away of no more than a fifth of the annual *increase* in capital.

THE LABOUR RECORD

Following this analysis, the criteria that suggest themselves for assessing the extent to which the Labour Government achieved a more equal distribution of wealth, are as follows:

1. How far was the taxation of wealth increased in relation to the approximate rate of annual appreciation of capital, and how far was such taxation geared to the most extreme inequalities of wealth?

2. To what extent were the main avenues of tax avoidance and evasion effectively blocked?

3. What efforts were made to increase capital ownership at the lower reaches of the income scale?

It is clear that the great bulk of Labour's measures in this field were directed towards the second objective, but all three will be briefly examined.

taxation of wealth

The table below traces the annual yield of the various capital taxes during the period 1965-69 and reveals that as a proportion of total government receipts from taxation, duties on wealth actually declined in the intermediate years and only at the end reached a level marginally higher than at the outset. Similarly, as a proportion of net national income, total taxes on wealth fell from 1.4 per cent in 1965 to 1.2 per cent in 1967, before rising to 1.8 per cent in 1969. This is despite in increase of £286 million in levies on wealth under Labour rising eventually to an estimated extra £400 million a year. Overall therefore no decisive shift of emphasis towards capital taxation is apparent and when total wealth duties represent probably no more than a third of the current long-term rate of appreciation of capital, it is manifest that inequalities of ownership have not been seriously impugned. This conclusion is not refuted despite the important innovations during this period of

NET RECEIPTS FROM TAXES ON WEALTH, UNITED KINGDOM, 1964-65 TO 1968-69

year	death duties £m	capital gains tax £m	stamp duties £m	investment surcharge £m	total taxes on wealth £m	total inland revenue duties £m	% of taxes on wealth to all duties
1964–65	296.5	—	80.0	—	376.5	4,072.0	9.2
1965–66	292.9	—	76.6	—	369.5	4,692.9	7.9
1966–67	300.9	7.5	76.2	—	384.6	4,997.3	7.7
1967–68	329.9	15.8	98.3	—	444.0	5,742.9	7.7
1968–69	381.9	46.9	124.5	67.3	620.6	6,546.4	9.5

source: *Inland revenue statistics*, p 2, table 1, HMSO, 1970.

a comprehensive long-term capital gains tax, a discriminatory impost on distributed profits, and a special one year charge on investment income in excess of £3,000 which rose to a rate above 100 per cent at the highest levels. Indeed, even concerning *recorded* wealth, the Gini coefficients of concentration declined no more markedly in the four years after 1964 than in the preceding four years.

Nor were these new measures brought into operation as vigorously as they might have been. The 1965 capital gains tax, for example, is considerably more generous to property owners than the tax treatment of marginal earned income, let alone unearned income, and by allowing realised losses to be set off against gains offers wide scope for mitigating tax liabilities. Also, the introduction of the tax in conjunction with the corporation tax has greatly undermined its efficacy. For in regard to the substantial amount of wealth held in "close" companies with high retentions, and hence paying relatively little income tax and surtax, the shift to the corporation tax provides tax savings that largely offset the capital gains tax. Another more general source of weakness is that it is limited to *realised* capital gains. For the more wealthy sections of the community can normally postpone realisation of their capital appreciation for a very long period, especially in the hope of a political change of climate. Unless therefore the rate of capital gains were geared to the length of the holding period, this inequity will continue to characterise any tax confined to appreciation rather than the capital itself. The only caveat to this stricture derives from the introduction by the Finance Act 1965 of the charge to capital gains tax on death, the associated 15 year levy on the increase in value of assets held by a discretionary trust. For the respective unpredictability in the timing of the one event and the regularity of imposition of the other levy preclude ready avoidance. If these new charges had been allowed to come to fruition, they might well have made significant inroads on some of the grosser inequalities of wealth, and it was presumably for this reason that the incoming Tory Government has given them such immediate priority for repeal under section 49 of the Finance Act 1971.

Indeed, it is precisely the failure to develop a tax on capital holdings per se which constitutes the central omission from the Labour strategy, a failure reinforced by the exclusion of a commitment to a wealth tax in the 1970 election manifesto. The administrative difficulties pressed by the Inland Revenue in the period 1968-69 against its introduction were apparently permitted to quash the overwhelming case, on grounds of international comparison as well as the overriding arguments of equity, for a direct tax on wealth. It is now widely recognised that for the majority of wealthy tax payers, death duties as a tax on the ignorant and the prematurely dead is an option they decline to accept. As one commentator has put it, "estate duty is now paid only by the misanthropic, the patriotic, the absent-minded or the downright unlucky" (O. Stutchbury, *The case for capital taxes*, p 2, Fabian tract 388). In fact, because of widespread avoidance, death duties are probably an extremely *regressive* tax in that the rate of tax actually paid often diminishes with the size of the estate. Yet no priority was allotted by the Labour Government towards resolving this problem through a supplementary gifts tax—the extension of the estate duty charge on gifts to seven years in 1968 was no functional substitute—nor did Labour embark on any more radical or far-reaching alternative such as a cumulative capital receipts levy. Yet only from such new devices might a significant redistribution of wealth be expected.

blocking of avoidance and evasion

A very wide-ranging and complex network of anti-avoidance legislation was nevertheless put on the statute book during this period, and this is briefly listed at the end of this chapter. The blocking of duty avoidance is not of course a monopoly of Labour administrations—and indeed section 28 of the Finance Act 1960 (now section 460 of the consolidated Income and Corporation Taxes Act 1970) designed to counter tax advantages from transactions in securities remains perhaps the most important single piece of anti-avoidance legislation since the War—but the blocking measures of the 1968-1969 Finance Acts were unusually comprehensive. To assess their impact, they will be briefly examined in relation to the main techniques of avoidance.

family settlements

In his 1969 Budget speech the Chancellor announced that he proposed to end the loophole whereby at the death of a beneficiary under a continuing discretionary trust, no estate duty was payable provided there was at least one surviving beneficiary, even though the deceased beneficiary may have been receiving the whole of the trust income. The Chancellor's original intention was that the charge should be calculated on the proportion which the income the deceased beneficiary had received over the time he was a potential beneficiary bore to the whole income of the trust property over that period. However, so extensive were the amendments at the Report stage of the Bill that the meagre yield of £10 million per year which was the Chancellor's original estimate of the additional duty from these changes is now likely to be only half that amount. When the new provisions actually reached the statute book, the reckonable period of income enjoyment by a beneficiary had been cut to the seven years ending with his death. Although the objections which eventually led to this more restricted basis of charge, such as the administrative problems facing trustees if a longer period were involved, were generally quite reasonable, they again underline the basic weakness in the concept of a mutation duty as a major source of revenue.

EVASION OF ESTATE DUTY, ENGLAND AND WALES, 1960-70

year ending 30 September	number	amount £	duty recovered as % of total estate duty receipts	prosecution for fraud
1960	104	67,728	0.030	1 (fine £500)
1961	95	156,392	0.066	—
1962	136	90,998	0.035	1 (fine £2,000)
1963	109	58,613	0.022	—
1964	94	151,723	0.049	—
1965	112	173,954	0.059	—
1966	113	111,402	0.038	—
1967	104	166,174	0.055	2 (fines £2,000 and £15,000)
1968	125	122,363	0.037	—
1969	156	274,503	0.072	—
1970	92	171,309	0.047	1 (fine £1,000)
total	1,240	1,545,159	—	—

source: *Hansard*, 22 March 1971, written answers, col 43.

More generally, since the central difficulty in taxing discretionary trusts, that of measuring what share of the total income of the fund any single beneficiary may be said to own, has been resolved by calculating what share of the total income of the fund has been paid out to him over the seven years preceding his death—a nil amount in many cases—then death duty liability will still often remain even under the new dispensation at precisely nothing. By ensuring that the only beneficiaries to whom income is paid are the young ones, little risk is incurred under the new rules, and where there are older beneficiaries who require income, steps can be taken to re-arrange their interests. Capital appreciation without income, such as is offered by life assurance endowment policies, is likely to be the aim of many trustees in the future, since this will overcome many of the problems presented by the new rules. More specifically, a number of potential sidestepping manoevres can already be predicted. Thus, a trust may be established with investments such as capital shares or works of art that yield no income at all. Or charities may be made objects of discretionary settlement and all the income distributed to them or one of them, coupled with low-yielding securities with a high capital return so as to restrict the amounts passing to the charities. Or provision may be made for a large class of minors to have an interest contingent on attaining the age of 18, but with a wide overriding power enabling income and capital to be paid to a larger class with a 21-year period of accumulation. In regard to existing discretionary trusts, duty can still be saved by reducing the whole trust income or that part which passes to a vulnerable beneficiary during the appropriate relevant period, for example, by accumulating the trust income or by paying out to less vulnerable beneficiaries.

Two quotations can perhaps best summarise the new position. The author of one recent text-book on estate duty avoidance has concluded: "Despite the changes under the Finance Act, 1969, it is considered that discretionary settlements are still a very worthwhile mode of avoiding duty and tax liabilities. Above all, a discretionary trust provides a greater measure of flexibility (provided the trusts and discretions are widely drafted) than is possible under the fixed type of trust . . . It is thought that for the future discretionary trusts should contain the widest possible powers and discretions, including power to have the trust administered outside the UK and to change the proper law of the settlement" (J. B. Morcom, Estate duty saving and capital gains tax, p45, 1969). More inviting still is the advertisement by First Investors and Savers Ltd. in the *Law Society Gazette*, June 1970, pxxi: "A Discretionary Trust is *still* the most flexible means of providing for dependents. The disadvantages caused by the Finance Act 1969 *can* be overcome and with skilful drafting and careful administration it is possible to avoid a charge to estate duty on the trust's assets on the death of any beneficiary; increase net income to the beneficiaries; and avoid the charge to capital gains tax normally made on the trust's assets every fifteen years."

gifts inter vivos

Since gifts have always remained the simplest and most effective method to circumvent estate duty, Governments have successively raised the exemption period from one year in 1894 to 3 years in 1910, then to 5 years in 1946, and finally to 7 years in 1968. Any further extension to 10 or 15 years, however, might present very real problems of recovering records of past transactions. To that extent the limit to this type of check has initially already been reached and, as has already been stated, Labour introduced no substitute mechanism to block this obvious form of avoidance.

life assurance loopholes

An important attempt was made in 1968 to stop the use of the "back-to-back" arrangement whereby the estate owner purchased for a capital sum a life annuity and at the same time effected a life assurance policy with an assured capital sum of up to 80 per cent of the cost of the annuity. The life policy was normally written on trust for the benefit of the assured's wife and family under the Married Woman's Property Act 1882, with the result that upon his death the policy proceeds formed a separate estate on the basis that it was property in which he never had an interest. Whilst the new legislation made it more difficult for the more unscrupulous advisers, the "normal expenditure" provisions introduced by the Finance Act 1968, together with the liberal attitude adopted by the revenue in interpreting these provisions, have largely compensated for the new restrictions.

aggregation

One other form of blocking device should be specially mentioned, namely the abolition of the non-aggregation rule whereby previously the investment income of infants had not been added to their parents' income for tax purposes. The aggregation rules introduced under section 15 of the Finance Act 1968 did not, however, affect the surtax saving achieved by a direction to trustees to accumulate income from settled property. For not only did the new rules not apply to income accumulated by the trustees, who are not liable to surtax, but in the same way such income is expressly excluded from being treated as that of a parent settled under the trust provisions now contained in part XVI of the Income and Corporation Taxes Act 1970.

Although the Finance Act 1968 ended "contingency claims" by minors whereby an infant beneficiary could make a substantial income tax repayment claim on attaining his majority in respect of the income tax borne by the trustees on the accumulated income, legislation promised on accumulation trusts in general never materialised either in 1969 or 1970, and now

COSTING OF CHANGES IN WEALTH TAXATION UNDER LABOUR, 1965-66 to 1970-71

year	tax changes	effect in full year £m
1965–66	surtax: withdrawal of relief for settlements in favour of individuals	+2
	capital gains tax: tax on gains realised by an individual on assets held for more than a year at 30%*	+10
1966–67	surtax: disallowance of relief for dividends received in 1965–66	+4
	estate duty: restriction of exemption given to certain British Government securities	+1
	capital gains tax: rate for life assurance companies to be 30%	+5
1967–68	stamp duty: increase of rate of duty on issue of loan capital to $\frac{1}{2}$% and extension of scope of duty	+6
	exemption of local duty authority stocks and bonds on conveyances on property other than stocks and marketable securities	−3
1968–69	income tax: aggregation of child's investment income with his parents' income	+25
	corporation tax: increase of rate to $42\frac{1}{2}$%	+98
	capital gains tax: exemption of gains of less than £50	−1
	estate duty: extension of inter vivos gifts period	+6
	aggregation of gifted insurance policies, &c.	+5
	special charge:	+67
1969–70	corporation tax: increase of rate by $2\frac{1}{2}$% to 45%	+120
	abolition of limits of directors' remuneration and loan interest to proprietors	−20
	preventing abuse of loss buying	+5
	capital gains tax: consequences of devaluation	−20
	exemption of gilt-edged securities	−7
	executor's gains to be treated as accruing on deceased's death	−3
	estate duty: raising of threshold to £10,000 and adoption of slice system	−8
	preventing avoidance by settlement	+10
1970–71	surtax: introduction of exemption limit of £2,500	−5
	estate duty: interest rate increased from 2% to 3%	+2
	stamp duties: abolition of cheque duty	−11
	abolition of receipt duty	−1
net total		+£285m

* rising to an estimated £125 million—total will rise to £400 million.
sources: Financial statements and budget reports, 1965-66 to 1970-71.

under section 10 of the Finance Act 1971 it is proposed to abolish even the limited basis of charge introduced in 1968.

In summary, therefore, it must be concluded that while some determined and important efforts were made to block some of the most glaring gaps and anomalies in the estate duty provisions, these were in virtually no case wholly successful. To the extent that the estate duty field remained pitted with openings for avoidance, severe doubt is cast upon the practicability of any complete solution, given the inherent nature of death duties as a form of tax.

On the question of the *evasion* (illegal) of death duties, it can only be said that the available evidence suggests neither a more strict nor a more relaxed application of checks against fraud in the later half of the 1960s compared with the earlier half. In both periods the number of prosecutions undertaken and the size of fines imposed appear minute.

dissemination of wealth

No concrete moves were made by Labour towards developing schemes for capital growth sharing such as are being currently established by European trade union movements, and discussion of the important question, so relevant to the redistribution of wealth, of means of allotting shares in undistributed profits for unions or workers is therefore dealt with later.

WIDER PROCESSES INFLUENCING THE DISTRIBUTION OF WEALTH

Apart from deliberate Government policies, other factors clearly influence the division of wealth holdings, and to round out the picture of the changing pattern of inequalities, certain relevant on-going processes should be briefly surveyed. Not all of these processes are of course quantifiable. Professor Meade, who examines the interaction of differential fertility, intelligence, social and occupational mobility, and inheritance of property, is forced to conclude merely that "there are at work the systematic biological and demographic forces of inheritance which are some of them tending to equalise and some of them to disequalize ownership. The striking inequalities which we observe in the real world are the result of the balance of these systematic forces working in a society subject to the random strokes of luck" (J. E. Meade, *Efficiency, equality and ownership of property*, p52, Allen and Unwin, 1964). Nevertheless, certain measurable flows in the economy can be considered in this context.

The most significant factor here has been company practice in retaining profits, sharply upgraded by the effects of constant post-war full employment policies, as investment reserves. The official statistics demonstrate that total undistributed post-tax profits reinvested by all UK companies on behalf of shareholders, net of depreciation and stock appreciation, rose each year from about £1,000 millions in the middle 1950s to £1,400 millions in 1959, and thence fluctuated at around this level beneath a peak of £1,600 millions in 1965 (*National income and expenditure blue book 1970*, tables 26, 27 and 58). Such massive, even if uninvited, re-investment, encouraged by the corporation tax ploughback philosophy, can even within a decade produce huge capital gains for shareholders. Nor can the explosion of growth stocks be dismissed as purely, or even largely, an inflationary phenomenon, though it may be exaggerated on these grounds. An annual survey by a firm of London stockbrokers showed that throughout the period 1919-60 the investment of £1,000,000 a year in a representative group of blue chip industrial equity shares, with the gross income annually re-invested, would have produced a constantly growing fund until, after a huge acceleration in the 1950s, it would have totalled £646,330,000 by 1960. Allowing for depreciation as well as gross income, the overall yield would have been 10.6 per annum (*The Times*, 24 March 1960). On this calculation, even the imposition of a so-called "penal" or "crippling" top rate of 80 per cent duty on the £1 million estate of its peculiarly improvident owner would allow a beneficiary with the £200,000 remainder entirely to recoup the fortune to its previous size in only 20-25 years.

This built-in escalator towards property inequalities, which even the severest of present taxation is unlikely to restrain, let alone reverse, is aggravated by two further considerations. One is the quite excessive degree of concentration of equity holdings in the hands of the very rich.

Lydall and Tipping found that, while the richest 1 per cent held two-fifths of Government and municipal securities and a quarter of land, buildings and trade assets as well as a quarter of cash and bank deposits, they actually held 81 per cent of stocks and shares in companies, 96 per cent of the latter being held by the richest 5 per cent (*Bulletin of Oxford University Institute of Statistics*, 1961, p90). This calculation included life funds, though not other forms of institutional holdings. Estimates were, however, made concerning pension funds that half their assets were owned by the wealthiest 10 per cent, while trust capital, almost exclusively concentrated among the very richest group, tilted the balance of ownership among omitted items of wealth towards a similar degree of inequality as that found for the known bulk of capital holdings. Conversely with this utterly disproportionate restriction to the extremely rich, even among property owners, of those assets generating the largest capital and income appreciation is the tendency for smaller property holdings to be located chiefly in "safer" assets with a lower capital and income yield. Thus a 1966 survey found that the DE socio-economic groups (semi-skilled and unskilled workers and state pensioners) had such holdings as they possessed chiefly in unit or investment trusts (British Market Research Bureau, *How does Britain save?* 1966).

In other words, while the rich can employ accountants and investment analysts to advise how a balanced growth portfolio can be increasingly devoted, with a smaller proportion of money kept unprofitably as a liquid reserve, to speculation for bigger and faster gains, small owners of assets are unduly confined to fixed interest saving. For some 30 million persons in Britain today hold about 22 million Post Office Savings Bank accounts and 11 million Trustee Savings Bank accounts. This picture is reinforced by *The Economist's* researches which reported in 1966 (15 January, p218) that cash and fixed interest securities represented 45 per cent of the wealth of individuals with less than £10,000, and equity shares only 5 per cent. By contrast, equities represented 56 per cent of the wealth of those with over £250,000, and cash and bonds only 22 per cent. Consequently, the average capital appreciation of the assets held by the wealthiest group was calculated, on this average composition, at 114 per cent between 1950 and 1964, while over the same period the assets of the £3,000—£10,000 group appreciated by only 48 per cent.

The second consideration exacerbating inequalities in wealth ownership is that ordinary shares appear to be a declining (though rather irregularly so) source of company funds. Thus, while undistributed profits maintained a fluctuating half share, loans and other increases in credit grew as a source of funds at the expense of equities as shown in the table below. By 1968, out of £4,800 millions of capital funds at the disposal of industrial and commercial companies, only 6 per cent was raised through equity issues,

PERCENTAGE SOURCES OF FUNDS OF QUOTED BRITISH COMPANIES

source of funds	1959	1960	1961	1962	1963	1964	1965	1966	1967
ordinary shares	14	16	23	14	8	9	8	9	13
long term loans and increases in credit	22	30	26	26	31	36	36	39	38
additions to reserves	61	50	47	55	56	54	54	49	41
other sources	3	4	4	5	5	1	2	3	8
all sources (£m)	1,881	2,434	2,135	1,901	2,310	2,856	3,154	2,836	3,397

source: derived from *Annual abstract of statistics, 1970*, p360, table 381.

whilst loans, debentures and all other borrowing accounted for only another fifth, and the whole of the remainder was financed out of retained earnings. (Bank of England, *Quarterly bulletin*, April 1969). Such a disposition must mean the restriction of future profits and long term growth very largely in the hands of the existing holders of ordinary shares who have already been shown to be to a quite exceptional degree a tiny number of the extremely rich. Such is the polarising dynamic in the growth of inequality of wealth in our society.

RECOMMENDATIONS FOR POLICY

What then is to be done? The argument for taxing wealth at its root can be made on several grounds. Firstly, since it confers not only considerable security and substantial economic and social advantages, but also great power, no proper redistribution of power can be achieved without a fundamental redistribution of wealth. Secondly, unless a more even balance is constructed between the taxation of income and capital, a strong incentive persists to transform the former into the latter in order to mitigate tax liabilities. Thirdly, though no direct trade-off is afforded between a wealth tax and reduced surtax levels since their economic effects are not complementary, a wealth tax in exchange for lowered surtax rates is likely to stimulate investment and growth.

It might also be expected to encourage greater risk taking enterprise by encouraging the transfer of resources from low yield to higher yield investment. Last, and by no means least, it might facilitate the establishment of a new social contract within which the planned regulation of other sectors of the economy would be acceptable.

wealth tax

Various objections have, however, been voiced to the idea of a wealth tax. One is the administrative cost. If the rate usually mentioned for a wealth tax were adopted, that is 1 per cent on fortunes over £25,000 with certain personal assets exempted as under the capital gains tax, then the effective starting rate would be almost £50,000, and the yield on the excess would approximate £150 millions a year, spread across 110,000 persons. Alternatively, the starting point could be raised, at least initially, to perhaps £75,000, which would make the administrative problem perfectly tolerable, but the higher yield could be recouped by establishing a mildly progressive rate of an extra 1 per cent on each successive £50,000 block up to an initial 10 per cent. The yield of such a scheme would be about £600 million (*Hansard*, 2 March 1971, written answers, col 387). Before this latter is challenged as punitive Socialist expropriation, it should be recognised that an estate of £1,000,000 geared largely towards equities and with an overall annual yield of 10 per cent would still be levied, at £70,000 in the first year, on less than the annual gross appreciation. Secondly it has been queried that if investments were shuffled to minimise tax by switching to higher-yielding portfolios, then lower yield growth shares. of which new issues are made, would suffer (H. Crawford, "Economics of a wealth tax," *The Sunday Times*, 4 February 1968). If such an effect were likely to be damaging, however, it could be offset by making the wealth tax impost deductible against income tax, as in West Germany, and surtax.

The central problem is undoubtedly valuation. Clearly, if the problem of capital splitting by gifts is to be effectively surmounted, the wealth of the spouses should be aggregated, as also should the wealth of unmarried infant children. Discretionary trusts, accumulation trusts where the ultimate beneficiaries are not known, and settlement with powers of appointment, revocation or advancement cannot be allocated to particular individuals except arbitrarily. Wheatcroft has suggested such problems might be handled by allocating the capital of certain trusts to the settlor during his life where reservations are retained to him or his wife, or by authorising the Special Commissioners to allot certain trust capital to persons they consider most likely to benefit from it, or to tax all trusts at a standard rate with a right both to the Revenue and the taxpayer to adjust the rate in accordance with the wealth of the beneficiary when the trust is distributed (G. S. A. Wheatcroft, "The administrative problems of a wealth tax," *British Tax Review*, November-December 1963). He also notes similar problems in regard to holdings of shares and debentures in closely controlled companies. "Where rights of voting, to dividends and to capital in a winding up do not correspond, the value of a share may be extremely difficult to assess. Special rules have been found necessary for estate duty purposes and for surtax direction purposes to arrive at arbitrary values and to make the company, in certain circumstances, liable for the tax." Such problems will undoubtedly impose considerable complexities in any consolidated statute, as well as further apportionment difficulties like accrued income not yet received and bad or doubtful debts.

Certain machinery for dealing with these problems does, however, exist.

Special provision, for example, is made in the Finance Act 1940 for estate duty purposes to value the shares of a controlling shareholder in a closely controlled company by reference to the underlying assets of the company and not on an earnings or dividend yield basis. Similar rules could be adopted for the wealth tax, with all the unquoted shares being valued on the "assets basis," but subject to a discount depending on the size of the total holding of a "family unit." The smaller the percentage holding, then the greater would be the amount by which the assets valuation would be reduced. A comparable practice is adopted by the shares valuation division of the Estate Duty Office in valuing unquoted shares for capital gains tax, except that family holdings are not generally aggregated in the manner suggested here.

capital receipts tax

There is therefore nothing inherently insuperable about the administrative complexities of a wealth tax, and indeed much of the cost of valuation could be reduced by the scissors device of allowing the tax payer himself to estimate the value of his assets for wealth tax provided that these estimates also formed the base values for capital gains tax. Nevertheless, unless the duty rates were raised substantially above the introductory levels and well beyond the threshold point at which the full value of the annual appreciation is reclaimed, no fundamental redistribution of wealth will be effected. Nor can any conceivable reform of the existing estate duty be looked to for this purpose. Of course, it is always possible to devise further steps, such as restricting the "normal expenditure" gift provisions in the Finance Act 1968, removing the exemption on property abroad secured by a foreign domicile and ending concessions on agricultural property since the absence of a time limit means that a death bed purchase of agricultural property still achieves a 45 per cent abatement. But the never ending war of attrition between avoidance and anti-avoidance and anti-anti-avoidance suggests it would be unrealistic to look to reinforced estate duties for any major reversal of wealth inequalities. This is confirmed by the failure of the tax since the last War to contribute even a twentieth of total government receipts from taxation and by its relative decline as a revenue raiser throughout the last 20 years despite the boom in equities and real estate.

Further supplementation is therefore required from some type of gifts levy. An inter vivos gifts tax purely according to the size of gift would not, however, be sufficient. For this would still enable wealth to be accumulated by the inheritance of money from many different sources. Nor even will the aim be secured by a gifts tax not only according to the size of the bequest, but according to the existing wealth of the beneficiary (*The Economist*, 22 January 1966, p 329). For the latter could always spend his way through his current wealth before accepting the next large gift. The solution must therefore lie in the recording on a register of successive gifts or legacies to the beneficiary through his lifetime, with a progressive rate of tax applied up to a ceiling point imposed where gifts could confer power or affluence unmerited by the donee's capacities or offering unreasonably advantageous opportunities. Stutchbury fixes this point arbitrarily at £20,000, rather less than sufficient to acquire control of any sizeable business (O. Stutchbury, *The case for capital taxes*, p 3, Fabian tract 388). Even if, given the current rapid inflation of money values, this was raised to £50,000, the application of a (say) 90 per cent rate above this point should produce a much wider dissemination in the transfer of wealth. Nor need such an inheritance tax necessarily yield less revenue than estate duty, for a scale which took account of the distribution of estates could be devised to produce a yield to the Exchequer equal to that of death duties (see C. T. Sandford, "Taxing inheritance and capital gains," table IV, p 59, IEA, 1965).

Of course it will be objected that such rates are confiscatory and that a lower rate would reduce the propensity to avoidance and increase the duty yield from a much wider base. The siren plea must, however, be rejected on two main grounds. One is that it would preclude the central aim of the policy which is to end the utterly indefensible concentration of wealth vested in the hands of the richest minority. Quite apart from the perverse inequality of power contingent on the accident of birth, the grotesque inequalities of the biggest estates represent the abnegation of any fair and proper system of incentives as the central economic motive. Secondly, historical evidence does not suggest that *any* tax level, even a much lower one, will not be viewed as unduly onerous by those to whom it is applied. In 1909, for example, it was argued that the proposal to increase estate duty—to a maximum charge of 15 per cent on unsettled estates—would "lead to a very considerable depletion of capital" which could "only be accompanied by scarcity of employment, growing greater from one year to the other" (*Hansard*, 20 June 1909).

wider dissemination of wealth

It must be added here, though there is no space to develop the argument, that the redistribution of wealth not only *from* the rich but *to* the four-fifths of the population who scarcely hold any wealth at all must be an equally important goal of policy. One such proposal is that corporation tax could be reformed in favour of an annual levy of, say 2 per cent of the replacement value of assets, to be collected at least partly in the form of an additional equity issue transferred to the State (J. Hughes, "The increase in inequality," *New Statesman*, 8 November 1968). The substantial, and growing, annual yield on these acquisitions could then be centralised in the hands of a national shareholding agency which would pay out dividends, on condition only that necessary investment levels were maintained, to all families in the country on a universal flat rate basis subject to clawback at least below the surtax level (M. H. Meacher, "A national equities issue to defeat poverty," *Poverty* 14, Spring 1970 and pamphlet forthcoming). This arrangement would combine several advantages. It would avoid the danger of profit-sharing or investment pay schemes in tying the worker's prospect of capital appreciation to his job security, and would prevent poorly paid workers being penalised through working in industries with the poorest records of productivity and growth. Some such scheme or a suitably modified variant should therefore, as much as a direct tax on wealth, constitute an early and fundamental priority for the next Labour Government.

chronology

July 1965	Finance Act, *Sections 19–45:* introduction of capital gains tax, and in particular of a comprehensive charge on settled property, including at the death of a life tenant, together with an associated 15-year charge on discretionary trusts.

sections 46–89: introduction of corporation tax and abolition of profits tax. Comprehensive anti-avoidance provisions deal with closely controlled private companies.

July 1966   Finance Act, *Section 41:* restrictions imposed on the exemption from estate duty for certain UK Government securities, under schemes involving the use of foreign companies and foreign settlements.

July 1967   Finance Act, *Section 22:* further restrictions imposed on the use of hobby farms and market gardens for the purpose of creating losses to offset against other income.

July 1968   Finance Act, *Section 15:* aggregation with parents' income of investment income of unmarried infants not regularly working. *Section 16:* restrictions imposed on the use of life assurance policies for investment purposes attracting income tax relief, including the introduction of a minimum 10 year qualifying period and the ending of "borrow-all" policies (where premiums are borrowed from the life office). *Section 23:* restrictions on the use of stock dividend options to avoid schedule F distribution charge. *Section 35:* estate duty charge on gifts inter vivos extended to seven years. *Section 36:* use of marriage gifts as a means of estate duty avoidance severely restricted. *Section 37:* concession given whereby gifts forming part of the "normal expenditure" of the deceased are ignored for estate duty and not subject to the seven-year period laid down in section 36. *Section 38:* Non-aggregation rules abolished for life assurance policies in which the deceased never had an interest. *Section 41:* special charge levied for 1967-68 on individuals whose aggregate investment income exceeded £3,000 in that year. *Miscellaneous schedules:* general tightening up of anti-avoidance rules, particularly those concerning groups of companies and capital gains tax.

July 1969   Finance Act, *Section 18 et seq:* disallowance of interest as a deduction for income tax and surtax (except in certain certain specially defined circumstances) checked the borrowing of money to pay life assurance premiums and school fees. *Section 30:* further restrictions imposed on relief for trading losses where there was a change of ownership in in a loss-making company. *Section 31:* restrictions placed on the sale by individuals of income derived from their personal activities for a capital sum. *Section 32:* comprehensive changes introduced relating to avoidance schemes involving land and land-owning companies. New rules give the Inland Revenue wide discretion to counter such schemes. *Section 36 et seq:* comprehensive changes in estate duty charging rules introduced including the imposition of a charge on the death of a beneficiary under a discretionary trust. *Section 39:* tightening up of estate duty rules on the use of works of art to avoid duty. *Miscellaneous schedules:* further tightening up of general capital gains tax and corporation tax anti-avoidance rules.

12. tax allowances and fiscal policy

A. J. Walsh

The purpose of this chapter is to assess the impact of changes in personal income tax allowances under the Labour Government 1964-70 and to indicate to what extent a future Labour administration could reduce the inequality in the distribution of income by use of such allowances. In the early part of the chapter we look at changes made in these allowances in the period 1964-70. Although we are primarily concerned with personal allowance changes it will be necessary to refer to changes in personal deductions and personal reliefs from time to time. Some of the major features of the personal income tax systems in the EEC countries are noted. The second part of the chapter is devoted to analysing the distribution of income in general and the effect of recent tax allowance changes on this distribution. From this general description we look at the effect of changes implemented by Labour on two representative groups—the agricultural worker and the manufacturing worker. The chapter concludes with suggestions for the future.

The United Kingdom personal income tax system works basically in the following way. The gross incomes of husband and wife and the investment income of unmarried minor children are aggregated. From the gross income which is treated as income for tax purposes various personal deductions are subtracted in order to arrive at net income. From net income the taxpayer deducts the personal allowances and reliefs to which he is entitled. The difference between allowances and reliefs is that allowances are of a fixed amount whereas reliefs are calculated as a proportion of income (usually subject to certain maximum amounts). The income which remains after these adjustments have been made, termed taxable income, is directly subject to the appropriate rates of income tax, and, where applicable, surtax.

The personal deductions which are charges against gross income serve two basic functions: firstly, they allow the taxpayer to subtract from his gross income expenses and losses incurred in the pursuit of this income and the granting of such deductions by the authorities is thus motivated by the desire to maintain equity between taxpayers; secondly, they allow the authorities to encourage expenditure by the taxpayer in ways which they consider economically or socially desirable, for example, the encouragement of home ownership and saving for retirement. This latter type of deduction is incentive motivated, and from the point of view of the taxpayer part of the cost of the expenditure which is encouraged is paid by the general body of taxpayers. If this type of deduction is to achieve its desired objective the expenditure which is encouraged must be responsive to changes in its price (see C. Harry Kahn, *Personal deductions in the federal income tax*, National Bureau of Economic Research, 1960).

The functions of the various personal allowances according to Seltzer are fourfold: first they exclude from tax the recipients of small incomes; secondly they provide a deduction from otherwise taxable income for the essential living costs of all taxpayers, and consequently, reduce effective rates of tax below the nominal rates at all income levels; thirdly they provide additional allowances for taxpayers with dependents and for the aged and the blind and thus recognise that capacity to pay tax is not solely a function of the size of income and finally they serve as a major instrument in the graduation of the tax rates, indeed, as far as income tax is concerned, they serve as the only instrument of graduation at present (L. H Seltzer, *The personal exemptions in the income tax*, p6, National Bureau of Economic Research, 1968). The terms "allowance" and "exemption" are synonymous.

The personal reliefs granted in the United Kingdom are the earned income relief, wife's earned income relief, small investment income relief, age relief and life assurance relief. The most important of these reliefs is earned income relief, the rationale for which has been extensively traced elsewhere (F. Shehab, *Progressive taxation*, Clarendon Press, Oxford, 1953; *Royal Commission on the income tax*, appendix 7 (b) pp54-56, HMSO, Cmd 615, 1920 and the *Royal Commission on the taxation of profits and income*, 2nd Report, pp 66-69, HMSO, Cmd 9105, 1954).

Suffice it to say that the earned income relief fraction allows the taxpayer to deduct from his pre-tax income extra monetary costs associated with earned income relative to investment income. The wife's earned income relief is based on this same principle—in this case the deduction purports to represent the extra expenditure incurred as a result of the wife working.

For individuals who are old with small or medium sized investment incomes and for the non-aged dependent upon small investment incomes this principle of differentiating between earned and investment incomes is suspended. For these groups of individuals it is felt that the size of the income is more important than its source. The relief for life assurance premiums is an example of the authorities encouraging taxpayer expenditure in ways which they consider economically and socially desirable.

Some measure of the magnitude of personal deductions can be gauged from the fact that for the tax year 1967-68 personal deductions for single and married persons reduced the tax base by £1,118 million (*Inland Revenue statistics*, 1970, table 61). The personal allowances and reliefs reduced the tax base by £14,385 million in 1965-66, the latest year for which figures are available (*Inland Revenue report*, 1967, table 32). By far the most important allowances and reliefs are the earned income relief which removed £4,750 million from the total amount of income subject to tax rates, and the single, marriage and child allowance which together with the wife's earned income relief removed a further £8,870 million in 1965-66.

The amount of income which is not directly subject to tax because of the various tax concessions depends of course upon the type of concessions used. In the United Kingdom we make use mainly of two types of allowance—the continuing exemption and the vanishing exemption. The continuing exemption excludes from tax those with incomes equal to or less than the amount of the exemption and deducts the same amount from otherwise taxable income of all larger incomes. With progressive tax rates use of this type of exemption means that the absolute amount of tax relief increases with income. Increases in the continuing exemption are costly in terms of revenue loss because they reduce the taxable capacity of all taxpayers. Very little of the revenue loss can be attributed to those with the lowest income—in 1965-66 the amount of income which came within the purview of the Inland Revenue authorities but which was kept out of the tax net because its recipients had incomes below the effective exemption limit was only £320 million. The effective exemption limit is roughly the single personal allowance grossed up by the earned income relief fraction.

The vanishing exemption excludes from tax liability net incomes which do not exceed the amount of the exemption and reduces in value as net income increases until it eventually disappears. This type of exemption, which is used, for example, in the case of the age exemption is consistent with the view that exemptions are only needed in full at the bottom of the income scale and that as income rises the amount of the exemption should be reduced and finally disappear. Because it is restricted to the lower income groups it permits a given amount of revenue to be raised with lower formal rates of tax than the continuing exemption. It avoids an abrupt separation of taxable and non-taxable income, but as used in the United Kingdom it leads to the imposition of relatively high marginal rates of tax upon income which is just in excess of the exemption limit.

We turn now to changes implemented by Labour in the period 1964-70—a period during which the overriding aim of government policy was to secure a healthy balance of payments surplus. In order to achieve this aim domestic consumption was continually restrained by massive increases in customs and excise duties, SET, and purchase tax. We became accustomed to budget speeches which claimed that "the vital thing this year and next is to put the balance of payments into substantial surplus" (*Hansard*, vol 761, col 261) and that "the main purpose of the Budget is to restrain current consumption" (*op cit*, col 1034). In the budget immediately prior to devaluation we were mis-guidedly told "We are back on course. The ship is picking up speed. The economy is moving" (*Hansard*, vol 744, col 1010). In no budget during this period was the aim of government policy a reduction in the degree of inequality in income distribution.

The first point to note is that had Labour introduced no changes in the personal income tax system the amount of revenue raised would have increased. This "buoyancy of the revenue," as it is euphemistically termed, arises from the fact that in a period of rising money incomes with a progressive tax structure money income is moving into brackets subject to higher tax rates. Over the period 1964-70 many of the allowances and reliefs were unchanged, these included: the earned income relief fraction and the maximum amount of earned income relief; the small investment income relief fraction; the child allowance and the limit of income which a child can receive before the child allowance is reduced £1 for £1; the housekeeper allowance; the dependent relative allowance in certain cases; the daughters services allowance, and the blind persons allowance. As a result of inflation the real value of these allowances in 1969-70 was only 81 per cent of their value in 1964-65.

Whilst the beneficiaries of these allowances were unprotected from the impact of inflation other groups were protected. Some of the old benefited directly from increases in the age exemption limits which together with the dependent relative's income limit were adjusted upwards as it became necessary to increase the amount of the flat-rate state retirement pension as money incomes in general rose. The better off amongst the old benefited from the increase in the age relief income limit implemented in 1969. Other individuals and married couples with low incomes benefited from the increases in the single personal allowance and marriage allowance. The effect of changes in these concessions upon the number of taxpayers is outlined in the table below.

NUMBER OF TAXPAYERS 1964-65 TO 1967-68 IN THOUSANDS				
	1964–65	1965–66	1966–67	1967–68
incomes above effective exemption limit*	21188	21684	21782	21800
entirely relieved from tax by allowances	2696	2356	2092	1790
chargeable with tax	18492	19328	19690	20010

*husband and wife count as one; the figures do not cover individuals with incomes below the effective exemption limit.
source: Inland Revenue annual reports.

The number of individuals chargeable with tax increases over the period 1964-65 to 1967-68 because the adjustments to the major personal allowances were only made in 1969-70. Since money incomes were rising throughout the period 1964-65 to 1967-68 and personal allowances failed to keep pace, more and more individuals were brought into the tax net.

changes made in personal income tax systems

The most important changes in the personal income tax system, in terms of their impact on revenue, started with the mini-budget announced in November 1964 when a 2.5 percentage point increase in the standard rate of tax was provided for: it was estimated that this would yield an additional £122 million for 1965-66 and that only 6.5 million out of 21 million individuals with incomes above the effective exemption limit would be adversely affected by the change (see Annual Financial statements).

In 1965 the allowance for national insurance contributions was abolished because of its regressive character. As Mr Callaghan stated "the contributor who is not liable to income tax bears the full amount of his contributions while the better off have the impact reduced by tax reliefs, including surtax relief" (*Hansard*, vol 710, col 293). The abolition of this allowance was coupled with an increase in the single personal allowance, marriage allowance and wife's earned income relief. It was felt that since the single individual, married man and the working wife all lost the same amount with the abolition of the allowance for national insurance contributions they should all be compensated with the same absolute increase of £20 in their personal allowances. The wife's earned income relief income limit was increased by £20 in line with the increases in the single personal allowance and marriage allowance. The yield from withdrawing the allowance for national insurance contributions was estimated at £140 million and the cost of the increase in personal allowances was put at £141 million on a full year basis. In effect the national insurance allowance and personal allowance changes were self-balancing. As a result of these changes married women and widows in employment and the retired were net beneficiaries and the surtax payers net losers.

In the same year tightening up on business entertaining expenditure and capital gains helped to reduce inequities in the tax system, and to the extent that this type of expenditure and capital gains are mainly of benefit to upper income groups inequality in the after tax distribution of income should have been reduced.

We have to wait until 1968 for the introduction of further significant changes. The 1966 Finance Act brought changes in some minor allowances and the 1967 Act brought a 10 per cent surcharge on surtax for 1965-66, payable on 1 September 1967. With increases in family allowance payments following the publication of *Circumstances of families* (HMSO, 1967) it was decided in 1968 to adjust the taxpayers personal allowances in order to reclaim in tax all or part of the additional benefit payment. Use of the "clawback" "would do the job for the standard rate payers with an almost tailor made precision" (*Hansard*, vol 761, col 293-4). This "clawback effect" brought in an estimated £83 million in a full year. This extra revenue was recouped from individuals paying tax before the clawback was introduced, and from those brought into the tax net because of the combined effect of the reduction in the amount of their personal allowances and the increase in their net income resulting from the higher benefit payment.

1968 also saw another significant change, in principle if not in terms of revenue, with the introduction of aggregation of the investment income of unmarried minors with the income of their parents. This change, which was expected to bring in £25 million in a full year, eliminated the inequity which had previously existed whereby two families, in otherwise identical circumstances, paid differing amounts of tax simply because in one case the child possessed property transferred to it by a grandparent, while in the other case the grandparent's identical property was inherited by the parent. As was pointed out in the *Royal Commission on the taxation of profits and income* "parents and children forming part of a single family normally share the same standard of living, and non-aggregation of children's income with their parents' involves the privileged tax treatment of those particular families whose children happen to be possessed of property given to them by someone else than their parents" (reservations to second report, *op cit*, paras 23-28). In addition, provisions covering life assurance relief were tightened in 1968 and a special charge on investment income was temporarily imposed on investment incomes in excess of £3,000. This special charge was expected to raise £100 million in a full year.

The tax years 1969-70 and 1970-71 were characterised by increases in the single personal allowance, the marriage allowance and the wife's earned income relief accompanied by offsetting adjustments in the reduced rates of tax. As we have seen, the number of taxpayers was increased each year over the period 1964-65 to 1967-68. Further, the amount of revenue realised from many of these taxpayers was very small in relation to the administrative costs involved in obtaining the revenue. The Government therefore decided to remove many of these taxpayers from the tax field by increasing the major personal allowances. However, because these personal allowances rank as continuing exemptions for income tax purposes, the cost in terms of revenue loss from such increases is great. In order to reduce the cost it was therefore decided to reduce the benefits derived from the reduced rates of tax. The net cost of the increase in allowances accompanied by adjustments to the reduced rates of tax was estimated at £14 million in 1969. The 1970 changes led to a decrease in revenue of £175 million. The changes in 1969 concentrated all the benefits on the low income groups, the changes in 1970 again helped these groups and also slightly redistributed the tax burden away from the married. By increasing the allowances Mr. Jenkins reduced the number of actual current tax years by an estimated 1.1 million in 1969-70 and by 2 million in 1970-71; the number of potentital future taxpayers was also reduced. Further, since those subject to the reduced rates of tax only also benefited from the changes, the proportion of tax revenues collected from the lower income groups would be reduced. The changes implemented in 1969-70 and 1970-71 should consequently have led to some reduction in the inequality of income distribution after income tax and surtax.

The 1969 Finance Act also abolished the principle that interest payments in general qualified for tax relief. This measure, which was expected to raise an additional £25 million in revenue, was introduced to discourage consumption in a budget which aimed at promoting increased saving. As the Chancellor said "Because of tax relief on loan interest, it pays anyone with a substantial taxable income to borrow as much as he can from his bank or from some other financial source . . . Moreover (the relief from income tax at the standard rate and surtax) is unfairly discriminating and regressive in its effect. Hire purchase does not attract tax relief, but bank overdrafts and credit sales do." (*Hansard*, vol. 781, cols 39-40.) The 1969 Finance Act also introduced increases in some of the minor allowances, notably the additional personal allowance, the age exemption and age relief and the dependent relative income limit. Further adjustments in these concessions were made in 1970 except in the age relief.

The provisions of the 1970 Finance Act removed from the tax net, as we have seen, over 2 million people who would otherwise have been paying small amounts of tax. However, to reduce the cost of increasing personal allowances the single remaining reduced rate band was abolished. In consequence, all taxpayers became subject to at least a 32 per cent marginal tax rate on their earned income. This 32 per cent represented the standard rate of 41.25 per cent adjusted for the two-ninths earned income relief. All taxpayers with investment income apart from some of the aged and those with small investment incomes became subject at the margin to a minimum tax rate of 41.25 per cent.

Mr. Jenkins was unwilling to reduce the standard rate of tax rather than increase the personal allowances because such a move "would take no one out of tax, and it would give no benefit to those not already paying at the standard rate. On the other hand, it would, of course, give very great benefits to those with large increases. It is," he declared "the most dramatic but also the most regressive of all income tax changes" (*Hansard,* vol 799, col 1249).

effect of changes

In the table below, we trace the estimated changes in the cost of the major personal allowances, reliefs and deductions. In the case of all three tax concessions the amount of revenue sacrificed varies with the number of people for whom concessions can be claimed, and the tax rate structure. In the case of allowances and reliefs the cost also varies with the amounts of the allowances and the fraction and income limit for reliefs. The cost will also tend to rise in the case of all three types of concessions in a period of rising money incomes because the amount of tax relief for many of the allowances and all the deductions and reliefs increases with money income up to the stated limits. The cost of personal deductions is also determined by other factors, for example, the cost of the mortgage interest deduction varies with the rate of interest charged by building societies and local authorities on their loans to the public.

COST OF TAX CONCESSIONS IN TERMS OF REVENUE FOREGONE: £ MILLION*

	1964–65	1965–66	1966–67	1967–68	1968–69
marriage allowance	1,280.0	1,480.0	1,520.0	1,550.0	1,600.0
single personal allowance	550.0	650.0	675.0	685.0	700.0
child allowance	440.0	500.0	580.0	630.0	675.0
wife's earned income relief	208.0	232.0	238.0	250.0	270.0
age relief	7.0	5.0	4.0	4.5	5.5
age exemption	10.0	13.0	13.0	13.0	14.0
housekeeper allowance	5.0	5.0	6.0	4.0	4.0
blind person's allowance	0.5	0.5	0.7	0.7	0.7
additional personal allowance	1.2	1.7	2.0	4.0	4.0
superannuation and retirement annuity relief	75.0	79.0	83.0	90.0	100.0
life assurance relief	66.0	68.0	70.0	75.0	84.0
mortgage interest deduction†	110.0	135.0	157.0	180.0	190.0

* the estimated figures refer to the cost measured for each year and are not those in the year. The estimates do not cover people with incomes below the effective exemption limit. Each cost is calculated on the *ceteris paribus* assumption, and therefore the amount involved by two or more concessions, could be more than the sum of the separate costs shown. The system allows for tax relief on covenants in favour of individuals; and the first £15 of interest in ordinary accounts with the National Savings Bank and the Trustee Savings Banks is exempt from tax. The value of these concessions is of the order of £20 million a year each.

† the cost, in terms of revenue foregone, of the mortgage interest deduction is estimated at £300 million for 1970-71 (*Hansard,* 27 November 1970, col 243).

sources: *Hansard,* vol 743, cols 208-212, vol 787, cols 129-130.

Because there are so many factors at work it is impossible to draw definite conclusions from this table. Further, we do not know what was the additional cost in terms of revenue loss for incomes below the effective exemption limit. The increase in the cost of those concessions whose money value remained unchanged over the period 1964-65 to 1967-68 can be explained to a great extent by the effects of rising money incomes, changes in the number of claimants, a decrease in the real value of the amount of the concession, and the 2.5 percentage point increase in the standard rate of tax. Taking the child allowance as an example, the number of claimants of this allowance increased from 7.3 million in 1967-68 to 7.8 million in 1968-69. Despite the reduction in the amount of the allowances resulting from the "clawback" the cost of the allowance increased from £630 million in 1967-68 to £675 million in 1968-69.

The increasing cost of the wife's earned income relief and the marriage allowance results in the main from increases in the number of claimants combined with increases in the income limit for the relief, and the amount of the allowance. The dramatic rise in the cost of the mortgage interest deduction, from £27 yearly per owner-occupier in 1964-65 to £47 in 1969-70, is to be explained largely by increases in the amount of advances made available to the public, and by increases in the rate of interest charged by building societies, other financial institutions and local authorities on their loans to public (*Hansard,* 18 December 1970, col 525). The growth of the private pensions sector over the period is demonstrated by the increasing cost of superannuation deductions, retirement annuity relief, and life assurance relief.

Taking the period 1964-65 to 1969-70 as a whole we can discern the following trends. There was a shift in the tax burden away from the single person and the dual earned income couple towards those taxpayers with families. This shift resulted from the influence of three factors—the introduction of the clawback; the money value of the child allowance remained constant; and the single personal allowance increased as proportion of the marriage allowance from 62.5 per cent in 1964-65 to 68 per cent in 1969-70. (No allowance is made for the fact that when the allowance for National Insurance contributions was abolished in 1965 it was felt that both the single man and married man should be compensated by the same absolute increase in their personal allowances).

The single allowance, marriage allowance and wife's earned income relief were adjusted upwards at the latter end of the period in order to remove from the tax net taxpayers with low incomes who paid little in income tax. The benefit of these allowance changes was confined, in the main, to the lower income groups by offsetting adjustments in the reduced rates of tax.

Many of the minor allowances were not adjusted to take account of price increases and increases in money incomes in general. The low-income aged, however, were singled out for special treatment—the age exemption and dependent relative's income limits were increased with increases in the size of the state retirement pension. Some of the better off amongst the aged with investment income benefited from the increases in the age relief limits. The increased sacrifice of revenue on account of the mortgage interest deduction, the superannuation deduction, retirement annuity relief, and the life assurance relief will have mainly been of benefit to the upper income groups. This situation arises from the fact that poor are unlikely to be in a position to obtain a mortgage, to be working in superannuated jobs, or to be able to put much aside to take out life assurance policies. Further, for any given amount of deduction the gain to the taxpayer rises with the taxpayer's income owing to the progressive rate schedule of the income tax.

Having studied changes in tax concessions under the Labour administration it is now time to stop and ask ourselves the question: "To what extent can tax concessions help reduce the degree of inequality in the distribution of income?" As regards the poorest citizens, the answer is very little, simply because no form of concession can ensure that every citizen has a minimum income. If our objective is to help the poor it can only be achieved through increased government transfer payments and payments in kind. It cannot be stressed too strongly that "the income tax system as such cannot be used to help people without income—those who most need help." (*Report of the Canadian Royal Commission on taxation,* vol 3, p21). At the same time it must be recognised that it is desirable to exclude from tax the recipients of small incomes and this is a basic function of our present single personal allowance and marriage allowance. Our personal allowances also serve the functions of adjusting the degree of progression of the tax rates to the personal circumstances of the individual taxpayer and of providing a brisk progression of the tax rates.

exemption methods used in the EEC

At this point, it seems relevant to examine some of the exemption methods and techniques used to adjust the tax burden to the personal circumstances of the taxpayer in other countries. As Britain is expecting to enter the EEC we shall confine our observations to the countries which form this customs union. It should be borne in mind that if Labour is returned to power in the next decade membership or non-membership of the EEC would impose few constraints upon the measures which could be implemented in the UK. Harmonisation of the personal income tax systems of member countries is very low on the list of EEC priorities.

We shall concern ourselves with looking at the size of the tax unit, the methods of differentiating between the units of different size but with equal net incomes, and the treatment of certain personal deductions in the countries making up the EEC. In making international comparisons it would be futile to talk about tax concessions before discussing the size of the tax unit. A correct definition of the tax unit is important because once the size of the unit is decided upon, be it the individual, the married couple, the family or the household, legal division of net income within the unit will not affect total tax liability of the unit.

In the UK we aggregate the incomes of husband and wife and the investment incomes of minors. Thus, we use a marital tax unit for earned income and a family unit for investment income. Support for the marital unit (and the family unit) is founded upon the case that most couples (families) act as a common income and expenditure unit so that the economic well being of each member of the unit is a function of joint rather than independently received income. If this argument is accepted it follows that the ability of the tax unit to pay tax depends upon the aggregated income. All the EEC countries accept the argument that aggregation, at least in the case of husband and wife, is consonant with economic reality in most instances (D. Y. Thorson, "An analysis of the sources of continued controversy over the tax treatment of family income," *National tax journal*, June 1965, G. P. Marshall and A. J. Walsh "Marital status and variations in income tax burdens," *British tax review*, no 4, 1970, pp236-249).

Holland, Luxembourg and Belgium use the same tax units as we do—marital units in the case of earned income and family units in the case of investment income. Germany uses the marital unit only, Italy relies upon the family unit as does France in most instances.

However, the methods employed to differentiate between tax units of different size with equal net incomes differ greatly between the EEC members and the United Kingdom. Such differentiation can be achieved by means of exemptions (personal allowances), income splitting or the use of separate tax rate schedules. There exist very broadly three approaches to this differentiation problem: the "unit" approach under which a single individual and a married couple pay taxes at the same marginal rate if their taxable incomes are equal; the "per-capita" approach under which the marginal rates of tax are equalized if per capita taxable incomes are equal; and a "combined" approach falling between these two polar approaches.

Under the unit approach differentiation between units of different size is achieved by means of exemptions, and the supporters of this approach have naturally tended to concentrate upon the magnitude and type of exemptions to be employed. The unit approach has been basically followed in the UK and Italy. Both countries accept the view that a married couple or a family with minor children should receive larger personal allowances than a single person but they have been unwilling to differentiate between different sized tax units by differential marginal rates of tax. The supporters of this approach have been faced with two difficulties, firstly at what level to fix the personal allowances in view of the fact that any standard of minimum necessity is relative to the customs of the particular income group involved, and secondly how to defend the view that incremental income received in excess of the exemption level has equal taxable capacity independent of family status. In terms of relative cost experience at different levels of income the unit approach treats harshly the married couple and the family *vis-a-vis* the unattached individual.

The per-capita approach has the opposite effect, it treats harshly the single individual, *vis-a-vis* the couple and the family. The incomes of husband and wife are aggregated and the total is divided by two. Each half of the total is then taxed as if it were the income of a single individual. If accompanied by per-capita exemptions this approach leads to the situation that a married couple with the same net income as that of a single individual pay twice the tax of the individual on one half his income. With a progressive tax rate structure such treatment of the married couple is very beneficial especially for those with high incomes. Income splitting results in a reduction in tax burdens of high income taxpayers relative to those at the lower end of the scale.

This approach is faced with the difficulty of reconciling two opposing considerations, namely, that incremental income in excess of the exemption level has a taxable capacity which varies directly with the size of the tax unit on a per-capita basis—it admits of no economies of joint-living—and that in the upper income ranges a steadily declining percentage of income is required to maintain an adequate standard of living as the margin of wants satisfaction moves from the physiological to the sociological and psychological.

France uses a "family-part" system which is a modification of the per-capita system. The incomes of the family are aggregated and then divided by the number of people in the family; husband and wife count as one person each, each child counts as one half. For a family consisting of husband, wife and two children aggregated family income would be divided by three and each one third of family income would be taxed as if it were the income of a single individual. No personal allowances are granted but the French system uses an exemption limit which relieves from payment of any income tax a married man with two children with an income equivalent to £1,160.

The Germans use a per-capita system for marital income and provide personal allowances for children. An effective exemption limit is provided for both single individuals and married couples. As we have seen the benefits of such a per-capita system as compared with our system are greater the larger the income of the couple, and the more unequal the amount of marital income received by each spouse.

Luxembourg and Holland use a "combined" approach, they use separate rate schedules, one for the single person, one for the married couple, and one for the married couple with children; in addition allowances are provided for children. In Holland three rate schedules are provided up to an income equivalent to £7,000 per annum. They then revert two schedules—the schedule for the married man with children disappears—and personal allowances and tax rebates are granted for children.

Most of the EEC countries place greater emphasis on per-capita family income than we do. If it is accepted that individual welfare is an important social goal, society must be interested in per-capita family income as well as total family income. This would suggest that we in the UK should differentiate more between tax units of equal net incomes but different size at least in the low and middle income ranges. Such differentiation could be achieved by separate rate schedules, or by a combination of differential exemptions and differential marginal rates (via bracket widths or splitting). In the upper income ranges differentiation in the marginal rate progression for tax units of different size could eventually disappear on the grounds that the power of the tax unit to command goods and services for personal use is a function of the aggregate income of the tax unit at high levels of income.

The treatment of expenses, at least for the employed, is much more lenient in the EEC countries than in the UK. However, Italy, Germany, Luxembourg and Holland do not differentiate between earned and investment income. The French provide an earned income relief of 20 per cent of earned employment income which is subject to no limit on the maximum amount of relief claimable; in Belgium an allowance equivalent to £84 can be deducted from earned income.

The Dutch allow all taxpayers to deduct a minimum expense allowance whether any expenses have been incurred by the taxpayer or not. If the taxpayer is prepared to provide proof that he incurred further expenses in obtaining his income he can deduct these expenses, including the costs of travelling to and from his place of work, from his gross income without limit. Germany also provides a standard deduction for employment income without any proof that this amount of expenses have been incurred. The French allow a 10 per cent expenses allowance for earned income without restrictions on the maximum amount claimable. This allowance is granted in addition to the earned employment income relief.

Unlike the UK all the EEC countries treat the major social security contributions as expenses which are deductible from gross income. As in the UK life assurance relief is claimable although the rules governing this relief vary from country to country. Deductions for contributions to superannuation funds are allowed in all these countries with upper limits which in some cases are on the generous side. The deduction for mortgage interest payments is allowed in the EEC countries subject to different rules in different countries.

trends in income distribution

We turn in this section of the chapter to look at trends in the distribution of income over the years 1964-69. Before doing so, however, it is necessary to state why we are interested in this distribution.

Income is important in a market system because the weight given to individual preferences in the market depends upon income. An individual must possess the means to purchase goods and services if his demand is to be effective. The income distribution, because it is a measure of the allocation of potential purchasing power, measures the weight given to individual preferences in making economic decisions. The distribution of income is consequently one of the most important allocative decisions. It should be noted that there is nothing in the market system, which generates incomes in the process of producing and distributing goods and services, that automatically achieves the desired income distribution. Consequently, there arises the need for government intervention via taxation, transfer payments and payments in kind, to alter the distribution of income determined by market forces to that desired by society.

The income figures which have been used to obtain the trends in the distribution of income are the figures of personal income as set out and tabulated in the national income and expenditure accounts for the UK. The problems associated with use of these figures are well known (H. F. Lydall, "The long-term trend in the size distribution of income," *Journal of the Royal Statistical Society*, series A, 122, part 1, 1959; R. Titmuss, *Income distribution and social change*, Allen and Unwin, 1962; R. J. Nicholson, "The distribution of personal income, *Lloyds Bank review*, January 1967; F. W. Paish, "The real incidence of personal taxation," *Lloyds Bank review*, January 1957). Firstly, they are based on data collected by the Inland Revenue who treat the incomes of husband and wife as one income whilst other incomes are treated separately. Consequently, the distribution of personal income could be affected by changes in the number of married people in the population, changes in the age of marriage and changes in the number of married women who work. Secondly, tax avoidance incomes and some claims on wealth, such as undistributed profits, are excluded from the definition of personal income. Finally, not all of personal income as defined in the national income accounts can be allocated by income range. In 1967 the amount of personal income which could be allocated by income range was only 84 per cent of total personal income. The 16 per cent which was not allocatable comprised of:

1.   Investment income of, for example, charities, life assurance companies and superannuation funds.

2.   Some income in kind and the imputed rent of owner occupied dwellings.

3.   Some non-taxable grants from public authorities like school meals and welfare milk.

4.   Accrued interest on national savings certificates; dividends of co-operatives; post-war credits.

5.   Depreciation allowances in respect of self-employed persons.

6.   Employees' and most of employers' contribution to national insurance and superannuation schemes.

7.   Mortgage interest, bank interest and other loan interest allowable as a charge against income.

8.   Incomes of less than £50 per annum.

Because these items cannot be allocated by income range if we concentrate wholly on allocated income we may draw incorrect conclusions about the trend in the distribution as a whole. In consequence, we also examine the figures of personal income analysed by form of income. Indeed, for the period 1967-69 we have to rely solely upon these figures because the figures on distribution of personal income by income range were discontinued after 1967.

The method we employ for determining the trends in the distribution is the percentile method which Lydall used in his study. As Lydall points out this method of percentiles is a convenient way of comparing changes in the level of persons at equivalent positions in the income distribution over time but we are unable to study the fluctuations in the fortunes of individuals (*op cit*).

The table below shows that there has been no significant change in the pre-tax distribution of allocatable personal income since 1957. In the period 1964-67 the amount of pre-tax income accounted for by the top 10 per cent of income recipients fell slightly from 29 per cent to 28 per cent, the middle 11 to 70 per cent slightly increased their share as did the bottom 30 per cent.

PERCENTAGE DISTRIBUTION OF INCOMES BEFORE INCOME TAX AND SURTAX*

group of income recipients	1957	1960	1961	1963	1964	1967
top 1%	8.2	8.5	8.1	7.9	8.1	7.4
2%–5%	10.9	11.4	11.1	11.2	11.4	11.0
6%–10%	9.0	9.8	9.7	9.6	9.5	9.6
11%–40%	37.6	38.5	37.6	39.0	39.1	38.9
41%–70%	23.1	22.1	23.5	22.6	22.3	22.8
bottom 30%	11.3	9.8	10.0	9.7	9.6	10.3

* the numerical results given in the table and the subsequent three tables have been obtained by double-log proportionate interpolation into the published distributions. The figures prior to 1964 are taken from Nicholson's article. Nicholson's figures are based on *National income and expenditure* 1965. The figures for 1964 and 1967 are based on *National income and expenditure* 1969.

The after tax position exhibits the following trends for the period 1964-67; the share of allocatable personal income going to the top 10 per cent fell slightly, this was in part the result of the special surtax surcharge. The share of the middle 11 to 70 per cent fell very slightly, and the bottom 30 per cent received a slightly increased share of personal income after income tax and surtax. As can be seen from the next table tax changes over the period 1957-67 led to a slight improvement in the relative positions of the middle and

PERCENTAGE DISTRIBUTION OF INCOMES AFTER INCOME TAX AND SURTAX

group of income recipients	1957	1960	1961	1963	1964	1967
top 1%	5.0	5.1	5.5	5.2	5.4	4.9
2%–5%	9.9	10.5	10.5	10.5	10.3	10.1
6%–10%	9.1	9.4	9.1	9.5	9.4	9.4
11%–40%	38.5	39.8	38.9	39.5	40.3	39.6
41%–70%	24.0	23.5	24.3	23.5	23.8	24.3
bottom 30%	13.4	11.7	11.9	11.8	10.8	11.7

upper income groups. However, taking the period 1964-67 in isolation, tax changes effected a slight improvement in the relative position of the bottom 30 per cent of income recipients.

The distribution of income tax and surtax raised from the specified groups of income recipients as presented in the following table shows that there was a shift in the distribution of the tax burden away from the top 10 per cent of income recipients. The proportion of income tax and surtax raised from the top 10 per cent fell from 58 per cent in 1964 to 50.1 per cent in 1967, that raised from the middle groups rose from 41.5 to 48.3 per cent, while the proportion accounted for by the bottom 30 per cent increased from 0.5 to 1.6.

PERCENTAGES OF TOTAL INCOME TAX AND SURTAX RAISED FROM SPECIFIED GROUPS OF INCOME RECIPIENTS

group of income recipients	1957	1960	1961	1963	1964	1967
top 1%	35.3	34.4	30.0	28.0	28.6	23.4
2%—5%	18.9	19.7	19.9	19.3	18.6	16.1
6%–10%	9.0	10.0	10.0	11.0	10.8	10.6
11%–40%	24.9	25.4	27.6	29.8	29.7	24.5
41%–70%	11.2	9.7	11.4	11.3	11.8	13.8
bottom 30%	0.7	0.8	1.0	0.6	0.5	1.6

This shift in the burden of income tax and surtax results in the main from a combination of changes in the system of personal income tax—changes in tax rates, personal allowances, reliefs and deductions—and from the lack of changes in the personal income tax system to take account of the fact that in a period of rising money incomes such incomes are moving into tax brackets which are subject to higher marginal rates of tax. As we have seen, the redistribution of pre-tax income away from the highest income groups has been very little and is likely to have had a negligible effect on the distribution of the tax burden.

The numerical results presented in the next table indicate that the percentage increase in the proportion of pre-tax income taken in the form of income tax and surtax for the specified income groups was a decreasing function of the size of income over the period 1964-67.

PERCENTAGES OF BEFORE-TAX INCOME OF SPECIFIED GROUPS OF INCOME RECIPIENTS TAKEN IN INCOME TAX AND SURTAX

group of income recipients	1957	1960	1961	1963	1964	1967
top 1%	45.5	46.1	41.5	39.1	41.3	43.0
2%–5%	18.4	19.7	20.0	19.0	19.1	19.9
6%–10%	10.7	11.6	11.5	12.5	13.1	15.0
11%–40%	7.1	7.5	8.2	8.4	8.9	12.1
41%–70%	5.2	5.1	5.4	5.5	6.2	8.2
bottom 30%	0.7	0.9	1.1	0.6	0.6	2.2
all incomes	10.6	11.4	11.2	11.0	11.6	13.6

Our results so far would indicate that there was no significant reduction in the degree of inequality of income distribution in the period 1964-67. In order to extend our analysis to 1969 and throw more light on the analysis of trends in personal income distribution for the period 1964-67 we now turn to an examination of changes in the make-up of personal income.

It can be seen from the next table that over the period 1964-67 total employment income and total income from self-employment have been growing at the same rate, and that rents, dividends and net interest have also been keeping pace. Paish and Lydall found that for the period 1949-57 there was a movement towards a more equal distribution of income with employment income growing faster than other forms of personal income. Nicholson found that this movement towards greater equality was halted during the period 1957-63 with the rate of growth of total employment income slowing down relative to the other main forms of personal income. He also found the income of professional persons was increasing faster than wage income and a dramatic acceleration in the rate of growth of rent, dividends and net interest which was the fastest growing form of personal income in the period 1957-63.

PERCENTAGE MAKE-UP OF PERSONAL INCOME BEFORE INCOME TAX AND SURTAX

	avearge annual rates of growth*				percentage of total personal income		
	1964-67		1964-69		1964	1967	1969
	money terms	real terms	money terms	real terms	money terms	money terms	money terms
wages	4.5	0.8	5.2	1.0	39.0	36.6	36.1
salaries	7.8	4.1	8.2	3.8	25.2	25.9	26.6
total income from employment	6.2	2.5	6.7	2.4	71.2	70.2	70.5
professional persons†	7.1	3.4	5.6	1.4	1.5	1.5	1.4
farmers†	4.3	0.7	3.7	−0.4	2.0	1.9	1.8
other sole traders and partnership†	6.7	3.0	5.6	1.3	4.9	4.9	4.6
total income from self employment†	6.2	2.5	5.1	0.9	8.5	8.4	7.8
rent, dividends and net interest	6.0	2.4	5.7	1.6	12.1	11.8	11.5
transfers	12.2	8.3	11.7	7.2	8.3	9.6	10.3
total personal income†	6.7	3.0	6.8	2.6	100.0	100.0	100.0
personal disposable income‡	5.6	2.0	5.9	1.6	84.5	81.9	80.4

* end-point ratios.
† before providing for depreciation and stock appreciation.
‡ before providing for additions to tax reserves. The personal disposable income figures are, of course, after tax.
source: *National income and expenditure*, 1970, table 19. For the period 1949-63 see J. L. Nicholson, *Economic statistics and economic problems*, p301, McGraw-Hill, 1969.

For the period 1964-67 our figures reveal that, with the exception of the income of farmers, wages have experienced the slowest rate of growth of all the forms of personal income.

Taking the period 1964-69 and comparing it to Nicholson's analysis for the period 1957-63 we find that only rent, dividends and interest have a slower rate of growth in the more recent period. He pointed out that this slowing down might occur with the introduction of corporation tax which gave a strong inducement to companies to retain profits. To the extent that companies have increased their plough back ratios the rate of growth of rent, dividends and net interest will have been under-estimated because undistributed profits are not treated as personal income in the national income accounts. Without allowing for this possible underestimation in our results it is interesting to note that rent, dividends and net interest grew at a faster rate than wage income in the period 1964-69. The incomes of sole traders and partnerships, professional people and salary earners, also grew faster than wages over this five year period.

The effect of these differential rates of growth on percentage shares of personal income can also be obtained from the table above. Salary income has run counter to the general trend of other forms of personal income since 1964 in that such income accounts for an increased share of total personal income over the period 1964-69. The distinction between salaries and wages is arbitrary, the former refers to administrative, technical and clerical employees, the latter to all other classes of employees (*National income accounts: sources and methods*, p121, HMSO). The reason for the increased proportion of personal income being in the form of salary income is largely accounted for by the increased number of salary earners. In the next table we look at wages and salaries in manufacturing industry. It can be seen that the increased share of salaries and decreased share of wages can be explained by that fact that average salaries and wages have increased by the same percentage since 1964 but, whereas the number of wage earners in manufacturing has fallen slightly, the number of salary earners has increased.

WAGES AND SALARIES IN MANUFACTURING INDUSTRY

	1964	1967	1969	% change 1964-69
wage-earners 000s	6150	6040	6060	−1.5
salary-earners 000s	1920	2025	2070	+9.2
average wage £	718	837	986	+37.3
average salary £	1041	1240	1418	+36.2

source: *National income and expenditure*, 1970, table 18.

The analysis of trends in the distribution personal income by income range and by form of income suggests that there was no movement towards a more equal distribution in the period 1964-69. This is not to say that the Labour Government did not introduce changes in the tax system that should have promoted greater equality, but that the changes implemented by Labour were insufficient to counteract forces promoting greater inequality in income distribution. The redistributive effect of social insurance benefits and grants from public authorities, listed as "transfers" in a previous table is not shown by the comparisons of before tax and after tax tabulations of personal income as presented in *National income and expenditure*. Such transfers are already included in the definition of personal income.

Because of the difficulties of using the national income figures and because they do not allow us to study the redistribution of income within groups of income recipients we turn now to look at the effects of the policies implemented by the last Labour administration on two representative groups of workers—the adult male manual worker in manufacturing and certain other industries and the adult male agricultural worker. The adult male manual worker is taken as being representative of the "average man," and the agricultural worker as being representative of the low paid.

It can be seen from the table below that the percentage increase in money income for the manufacturing worker with less than two children was the same irrespective of family size. This result arises from the fact that the single man, the married man and the married man with one child receive the same income and no family allowance. For the tax year 1964-65 their annual income was £941, by 1969-70 it was £1,290. For the manufacturing workers with two or more children the percentage increase in money income before tax was slightly larger because they receive family allowance payments for the second and subsequent children. For the worker with four children average earnings plus family allowance payments amounted to £1,014 in 1964-65 and £1,440 in 1969-70.

When we look at the position after direct taxation we find the main beneficiaries from Labour's policies were the single man and the married man with four children. It should be remembered that redistribution of income is affected not only by the impact of direct taxation as dealt with in this chapter but also by indirect taxation and by social insurance benefits and grants from public authorities. The answer to why the single man did well relative to other married men and married men with families is to be found in the changes in

PERCENTAGE INCREASE IN THE MONEY INCOME: MONEY AFTER INCOME TAX AND MONEY INCOME AFTER DIRECT TAX IN CONSTANT PRICE TERMS OF THE ADULT MALE MANUAL WORKER IN MANUFACTURING AND CERTAIN OTHER INDUSTRIES 1964-65 TO 1969-70*

size of tax unit	money income	after direct tax	money income after direct tax in constant prices
single	37.0	30.1	5.6
married	37.0	28.7	4.4
married and one child	37.0	28.3	4.1
married and two children	38.9	27.2	3.3
married and three children	40.5	27.2	3.3
married and four children	42.1	30.6	6.0

* these figures are based on the October earnings figures for these workers as published by the Department of Employment and Productivity. The figures for the annual average earnings of adult male agricultural workers were obtained from the figures of average weekly earnings as published in the *Annual abstract of statistics* and by the Department of Employment and Productivity. In the case of both groups the figures were adjusted to take account of family allowance payments payable for the full year and the effects of the clawback. In order to obtain the money figures in constant price terms they were deflated by the all item January 1962 based index of retail prices. The figures assume that all income received is earned income and that the husband is the sole income recipient in the tax unit. The ages of the children are assumed to be: under 11 years of age for the first two children, over 11 but under 16 for the third child, and 16 or over for the fourth child. The figures for income after all direct taxation refer to money income before tax as adjusted for income tax payments, national insurance flat rate employee contributions and the graduated contributions.

the personal allowances. Child allowances remained constant prior to 1968-69 but with the introduction of clawback the amount of these allowances was subject to reduction in the case of families with two or more children. The effect of the clawback was to dramatically increase the tax liability of the average manufacturing worker who benefited from the increased family allowance payments. The married men did relatively worse than the single man because the single personal allowance, as a percentage of the marriage allowance, increased from 62.5 per cent in 1964-65 to 68 per cent in 1969-70. As a result, the money income after direct tax of the single man increased by 30.1 per cent whilst that of the married man increased by 28.7 per cent over the period 1964-69. The married man with one child did relatively worse than the single man because of the increase in the size of the single allowance relative to the marriage allowance and because the child allowance remained unchanged over the period. The relatively larger increase in the income of the married man with four children *vis-a-vis* other manufacturing workers with fewer children can be explained to a large extent by the fact that we have assumed that the age of the children, and hence the size of the child allowance, increases with family size.

We may note in passing that the increasing size of wage demands in recent years may be a reflection of the fact that trade unions realise that they have to secure larger and larger increases in money terms in a period of inflation and increasing taxation in order to obtain a marginal increase in the real disposable incomes of their members.

The fortunes of our representative low-paid worker—the adult male agricultural worker—are illustrated in the table below. The single worker, married worker, and the married worker with one child all increased their money income by the same amount, that is from £665 in 1964-65 to £913 in 1969-70. For those workers who benefited from family allowance payments the percentage increase in pre-tax money income increased with family size. The income of the married worker with four children rose from £738 in 1964-65 to £1,063 in 1969-70. The after tax position showed families with three and four children benefiting quite significantly from the increase in family allowance payments. The single individual again improved his position relative to the married couple and the couple with one child, and for the same reason as the single

PERCENTAGE INCREASE IN THE MONEY INCOME: MONEY INCOME AFTER INCOME TAX AND MONEY INCOME AFTER DIRECT TAX IN CONSTANT PRICE TERMS, OF THE ADULT MALE AGRICULTURAL WORKER 1964-65 to 1969-70*

size of tax unit	money income	after direct tax	money income after direct tax in constant prices
single	37.2	30.3	5.8
married	37.2	28.0	3.9
married and one child	37.2	28.1	4.0
married and two children	39.9	29.7	5.3
married and three children	42.1	35.0	9.6
married and four children	44.1	41.0	14.4

* see note to previous table.

manufacturing worker—the relatively greater increase in the size of his personal allowance.

As we would have expected the increase in family allowance payments together with the clawback has improved the relative position of the low paid worker with two or more children as compared with the childless couple and the couple with one child. The childless couple and the couple with one child also did relatively worse than the single person. On the basis of these results it would seem that a strong case can be made for the payment of family allowances to the one child family.

recommendations for the future

In the space available it is impossible to make specific recommendations concerning every tax concession at present in operation. However, an outline can be sketched of a more equitable system of personal income taxation. Such a tax system is not to be confused with an egalitarian tax regime. Whereas an equitable system of taxation requires equality of treatment between people who are similarly situated, an egalitarian tax system uses taxation as an instrument to promote greater economic or social equality within the community (see N. Kaldor, "The reform of personal taxation," in *Essays on economic policy*, vol 1, Duckworth, 1964). This sketch, which is based upon the work of Henry Simons (*Personal income tax*, Chicago University Press, 1965), received firm endorsements from the Carter Commission and from the signatories to the Memorandum of Dissent. (*Canadian Royal Commission on taxation*, op cit; *Royal Commission on the taxation of profits and income, Final Report, Memorandum of Dissent*, paras 2-3, HMSO, Cmd 9474, 1955).

The main recommendation is that we move towards as exhaustive a definition of income as is administratively practical. The tax laws, which define what is to be included in the tax return as income, should be framed in such a way as to be logically coherent and include as income anything which adds to the ability to command resources of individuals and families.

Starting from the basic premise that an income tax is a tax upon income and that the tax burden should be distributed in accordance with the taxable capacity of different members of the community " . . . it follows that equity between persons cannot be secured—however nicely the effective rate of tax is graduated according to an individual's total taxable income and however meticulously it is differentiated to allow for personal circumstances—unless the tax base itself (that is to say the definition of income for tax purposes) provides a measure which is uniform, comprehensive and capable of consistent application to all individuals.

Impartial assessment of the relative taxable capacity of individuals is impossible if the definition of taxable income is unduly restricted, ambiguous or biased in favour of particular groups of taxpayers.

A system of personal income taxation which operates without any clear definition of what constitutes "income" is exposed to a double danger. On the one hand the simple view that income is an unambiguous word, not subject to various interpretations, may ensure general complacency, and the particular notion of "taxable income" hallowed by legal tradition tends to become identified with taxable capacity as such. On the other hand, in the absence of any clear underlying principle, revisions and interpretations of the law proceed, in the light of particular considerations, to introduce successive concessions which have the effect of constantly shifting the tax burden in a manner which is no less far reaching for being unobtrusive. Lacking a firm basic conception, neither the public nor the legislature nor the courts are conscious of the extent to which the tax system, behind a facade of formal equality, metes out unequal treatment to the different classes of the taxpaying community" (*Memorandum of Dissent*, loc cit).

The absence of a comprehensive definition of income leads to the dangers referred to above. It leads to the situation where "wage earners pay according to their code number, company directors pay according to the ingenuity of their accountants and the self-employed pay according to their honesty." (*Taxes*, January 1965, p21). Understatement of taxable income in relation to "true" income by all taxpayers does not in itself result in inequities. The horizontal inequities arise from inequalities in the differing degrees of understatement of taxable income by taxpayers with the same "true" income.

However, it leads on to the situation that there is no logical place to stop erosion of the tax base. Once concessions are granted to one group of individuals another group claims similar concessions in order to maintain "parity." The pressure to enact further concessions increases and "instead of promoting growth, tax privileges put a premium on earning and disposing of incomes in a tax sheltered form and distort economic activity" (J. A. Pechman, "Report of the Canadian Royal Commission on taxation: a summing up," *The Brookings Institution, studies of government finance,* report no 134. p4).

Over time, this erosion of the tax base forces governments to raise tax rates to high levels in order to maintain the revenue yield because the rates are applied to only a fraction of total personal income. The use of high tax rates intensifies the inequities of the system, leads to further pressure for the enactment of tax privileges, and may have adverse effects upon the incentives to work and save by the community at large. Governments become aware of the potential disincentive effects and concentrate upon financing further government expenditure by imposing increased taxes upon consumption. As levied in the UK such taxes violate the criterion of vertical equity because they do not distribute the tax burden in accordance with changes in the ability of individuals and families to command resources. The next Labour Government should make increasing use of those taxes which can be imposed directly upon individuals because such taxes can be levied in accordance with the ability to pay of each taxpayer.

The introduction of a comprehensive tax base would require a thorough overhaul of our present system. On an ideal level all gifts, inheritances, transfer payments, capital gains, gratuitous receipts and imputed income would be included in the tax base. As a long term measure we should be working towards such an ideal tax base. Some method of income averaging would have to be devised to avoid discriminating against those taxpayers with fluctuating annual incomes. In the short term changes in the following concessions would be practical and could lead to a more equitable tax system.

1. Introduce a deduction for the employee national insurance contribution. This contribution in a pay-as-you-go system is a poll tax which is regressive with respect to the incomes of those subject to it. Because the tax reduces the taxable capacity of all who are subject to it the granting of a deduction would refine a person's net income and make the definition of "equals" for tax purposes more meaningful. As a long term measure abolition of the employees' and employers' national insurance contributions would prove a powerful redistributive measure. The revenue lost could be replaced by an increase in the scope of the income tax and the income tax rates if necessary with similar adjustments to the corporation tax rates.

2. Regard "fringe benefits" as income of the employee.

3. Place the employed and self-employed on the same footing by allowing the employed to deduct from their gross income expenses reasonably related to earning income.

4. Since the imputed net rent from owner occupation is no longer taxable there seems little ground for allowing the mortgage interest deduction.

The tax system to be consistent should allow either all forms of imputed net income to be included in the tax base or exclude all such forms of income. At the present time we not only exclude the imputed net rent from the tax base but also allow the taxpayer to deduct from his gross income mortgage interest payments. In consequence we discriminate against all taxpayers in rented accommodation.

Additionally, there seems to be no logical reason why if any concession is to be made to house purchasers it should take the form of a deduction. The justification for the mortgage interest deduction is not to refine net income, in which case a concession in the form of a deduction is appropriate, rather the concession is allowed to encourage this specific kind of private activity (owner occupation) which is deemed to be in the social interest. With this latter type of objective the granting of a tax credit in place of a deduction may be held to be more appropriate. A deduction allows the taxpayer to reduce the base upon which the tax is levied, and thus prevents him from reaching as high a rate of tax as he would otherwise have done, or he will have less income to be taxed at his highest rate. For a given amount of deductible expenditure the gain to the taxpayer rises with income. A tax credit allows the taxpayer to reduce the tax that has already been computed on a determined base—it is a sum that is deductible from the taxpayers tax bill. A tax credit of a fixed amount grants, for a given deductible expenditure, a tax reduction that is the same for almost all taxpayers regardless of income size.

5. Abolish the housekeeper allowance granted to a widower or to a widow without reference to the care of young children. The abolition of this allowance was suggested by the Royal Commission on the taxation of profits and income (op cit, 2nd report, para 224).

6. Abolish the age relief and raise the age exemption age limit to 75. Evidence has yet to be presented to support the belief that the aged with low or modest income require additional financial assistance relative to younger people with equally low incomes. (The case for a special tax concession for the aged would be greater if the age limit was increased. See *Report of the Committee on the economic and financial problems of the provision for old age*, para 184, HMSO, Cmd 9333, 1954.) In addition whether changing the income tax structure is the way to achieve an improvement in the conditions of the low income aged is very debatable. In the first place, for the aged with very low incomes the granting of a special tax concession is an illusory gain because their income is so small that even without a special exemption they would pay little or no tax. Secondly, if the granting of the special tax concessions is a good policy for the aged then surely it should be extended to include other low income groups. As we said earlier in the chapter tax concessions cannot be used to help people without income, what they require is positive assistance, either more income or more income in kind.

During the years "out of power" the Labour Party should closely analyse the justification for all the tax concessions which are now granted in the UK income tax system. It should bear in mind that use of special concessions which aim at promoting increased savings, and thereby a faster rate of economic growth, also at the same time necessitate a switch in the tax burden between groups of citizens if revenue is to be maintained. In effect by using such concessions we are removing taxes from those who save and transferring them to those who do not save or are unable to save. This saving allows society to acquire additional capital resources against which "are mortgages, property rights, in the hands of those freed from tax. While the saving will really have been done by those at the bottom of the income scale" (those who in order to meet the increased tax burden have to reduce consumption and/or savings), "those free from tax and their assigns will enjoy the reward. This method of fostering increase in productive capacity thus increases the concentration of property and aggravates inequality" (Simons *op cit*, p25).

As Simons demonstrates in this argument the proposition that the only effective way of dealing with the poverty problem is to increase the rate of growth "implies that those at present in poverty should be asked to pay a share of the cost of increasing the growth rate against a hope that if success attends the efforts made society will be able to 'afford' to deal with their problem" (R. W. Houghton, unpublished paper).

other major tax changes

The major changes in income tax in the period 1964-70 have already been reviewed in earlier sections of this chapter and, consequently, we concern ourselves here with other major tax changes in the same period.

The mini-budget of November 1964 saw increases in hydrocarbon oil duty and the imposition of a temporary charge on imports coupled with an export rebates scheme. The increased revenue obtained from these changes was required to help finance an increase in social security benefits and to restrain domestic consumption. The budget of 1965 was the major innovating budget of the period of Labour Government. The two tier system of income tax and profits tax was to be replaced by the corporation tax and the short term capital gains tax of 1962 was greatly modified and extended in scope. Large increases in the duties on tobacco, alcohol and motor vehicles were also announced in this budget.

1966 will be remebered for the introduction of SET and the betting tax. The traditional revenue raisers—the duties on tobacco and alcohol—had, as we have seen, been greatly increased in 1965 and increases in purchase tax and income tax would not provide "positive incentive to bring about structural changes in the economy" (*Hansard*, vol 727, col 1457). The Chancellor turned, in consequence, to SET, the rationale for which was to encourage the movement of manpower into the manufacturing sector of the economy and thereby stimulate a faster rate of economic growth. The importance of a manpower shortage and the need to switch manpower into the manufacturing sector was stressed in the National Plan and in the writings of one of the Labour Government's chief economic adviser's N. Kaldor (see his *The causes of the slow rate of growth of the United Kingdom*, Cambridge University Press, Cambridge, 1966).

A complete package of measures comprising of HP restrictions, increases in purchase tax; and duties on hydrocarbon oils; beers; wines and spirits; a surtax surcharge; deferment of public sector investment programmes; defence cuts; and tighter control of private sponsored construction works; was introduced in July 1966 in the face of a weakening balance of payments situation. No major changes were made in 1967.

Following devaluation of the pound in the autumn of 1967, the 1968 budget introduced massive increases in taxation estimated to bring in an extra £923 million revenue in a full year. Coupled with a 2.5 percentage point increase in the corporation tax rate were increases in betting and gaming duties; the duties on alcoholic drinks; tobacco; hydrocarbon oils; purchase tax; vehicle and excise duties, and the SET. Further consumption restraining measures were taken in the budget of 1969 with an extension in the scope of purchase tax. Increased revenue was to be obtained from betting and gaming, wines, and hydrocarbon oils. The corporation tax rate was increased again by 2.5 percentage points and changes in estate duty were made by raising the threshold to £10,000 and by adoption of bracket progression in place of the system of totality progression which had previously existed. SET rates were increased in preference to either purchase tax or income tax rates because the Chancellor maintained a purchase tax change could lead to a considerable cost of living increase whereas an income tax increase could have possible disincentive effects on work effort and willingness to save. 1969 also saw the introduction of save-as-you-earn. The major tax changes in 1970 were concerned with income tax and have been discussed in earlier parts of this chapter.

13. selectivity for the poor

Michael J. Hill

The chief difficulty involved in dealing with the subject of selectivity for the poor lies in the fact that the role of the selective social services has been, at least since the social security reforms of the 1940s, to fill the gaps left in the more universalistic services. Therefore it is very difficult to discuss selectivity in isolation from the other services. Changes in the universalistic services have in many ways a greater impact upon the scope and adequacy of the selective services than do changes in the selective services themselves.

In the years since Beveridge, to judge by the things that have been written on this subject, it would appear to be the case that most socialists have come to accept his view that the place of selectivity is merely to fill the gaps in a universalistic system which is as comprehensive as possible. In *Signposts for the sixties* (1961), the Labour Party attacked the Tories for their readiness to contemplate extending selectivity; and in *New Frontiers for social security*, published in 1963, a very clear stand was taken on national assistance: "As a result of our proposals (to extend the scope of national insurance), the National Assistance Board will gradually cease to supplement inadequate national insurance benefits, and so revert to its original purpose of providing a "safety net" for those who do not qualify for national insurance. This will mean for those still on national assistance more generous treatment and greater care and attention from the staff. This group will also be given its fair share of rising national prosperity by tying national assistance rates to the level of national average earnings" (*New frontiers for social security*, p19).

What is clearly envisaged here is a system which provides "universal" benefits to all people who fit into a number of common categories of need, by virtue of sickness, old age or unemployment, in particular. Selectivity, involving the use of a "means test" to discriminate between people with different material circumstances, is thus confined to a minority who do not fit into the broad categories covered by the universalistic system.

Of course, every social service is selective in a wider sense of the word, and for this reason confusion can sometimes arise from different uses of the word "selectivity." Thus two of the leading opponents of selectivity in the sense it is defined above, Professors Titmuss and Abel-Smith, argue in favour of certain other forms of selectivity, the former calling for "positive discriminatory services to be provided as rights for categories of people and for classes of need in terms of priority social areas and other impersonal classifications," (R. M. Titmuss, *Commitment to welfare*, p135, Allen and Unwin, 1968), and the latter arguing "Selectivity in the form of means tested benefits for poor families is already playing too large a role. Our need today is not for more means tested benefits but for less. This can be achieved by introducing 'selectivity' in our social security payments by grading them according to capacity to pay," (Brian Abel-Smith in *Social services for all?*, p122, Fabian Society, 1968). I certainly do not intend to challenge the "doctrine" on selectivity so admirably set out in *New frontiers for social security*, but rather to ask whether Labour's record lived up to its own ideals in this sphere. When Labour came to power the main forms of selectivity in operation were as follows:

1. A national assistance scheme that had been left substantially unchanged since 1948, but which had grown in importance because of the failure of statutory benefits to keep up with needs, probably particularly as far as rent levels were concerned. It had also grown as a result of various attempts to encourage people to make use of the scheme despite its traditional stigma.

2. The refund of National Health Service charges by application to the National Assistance Board, which operated an assessment scale based upon, but slightly more generous than, its normal scales and without the rules preventing payments to persons in full time work.

3. A legal aid scheme, also largely operated by the National Assistance Board, but on rather different lines and taking in a much wider range of needs.

4. A large number of means test schemes operated by local authorities, estimated to be in excess of 3,000, of which the most important were rent rebate schemes, and assessment schemes associated with the supply of free school meals, educational grants and day nursery facilities (see Mike Reddin in *Social services for all?*, Fabian Society, 1968).

In 1964 there were about 1,961,000 weekly national assistance allowances in payment covering the needs of about 2,770,000 persons. The great majority of the weekly allowances, 73 per cent, were to supplement inadequate national insurance benefits, above all retirement pensions. The figures can be broken down to show 69 per cent payments to the old (1,342,000), 7 per cent payments to the unemployed (131,000) and 24 per cent payments to others including the sick and unsupported mothers (*Annual report of the National Assistance Board for 1964*, HMSO, 1965).

By the end of 1969 the Board's successor, the Supplementary Benefits Commission, was paying out 2,688,000 weekly allowances providing for the needs of 4,097,000 persons. 70 per cent of the recipients of these allowances were the old (1,875,000), 8 per cent the unemployed (228,000) and others accounted for 22 per cent (*Report of Department of Health and Social Security for 1969*, HMSO, 1970).

Over this period the number of retirement pensions in payment under the national insurance scheme increased from 6,157,000 in 1964 to 7,130,000. This means that supplementary pensions increased from 22 per cent to 26 per cent of all retirement pensioners.

The proportion of the unemployed in receipt of supplementary benefits, on the other hand, fell quite considerably. At the beginning of January 1965 the number of men unemployed was 274,000, while in January 1970 it was 505,000. The proportion of the unemployed assisted by the Supplementary Benefits Commission dropped from 49 per cent in winter 1964-65 to 45 per cent in winter 1969-70. (These figures are taken from the *Ministry of Labour*

Gazette, February 1965 and the *Department of Employment and Productivity Gazette*, February 1970. The counts were taken early in January and are therefore the nearest ones to the counts of supplementary benefit recipients taken in late November.)

The introduction of earnings related unemployment benefit will undoubtedly have contributed to the fall in the proportion of the unemployed receiving supplementary benefits. In this respect the figures show a relative move towards universality. On the other hand, the very large increase in unemployment totally wiped out any possibility of any absolute gain in this direction.

But the figures are rather difficult to interpret because they are not only complicated by changes in the amounts provided under both the national insurance and the supplementary benefits systems but also by changes in the social and demographic characteristics of the population. Furthermore the general rise in the number of people covered by the "safety net" part of the system may be attributed either to the Labour Government's *failure* to develop the universal benefits system adequately, or to its *success* in increasing the "take up" of supplementary benefits on the part of the needy people who had hitherto failed to claim their rights, or to its *success* in providing more adequate supplementary benefits. The Government would have had to increase the universal benefits very much more than it did to be able to score successes on all these three points, and in fact the evidence is that as far as pensions were concerned, it was more successful in raising supplementary pensions relative to national insurance pensions, and thus failed entirely to push insurance pensions up to levels at which the supplementary pensions system could begin to wither away. The following table shows how supplementary pension rates and national insurance rates moved together over the period after the 1966 Act, with supplementary pension rates improving for those who acquired the long term addition, if they did not loose large discretionary additions, while insurance rates improved for those getting income related supplements to sickness or unemployment benefits.

INCREASES IN NATIONAL INSURANCE AND SUPPLEMENTARY BENEFIT RATES, 1966-69

	national insurance		supplementary benefits	
dates	single people	married couples	single people	married couples
November 1966*	—	—	5s 0d†	7s 6d†
October 1967	10s 0d	16s 0d	5s 0d	8s 0d
October 1968	—	—	5s 0d	8s 0d
November 1969	10s 0d	16s 0d	5s 0d	8s 0d
total	20s 0d	32s 0d	20s 0d	31s 6d

*income related supplements were introduced in 1966 to enhance the rates of sickness and unemployment benefits for those not on the lowest rates of pay.
†9s long term addition also given; raised to 10s in October 1968.

Although the Ministry of Social Security Act was expressly designed to increase the "take up" of selective benefits, Tony Atkinson concluded that "between a half and two thirds of the increase between December 1965 and November 1968 in the number of retirement pensioner households receiving assistance can be attributed to the more generous assistance scale" (A. B. Atkinson, *Poverty in Britain and the reform of social security*, p75, Cambridge University Press, 1970). The general position was not markedly changed in 1969 when a ten shillings retirement pension increase was accompanied by a five shillings supplementary benefits increase for single people (the new amounts were 16 shillings and eight shillings respectively for married couples). This change checked the rate of growth of numbers of pensioners dependent upon supplementary benefits very slightly, the absolute numbers increased only about 30,000 between the annual counts of 1968 and 1969. These figures do not provide any evidence on the adequacy of the various rates of benefit paid, this task has been undertaken by other contributors to this volume, but simply show that as far as social security is concerned no really effective assault on selectivity was mounted by the Labour government. Yet, at the same time, judging by Atkinson's figures, the notion of a "right" to supplementary benefits did not appear to become established in the minds of the poor. Although the increase in numbers of pensioner households in receipt of help of this kind was close to the half million the government estimated to be failing to claim assistance in 1965, when the increase in the number of pensioners and the impact of increased assessment rates are taken into account it becomes certain that only a small proportion of that half million have in fact been found (see *Report of the committee of inquiry into the impact of rates on households*, Cmnd 2582, p117, HMSO, 1965).

In *New frontiers for social security* where the idea, put into practice in the 1966 Act, of a ministry combining responsibilities for national insurance and national assistance was first suggested by the Labour Party, it was claimed that "a change of name which leaves the essential evil unchanged makes little appeal to us." Yet, as far as the balance between the two systems of social security and as far as the take up of benefits are concerned there seems to have been little change. Were there, therefore, any changes of real importance as part of, or associated with, the 1966 Act?

The development of a single department was aimed to have the effect of blurring the distinction between the two types of benefit. An immediate gain here was the provision of single order books to enable pensioners to cash their supplementary benefits without being conspicuous. A longer term objective was to get rid of the situation in which members of the public had to deal with unco-ordinated departments. However the integration of the two departments is proving a slow process, and one moreover which is causing resentment on the part of many members of the smaller of the two departments, the National Assistance Board. This is, in itself, a cause for concern because any lowering of morale on the part of civil servants with responsibilities of this kind will have an impact upon the service given to the public. Furthermore, the merger has naturally to some extent led to the dominance of former members of the larger department, where there was no substantial tradition of individualised service to the public such as was growing up, perhaps sometimes rather halfheartedly, in the National Assistance Board. Accordingly, the *New frontiers for social security* objective of "greater care and attention" is certainly not being achieved.

The 1966 Act laid greater emphasis upon entitlement to benefit, this produced some liberalisation of policy. Yet, at the same time discretionary powers were retained in the hands of the Supplementary Benefits Commission which could be used to undermine any progressive developments. This is what seems to have happened as far as the treatment of unemployed men was concerned. Under the Social Security Act newly unemployed people were no longer denied help during their first month of unemployment on the grounds that they could manage on savings as some of them had been under the National Assistance Act. Similarly men who had their unemployment benefit disallowed for six weeks, on the grounds that they had been at fault in losing a job, were no longer subjected to the harsh rule applied by the National Assistance confining their payments to below "benefit rate"; instead a policy was adopted of paying them their full entitlement less 15 shillings.

However, in 1968 the government became influenced by a hysterical campaign alleging abuses of the system by unemployed men. Perhaps they allowed themselves to be swayed by this campaign on account of their own eagerness to disclaim responsibility for a rising unemployment rate. It became convenient to explain the failure to maintain as low a rate of unemployment as had existed for most of the 13 years of Tory rule in terms of the unwillingness of men to work rather than in terms of either a failure of economic policy or a failure to train and equip low skilled and low paid workers to compete in the labour market. As far as supplementary benefits were concerned two policies were adopted, a considerable increase in the staff employed to harry the so-called "voluntary unemployed" and a rule that young, single, unskilled men living in low unemployment areas should have their supplementary benefits stopped after four weeks. Then, later, in the Superannuation Bill which came before Parliament in the session 1969-70 a provision was included restricting allowances to people disallowed unemployment benefits to one third of the "normal scale rate" with rent and children's requirements to be met in full. This was subsequently amended to one quarter of the scale rate, but of course the Bill never became law on account of the dissolution for the general election.

Some of the efforts to limit the discretionary powers of supplementary benefits officers were also not as successful as they initially appeared to be. For example, a long term addition of nine shillings a week (subsequently raised to ten shillings) was provided for the allowances of all pensioners and for the long term sick. This was designed not merely to raise the resources of people in long term need but also to eliminate some of the discretionary additions which had been given to such people under the national assistance system. When the bill was debated by the Lords, Lord Ilford pointed out that a "long term addition" of nine shillings a week could hardly be expected to eliminate discretionary additons which were at that time averaging 9s 6d per week.

What has in fact happened is that the long term addition has reduced the sensitivity of the system's response to special needs, since a very fit and active pensioner will get the addition like everyone else but an unfit one will have his special needs, for more expensive foods, help with laundry, extra heating and so on, offset against the addition so that his allowance will only be increased by the extent to which his extra needs are calculated to exceed ten shillings a week. The scope of discretion has been reduced at the cost of sensitivity to diverse needs.

In the same way the Commission have tried to regularise the operation of the wage stop, a welcome development in the light of the inconsistencies which had been demonstrated to occur under its operation by the National Assistance Board. But what this means in some cases is explained in the *Supplementary benefits handbook* (1970) as follows: "In the case of labourers and light labourers who have been unemployed for some time . . . there may be such a variety of possible jobs that it is not possible to take either an individual earnings figure or the standard earnings figure in a particular industry in a particular locality. If so, the wages fixed for labourers and light labourers by the National Joint Council for Local Authorities (Manual Workers) are used as a measure of earnings capacity" (p21). This would seem good sense were it not for a fact that such "basic" rates tend to be markedly below normal earnings rates in some areas. Thus it tends to be a liberal policy in low pay areas, like the North East, but an illiberal one in the Midlands and South.

In general the attempts in the Act to reduce the discretionary powers of supplementary benefits commission officers were unsuccessful, and the commission has subsequently done little to advance beyond this situation. In many respects such advance is impossible, as is demonstrated by the fate of the "long term" addition, without a substantial increase in the basic rates. Having left the staff of the supplementary benefits commission with substantial discretionary powers there were a number of things which the government could have done to make these powers more subject to control. There could have been included within the 1966 Act some clear definitions of circumstances that would be considered "exceptional," particularly where reductions or refusals of allowances were likely to be involved. At present there is little more on this subject than a vague passage in Schedule 2: "Where there are exceptional circumstances—(a) Benefit may be awarded at an amount exceeding that (if any) calculated in accordance with the preceding paragraphs; (b) a supplementary allowance may be reduced below the amount so calculated or may be witheld—as may be appropriate to take account of these circumstances." After a prolonged attack by the Child Poverty Action Group upon the fact that discretionary decisions of this kind are based upon secret rules set out in manuals or codes, of which the "A code" is the most important, which should be made public, the commission published a short handbook. This book is a reasonably accurate digest of most of the important instructions found in the codes, so the Child Poverty Action Group have scored a small victory on this issue. But this publication is designed for social workers and is not readily available to clients seeking their rights. More seriously the handbook, and for that matter the codes, do not contain rules but only guidelines. (For further discussion of some of the following points see *Poverty* 15, 1970.) It is not possible to find a clear definition of what constitutes an "exceptional need," or an "unreasonably high rent," or "cohabitation" as a grounds for the refusal of help to a woman. It is also not possible to use the handbook guidelines as a firm basis for an appeal. In other words, the 1966 Act remains the sole source of law on supplementary benefits.

Supplementary benefits appeal tribunals thus have a very slight legal framework within which to operate. Furthermore, they are not able to establish case law; no decision of a tribunal provides any precedent for that or any other local tribunal. While there may be a strong case against developing a system in which administrative innovation is largely controlled by a legal body (see R. M. Titmuss, "Welfare rights, law and discretion," *Political Quarterly*, April 1971), the present system is exceptionally confusing to appellants because of the lack of consistency.

Another serious defect of the appeal system is the onus that is put upon the member of the public to prove that he has been unreasonably treated after his allowance has been reduced or refused. Surely the system could be operated in such a way that the individual is informed that the department proposes to use its discretionary powers to reduce or stop an allowance; and, if he avails himself of his right of appeal, action could be stayed until the appeal tribunal has confirmed the department's action.

Finally, there are still grounds for concern that many members of the public who are forced to seek help from the commission are entirely unaware of how their entitlements are worked out. Lena Jeger MP sought to have a provision included in the Act that claimants should have a statement setting out exactly how their allowances are calculated. She was persuaded to withdraw her amendment after the Minister had pleaded that staff were too hard pressed at that time, but had promised that such statements would be provided in due course. This innovation is still awaited.

It can be concluded about the Labour Government's actions with regard to the main planks in the social security system that no significant changes were made to diminish the importance of selectivity. But, if we turn now to the area of local authority means tests we will find that it also adopted a number of policies which led to a growth in the significance of selectivity. When it increased the price of school dinners it naturally made the means test involved for applicants for free school meals more important. At the same time it sought to rationalise and publicise these schemes, and adopted a policy of allowing free meals for the fourth and subsequent children from families regardless of means. For no apparent reason, it subsequently withdrew this last provision.

More important changes were made in the field of housing "means tests." Here the government introduced a rates rebate scheme, and also encouraged local authorities to develop or extend rent rebate schemes.

The report of the Ministry of Housing and Local Government for 1967 and 1968 provides the following statement on the rates rebate scheme: "During the period under review, householders with small incomes (if their liabilities were not being covered by supplementary benefits) could claim rate rebates. In 1966-1967, the first year of the scheme, 986,000 householders got rebates averaging £14 18s for the year. In 1967-68 the corresponding figures were 786,000 and £15 13s." (*Ministry of Housing and Local Government report for 1967 and 1968*, p98, HMSO, 1969).

Despite the Ministry's protestations that widespread publicity was given to the scheme it is clear that a high proportion of the householders entitled to rates rebates do not claim them. One of the main troubles here seems to be that local authorities are often not at all skilful at publicising matters of this kind, the great majority still taking the view that the public should come to seek them out and not that they should seek to inform the public. Another difficulty lies in the fact that many tenants, including of course local authority tenants, pay rates not as a lump sum but as a small, and not necessarily very obvious, weekly addition to their rents. Finally, in explaining the failure of the rates rebates scheme one must not overlook the potential for misunderstanding, misapprehension and just plain dislike present in any new means test scheme (see T. Lynes "Rate rebates: what went wrong," *Poverty* 1).

The Labour government's position on rent rebate schemes was set out in a White Paper on the housing programme published in 1965: "Rent policies are also for local decision. But if the extra subsidies now to be provided are to be used, as they should be, to relieve those with the greatest social need, these policies should reflect the fact that the financial circumstances of council tenants vary widely. This means that subsidies should not be used wholly or even mainly to keep general rent levels low. Help for those who most need it can be given only if the subsidies are in large part used to provide rebates for tenants whose means are small. A number of authorities have had the courage to adopt thorough going rent rebate schemes and have found that it does not entail general rent levels beyond the means of the majority of their tenants. The more generous subsidies now to be provided create an opportunity for all authorities to review their rent policies along these lines. In doing so, they will be able to take into account the higher standards of accommodation which will increasingly be provided with the aid of the new subsidies" (*The housing programme 1968-70*, cmnd 2838, p15, HMSO, 1965).

At the end of 1966 the minister set up a working party of ministry officials and local authority representatives to examine the question of rent rebates. After the working party reported in 1967, a circular was issued which reiterated the views of the White Paper and provided an example of the sort of scheme the ministry would like to see in operation. This circular also strongly recommended that no tenant should be asked to declare his income unless he applied for a rebate, a view which involved taking a strong line on privacy at the cost of comprehensive coverage of those in need (*Ministry of Housing and Local Government circular 46/67*).

Before the circular was issued only about 40 per cent of local authorities had rebate schemes. By the time the Prices and Incomes Board studied this subject in March 1968 53 per cent had schemes, including a high proportion of the larger authorities, so that about 70 per cent of tenants were covered, though not necessarily in receipt of rebates: " . . . 495 authorities operated rent rebate schemes, and the £9.5 million total rebate went to over a quarter of a million tenants, representing nearly 12 per cent of the total housing stock. The average rebate, 13s 9d, amounted to one third of the average rent." By now the situation is that 60 per cent of local authorities have schemes and about 80 per cent of tenants are covered.

The Prices and Incomes Board considered the question of rent rebates in 1968 in connection with the subject of local authority rent increases. They decided that the introduction or extension of a rebate scheme by a local authority could be regarded as a justification for a rent increase, thereby further intensifying the pressure on local authorities to set up schemes. The board also recommended that local authorities should be required to adopt a uniform scheme for rebates and that they might also be given powers to grant rebates to tenants of private landlords. The Labour Government took no action on these two recommendations, though it is now clear that the Ministry must have undertaken a study of their implications and the Government did in fact allow Birmingham to pass a Private Act making the implementation of the latter proposal possible in their area (NBPI, *Increases in rents of local authority housing*, cmnd 3604, HMSO).

During the Parliamentary session of 1968-69 the Estimates Committee took a look at the subject of housing subsidies. In the course of their enquiries they were given some disturbing evidence about the way some local authority rent rebate schemes were working out in practice. They discovered that some authorities were attempting to maximise rent income by refusing to allocate poor tenants to good quality dwellings where they would require large rebates, and that others were excluding some modern properties from their rent rebate schemes (*Fourth report of the Estimates Committee, session 1968-69: housing subsidies*). The Committee also received evidence on the relationship between the supplemntary benefits scheme and local rebate schemes. They summarised the general situation in the following passage: "Local authorities, in increasing numbers, have been refusing to grant rebates to tenants on supplementary benefit on the grounds that the Supplementary Benefits Commission make full provision for rent when assessing entitlement to benefit, and benefit would be reduced by an amount corresponding to the rebate. Rebates are however granted in wage-stop cases (where the claimant will benefit from a reduction in rent) or in cases where supplementary benefit is payable over short periods. . . ." (*op cit*, p54).

There is no question that lying behind this simple statement of the relationship that has been achieved there lies a saga of conflict between a central government department and some local authorities over who should give support in many cases, and that many tenants suffered during the period in which the local authorities were engaged on forcing the Supplementary Benefit Commission to assume responsibility for full rents. It seems unlikely that, even now, there are not instances in which there are arguments, which may temporarily affect the circumstances of individuals, over whether certain people should be regarded as "short term" or "long term" cases. More seriously there were examples quoted to the Estimates Committee in which claimants for supplementary benefits living in local authority houses were refused full rent allowances on the grounds that their rents were too high (*op cit*, p323 evidence provided by J. C. Swaffield on behalf of the Association of Municipal Corporations). In these cases tenants were pushed into hardship in what can only be seen as an indirect effort to get local authorities either to move them to cheaper accommodation or to grant them rebates.

The general conclusions that can be drawn about the impact of the Labour government upon the nature and extent of selectivity for the poor are as follows: They did very little in practice to alter the national assistance /supplementary benefits system despite a declaration that they were establishing the principle of "entitlement" much more clearly. The introduction of the long term addition provided a slightly more generous approach to the support of pensioners and other long term cases, and it is hypothesised that the increase in the number of benefit recipients stems largely from this change, but its impact was to a considerable degree negated by the fact that additions for special needs were, and are, offset against it. The absence of clarity in many of the rules surrounding supplementary benefits, and the fact that recipients do not receive statements setting out how their allowances are calculated, means that the system still appears to many people as one in which they have to persuade an all powerful official to regard them as deserving of help. The unmarried mother, the deserted wife, and the able bodied unemployed man still have to face situations in which, in order to establish their case for help, they may have to endure humiliating interrogations. By contrast officials generally bend over backwards to make clear their readiness to assist the elderly, but the elderly have very long memories and many are still unwilling to apply for help.

However, the most striking developments in selectivity during the period 1964-70 came not so much in the social security field as in the housing field. Here rapidly rising costs brought large numbers of local authorities face to face with the problem of spreading rent rises in an equitable way. Despite generous increases in subsidies, the very high cost of new developments began to make it difficult for authorities to continue to push new costs onto existing tenants by "rent pooling." In this situation the Government, which also responded to increasing concern about rate rises by introducing a selective scheme rather than by reforming local taxation, decided to follow their Conservative predecessors and encourage local authorities to develop rent rebate schemes.

In general, then, we can take it that the Labour government largely failed to live up to its commitment to reduce the importance of selectivity in our social security system. They found it only too easy to meet problems of rising costs and emergent needs by new extensions of means testing. The net result of six years of Labour rule is an even greater tangle of means tests than existed before, and accordingly there is today rising concern about the fact that the large number of schemes provide in effect a special and severe kind of tax upon low wage earners. This paradoxical effect occurs because as low wage earners gain increases they lose means tested benefits, to such an extent that a £1 increase in wages can sometimes leave them worse off than before.

The full seriousness of this effect is only just beginning to be fully recognised, simply because of the complexity of the muddle that has been created. Furthermore the fact that many poor people are not aware of, or do not avail themselves of, their rights under the multitude of schemes means that few people actually feel the full "taxation effect." Accordingly the more effectively the low "take up" problem is tackled the more serious will the "taxation effect" problem become.

As the weaknesses inherent in the present mixture of schemes become apparent there will be an increasing demand for rationalization. The obvious form some of those demands will take will be the deployment of the case for the introduction of "negative income tax." The case against negative income tax has been widely argued in the publications of the Fabian Society, and elsewhere. There are severe objections to it on administrative grounds, particularly because many of the most needy at present do not make tax returns, and because tax assessments are not very sensitive to variations in personal needs. But more seriously, negative income tax would do incalculable harm to our economic and social structure, creating a permanently subsidized "under class" and making any moves towards real social equality exceptionally difficult (see, for example, Peter Townsend "The difficulties of negative income tax," *Social services for all?*, p106-111, A. B. Atkinson, Poverty *in Britain and the reform of social security,* Cambridge University Press 1970 and D. Piachaud "Poverty and taxation," *Political Quarterly,* January-March 1971).

The failure of the last Labour government to move effectively towards achieving greater universality in the social security system should not lead the Party to abandon its commitment to that principle. The right way to attack selectivity, and to clear away the present tangle of means tests, is to develop policies which enable them to wither away. The improvements that were made to the sickness and unemployment benefit schemes, and above all the ill fated pensions scheme, pointed in the right direction. Greater improvements in these, together with the development of much more adequate provisions for the disabled and of allowances for unsupported mothers, are still needed. Family allowances, too, must be substantially increased, and an effective assault must be made upon low wages. Finally, the rising cost of housing has been a critical source of extensions of selectivity. A future Labour government must take steps to spread the burden of housing costs so that they do not fall so disproportionately heavily upon people with low incomes.

I, therefore, conclude as I began with a reminder that an attack on selectivity depends upon an extension of universalistic services. The real solutions to the problems associated with selective services for the poor lie in the development of services beyond the concern of this chapter; the reader will find the necessary policies outlined more fully in other contributions to this volume.

chronology

November 1965	White Paper *The Housing Programme 1965-70* asking local authorities to consider rent rebate schemes.
March 1966	Rating Act, making provision for rate rebates.
November 1966	Implementation of Ministry of Social Security Act 1966.
November 1966	Local authorities told in White Paper *Prices and incomes standstill: period of severe restraint* that they should adopt rebate schemes if forced to raise rents.
June 1967	Ministry of Housing and Local Government published a recommended rent rebate scheme in circular 46/67.
November 1967	Devaluation, accompanied by deflationary measures including re-imposition of prescription charges and an increase in school meals charges.
May 1970	Publication of *Supplementary benefits handbook.*

14. social administration and human rights

Rosalind Brooke

In this review I shall be arguing firstly that the Labour Government's record on rights was inadequate, but better than that so far of the present Conservative administration. The latter promised in October 1970 that the "Government will make it their *special* duty to protect the freedoms of the individual under the law" (*Hansard,* House of Lords, 26 November 1970, col 246) but this promise was forgotten very quickly in, for example, the Dutschke case, the Immigration Bill, the Industrial Relations Bill and Family Income Supplements Bill. But the Labour Government was inconsistent. It did not set up an inquiry into administrative law as it had been urged to do by the Law Commission, but did set up a strait jacketed one into privacy. Kenneth Robinson set up a committee of inquiry into the Ely Hospital but the publication of its report had to await a decision by Richard Crossman. Mr. Robinson had testified to his belief in rights, yet he failed to sort out the wheat from the chaff in the AEGIS inquiries and make sure that the issue of rough treatment of elderly patients was properly, and independently, investigated. The Government failed to do anything publicly about the problems of homeless families in June 1970 before the presentation of the Greve report about temporary accommodation for the homeless. As a final example, action on the problem of mental handicap was slow in the early months of 1970, after a good Ministerial campaign earlier.

There were some notable advances in areas of private morality under Labour rule, for example abortion, homosexual and divorce law reform. It should be pointed out however that the improvements in most cases were initiated by private members, although the Labour Government, notably when Roy Jenkins was Home Secretary, helped by allowing extra time and with drafting help. However, these measures are not discussed in this review.

Again, it would be possible to discuss rights in relation to the abolition of capital punishment, (see P. G. Richards, *Parliament and conscience,* 1970) Labour's record on race relations, the setting up of the Urban Aid programme and the treatment of Commonwealth citizens and stricter controls on entry. Some of these matters are discussed elsewhere in this book. I shall confine myself to a discussion of rights within the social services—an area neglected by so many—and access to services designed to help people obtain their rights. The issues spread across a number of different services and I shall try to pick them out and discuss them rather than adopt a more conventional narrative account of events.

legal principles

There are some important questions which need examination by lawyers, social administrators and social workers, since these involve fundamental liberties within the "welfare state." One constitutional lawyer has written, "The expansion of individual liberty (in one sense) as a result of the development of social services and of the acceptance of principles of social security, as well as the general growth of state activity, all create problems of the protection of individuals. Every measure which produces the possibility of beneficial state action necessarily produces at the same time a possibility of the abuse of power" (J. D. B. Mitchell, *Constitutional law*, p323, 1968).

The twin problems of individual liberty and abuse of power are not helped by the piecemeal development of the social services. R. H. Tawney, 40 years ago wrote that "The services establishing social rights can boast no lofty pedigree. They crept piecemeal into apologetic existence, as low-grade palliatives designed at once to relieve and to conceal the realities of poverty" (*Equality*, p127, Allen and Unwin, 1964).

One of the problems arising out of the lack (or denial) of rights within the social services is that earlier, well-intentioned legislation may have been designed to remedy an earlier difficulty or abuse, but creates a new set of problems. For example, it is generally desirable to clear out of date, slum housing with no bath and an outdoor lavatory. But some local authorities acquire property for redevelopment years in advance of their being pulled down so that comparatively adequate housing is unoccupied for years—housing which in the eyes of a family evicted from a rat infested, two roomed "furnished" flat is utopia. Or plans will be announced for redevelopment, and residents may then be left with no news for years. Similarly, it may be desirable to speed traffic in inner city areas, but this creates intolerable problems for those living within yards of the urban motorway. A third example can be drawn from our social security system which is designed to maintain the income (at least to a certain level) of the disabled, sick, injured, unemployed, fatherless or elderly but the administrative machinery for the claimant with its complex battery of forms, qualifications for entitlement, and bewildering variety of times within which a claim has to be made, may prevent the fundamental aim of maintenance of income and prevention of want (to use Beveridge's phrase) from being fulfilled.

We need some framework within which to examine rights within the social services, even as the economist will be using his analytical framework of supply and demand theory, of how allocation of services operates within the private market and what limitations may arise therefrom, and of cost benefit analysis. What set of questions should a lawyer, concerned with the consumers of social services, ask? One useful frame of reference can be found within certain articles of the European Convention on Human Rights, with its emphasis on rights to privacy, and to information, with fair hearings and no unjust denial of rights. Articles 6 and 8 of the Convention deal with these topics:

Article 6: (1) In the determination of his civil rights and obligations or of any criminal charge against him, everyone is *entitled to a fair and public hearing within a reasonable time* by an *independent and impartial tribunal* established by law. Judgment shall be *pronounced publicly* but the press and public may be excluded from all or part of the trial in the interest of morals, public order or national security in a democratic society, where the interests of juveniles or the protection of the private life of the parties so require, or to the extent strictly necessary in the opinion of the court in special circumstances where publicity would prejudice the interests of justice.

Article 8: (1) Everyone has *the right to respect for his private and family life,* his home and his correspondence. (2) There shall be no interference by a public authority with the exercise of this right except such as is in accordance with the law and is necessary in a democratic society in the interests of national security, public safety or the economic well being of the country, for the prevention of disorder or crime, for the protection of health or morals, or for the protection of the rights and freedoms of others.

No doubt it is difficult to agree on criteria by which these principles may be applied and tested but the general questions that we should be asking are reasonably clear. Are particular services being fairly administered? Is the recipient being given adequate notice of a hearing to curtail his benefit? Is any opportunity being given to the recipient of stating why something should or should not be done in the social services? Is proper respect being paid to his "private and family life, his home and his correspondence"? Is firm and reputable evidence being used as a basis for allocating (or curtailing) some right or benefit? Is social service legislation being implemented and interpreted in accordance with the intention of Parliament and the spirit of the Act? Does the parent Act give discretionary power and what indications, if any, have been given as to how it should be exercised? Are mandatory provisions, although clearly mandatory, treated as if they were cast on a discretionary basis? To what extent have services, clearly designed for individuals and not for the administrators, been publicised and made accessible to the intended recipients?

Because too often there is a fuzzy and woolly approach to the whole question of rights, it is perhaps necessary to distinguish between procedural and substantive rights (see C. Glasser, *Poverty*, 15, 1970 p11). By procedural rights I mean whether there is a right to an appeal or a fair hearing, whether the administration of the service is fair and just, whether there is adequate information and publicity. For example, is there an opportunity to appeal against refusal of benefit or prohibition on an immigrant wanting to land? By substantive rights I mean whether there is a right (or a privilege to claim) a benefit or a service, for example is there an unqualified right to benefit, or a privilege that one may be considered eligible, for instance to a rent rebate. The question of the philosophical basis of rights—natural rights, contractual rights—cannot be discussed here. Nor do I propose discussing the intangible "moral rights" to "courtesy and understanding relationships" (*Supplementary benefits handbook,* p1, HMSO, 1970).

substantive and procedural rights within the social services

Labour's record on substantive rights has been covered in part in the chapters in this book: for example, questions of the extension of substantive rights to social security payments, improved medical care, and greater choice and freedom in education are discussed. An extension of substantive rights depends in the end on a political decision to switch resources from, for example, the surtax payer to the elderly, or to make further resources available for a specific service. In some areas there has been no improvement in substantive rights. There is no "right" to housing, only a possibility that one may be privileged in being considered eligible. Despite this, large families (which is one group most likely to be in need and is therefore specifically mentioned in the 1957 Housing Act) may not be offered council housing for a long time because few large houses are built (MHLG, *Council housing, purposes, priorities and procedure*, para 39, HMSO, 1969).

Despite the obvious need to improve and extend many substantive rights—housing, social security, welfare benefits—there may still be important barriers to the obtaining of those rights if procedure is unclear or faulty. A substantive right can be created by cutting out discretion, but one American lawyer, commenting on the pressure to reduce discretion in the American welfare system, has pointed out that "It is one thing to specify objective criteria in the books . . . it is quite another matter to ensure that welfare officials will communicate these rights to the clients and that the clients will understand what they are entitled to and will demand what is due them rather than rely on the good will of the case worker . . . there is the danger that expanded, improved service programs will increase client dependency and coercion" (J. F. Handler and Ellen T. Hollingsworth, *The administration of social services and the structure of dependency: the views of* AFDC *recipients*, pp416-17).

It is essential therefore to look at the social services from the standpoint of the delivery of the services, their administration, and not only to be concerned, as so many economists are, with the rise (or fall) of 0.1 per cent in GNP spent on this, that or the other service. It may mean so little to the consumer at grassroots whereas access to and administration of the service will be vital. Professor K. C. Davis has argued that procedural reforms can often achieve more by "better confining, structuring and checking of discretion of administrators. Discretion should be more fully guided by rules (classified statutes, regulations and instruction manuals), and strictly enforce the rules against their subordinates" (*Discretionary justice*, pp180-81).

I shall discuss four important areas of procedural rights, using examples of Labour's record in the social services, namely: privacy, information and secrecy, administrative complexity and refusal to make decisions, and fair hearings.

There is no need to marshal a great mass of evidence about official invasions of privacy. There have been recent examples of a local authority which kept in its files newspaper cuttings about criminal charges against tenants or the DHSS officials who in order to investigate whether a woman was cohabiting went to the man's place of work with the result that he lost his job. There is the case of the clerk of a supplementary benefit tribunal who wrote to an appellant's doctor without informing the appellant or her representative or obtaining their consent, and the doctor who gave his views to that clerk in writing. (Incidentally, this is an interesting reflection on medical ethics.) It may be argued that all these infringements of privacy were necessary, no doubt to ensure only "deserving" people are tenants, only "deserving" women receive the state's money payments and only "deserving" long term sick get discretionary payments. But nonetheless, these are infringements of privacy: would a surtax payer welcome an inland revenue inspector contacting his doctor and consultant behind his back? Unless we are really concerned that there are equal standards of administration, these infringements will recur. In great part they stem from the low status accorded to many of the welfare services and their clients. It cannot be said that the Labour Government did anything notable or striking in issues of privacy, beyond setting up the Younger Committee on Privacy with limited terms of reference. Yet "The right to be let alone," as American Supreme Court Justice Brandeis states, "is the most comprehensive of rights and the right most valued by civilised men" (quoted in A. M. Bendich, "Privacy, poverty and the constitution" in J. tenBroek (ed), *The law of the poor*, p84).

Secrecy has two aspects: the lack of openness in the decision making process about general policy and the failure to make available to an individual facts and reasons for a decision involving him. The sin of secrecy is not a rare one and is probably even more prevalent amongst local government civil servants, where decisions often affect so closely individuals' rights. Excessive secrecy is, in some contexts, one of the dominant characteristics of central and local government decision making. The Cullingworth Committee had some tough things (for an official committee) to say on some local authorities' reluctance even to divulge the basis of their allocation points system (MHLG, *Council housing purposes, procedures and priorities*, para 75, HMSO, 1969). This was true of over 25 per cent of housing authorities in the Committee's sample. If this is so, then it is even more likely that little information is given to individuals about their own housing applications. Lack of information is also to be found far too often in supplementary benefits. One separated mother with two children of $2\frac{1}{2}$ and 5 had her supplementary allowance altered and withheld about 5-6 times in as many months: it veered from £3 to over £12 and was stopped for some months. She could not get an explanation for this and it was forthcoming only when I wrote as a lawyer saying it was necessary to have this in order to advise her about her grounds and evidence for an appeal.

One of the obvious problems of, and no doubt a reason for, this secrecy, is the difficulty of contesting a decison which has been made in secret. It is true that if there is bureaucratic wrong doing there may be recourse to an MP or to the Parliamentary Commissioner—only in some central government matters—while there may be the possibility of going to the High Court to ask the judges to review what has been done. Apart from people's knowledge of such a possibility, the expense of such action, the availability of legal aid, and the willingness and competence of solicitors and barristers to take on such cases there is the major difficulty of getting the case on its feet. "A person aggrieved may never be appraised of facts which, if known, would afford a cause of action: departmental decision-making has been screened by Crown privilege and canalised onto the concept of ministerial responsibility to Parliament . . . other public authorities in England are not conspicuously indiscreet in distributing ammunition to potential adversaries; the courts . . . have been reluctant to place the worst interpretation on the face of the sphinx" (S. A. de Smith, *Judicial review of administrative action*, 2nd edition, p3).

This failure to provide relevant information, and the claiming of privilege is particularly important as since 1942, "There has been an enormous increase in the extent to which the executive impinges on the private lives of the citizens. New ministries have been created and the old have been enlarged. Inevitably the mass of documentation has proliferated. It now bears little relation to the "State Papers" or other documents of government to which some of the older cases refer. Yet the same privilege has been sought (and given) under the argument that the necessary candour cannot be obtained from civil servants if their documents are to be subjected to an outside chance of production in a court of law" (*Conway v Rimmer* (1968) I All ER p909).

One of the most significant attacks on the secrecy syndrome has been made by the judges, the often fitful guardians of citizens' rights. In the police constable's torch case, the House of Lords would not accept Roy Jenkins' (then Labour's Home Secretary) refusal to produce the Chief Constable's and the Police College's reports on a probationary police constable who was asked to leave the force. This was an important ruling the House of Lords did not follow the 1940s submarine cases which had upheld the executive's refusal to divulge information on national security grounds, but went on to establish their right to reject a minister's decision to withhold documents even from the court. Lord Reid urged the "House might now decide that courts have and are entitled to exercise a power and duty to hold a balance between the public interest, as expressed by a minister, to withhold certain documents or other evidence, and the public interest in ensuring the proper administration of justice" (*op cit*, p888). Their Lordships agreed that "the state of affairs cannot be allowed to continue . . . the judiciary must regain its control over the whole field of the law" and Lord Upjohn then went on to outline certain tests for the production of documents. It remains to be seen whether this case becomes an important weapon in counteracting the strength of departments in denying information—will this ruling extend to social security and welfare cases?— and become another *Donoghue and Stevenson* (the snail in the ginger beer case) in the field of civil rights. It is unlikely that it will have any dramatic effect as its principles cover discovery, not the earlier stages of preparation when it is vital to know what documents, if any, exist.

The Law Lords' comments in *Conway v Rimmer* were echoed in the report of the Fulton Committee set up by Labour to look at the Civil Service. That Committee stressed that "Ordinary citizens confront the state at many points in their everyday life: it taxes them and determines their rights to social benefits, it provides for the education of their children and the protection of their families' health. As householders many are dependent on the State's housing policies, as employers and employees they are deeply affected by its success or failure in its management of the national economy. In practice, most people can discharge many of their obligations to their families only with the help of the services provided and controlled by the state" (*The Civil Service, report of the Committee 1966-68,* vol. 1, para 290, HMSO, Cmnd 3638). The Fulton Committee on the Civil Service drew attention to the secrecy involved in decision making and gave its view that "The public interest would be better served if there were a greater amount of openness" (*op cit*, para 277). The only apparent step taken by the Labour Government was to publish a statement of intent asserting its belief in making more information available (*Information and the public interest,* Cmnd 4089, HMSO 1969). But the White Paper concentrated on information on policy issues, not for the individual, and did not deal with the question of information and local government.

Lack of information and secrecy can operate at top policy level, but also at individual level. This then involves two questions: to what extent does an individual have a *right* to specific information, like scale rates for educational welfare benefits? Secondly, how adequate should the information be? On the first question, the Labour Government did in 1970 make an important move: a summarised selection of the guidance notes to supplementary benefits officials was published, in the Supplementary Benefits Handbook. This handbook is too short and compressed, (as can be seen by comparing the information on definitions of cohabitation with that on normal occupation), but it represents a major advance in applying the principle of publishing information. Moreover, this "advance" is offset by so many other instances in which no, or inadequate, information is provided.

Some, so-called, explanatory leaflets obscure more than they reveal, particularly in social security. Recently the National Insurance Commissioners allowed an appeal by an unemployed man who was refused benefit on the ground he had delayed too long in claiming. The Commissioner decided that since it had not been possible to describe the administration of that part of social security accurately in leaflets and on forms, the system was not easy for claimants to understand with the result that the appellant had been misled by the claim form (R(U)3/70). Another leaflet from DHSS although not positively misleading like the one on unemployment benefit, appears more daunting, namely leaflet NI95, which applied before the recent divorce law reforms, for women whose marriage was ended by divorce or annulment. Apart from telling her to report to her local office, with its slightly sinister overtones of a ministry of moral behaviour, it has on the first page this statement: "Broadly the position is that the special rules set out in this leaflet apply to a marriage which has been annulled as being voidable, but not to one annulled because it was void." How many people here carry in their heads the knowledge of what makes a marriage void or voidable?

Local authorities are possibly the worst offenders. Some will not publish information about scale rates for welfare benefits, for example one county borough in the Midlands does not divulge information about its educational welfare benefits. Others will not make available leaflets and forms to agencies endeavouring to publicise benefits. An outer London borough would not give forms on rebates and educational benefits to the local citizens' advice bureau when it was running a one day welfare benefits bookstall in Autumn 1970.

Lack of knowledge about available benefits has been fairly well documented: large families in London who did not know about educational maintenance allowances (Hilary Land, *Large families in London,* p101); unsupported mothers who did not know about national assistance (now supplementary benefit) (D. Marsden, *Mothers alone,* p178); disabled men who did not know about benefits; students who do not know about statutory legal advice.

Decision making processes may be unbelievably slow and bureacratic, both in central and local government services. These difficulties may stem from low status and pay for the officials, coupled with inadequate training and supervision. Indeed it might be argued that slowness on the part of the SBC is an indication of a high level of takeup, but this in turn presupposes that one accepts the dominant role played by the SBC in income maintenance, compared to the comparatively minimal role accorded to its predecessor by Lord Beveridge. If Labour had fulfilled some of its promises in this area, perhaps the SBC would not have been so overloaded: in 1969 there was over 2,688,000 supplementary benefit recipients, compared with 2,495,000 in 1966 (*Civil appropriation accounts, 1969-70 report*, pxviii). In one case I handled when at the Child Poverty Action Group, it took DHSS from April 1969 to January 1970 to decide that a man who was in the process of appealing against a national insurance local tribunal decision was however entitled to supplementary benefit. Delays arose from SBC difficulties in contacting the man, files were lost, and vital and necessary questions were omitted at the first interview. A decision was only reached because we were prepared to go to the Divisional Court for an order of mandamus (see *The Times*, 9 August 1971). This may well have been an exceptional case: but it happened. Local government wheels grind slowly too, particularly over housing allocations. Administrative slowness may enable administrators to reach a right decision in the end, meanwhile the individual is worrying himself sick, or starving while the process goes on. Slowness is also apparent in social security dealings with unsupported mothers. Here it resembles somewhat the mediaeval test for witches: if you survived, you must have a source of income, if you did not—what a pity, you were obviously innocent. In a recent welfare case under the Illinois AFDC program, the court stated that a determination as to eligibility must be made within 30 days from the date of application (*Clearinghouse review*, December 1970, p390). This type of requirement has been written into the American Medicaid programme which states that applications must be processed promptly, and a decision reached within 30 days unless additional medical information is required (*Clearinghouse review*, October 1970, p251).

One way of tackling the problems of secrecy, infringement of privacy and administrative slowness might be to give many more opportunities of fair hearings or appeals and to institute pre-termination hearings. For example a tenant could be given the opportunity of an impartial hearing, independent of the local authority so he could hear why he is to be evicted and why he should not be evicted. (It is true he cannot be evicted without a court order, but if proceedings are in the magistrates' court, the magistrates have little option but to make the order.) In the USA courts have established that local housing authorities cannot deprive tenants of their right to public housing without notice and hearing. This is required under the appropriate regulations and the due process clause of the 14 Amendment (*Clearinghouse review*, June 1970, p54). A recent American Supreme Court decision has established that a pre-termination hearing must be held before public assistance payments to a welfare recipient are discontinued (*Goldberg v Kelly*, 90 S.Ct 1011, 1970). If we had a similar provision, the position of the deserted mother on supplementary benefits discussed earlier would have been radically altered: the onus of proof is on the agency to show why benefit should be cut, rather than withdrawing it and leaving the recipient to know about and use existing rights of appeal.

There are many other occasions where it might be just and fair to give the user/client/recipient an opportunity of being heard. But in the USA some lawyers are arguing that appeals and fair hearings if extensively used can slow up the decision-making process. The relevance of this can be seen in this country over town planning inquiries. Some Americans go on to argue that excessive enactment of rights and provision of hearings ignore the more fundamental realities of the processes of administration, particularly the informal process (Joel Handler in J. tenBroek, *op cit,* p166).

In the field of supplementary benefit appeal tribunals—procedure and composition—Labour's record was disappointing. There were difficulties over procedure: a second representative was not allowed by some individual tribunals, evidence was treated in a cavalier manner, documents were not made available to the appellant or his representative. Informality in procedure could lead to a denial of justice. For example on one occasion when I was at an appeal the presenting officer went back into the tribunal room within minutes of the end of the case. On some occasions considerable time elapsed before the appeal hearing date was fixed although this is not usually so. Putting in for an appeal is an occasion for an internal review of the case so that sometimes all the papers are sent to regional or head office. This practice would appal not only followers of Dicey with the blurring of the distinction between what is judicial and what is administrative but appal any person concerned with rights.

One positive step towards improvement was made when agreement was reached that conferences of Chairmen should be held (Council on tribunals, *Annual report, 1969-70,* para 27, HMSO, 1970). Other notable improvements have taken place since Labour left office: acceptance that two representatives are allowed, that documents should be sent to the appellant and that reasons should be in writing (*The Supplementary Benefit (Appeal Tribunal) Rules* 1971, SI 680, sections 11-12).

Supplementary Benefit Appeal Tribunals should be grouped, with full time chairmen, and properly trained staff with a separate career structure, and offices from DHSS. Labour however had proposed yet another separate tribunal for appeals for attendance allowances in the draft National Superannuation and Insurance Bill (Council on Tribunals, *op cit,* paras 47-48). At present we have a piecemeal system of tribunals for social security and related matters, with varying degrees of adequate procedure. The Council on Tribunals has argued for a proper policy on tribunals because legislation on tribunals is "shaped by the short term exigencies of political and administrative convenience rather than by any coherent long term policy" (*op cit,* para 10) with the result that we have relatively weak tribunals with awkward divisions of jurisdiction.

discretion and ministers' powers

As pointed out earlier, few major new substantive rights within the social services were created during 1964-70. Discretion in legislation for the social services is one of the rationing devices. A local authority may charge "reasonable rents" (*Housing Act* 1957, section 111) or may give financial help to families in need to prevent a child being taken into care (*Children and Young Persons Act* 1963, section 1) or provide "temporary accommodation for persons who are in urgent need thereof, being need arising in circumstances which could not reasonably have been foreseen or in such other circumstances as the authority may in any particular case determine" (*National Assistance Act* 1948, section 21). Discretion can also be seen in the interpretation of phrases (often of the utmost significance) in legislation. In section 4 of the 1966 Ministry of Social Security Act a person has a right to help if his resources are inadequate to meet his requirements. But what is meant by "requirements"? This will depend partly on what rent he pays, so what is a "reasonable rent"? But requirements will be limited in part by the operation of the wage stop so what are his "normal earnings"? Some of these words have not been clearly defined by Parliament in the Act, so what becomes important is how officials work out these phrases.

In some welfare legislation, often in those Acts which set out no clearly defined set of rights for the individual, clearly defined default powers were given, enabling the Minister to take action to ensure the provision of a particular service. Here the Minister is being given more than the umpire's role between individual and local authority: he is being given powers to redress the position of some groups of individuals too weak to secure the minimum of standard and service. These default powers can be found in the National Assistance Act 1948, part III, in the National Health Service Act and legislation on education, housing and town and country planning. In some cases the Minister may be able to step in, or compel the authority by mandamus to do what is failing to do as a court is sometimes reluctant to entertain an application by an individual (S. A. de Smith, *op cit*, p569). But it is rare for a Minister to intervene publicly. Mr. Crossman, as Secretary of State, did not in the Spring of 1970 intervene in one or two London Boroughs notorious for the inadequate provision which they made for homeless families but waited for the result of the enquiry under Professor Greve, set up by him, and finally published in May 1971.

It is not possible for the obvious political reasons of scarce resources to say that discretionary powers should be made mandatory. Anyway clear mandatory duties are not necessarily performed. Medical officers of health have a duty to order the closure of housing which is in bad condition. But this is unlikely to occur if there is a shortage of housing, particularly in the decaying inner areas of large cities. So mandatory powers can be a fitful, paper protection. Here public health inspectors are exercising that flexible discretionary power, so praised by the SBC in its handbook. Discretionary power can also be unfair and inconsistent. Public health inspectors cannot take notice of the hundreds of houses in poor condition, so they have to exercise their discretion as to which houses they will notice, even as the Queen exercises her discretion as to which guests she will talk to at a Royal Garden Party.

Recently, however, the House of Lords stated that ministerial discretionary powers should not be exercised arbitrarily. In *Padfield v The Ministry of Agriculture* (1968) I All ER, p694), the Law Lords refused to accept the Minister's claim to have unfettered discretion whether to refer a complaint from a group of farmers to a certain committee set up under the milk marketing scheme. Lord Reid said that "Parliament must have conferred the discretion with the intention that it should be used to promote the policy and objects of the Act . . . (that) must be determined by construing the Act as a whole, and construction is always a matter for the court . . . but if a Minister . . . so uses his discretion as to thwart or run counter to the policy and objects of the Act, then our law would be very defective if persons aggrieved were not entitled to the protection of the court" (*op cit*, p699). This contribution by the House of Lords to the control of discretion should not be overlooked. It is not certain how far the courts will be prepared to go, but this decision might be capable of extension, particularly if lawyers demonstrate an "aptitude for verbal gymnastics" (S. A. de Smith, *op cit*, p80) since "the usual meanings of words can be stretched, contorted and stood upside down" in this uncertain area of judicial review.

information and advice services: access to the courts

Many years ago Tawney wrote that "if the rights essential to freedom are effectively to safeguard it, they must not be merely formal, like the right of all who can afford it to dine at the Ritz, but must be accompanied by conditions which ensure that, whenever the occasion to exercise them arises, they can in fact be exercised" (Tawney, *op cit*, p80). The trouble is that those rights which do exist cannot often be exercised unaided—this is why the network of information and advice services and the role of lawyers and social workers are so important for the exercise of rights.

Lord Beveridge had in 1942 seen that "one of the serious disadvantages of the present division of security functions between so many different agencies is the difficulty experienced by insured persons in understanding their rights and duties. This, apart from the direct loss and delay to insured persons, leads sometimes to unjustified resentment and sometimes lack of interest." He realised that a new system based on his proposals would still be complicated and that citizens could not be left to find out all about it by reading official pamphlets, however clearly written. He proposed an advice bureau in *every local* social security office (*Social Insurance and Allied Services: Report by Sir William Beveridge*, Cmd 6404, para 397, HMSO, 1942). The Ingleby Committee, the Molony Committee and the Seebohm Committee all reinforced the need for adequate advice and information services available to everyone on a variety of problems. A recent study in Sheffield demonstrated that some people often too easily accept a brush-off by a central or local government official and that a quarter of the respondents were not prepared in such a situation to seek further advice and help (W. Hamilton, *Democracy and community*, p139). Such an attitude was most "particularly marked among those who have received only the minimum of schooling and who are employed in unskilled occupations. People in these groups are often in need of advice when dealing with authority, but it is clear that they do not always receive it; nor do they always realise their need" (*op cit*).

Information services alone, as run by a local authority, may be inadequate since what may be essential is a skilled advocacy service for example which will ensure the writing of letters, making of telephone calls and putting the enquirer's case firmly and, if necessary, representing at a hearing. Conflicts of interest are bound to arise in a service run by a local authority. The last Labour Government did not take the opportunity to begin to improve and strengthen information and advice services which would have indicated a real concern for the rights of the individual. We have recently in the last two years seen much interest in the provision of legal services—indeed it is becoming one of the fashionable bandwagons—while little attention is paid to the front line advice and information services, which are under financed and not uniformly distributed. From my present survey financed by the Nuffield Foundation it appears that some citizens' advice bureaux even exist on a £50 budget, while one had an office in the ladies cloakroom. An independent, national service with a preponderance of trained, full time workers would seem essential to sort out the complexities of our present welfare state services, and to act as a competent referral agency for specialists' services. Advice centres could be modelled on the *Which?* Advice Centre in Kentish Town by having all the relevant information about central and local government services, like application forms and eligibility criteria on display. Really comprehensive information and advice services could well be linked to the Parliamentary Commissioner and the proposed local authority commissioners.

In addition much more extensive publicity about services and how to apply should be carried out on television, as well as by posters on public transport which might help to disseminate information and break down the barrier between "charitable" and non-charitable services. But unfortunately many people for whom these services are designed cannot always understand the forms or perservere with their applications, so that more publicity and effective training should be given to the front-line helpers, (advice and information services and social workers). Indeed the growth in self-help oranisations, claimants' unions, squatters, unemployed claimants and specialist advice services given by some pressure groups like CPAG and NCCL in part indicates a need on the part of recipients (and their advisers) for more competent help over certain types of problems. It might be beneficial for some of these consumer organisations to press for a right to have a desk and workers within social services and other offices, as has been done in the USA by the Philadelphia Welfare Rights Organisation. It has been argued in the States that this is a constitutional right, based on the first amendment right to speak, to associate and to petition the government for redress of grievances (*Clearinghouse review,* June 1970, p58).

During 1964-70 little was done for consumers in developing strong information and advice services. These could operate most effectively if in the last resort there were opportunities of asserting rights through the legal system. This requires an accessible and competent legal profession and accessible courts and tribunals. As Lord Gardiner, Labour's Lord Chancellor, pointed out in the debate on the state and the individual, "The Labour Party has always recognised that it is no good people having legal rights if they cannot afford to enforce or defend them" (House of Lords, *Hansard,* 18 June 1969, col. 1041). In that debate, however, he was essentially historical, dwelling on Labour's role in 1945-51. But this does not advance access to legal services in 1964-70. Legal advice financial eligibility limits were raised just before the election, to take effect after. But the increase (the limits had been unchanged for 11 years) was minimal, as I have shown elsewhere, (*Rights in the welfare state,* Poverty pamphlet 4) and the only tribunal to which legal representation was extended by Labour was the Lands Tribunal. The question of neighbourhood law firms and extension of legal advice services has been under considerable discussion, but the Lord Chancellor's Advisory Committee made weak recommendations, which were not implemented (see Rosalind Brooke, *Modern Law Review*, July 1970, p432).

During the Labour administration, as in America, it would be possible to argue that "undoubtedly the poor have failed to secure the fullest measure of their legal rights too because they have not been able to afford the services of lawyers. The very paucity of judicial precedents and the lack of decisions construing the rights of welfare recipients testify to the fact that their cause has seldom been free to interpret the legislative command almost at will" (Miller in tenBroek, *op cit*, p78).

Apart from problems of access to courts and lawyers, there is the major assumption that the majority of English lawyers would be helpful in obtaining the rights of poorer people. The situation is little different here from the American one described by Ralph Nader: "Possibly the greatest failure of the law schools was not to articulate a theory and practice of a just deployment of legal manpower. With massive public interests deprived of effective legal representation, the law schools continued to encourage recruits for law firms whose practice militated against any such representation even on a sideline, *pro bono* basis. Lawyers laboured for polluters, not anti-polluters, for sellers not consumers, for corporations, not citizens, for labour leaders, not rank and file, for, not against weak standards before government agencies . . . for agricultural subsidies to the rich but not food stamps for the poor" (*The New Republic*, p21, 1969). Recruitment and training of lawyers is a crucial matter. On this Lord Gardiner set up the Ormrod Committee to look at professional training (*Report of the committee on legal education*, Cmnd 4596, HMSO, 1971). But we needed to know far more about the work and remuneration of both barristers and solicitors. The NBPI did look at solicitors' remuneration (*Remuneration of solicitors*, report 54, Cmnd 3529, HMSO, 1968) while the Monopolies Commission looked at lawyers and other professional restrictive practices (Cmnd 4463, HMSO, 1970). Neither branch of the profession apparently felt sufficiently secure to tolerate a comprehensive and independent survey into their activities: nor did the Labour Government set such enquiries going.

conclusion

On rights within the social services the Labour Government's record was inadequate. Certain committees and research enquiries for the time honoured reasons of avoiding making a quick decision on important issues, like the provision of legal services, or the extent of accommodation for homeless families, were set up.

The Labour Government set up certain institutional devices like the Parliamentary Commissioner. But there were problems over the definition of "maladministration" and limited areas of review with the result that this new device did not fulfill the hopes of Mr Crossman in the debates on setting up the Commissioner. Despite the evidence from the Ely and AEGIS enquiries and the need for a hospital complaints service, Labour set up a hospital advisory service with personal complaints excluded. Protection against harassment was contained in the Rent Acts and the Rent Officer service was provided to give security of tenure for unfurnished tenants, but similar protection for furnished tenants was denied. The Labour Government salved its conscience by setting up the committee under Mr. Francis to investigate the matter.

Far more important was the total failure on the part of the Labour Government to do anything to help people obtain their rights by improving advice and information services, and access to legal services. Despite some measure of reorganisation of the courts following the Beeching Commission, nothing comprehensive was done about the organisation of tribunals. Legal representation was extended only to the Lands Tribunal while the new income limits for legal advice and legal aid were inadequate. Nor was anything done about the important problem of geographical access to legal services tackled. The very real problem of lack of sufficient and systematic review of legislation and the general state of English and administrative law was not tackled. But even had Labour's record on these points been better, the problem of rights would not have been solved. "But neither representation nor participation will prevent the abuse of power or secure redress to the person who is harrowed by such abuse" (Anthony Lester, *Democracy and individual rights*, Fabian tract 390). A Bill of Rights is needed since there are "too many limitations by the democratic process in protecting individual and minority interests." Justice Douglas of the American Supreme Court has said that "It is not without significance that most of the provisions of the Bill of Rights are procedural. It is procedure that spells much of the difference between rule by law and rule by whim or caprice—steadfast adherence to strict procedural safeguards is our main assurance that there will be equal justice under the law" (*Inquiry into civil rights, report 2*, vol 4, p1464, Queen's Printer (Ottawa) 1969). The emphasis in this chapter has been on the importance of procedural rights, and it is disappointing and discouraging that the Labour Government rejected the various proposals during their years in office for improving the situation of the individual by introducing a bill of rights. A bill of rights would not of itself improve the individual's rights, access to information, or reduce arbitrary invasions of privacy. But it would help to develop a consciousness of equitable procedures, particularly in test cases and appeals, and create the framework of values within which substantive reforms by a future Labour Government could be successfully introduced. The American Constitution has served a number of different functions over the years. For years it was used to uphold slavery and then segregation, but recently under a liberal bench, it was used to extend individual's rights in ensuring representation in juvenile courts and pre-termination hearings for welfare recipients.

The weak position of the individual needs strengthening in this country. As the Canadian Royal Commission on Civil Rights pointed out, the "sole purpose of the democratic state is to regulate and promote the mutual rights, freedoms and liberties of the individuals under its control. State power is something in the nature of a trust conferred by the people on all those in positions of authority" (*op cit*, vol 1, p2). Excessive and unnecessary power, or power exercised arbitrarily, corrupts and destroys democratic institutions. Guidelines for the exercise of these powers could be given by enacting a Bill of Rights. It cannot of itself secure rights: they have to be tested and fought for. Alone, it is inadequate. We need grassroots participation, information and rights at an individual level. Then we need action on a grand scale, mobilising the legal

260

system and here a bill of rights could help by establishing for individuals greater procedural rights in appeals and administrative decision making, and substantive rights which have been wrongly denied. This would be using law as a weapon, not a shield, to protect and regulate the respective rights, freedoms and liberties of individuals within the social services.

chronology

September 1965	Rent Act.
November 1965	Abolition of the Death Penalty.
August 1966	Ministry of Social Security Act: "right to benefit".
March 1967	Parliamentary Commissioner set up.
December 1967	Ormrod Committee on legal education (appointed).
July 1968	AEGIS enquiries: report.
March 1969	Ely Hospital Report.
April 1969	Mr. Crossman commissioned enquiry into homelessness under Professor John Greve.
June 1969	White Paper on Information and the Public Interest published.
July 1969	Skeffington Report on *People and Planning* with mention of need for participation published.
September 1969	Royal Commission on Assizes and Quarter Sessions: report published.
October 1969	Committee on the Rent Acts appointed.
November 1969	Hospital Advisory Service set up.
February 1970	White Paper on Local Government Reform with suggestion of Local Commissioners for Administration published.
May 1970	SBC Handbook published. Income limits for civil legal aid and advice raised. Younger Committee on Privacy appointed.

15. planning and the environment

Peter Hall

To understand the impact of the 1964-1970 Labour government upon planning as a whole, we need a systematic framework of analysis which relates physical planning, in the strict sense, to related policies in the fields of transport, housing, agriculture, public enterprise, and economic policy generally. Little attempt seems to have been made anywhere, up to now, to provide this framework, probably because no one appreciated the relationships. Planners, as we have seen, have been concerned to separate their policies on urban growth and change from the wider bundle of policies in related fields. But despite this the inter-relationships have necessarily continued to operate, and it is necessary to understand them.

The starting point is to develop a check list of *alternative policies with regard to physical forms of urbanisation*—the central concern of the physical planner in the quarter century after world war two, and then to develop a parallel list of *alternative policies in the related fields*. Particularly important here are alternative housing policies, transport policies and industrial location policies. But of only slightly less direct relevance are policies in agriculture, local government reform, land, and the general management of the economy. The analysis of alternative physical forms can be extended to include a great variety of alternative job distributions, population distributions and urban forms, which can be permuted or associated with each other in fairly systematic and logical ways. Some of these are considerably more likely than others, and these are the ones chosen for closer analysis in the study. They include:

1. *Peripheral growth* of cities and conurbations on the pattern of the 1930s, often condemned as "urban sprawl" by the planning writers of that time;

2. *New towns* of freestanding character away from the major cities and towns, as provided for in the 1946 New Towns Act;

3. *Town expansions* of existing small and medium sized country towns well away from the major cities and conurbations, as provided for in the 1952 Town Development Act;

4. *Polycentric planned urban agglomerations* including a great variety of different settlement types, as advocated in the final chapter of Ebenezer Howard's classic work *Garden cities of tomorrow* (1898/1901).

5. *Dispersal* of the population freely at low densities over the land surface. The problem then is to see how each of these alternatives may be encouraged, or discouraged, by policies in related fields as well as by the direct application of planning policies.

the record: 1945 to 1964

At the end of world war two, it can be argued there was a reasonably consistent bundle of policies offered to the British public by devoted campaigners like Patrick Abercrombie, Frederic Osborn of the Town and Country Planning Association, and others. It would have involved giving total, centralised control to the planners. Powers over land use would have been given to a central agency which would have decided how much land was to be released for urban growth, and where. This agency would also have had powers over the generation of new employment. All development rights would have been nationalised; all development (save perhaps for individually built houses for owner occupation) would have been carried through by compulsory purchase on the part of the central planning authority. The result would have been a pattern of urban growth closely corresponding to the new town, expanding town, planned conurbation models. The growth of the conurbations would have been strictly limited; virtually all urban growth would take place in new towns or planned town expansions.

This solution offended too many groups of people: intending owner occupiers seeking spec-built housing, the big cities, the counties. So it proved too radical even for the Labour government of 1945-1951, which allowed it to be buried under a set of other, often contradictory policies. The Labour government did nationalise development rights and did try to take all development profits for the State. It did concentrate its building programme on public housing; in four years (1946-1950) it designated eight new towns round London and six in other parts of Britain. It set up strong planning authorities to control land use, armed with real powers; it issued manuals of guidance which stressed the importance of protecting agricultural land. It inherited an Act (passed by the coalition government in its last days) which allowed it to control employment, even if the power extended only to factory employment. It began work on a bill to encourage planned town expansion. It sought to control the rate of inflation by quite draconian measures. It nationalised transport, mainly inter-urban rail transport and (indirectly) the bus companies in the countryside, but including London Transport; it tried to encourage good public transport at a time when cars were still luxury goods.

On the other hand, the 1945 government failed to do many things which needed to be done if a consistent set of policies was to be pursued. Above all, it failed to reform local government in a way that would allow cities and their surrounding rural land to be planned together. (It did, however, set up a strong chain of regional offices within its planning ministry, to provide a strong lead in regional development policies). It failed to take completely centralised power to regulate development, as the expert Uthwatt committee on compensation and betterment had recommended in 1942, preferring instead a system which depended on regulation of the market and 100 per cent taxation of its profits, a system which, on the financial side, proved quite unworkable. These were perhaps minor blemishes on a reasonably consistent record. But they were to prove a source of weakness once Labour were out of office.

The Conservative period from 1951 to 1964 was by no means a homogeneous one in terms of planning and related policies. In particular, we have to distinguish a period up to about 1960, when the tide against planning ran particularly strong; and the period after that, when a counter flow set in. During the 1950s, ministers like Macmillan, Sandys and Brooke pursued a fairly consistent line of reversing many of the strands of Labour policy. They shifted the pattern of housebuilding away from public and towards private building for sale. They virtually abandoned the new towns policy, starting no new towns in England (and only one in Scotland); in 1957 they even announced that no further new towns would be built. They preferred instead to concentrate on the machinery of voluntary town expansion by agreement between exporting and importing authorities, as provided by the 1952 Town Development Act (a Labour measure which they took over and passed on coming into office); a machinery which proved conspicuously unsuccessful in providing for large scale overspill up to 1960. They failed to make any fundamental reform of local government, though they appointed a Royal Commission to investigate London government, and a Local Government Commission with limited powers to recommend changes elsewhere. They dismembered the financial provisions of the 1947 Planning Act, though they retained the nationalisation of development rights which was its central feature. They were, as the Town and Country Planning Association felt bound to point out, relatively strong on negative controls for the defence of the countryside (like green belts); relatively weak on positive polices to ensure urban dispersal. In more than one major planning battle, they insisted on the comfortable formula that the cities should as far as practicable rehouse their populations at high densities in preference to invading rural acres. In themselves, these were perfectly consistent policies; the trouble is that they accorded ill with the basic promises and philosophy of the 1947 Act. The result was a policy of peripheral additions to existing urban areas wherever space was available; a policy dictated by sheer necessity rather than by any coherent overall regional plan.

The short period from 1961 to 1964 saw a profound re-orientation of Conservative policy. New town building started again in earnest: two new towns for the West Midlands, two for Merseyside, one for Glasgow were designated. The Town Development Act was made more effective and began to produce the promise of houses on a larger scale. Fundamental and far ranging inquiries into regional strategies were begun in the south east, the west midlands, the north west, the north east, and central Scotland (and, in three of these areas, were complete during the Conservative period of office). Local government in Greater London and the west midlands was reformed, though less radically than many had hoped. But even then, the Conservative government found itself unable to grasp several politcal nettles. It could not embark on a really fundamental reform of local government on a town plus country basis, because of the opposition of the counties to urban invasion. It could not act to deal with the increasing scandal of speculative profits on building land, where fortunes could turn on accidents of planning permission, despite the continued nominal fiction that all development rights really belonged to the state and that there was provision to compensate for any historic rights lost at the passage of the 1947 Act. Thus it continued to encourage an increasing proportion of the population into owner occupiership, while its policies guaranteed that the prices of the houses thus occupied would be escalated by land shortage and speculation. At the same time, while it began new towns to take overspill from the conurbations, it continued operating the high rise and expensive-land subsidies which in effect encouraged the major cities to rehouse as large a proportion as possible of their populations within their own boundaries, at the expense of the general taxpayer. Meanwhile, since the overspill programme did not provide for the owner-occupier, by and large, he continued to be housed in peripheral additions to the cities and towns. Documents like the *South East Study* (1964) were conspicuously silent on a positive planning policy for new private housing developments.

the Labour record

It might have been supposed that many of these policies would have been reversed by a Labour government determined to introduce a consistent set of policies throughout the field of urban development. But in fact, between 1964 and 1970 that was far from being the case. Too many existing policies reflected an untidy political concensus; and this in turn reflected similar political pressures which exerted themselves on both parties. Labour enthusiastically continued the policy of designating further new towns, though many of them suggested in regional policy documents published, or at least initiated, by the previous administration; it supported a welcome departure in policy, which suggested that 50 per cent of new homes in new towns should be built for owner-occupation; yet at the some time it continued to pay the differential subsidies on high-density redevelopment within the cities, though in the 1969 Housing Act it substantially modified the subsidy structure to discourage the expensive and unpopular high rise structures; and it did little to encourage lower income groups to leave the areas of housing stress in the conurbations. It continued at the same time to give a generous subsidy to owner-occupiers through income tax relief on mortgage payments (and even, in the case of insurance linked mortgages, to repayments of principal), though it was general knowledge that this was a sharply regressive subsidy giving maximum benefits to the rich. Though it made heroic attempts to curb inflation by wage freeze and income norm, the inflation that did occur further encouraged the move to owner occupation and so, indirectly, the flight to the suburbs; the 1966 Census recorded massive population losses from most major cities, on a scale never before witnessed save during the wartime blitz. Though it revolutionised the administrative structure of public transport and provided a new subsidy structure for unprofitable services under the 1968 Transport Act, it could do nothing in practice to stem rising car ownership and, like its predecessor, found itself committed to a steadily rising expenditure on road construction. Though it increased taxation of the motorist at a faster rate than the previous administration, the cost of motoring still rose more slowly than the costs of public transport, which were swelled by labour cost inflation: yet another case of a trend which hit the poor hardest and the rich least, and which (together with the subsidy for owner occupiers) could only encourage further suburban decentralisation and car-based commuting. In this respect, indeed, there is the closest parallel between the policies of Labour and Conservative governments alike, and the policies of successive American administrations since World War Two.

In precisely three respects the Labour government of 1964-1970 made major innovations. The first was the Land Commission. This essentially was supposed to achieve two objects: to bring in what was in effect a special capital gains tax on development land, and to provide a central agency to buy land and release it for development on a large scale. The first of these corrected an anomaly: it was a useful reform which in itself did not need a special agency to manage it. The second was quite radical: it was an attempt to alter the balance between rural conservation and urban development, by creating a strong, independent new land development agency. This in time would have done on a larger scale what the New Town Development Corporations did for their respective areas, and it would have achieved much of what the Uthwatt Committee were calling for in 1942. It was called nationalisation by stealth, and that is no bad description of what it would have become.

In an important sense the second major innovation had precisely the same objective. This was the fundamental reform of local government, on which the government embarked when they set up the Redcliffe-Maud Commission for England and the Wheatley Commission for Scotland, in 1966. It is generally agreed that any such fundamental reform must be based on a union of city and countryside; and that in itself, in a country where 80 per cent of the population are officially counted as urban and where the real proportion is probably nearer 90 per cent, must represent a profound shift of power away from the shires and towards the urban interest. But there are various ways of doing this, more or less radical. The solution proposed by Redcliffe-Maud for England, in 1970, was about the most radical possible. Over the great bulk of the countryside, unitary authorities controlling town and countryside, but controlled fundamentally by the townspeople who had hitherto been segregated in the county boroughs; in and around the conurbations, metropolitan two tier authorities where the top tier would have the basic responsibility for preparing plans, extending widely across the green belts and striking deep into the traditional territory of the counties. In effect, around Manchester and Liverpool and Birmingham this would have given the urban interests control over as much building land as they could conceivably have used, for many years ahead; the extremely wide extent of the boundaries meant that they would not be constrained to adopt narrowly self interested planning policies. There was in fact no alternative in good planning terms between this and the opposite extreme of conurbation authorities cut back to the physical boundaries of the conurbations, as the Conservatives recognised when they preferred the latter solution in their revised local government map of 1971.

The two major innovations, then, were both fundamentally intended to shift the balance of power between urban development and rural conservation. Their long term effect must have been to encourage more planned development, both for public rented housing and for sale, in the form of medium density housing beyond the conurbation boundaries, and conversely less in the form of high density renewal within them: a change which would have been socially and psychologically beneficial to the families affected, and economically beneficial to the community as a whole. Even if a proportion of the overspill population could not find local jobs, but were constrained to commute back to the conurbation daily for work, there can be no doubt, from the work of Dr. Stone and others, that this last statement would be still justified. But with clear evidence from the 1966 census that jobs were beginning to follow people in the migration from the big cities, this is perhaps a problem of decreasing force.

The third main innovation was related to the other two, though it seems to have become an arm of physical planning policy almost by accident. The

Regional Economic Planning Councils and Boards were introduced in 1965-1966 with the explicit aim of promoting regional economic development; it was only in the course of their actual work, especially in dynamic regions like the south east and the west midlands, that it became clear that the internal distribution of activities and people within each region must be one of their central concerns. Ironically, it was about this time (1969) that the Department of Economic Affairs was abolished and that the Councils were made responsible to the Secretary of State for Regional Planning, later, under the more fundamental Conservative reform of the Whitehall planning structure, the Secretary for the Environment. There, the Councils live in a curious half-world, pending the recommendations of the Crowther Commission. In the South East and again in the North West, both Labour and Conservative governments have displayed their preference for a new ad hoc form of regional study, produced by a specially gathered team and commissioned jointly by the Planning Council and by the standing regional body representing the local planning authorities. It may seem untidy and it does not provide in any clear way for monitoring or follow up after the report is finished; but it does provide a way of reconciling the necessary tensions between local and central interests on the subject of regional growth.

Against this background, what did Labour policies on planning do to reduce inequality? If they could have been consistenly followed through over a fifteen or twenty year period—something that does not now seem likely to happen—they could have exerted a strong influence on the living standards and living styles of certain large sections of the population. They could have allowed a given quantity of housing resources to have been employed more economically, providing for more people in the low middle income ranges to enjoy new housing of modern standards, either through owner occupiership or through public renting. (In the short run, while it operated, the Land Commission almost certainly had the reverse effect: that was inevitable, and should have been expected). What these policies would not have done, automatically, was to improve the lot of the very poorest. As Ray Thomas has shown in an important piece of research, the new towns policy has worked consistently since 1945 to improve the lot of the relatively skilled manual worker, who forms a disproportionately large part of the population in all of them; it has consistently failed to attract the low income service trade worker in the conurbations, who has remained trapped there in a vicious circle of low money income, poor privately rented housing and poor knowledge of employment and training and housing opportunities elsewhere (R. Thomas, *London's new towns*, 1968).

In her study of housing in Camden, Ruth Glass has clearly shown the haphazardness of current housing policies even in a progressive local authority area. Only about 30 per cent of all households of semi-skilled or unskilled workers were in the council sector, while of those in unfurnished privately rented dwellings no less than 45 per cent had less than £16 a week, 28 per cent of them less than £12. (The corresponding figures for furnished, privately rented accommodation were 54 and 26 per cent). Of those with under £12 a week, no less than 45 per cent of the unfurnished and 78 per cent of the furnished tenants were paying one third of more of their income on housing. As Ruth Glass comments, the poor are paying more, because many are paying no less than three supplementary housing taxes: on central area accommodation, on furnished accommodation and on accommodation for newcomers. These are the people who continue to suffer most from the existing bundle of policies (R. Glass, "Housing in Camden," *Town Planning Review*, 41, 1970).

The more prosperous, in contrast, have done not at all badly. The skilled worker enjoys his subsidised council or new town dwelling, and may use some of the surplus income to buy a car which gives him additional mobility, in seeking jobs for instance. He is in a similar position to the middle class white collar house buyer whose mortgage payments, though they have risen due to steepening interest rates, have been cushioned by the regressive tax relief arrangements. The fact here is that now, the white collar worker and the skilled blue collar worker find themselves on the same side of the real dividing line in British society. The really unfortunate, the unskilled, the immigrants, the old, the problem families, in many case find themselves on the other. It might seem surprising that Labour policies have not greatly changed this situation. But that would ignore that the Labour party is mainly run, at local level, by the lower middle and upper working class members who tend to forget it. They have a good reason to do so, because they are among the beneficiaries.

As a result, the general verdict must be that many policies which were good in themselves were less good than they might have been, simply because they failed to extend their benefits widely enough. It was certainly not wrong to build new towns, indeed there might well have been a bigger programme: but they failed to benefit the most disadvantaged anything like as much as the more advantaged groups. It was not wrong either to encourage home ownership: but the precise means chosen for the purpose had the effects of giving the biggest possible benefits to the rich, and next to no benefits (at least up to the option mortgage scheme) to the poor.

Many of the policies are concerned more narrowly with housing than with planning proper. But in logic and in practice, as I have sought to show, the policies are not readily separable. Planning is centrally concerned with spatial arrangements of people and activities. After twenty five years of effective town and country planning, nearly half of them under Labour, we find that the main distributive effect was to keep the poor, or a high proportion of them, poor.

One reason is that planning has not concerned itself specifically enough with such questions of distribution. For this reason it seems to have failed to discover even the facts. Far too little is known about the critical relationships between income, occupational skill, training, geographical location and housing conditions in the cities—though the Glass report on Camden provides important evidence and the Greve report on London housing, provides more. Far too little is being done, on an experimental basis coupled with action research, to develop experimental programmes which would bring employment and housing opportunities simultaneously to the forgotten millions in the inner city areas. These should be priorities for Labour's next period of office. But for the recent past, it is clear that policies of this kind were not pursued energetically, because the implications of planning for income distribution were not clearly realised.

the new approach to planning

It is only very recently (1970-71), in fact, that the theme of inequality has begun to appear prominently in writings about planning. As yet the main contributions are American; and some of the more important ones, both British and American, are not yet published (in particular Harvey's contribution to the 1970 Colston Symposium and Ray Pahl's British Sociological Association paper). The second half of this chapter is a very summary attempt to set out the central message of the new approach.

Some pioneers of the planning movement were implicitly interested in inequality. Thus writing at the time of the early Fabians, Ebenezer Howard advocated the garden city as a way of curing simultaneously many of the deprivations of poor city dwellers and poor ruralites. But more recently, planners in Britain have been conspicuously uninterested in the problem. One can say that by about 1940, an ideology of planning had developed, and it was this which was the basis of the whole legistlative and administrative effort after World War Two (H. Gracey in P. Hall *et al: Megalopolis denied* 1972). According to this ideology, the problems planning had to solve were defined in physical terms—urban sprawl, loss of open contryside, lack of cohesion in urban structure—and the remedies were similarly physical—urban containment, countryside protection, the creation of self contained and balanced communities. It was assumed, almost as an article of faith, that the problems were self evident to all men of intelligence and goodwill, and that the remedies would generally be to the benefit of the entire community; conflicts of interest between individuals and groups could not arise. This comfortable assumption suited the *unitary* style of decision making, which some American observers of British planning have noted as one of its most distinctive features (*cf.* D. Foley, *Controlling London's growth,* 1963). These same American observers have noticed that a unitary approach is typical of a paternalist system of government where an established ruling class is sure of its own values, so sure that it can impose them without question on the rest of the community, (M. Meyerson and E. C. Banfield, *Politics, planning and the public interest*, Glencoe 1955).

Little change in the assumptions and the values can be observed since then in the great bulk of the professionals and the ideologists of planning. The main change of the 1960s, the adoption of quantitative methods of forecasting and of evaluation, made no basic difference. For an essential tenet of cost benefit analysis is that the community *as a whole* can arrive at the best course of action. Though individual costs and benefits arise, they are all subsumed in arriving at the greatest good of the greatest number. Cost benefit analysis, however, did represent an advance in that it at least recognised the existence of costs and benefits.

Similarly, the belief remained strong that physical planning, or spatial planning, was a reasonably self contained activity with its own justification and its own rules. By the end of the 1960s there was a strong movement for the integration of transport planning with other aspects of spatial planning, a movement which reached its apogee in the Lady Sharp report (Sharp, *Transport planning: the men for the job*, HMSO, 1970). But here, as elsewhere, there is no attempt to question the validity of spatial planning as a separate, compartmentalised activity.

The real change has come in two ways, both felt first, and with great force, in the United States. First was the attempt to introduce output budgeting (PPBS) techniques throughout government (cf. P. Else, Public expenditure, Parliament and PPB, 1970). This proved difficult and Daniel Moynihan has recently pronounced it a costly failure (D. P. Moynihan, SSRC *Newsletter*, 10, November 1970). But it focussed thinking in government, both at central and local level, on the need to measure the value of any policy not in terms of *inputs*, which has been the traditional method, but in terms of *outputs* defined in terms of the achievement of given objectives which are common to the whole local or central government system, not to the particular agency being considered at the time. As example, the success of a public transport system could no longer be measured in terms of input criteria like the number of buses per hour, but in terms of output criteria such as the success in giving low income workers better accessibility to job opportunities. And this latter objective might more economically be secured by quite different policies, not provided by the transport agency at all—by better job information for instance. Output budgeting potentially provided a way for judging the policies of different departments or agencies against each other. The second development was the realisation, against this background, that physical planning was doing little to aid social objectives concerned with improving the condition of the American poor. Urban renewal, in the ironic phrase, was often synonymous with negro removal. Physical planners became more and more interested in non-physical programmes. As a result, many of them in America today would better be regarded as social administrators than as planners in the traditional British sense. The truth, however, is that in America and now increasingly in Britain, "planning" has two different meanings: a traditional meaning concerned with the working of the physical or spatial planning agency, and a new meaning concerned with the higher level general policy making function of the entire government system concerned. The second, increasingly, will vet the proposals and the policies of the first. It is a simple but a revolutionary change, since it destroys the autonomy of the professional in local authority work.

the new focus on distribution

Previously, though physical planning eschewed general statements of basic aims, the implicit focus was on improvements in economic *allocation*. Planning was supposed to make for more efficient, that is more economical, use of resources and so aided the achievement of a high rate of economic growth. In the new style of planning, there is a strong shift towards a focus on the consequences in terms of *distribution* of rewards. In particular, it is realised that many public policies, individually but also in their cumulative effect, act as "hidden mechanisms of redistribution" in David Harvey's phrase. This applies particularly not to the services popularly known as the "Seebohm services," where the re-distributive effect may be quite open, but to the area of spatial planning which affects the provision of "Impure public goods." Impure public goods, in the jargon of welfare economics, are provided publicly in the sense that they are not paid for directly when they are consumed, but they are not completely free goods like air; they are spatially distributed, and those located conveniently in relation to them will enjoy a more generous supply and/or a lower cost supply. Examples include schools, public transport, clean air and freedom from noise.

Sociologists have come to realise that people will organise together to get a better supply of these goods. And as the rich will use their money to buy more private goods in the market place, so they will tend to use their knowledge and influence to unite more effectively in the pursuit of impure public goods. Since these goods tend to loom larger and larger in the total pattern of consumption in advanced societies, it can be expected that the richer and better advantaged sections of the population will tend to transfer their energies progressively from the market place to the political forum. In doing so they will naturally tend to argue in "unitary" political terms, i.e. that the defence of their interests is in the interests of society as a whole. This may or may not be true. It needs to be very carefully examined, in particular for its consequences to other groups elsewhere. The poor seldom protest against motorways or airports. Indeed, as Mr. James Curran argued at the Roskill inquiry, they may actually benefit from an airport.

This raises the extremely difficult problem of cultural values. It is quite probable, indeed it would be surprising if it were not, that poor people have different attitudes to noise, air pollution, and inconvenience than rich people. Even if we do not make the mistake of the cost benefit analyst, and try to rank the poor man's shilling (which means a lot to him) against the rich man's (which means virtually nothing), we are left with the paradox that the disadvantaged may well care less about amenity, just as they cared less (and perhaps still care less) about education. There is a basic problem of paternalism here, which hinges on the values of different generations. The poor might not have voted for Foster's 1870 Education Act, and doubtless at the time a good many of them suffered from it (by withdrawal of family purchasing power); how far was it justifiable to sacrifice one generation for the next? Similarly, the benefits today of clean air or peace and quiet have to be placed against the benefits of dirty air (free coal for Yorkshire miners) or noise (well paid airport jobs); the poor may choose the immediate advantage because they are more desperate.

There is no easy way out of this paradox: a political line has to be drawn, and it should be a central task of Labour politics to help draw it. But it does lead to great difficulties in judging how much disbenefit people (or defined groups of people) suffer from environmental "spillovers." At Social and Community Planning Research, great hope is being placed on the Priority Evaluator, a game playing technique which tries to aid people to derive their own preferences in a rigorous way (Social and Community Planning Research, *Annual Report*, 1970). Still simple in form at present, it could be greatly improved by the use of film, television and teaching machine techniques; scpr and the University of Reading, in association with the Road Research Laboratory, plan to develop it in this way to evaluate the impact of motorways on people's environment. But it does remain true that people's attitudes to impure public goods of all kinds will be affected by birth, education, life experience and exposure to conditioning. For this reason, Conrad Jamieson has doubted the whole validity of techniques like these and has advocated the use of full blooded techniques of "hidden persuasion" to market public goods, (C. Jamieson, *Architectural Design*, 1971). This argument has a lot to commend it; certainly the producers of public goods have been notably backward, with a few exceptions, in harnessing the techniques of marketing. But it still avoids the essential problem of deciding public priorities, which new style local authorities are now beginning to face.

some examples

Despite these great conceptual and technical difficulties, it is possible to give a few fairly obvious examples of the questions which arise when planning policies (in the strict, spatial sense) are considered for their distributional effects.

An obvious case is *transport*. In any city or region, the transport system is only partly a reflection of current needs; the infrastructure in particular reflects past conditions and cannot easily be changed. At the same time, new investment is made to deal with needs which can be measured readily, and which score heavily on the evaluation system being used. This means for instance, that an inner city area may have a poor public transport service because it was once occupied by the rich, who did not need public transport, and because the cost benefit evaluation now being used puts little weight on the increased job opportunities that would be generated for the inhabitants. In this case, there would be an *a priori* case for public transport investments which would connect the area to job opportunities (and also educational and social opportunities) not now accessible. Investments like the Victoria Line extension to Brixton, or the Fleet Line in south east London, would gain an extra justification; investments like the Aston Expressway in Birmingham, whose main function is to connect rich commuters and shoppers with the central business district, would get rather less. But this does not mean simple minded justification of all public transport schemes and vilification of all urban motorway schemes. Some expensive tubes may benefit the better off (the proposed Wimbledon Line via the King's Road for instance), motorways may open up valuable circumferential routes and dramatically increase job accessibility, especially if accompanied by express bus services (London's Ringway Two for instance). In any given instance, a meticulous examination of the likely effects for different groups of the population would be needed. But it will have to be faced that some of the evaluation will be difficult, especially where it concerns environmental spillovers. The new motorway through a poor area may *appear* to cost less environmental damage if we measure people's ostensible reactions. But its effect on lives may not be measurable—particularly if it hinders the educational process which provides one escape route from the area.

Housing conveys two attributes over and above the bare minimum of shelter; accessibility to urban goods and services, and amenity. If provided publicly (and even if provided privately on land allocated by a plan) it is a particularly good example of the impure public good. Poorly located housing may restrict the opportunities of its inhabitants in the urban job market and the urban service market; Roehampton has been criticised on these grounds, many of

Glasgow's peripheral estates even more so. New towns convey a high degree of local accessibility to a certain level of jobs and services within one or two miles (at least when they are fully developed); but they suffer in comparison at the wider regional scale, because green belt restrictions mean very few additional jobs in the two to twenty mile range. These same green belt restrictions may be justified in forms of access to recreational opportunities in the countryside; but if the family lacks a car, these opportunities may be meaningless, and even if the car is there, they may not be wanted or appreciated.

The question of housing density is a particularly good example of the difficulty of reconciling contradictory facts. Allocationally, it is known that high-density high rise housing is extravagant of communal resources, in that it is possible to house more people for the same money in less expensive structures. (The same argument does not necessarily apply to high density low rise developments.) But distributionally, high density schemes may be justified because of the accessibility they give to big metropolitan labour markets and services. They may be less prone to "ghetto formation" than new towns, which have tended to house a rather narrow socio-economic spectrum of the population (Thomas, 1968) and so they may aid social mobility through the mechanism of the heterogeneous comprehensive school (as in many ILEA schools). They may help the maintenance of an informal support system through relatives, which can at least help reduce emotional strain and may even raise family incomes through baby minding services. But all this is speculative and little researched. Some light may be thrown on certain aspects by the studies of comparative urban time budgets, now being conducted simultaneously in several European countries. Though cost-benefit analysis would suggest that time is less valuable to low income families, common sense suggests that this is nonsense: the needs for work, sleep, and other basic functions are broadly the same, and the logistical problems of occupying time and space may be immeasurably more pressing for the non-car owning family than for the family where both husband and wife have individual transport (a result already observed in the Swedish time budget study). But this last example also reinforces a point which should be obvious: transport, and particularly convenient individual transport, can more than counteract the disadvantages of a poor housing location. Otherwise we should not find so many of the best informed and most privileged of the population living in the remote countryside. The sociologists would add a further point: in order to exploit the urban system, it is necessary to understand it. The poor may remain trapped in the inner areas of the large cities not merely because their jobs are there and they are immobile, but because they lack the knowledge to escape. To them, geographical distance acts as a constraint; to the rich it acts as an opportunity and a stimulus, which they can exploit through good transport to gain the amenities they desire. Here is a clear case of inequality which cannot be remedied in any simple way. Studies of the perception of geographical space by different groups, which form a currently popular research area in geography departments, will help us understand the phenomenon better; they will not help cure it.

Open space is another classic case of the public good with a very uneven geographical, and hence a very uneven social, distribution. From the early nineteenth century onwards, town planning has sought to remedy this by bringing open space into the city; Birkenhead Park, and Victoria Park in London's East End, were examples. Later, in the writings of Ebenezer Howard, it sought to take the people into the country. But the arrival of mass private mobility, through the spread of car ownership, has completely altered the dimensions of the problem. The average skilled worker with a small car has greater potential mobility than the aristocrat in any period up to the end of the nineteenth century, though his ability to exploit the potential will again depend on his perception of geographical distance and on his knowledge of the available opportunities. But the average unskilled worker without a car is more deprived in a relative sense than ever he was before. Car ownership, in this as in the work situation, is probably one of the key sources and indicators of inequality in our contemporary society; and at the present time, it reinforces the notion that the key class distinction is between the skilled and unskilled working class. For the mobility which the car potentially conveys offers *opportunities* of all sorts, economically, socially, and in terms of use of leisure, which represent a sort of non-money income.

These examples will perhaps help demonstrate a point being strongly made by some contemporary sociologists: that our research knowledge of the geography of inequality is very poor indeed. If we consider the archetype of the most deprived groups today, the family of the unskilled service worker living and working in the inner area of a great city, then we can guess, in intuitive terms, that their poverty is not simply a matter of low income. It is reinforced, paradoxically, by the poor supply and the low quality of many of the public goods supplied to them. Poor schools, with little opportunity for the acquisition of the skills that modern society needs; poor and deteriorating public transport, shutting off access to the better paid jobs which increasingly (in the case of factory industry) relocate in the suburbs; poor housing, with limited information about opportunities elsewhere; poor open space facilities; all these combine further to depress the real income of these families, and to deny them the possibility of improving that income in the future. But there is very little precise knowledge of what the true extent of this deprivation is, and who suffers most from it. All this partly reflects the traditional indifference of town planners to research and to problems of distribution. It is high time that both were changed.

16. social planning and the control of priorities

Peter Townsend

It is as difficult as it is necessary to assess some of the Labour Government's achievements and shortcomings. Difficult because a lot of information is not yet available: some legislation has only begun to take effect; the Official Secrets Act shrouds many decisions and events and there are straightforward statistical data, especially for 1969 and 1970, which will not all be published for a long time. Necessary because socialists need to know what progress has in fact been made towards equality and what important lessons for future policies are to be learned from the experiences of 1964 to 1970. Future policies are unlikely to carry much conviction either with Party stalwarts or disenchanted young voters unless they are shown to be critically related to experience.

The analysis presented in this chapter therefore has to be treated as a kind of working draft which has to be submitted to the tests of further evidence. It pursues three steps. First, an attempt is made to sum up the evidence about the trends in the unequal distribution of resources. They suggest, in general, that there has been no marked change in the distribution in recent years. Second, some of the successes and failures in reducing inequality and poverty are traced. On the whole the achievements are found to be rather meagre. Third, the kind of planning required in any future Government programme to reduce the unequal distribution of resources and some of the conditions required to implement it are discussed. Some account is given of developments in planning, including cost-benefit analysis and output budgeting, and of the ways in which incomes, fiscal and social service policies can be interrelated and based on conceptions of need.

the distribution of resources

I shall attempt to review trends in income distribution, the prevalence of poverty and expenditure on the social services. For 1964 to 1967, the Inland Revenue data on the distribution of pre-tax and post-tax personal incomes indicate little change. According to R. J. Nicholson, "The trend towards the reduction of inequality in the distribution of personal income seems to have come to an end by 1957" ("The distribution of personal income," *Lloyds Bank Review,* January, 1967, p18).

With minor fluctuations the richest 5 per cent of income recipients have continued to receive since the late 1950s about 15 per cent of personal income after tax and the poorest 30 per cent around 12 per cent. But these data are very general and do not properly represent the distribution of resources. Recipients of income are ill-defined in the Board's figures and include a mixture of individuals and income units. Estimates for incomes below the tax exemption limits have to be added on and are bound to be imprecise. The Board's definition of income is limited and does not include important forms of capital appreciation and benefits in kind from employers. As R. J. Nicholson concedes, "Indeed if, as is sometimes suggested, certain 'tax avoidance' incomes and other claims on wealth outside personal income have increased over the last decade and are concentrated more among higher income recipients, it is possible that the distribution of incomes on some wider definition may have moved towards greater inequality" (*op cit*, p18). A searching analysis of the Board's statistics, and of the uses to which they have been put, is given by Richard Titmuss in his *Income distribution and social change* (Allen and Unwin, 1962).

The data from the annual Family Expenditure Survey (FES) provide an alternative source of information which is in some respects less trustworthy but is more comprehensive. The response rate has fallen below 70 per cent and information about income cannot be checked, but income units are defined more rigorously (and can be grouped according to composition) and the effects upon income both of indirect taxation and social service benefits traced.

INCOME AFTER ALL TAXES AND BENEFITS, FOR DIFFERENT TYPES OF HOUSEHOLD, 1961, 1965 AND 1969

type of household	as percent of income in 1961			as percent of income of one adult		
	1961	1965	1969	1961	1965	1969
one adult*	100	131	160	100	100	100
two adults*	100	120	153	181	167	173
two adults, one child	100	124	147	206	194	189
two adults, two children	100	120	158	230	210	227
two adults, three children	100	126	162	248	238	250
two adults, four children	100	121	158	276	254	271
three adults	100	121	156	255	235	249
all households†	100	123‡	156‡	208	192	196

* excludes pensioners.
† including pensioner and other types of households not listed.
‡ estimated in terms of 1961 distribution by size of households.
source: based on *Economic trends*, February 1970, table 5, pxlv and February 1971, table 5, ppxxxv-xxxvi.

The first three tables in this paper bring together some of the evidence of trends in distribution. It must be remembered that the results of the Family Expenditure Survey for different years, particularly when divided into results for different types of families, are subject to sampling variation. The table above shows that after allowing for all taxes and social service benefits none of the gains made by different types of family in the 1960s were striking. Families with two or more children gained slightly more than average but so did single person households. In relation to one-person households, as the second part of the table shows, there was little change in the structure of net income during the period. Households consisting of two adults and one child gained rather less than average.

Information is not available for pensioner households for 1961. However, compared with 1963 single pensioners had in 1965 increased their final incomes by 21 per cent and in 1968 by a further 23 per cent. Pensioner couples had increased their final incomes by 15 and 21 per cent respectively. By contrast, single person households (excluding pensioners) increased their

LOWEST AND HIGHEST QUINTILES AS PER CENT OF MEDIAN
INCOMES AFTER ALL TAXES AND BENEFITS, 1961, 1965 AND 1969

type of household	lowest quintile as per cent of median			highest quintile as per cent of median		
	1961	1965	1969	1961	1965	1969
one adult*	70	72	71	162	155	162
two adults*	70	72	69	151	142	142
two adults, one child	74	75	73	133	132	136
two adults, two children	73	75	76	132	134	128
two adults, three children	78	73	78	128	128	134
two adults, four children	86	77	79	144	129	128
three adults	74	75	73	132	128	135
three adults, one child	80	76	79	134	130	128
three adults, two children	80	76	77	121	130	135
four adults	81	78	78	131	127	132
all households†	56	55	54	150	151	151

* excluding pensioners.
source: based on *Economic trends*, February 1970, table 2, ppxxxii-xxxiii,
and February 1971, tables 4 and 5, ppxxxiii-xxxvi.

final incomes by 13 per cent and 15 per cent respectively (and families with
four children by 15 per cent and 20 per cent).

The second and third tables are more chastening still. For each type of household, the table above shows income at two points in the distribution of
income at the lowest and highest quintiles. For each group of households the
lowest quintile is such that 20 per cent have lower and 80 per cent higher
incomes. The highest quintile is such that 80 per cent have lower and 20 per
cent higher incomes. Bearing in mind the liability of survey results to fluctuate
a little from year to year because of sampling variation, there is no evidence
of an equalising trend. If anything there is a very slight reverse trend. For
seven out of the ten household types, the lowest quintile was slightly lower in
1969 than in 1961.

In analysing trends in the distribution of final incomes the effects of Government taxes and benefits need to be distinguished. The table on the next page
gives just one illustration. It shows incomes after all taxes and benefits, as
a percentage of original incomes, for the lowest and highest quintiles within
each type of household. During the 1960s real incomes increased and the
proportion of incomes taken in tax also increased. But it does not reflect any
noticeable priorities. The poorest among families with one child, two children
and three children retained proportionately less of their original incomes in
1968 than they did in 1961. The poorest households with three adults and two
children also lost ground. Those with three adults and one child and two
adults and four children just about held their 1961 relativities to original
income. Taxation had not become more progressive. An official report
prepared jointly by the Central Statistical Office and the DHSS concluded that
the data for 1961 to 1968 showed that "for each type of family, direct and
indirect taxes combined form a remarkably stable proportion of income over
a wide range of incomes; and generally form a smaller proportion of the

INCOME AFTER ALL TAXES AND BENEFITS AS PER CENT OF ORIGINAL INCOME

type of household	quintile	1961	1965	1968
one adult	highest	80	72	70
	lowest	186	158	196
two adults	highest	77	72	69
	lowest	97	95	113
two adults, one child	highest	80	78	76
	lowest	85	83	80
two adults, two children	highest	88	87	85
	lowest	92	91	87
two adults, three children	highest	101	99	93
	lowest	107	100	102
two adults, four children	highest	111	103	106
	lowest	121	121	123
three adults	highest	73	74	71
	lowest	88	81	86
three adults, one child	highest	80	83	76
	lowest	92	89	93
three adults, two children	highest	86	98	92
	lowest	103	98	98
four adults	highest	72	72	70
	lowest	87	82	77
all households average income		87	86	84

source: *Economic trends*, February 1970, table 2, ppxxxii-xxxiii.

income of large than of small families, but the differences are not very marked" (*Economic trends,* February 1970, pxvii). For each type of household the report listed (table C) the proportion of original income (plus cash benefits) paid in taxes by different income groups. Altogether, 17 income groups paid fewer taxes than, or the same taxes as, the lowest income group and 21 paid more (mostly only slightly more).

Neither were there signs of priority being given in tax and social service policy for families with children. An official analysis of the 1969 survey shows that between 1961 and 1969 income after all taxes and benefits, expressed as a percentage of original income, fell for a couple with one child by 5 per cent, with 2 children by 8 per cent, 3 children by 9 per cent and 4 children by 2 per cent, compared with a fall among all households of 5 per cent (*Economic trends,* February 1971, ppxxxv-xxxvi).

However, the FES data can be criticised in make up and coverage. In some respects they may understate the reduction in inequality. For example, up to 1969 employers' national insurance contributions were counted as part of employees' original income and as a tax on their income. From 1969 onwards, however, this has been changed. Instead of regarding the employer's contribution as part of the employee's income it will be treated as an indirect tax included in the prices of all goods and services.

In others they may overstate the reduction in inequality. For example, capital gains and employers' fringe benefits are not included in income. The value of certain social service benefits in kind to families like education and health services are also averaged crudely, although it is likely that some middle and high income groups benefit disproportionaely, at least from the education system. Again, housing subsidies to council tenants are added to income but not improvement grants nor the increase in capital value of owner occupied houses which might reasonably be attributed to that part of the monthly payments of mortgage interest which is covered by tax relief.

Finally, they do not take account of differential changes in the cost of consumption and use of assets. Between 1956 and 1966 D. G. Tipping has estimated that prices had risen by 4.3 per cent more for the poor than the rich (D. G. Tipping, "Price changes and income distribution," *Applied statistics*, 1, 1970). The price index for pensioners excluding housing costs has kept slightly ahead of the general price index in recent years (*Employment and productivity gazette*, November 1970, p1024). But despite these reservations, which are intended only to make the point that we need to have information on the total effects upon family living standards of different policies rather than the effect of single policies, the FES data are the best that are available. Since they are based on the actual situation of families they are better than abstract examples of the nominal effects of tax and social security rates upon families which are usually quoted by government ministers.

indicators of poverty

So far we have been able to establish only a very rough picture of structural inequality and mainly of rigidities rather than shifts over time in that structure. A distinction has to be made between differences in levels of living and the proportion of the population at different levels of living. Differentials can remain approximately constant but there may be large displacements of population. In fact in Britain there seems to be a continuing expansion of the numbers in the upper and middle income groups, balanced by a corresponding expansion of numbers in the lowest income groups. Otherwise it would be difficult to explain the comparative rigidity of differentials. Since the mid-1950s salaries as a proportion of salaries and wages have grown from 34 per cent to 43 per cent. This might have been expected to result in a reduction of differentials between the two, but in fact there is no evidence of any marked change.

The fact that the numbers of people of pensionable age have increased from 13 per cent of the population just after the war to 16 per cent in 1970, is well known. The proportion is now levelling off. But the fact that there has been a steep increase in retirement is not so well understood. In 1959 only 47 per cent of men retired at the age of 65 but ten years later the figure had increased rapidly to over 70 per cent. As the supply of prospective retirees of pensionable age runs out their place may be taken increasingly by men in late middle age, so that the swelling salariat of managers and professional and technical staff can continue to be financed at the standards which have traditionally been expected—averaging between a third and a half higher than wages, depending on definition.

More men are retiring prematurely in the sense that they are still physically active and prepared to take paid employment. There is a steady increase in the numbers of people who are disabled in middle or late middle life, although to a certain extent the rates may be unreal because a number of people who were formerly employed may have opted for long term sickness benefit rather than unemployment benefit. Since 1966 the number employed has contracted by about a million from the figure originally projected for 1970. The unemployment rate has grown from about $1\frac{1}{2}$ per cent to nearly 3 per cent. (For a discussion of employment levels in relation to low pay see N. Bosanquet, "Jobs and the low paid worker," *Poverty*, 15, 1971.) For the three years 1967-69 the number of men wholly unemployed for more than two months averaged about 250,000. During 1970 the number was close to 300,000. Whether or not these trends in employment and unemployment are short term or long term they mean that disabled workers have found it harder to get, and keep, work; the working lives of some men have been shortened unnecessarily; the chance of supplementary occupation and earnings has been ruled out for some women; improvements in the lowest rates of pay have been discouraged and more families have found themselves in poverty or on its margins. Strangely enough the social and financial repercussions of changes in the employment and unemployment rates do not seem to have been fully documented.

There are of course other factors which contribute to overall dependency. Between 1961 and 1966 the number of fatherless families increased marginally from 7.3 to 7.5 per cent of all families. (*Social trends*, 1970, p59, HMSO.) In 1966 these families contained nearly $\frac{3}{4}$ million children, or nearly 6 per cent of all children. Finally, there are the trends in the numbers of large families. After a fairly rapid proportionate increase in the 1950s and early 1960s the number has levelled off in recent years. The number of families with four or more children in Britain grew, for example, by 17 per cent between 1961 and 1966 but by only a further 4 per cent between 1966 and 1969 (*op cit*, p101). They account for nearly a quarter of all children, (*ibid*, p101). These figures are taken from returns for family allowances and refer to the number of dependent children at a point in time. Of course, a higher fraction of the population are brought up in completed families of this size (see H. Land, *Large families in London*, Bell, 1969).

A high proportion of these groups are in poverty, and others are on the margins of poverty. The table below illustrates this from two Government reports. There are far more people marginally above the poverty line than below it. Allowing for married couples, for example, there are over two million old people with an income after supplementation of less than £1 above the Government's bare subsistence standard. Small changes in the interrelationship between incomes, prices and officially sanctioned standards of subsistence can transform the numbers found to be living below such standards. If there is a rise in rents without a corresponding increase in earnings, if family allowances are not increased as much or as often as supplementary benefits and if a pensions increase is delayed or the rate of inflation is exceptionally high between increases, then the numbers in poverty will grow quickly. This in itself suggests that no reform is likely to be of lasting value unless those with low incomes as well as those in poverty are helped. For one thing the families themselves tend to circulate between strata.

NUMBERS OF FAMILIES AND OLD PEOPLE LIVING BELOW OR JUST ABOVE GOVERNMENT SUBSISTENCE STANDARD

amount income above or below subsistence standard	families with two or more children—father in full time work (thousands)		retirement pensioners (thousands)	
	families	people	married couples	single and widowed people
£5 or more above	2,077,1	9,580,2	201,2	145,9
£2—£5 above	382,7	1,868,1	243,0	239,6
£1—£2 above	66,0	336,0	174,7	249,7
under £1 above	74,7	377,2	376,8	1,400,9
under £1 below	27,3	158,4	161,9	614,4
£1—£2 below	15,4	93,0	30,0	93,2
£2 or more below	20,5	107,8	5,6	14,2
total	2,663,7	12,520,7	1,193,2	2,757,9

sources: Ministry of Social Security, *Circumstances of families*, p142, HMSO, 1967. Ministry of Pensions, *The financial and other circumstances of retirement pensioners*, HMSO, 1966. Estimates made on basis of combining Tables III.4, III.5 and BR.8, and assuming (a) that those receiving national assistance had incomes above the standard to the extent indicated by the amount of income disregarded, as in Table III.10; (b) that those with unprotected capital of over £600 whose needs exceeded resources were less than £1 below standard.

There are two kinds of changes which affect any accumulation of people at the foot of the income scale: change in the proportions of the social and occupational groups making up the social structure, and change in the distribution of resources between or within these groups.

The Labour Government introduced a number of measures which improved the living standards of many of those with low incomes. Some of these have been discussed in earlier papers in this volume. In March 1965, rather than delay some months at least in order to press through the wholesale reconstruction of social security, which had been anticipated before the 1964 election, existing retirement pensions and other national insurance benefits were raised substantially. Later that year the Rent Act was passed. In 1966 three schemes were introduced: to pay earnings related supplements for the first six months of unemployment or sickness, to replace national assistance by supplementary benefits, and to pay rate rebates. In 1968 family allowances were raised substantially and both the urban aid and educational priority area programme were launched. The tax threshold was raised, particularly in April 1970, and among the routine increases in social security rates of benefit certain groups, such as widows, were treated very favourably.

But the impact of these measures on inequality and poverty does not seem to have been great or lasting. An early decision was taken which led to a temporary and then an indefinite postponement of the introduction of an overall plan for reform of either social security or incomes distribution as a whole. What had begun to take shape as an overall strategy was parcelled up into smaller fragments which were left very much to the energies or staying power of individual Ministers. Partly this seemed to be to serve economic planning (the singling out of the schemes for redundancy payments and short term earnings related benefits for unemployment is an example) and when economic planning fell into disrepute in 1966, social planning also seemed to lose support and coherence. Lacking an adequate monitoring service (despite the two valuable reports on families and pensioners prepared while Peggy Herbison was Minister of Social Security) Ministers seemed to forget that such an emphatic assertion of social priorities as that made in March 1965 could be rapidly undermined by other developments, some of them partly or wholly outside their control.

The effects for pensioners, the unemployed and low paid with families will be considered briefly. The relative growth as a whole of the incomes of pensioners living alone or as married couples seems to be one outcome of the period 1963 to 1968. But it is possible that the absolute numbers of pensioners living below the Government's subsistence standard may not have decreased and may even have increased since 1965. The incomes (after all taxes and benefits) of pensioners are expressed in the next table as a percentage of the incomes of other adults living alone or in couples. This is felt to be the best available guide to income relativities, and better than comparisons which relate pensions only to gross earnings or to earnings net of direct taxes only. By 1964 the single pensioner's income had fallen, relative to other adults living alone, but by 1966 recovered to the level of the early 1960s. By the late 1960s the income of two pensioner households had increased, relative to other two person households, compared with income at the beginning of the decade. Between 1963 and 1968, then, there was a relative increase in the incomes of retirement pensioners living alone and a smaller one for married couples.

INCOMES OF PENSIONERS LIVING ALONE AND IN PAIRS, AFTER ALL TAXES AND BENEFITS*

year	single pensioner households as per cent other one adult households	two pensioner households as per cent other two adult households
1961	51.0	42.6
1962	52.0	44.7
1963	45.6	45.4
1964	43.7	43.0
1965	48.9	46.8
1966	51.1	46.6
1967	51.4	48.1
1968	52.5	48.2

* strictly pensioner households should be compared with single person and two person households which do not include any retired adults (some of whom do not, according to the cso definition, comprise pensioner households), but the appropriate data for certain years are not available.
source: *Economic trends*, July 1968 and February 1970, supplemented by information provided by the cso.

But this outcome is by no means just due to changes in the rate of retirement pension. The single pension was raised by 10s in May 1963 (the first year it moved substantially ahead of 1948 values in relation to manual earnings) and was raised by 12s 6d by the Labour Government in March 1965, by 10s in 1967 and by a further 10s in 1969. The next table indicates the movement in the rates, relative to gross earnings. The best increase was in March 1965, but subsequently the attempt to narrow differentials was not pursued. When Labour took office in 1964, 18 months after the previous increase in the rates, the single pension was 18.7 per cent of average gross industrial earnings.

When it left office, 7 months after the latest increase, the single pension was approximately 18.6 per cent of average gross industrial earnings. During 1971 pensions reached the lowest level relative to earnings since 1957.

BENEFIT RATES AS A PER CENT OF INDUSTRIAL EARNINGS OF MALE MANUAL WORKERS AGED 21 AND OVER

	single pension	supplementary benefit for single person	family allowances for four children
1948 October	18.9	17.5	10.9
1961 April	19.1	17.8	9.3
1962 April	18.4	17.1	8.9
1963 May	20.8	19.5	8.6
1964 April	19.2	18.1	8.0
October	18.7	17.6	7.7
1965 April	21.2	20.1	7.4
October	20.4	19.4	7.1
1966 April	19.8	18.8	6.9
October	19.7	20.0	6.9
1967 April	19.4	19.7	6.8
October	21.0	20.1	7.7
1968 April	20.2	19.3	11.9
October	19.6	19.8	12.6
1969 April	18.8	19.0	12.1
November	20.0	19.2	11.7
1970 April	19.0	18.3	11.3
November	17.6	18.3	10.2
1971 March (est)	17.3	18.0	10.0

source: based on statistics of weekly earnings, *Employment and productivity gazette*.

There are three other factors contributing to the improvement of incomes relative to those of other adults between 1963 and 1968. Pensioners with increments which are added to their retirement pensions for deferred retirement or with small amounts of graduated pensions have been increasing as a proportion of all pensioners. In 1965 the Government raised the national assistance rate to a higher level relative to earnings (higher than the figure achieved in May 1963) and, through annual adjustments, broadly maintained the rate at between 19 and 20 per cent of gross industrial earnings until the beginning of 1970. But, as predicted when they were announced in the early summer of 1970, the November increases have fallen considerably short of restoring the rate to the level of previous years.

The third factor is the long term addition of 9s which was introduced with the 1966 Social Security Act for all pensioners receiving supplementary benefit and for others (except those required to register for employment) receiving supplementary benefits for two years. The net effect of this, however, was more to increase the proportion of people receiving any kind of addition to the basic scales than to increase the incomes of those already receiving discretionary additions. In December 1965, 73 per cent of retirement pensioners who received supplementary benefit from the former National Assistance Board received on average an extra 10s 1d or 13 per cent of the basic scale rate for a single householder, in discretionary additions. (The figure is 9.7 per cent if averaged for all supplementary pensioners.) In November 1969 nearly all pensioners were receiving the long term addition, by then 10s, which represented just over 10 per cent of the scale rates, and only 20 per cent (a decline from 23 per cent in 1968) of them were getting an average of 5s 6d in discretionary additions (meaning they received a total of 16 per cent in addition to the scale rates).

The 1966 Social Security Act did not reduce the numbers of retirement pensioners eligible for supplementary benefit but not applying for it by as much as was believed at the time (A. B. Atkinson, *Poverty in Britain and the reform of social security*, CUP, 1969). It probably did not bring resources to as many of the poorest as a shrewdly chosen universal measure—say, a disability supplement awarded by right to the oldest pensioners. Neither did it sharply improve the financial circumstances of those in greatest need among existing recipients but instead, by raising the minimum conditions of eligibility, extended state assistance to the band of incomes next to the lowest.

Rents are a complicating factor in this whole analysis. Increased payments by pensioners for rent may, though to a small extent, reduce the slight improvement indicated in the table. Between 1965 and 1969 rents paid to people receiving supplementary benefits increased much faster than general housing costs—by 36 per cent for single householders and 38.5 per cent for families with children, compared with 22 per cent generally (DHSS, *Annual report*, 1969, p95; NAB, *Annual report*, 1965, p70). It seems reasonable to infer that old people and families with low incomes who were not in receipt of supplementary benefit were also paying bigger rent increases than average—and for many they were not offset by rate and rent rebates, because of patchy coverage and low "take up" of these benefits.

The earnings-related benefit scheme which was introduced for the unemployed and sick is not particularly socialist in conception. There is little or no element of redistribution, and contributions and benefits do not, unlike the former national superannuation plan, favour the low paid. Indeed the introduction of the wage stop into benefits means that some low paid men with children will be paying contributions without receiving any benefits. The scheme is unfair to those whose earnings record has been affected by sickness. The short term and long term unemployed are ineligible. Benefits are not started until after the second week of unemployment and cannot be drawn for more than 6 months. Because of previous low earnings some men qualify to receive only a few pence. In November 1969, when there were 550,000 unemployed (including about 160,000 unemployed for 6 months or more and 100,000 for 2 weeks or less) about 280,000 received flat rate unemployment benefit and only 92,000 of them earnings related supplements. At any single time only about one in six are receiving such supplements (though some unemployed for more than six months will have received them previously). The SBC has also become less generous in treating the unemployed. In 1968 a tough new rule terminating benefits for single men under 45 was introduced. The wage stop was not abolished and despite announcements of the relaxation of certain rules after a review of the wage stop in 1967, the numbers of men whose benefits were reduced declined only marginally from about 13 per cent to 12 per cent of all the unemployed receiving supplementary benefit. Finally, in 1965, 16 per cent of those whose unemployment insurance benefits were supplemented by the NAB received discretionary additions but in 1969 the figure had dropped to 7 per cent. Even the absolute number diminished during a period when the number of long term unemployed nearly doubled. In these senses some of the unemployed were relatively poorer than their predecessors. The whole record on unemployment while Labour was in office was harsh.

The needs of the low paid, especially with families, began to attract attention. Rates of pay seem to have lagged, even when demand for workers was high. The next table gives some indication of the problem. Evidence presented by the NBPI showed that minimum weekly wage rates and average earnings for men in the lowest paid industries increased by about the average amount between April 1965 and April 1969 but lagged in the following 18 months. The same was true of 32 wages council industries. The earnings of individual low paid workers also lagged slightly between September 1968 and April 1970. However, those covered by collective bargaining arrangements did slightly better than average but those not so covered did considerably worse. "What little improvement took place in the relative position of the low paid in the earlier years of the prices and incomes policy was later lost" (NBPI, *General problems of low pay*, report 169, Cmnd 4648, pp14-17 and p41, HMSO, April 1971). Clearly any postponement of increases in family allowances, any increase in regressive taxes or any differential increase in prices (for example local authority rents, or even "fair" rents under the new legislation) puts men with families at risk of poverty.

THE LEVEL OF GROSS EARNINGS OF THE POOREST TEN PER CENT OF MALE MANUAL WORKERS (1964-1969)

	per cent of the median					
	1964	1965	1966	1967	1968	1969
lowest decile	71.6	69.7	68.6	69.7	68.9	68.4

source: reports of the FES.

The Government announced increases of 7s to each family allowance for 1968 and then, as a consequence of devaluation, a further 3s. For many families these gains were offset not only by increased prices, but by increases in the price of school meals and welfare milk, and the withdrawal of free milk in secondary schools, as well as the reintroduction of prescription charges.

Right-wing governments, as in France, had made more concessions to those on low incomes when devaluing their currencies than had the Labour Government. Flat rate insurance contributions, which had been raised by 2s as lately as October 1967 were raised by a further 1s in May 1968.

Labour leaders had frequently opposed these increases in principle. In a speech at Swansea on 25 January 1964, for example, Mr Harold Wilson said, "The Conservatives in the last four years in times of crises increased stamp contributions to bear most heavily on those whose needs are greatest and whose incomes are lowest." In Parliament on 28 January 1963, Mr R. H. S. Crossman had said, "A flat rate increase of 1s for low paid workers is a heavy imposition indeed. . . . Each time the Government puts a shilling on tax they make the burden more intolerable." Between 1964 and 1969 the Government increased the flat rate contribution by over 50 per cent.

The reduction of numbers of families in poverty was therefore smaller than it might have been. The Government itself never claimed that the reduction would be more than about half. But during 1969 and 1970 unemployment grew, the wage rates of the low paid lagged, the cost of living rose differentially and supplementary benefits were raised twice to keep step with earnings. The tax allowance for single persons and married couples was increased in the budget of April 1970 but though this helped the man with children it did not help him more than it did the man without children, and indeed helped far more people without than with children. As a redistributive measure it was clumsy. It was far less efficient in reducing poverty, and far more inequitable, than raising family allowances. It was also balanced by the final abolition of reduced rates of tax which, in a time of rapid inflation, meant that some families living in poverty were paying the standard rate of tax for the first time in their lives by the autumn.

It is hard to thread all the events, without distortion, into the picture. Rate rebates now help just under a million households, but many are owner occupiers and are retired people rather than families with children. Seaside resorts such as Clacton and Morecambe have relatively eight or nine times as many claimants as city areas such as Tower Hamlets and Islington. A publicity campaign raised the fraction of children eligible to get free school meals, perhaps to a half, but this still left the other half paying increased charges or finding a substitute for such meals. One index of inequality and of poverty is provided by the annual reports of the National Food Survey. The table below shows little change in the 1960s in dietary inequality (in fact astonishingly little change in the structure of nutritional inequality has taken place throughout the 1950s and 1960s). From 1964 up to 1968 there was little improvement in the nutritional content of poor families' diets, despite the continuing increase in real incomes.

Family poverty seems to have afflicted half a million people including a third of a million children of working or unemployed men throughout the 1960s. The Government had been rather shy of publishing secondary analyses from the Family Expenditure Survey. Some information was given to the House of Commons in November 1970 by Sir Keith Joseph, Secretary of State for Social Services, at the time of the introduction of the Family Income

INTAKES OF PROTEIN AND CALCIUM AS A PERCENTAGE OF INTAKES RECOMMENDED BY THE BMA

	man and woman only with high income		3 children		man and woman with low income and 4 children		children and adolescents	
year	protein	calcium	protein	calcium	protein	calcium	protein	calcium
1960	136	151	90	89	82	80	81	88
1961	138	155	90	92	87	86	83	90
1962	139	156	93	93	84	81	85	91
1963	138	153	95	94	87	83	84	87
1964	128	145	93	92	90	84	89	90
1965	136	152	95	91	86	80	82	86
1966	134	150	95	96	88	85	86	88
1967	136	147	97	97	91	89	85	89
1968*	131	143	93	95	92	91	91	91

* a different standard has been adopted by the DHSS and these are estimated from the new data.

source: *Household food consumption and expenditure*: annual reports of the National Food Surveys for the appropriate years, and especially for 1966, p39.

Supplements scheme. He said then that his estimates were based on the special analysis of the Family Expenditure Survey of 1968, adjusted to August 1970 with information from the latest survey of earnings. According to the survey carried out by the Government in 1966 there were 95,000 families of men in full time work and 15,000 of unemployed men subject to the wage stop, in addition to other groups, such as one-parent families, who were living below the level of the National Assistance scales. Sir Keith Joseph gave comparable figures for April 1970 of 110,000 and 24,000 respectively, who would qualify for help under the new Family Income Supplements scheme. However, he went on to admit that the measure would help only between one half and two-thirds of working households below the supplementary benefit level (*Hansard*, 10 November 1967). Throughout the debates on the Bill and subsequently, the Government dodged any commitment to detailed estimates.

In 1966 there were estimated to be 70,000 families with a father in full time work (that is, the 63,000 below the standard shown in the table on page 280 plus an estimate to cover those not responding to the Survey) with a very rough estimate of 25,000 one child families in addition (*Circumstances of families, op cit*, paras 22 and 40).

The results for June 1966 are preferred to the estimates for the end of 1966, both of which are given in the DHSS report published in 1971. The survey was carried out in June. Earnings had risen, and may have risen differentially, by the time that the supplementary benefits scheme was introduced at the end of 1966. The figures for different years summarised in the table below are a little difficult to interpret. Fluctuations could be attributed to sampling errors in the successive surveys. On the other hand, some of them could be attributed to the differential impact of inflation and increases in wages, family

NUMBER OF TWO PARENT FAMILIES IN POVERTY, FATHER IN FULL TIME WORK OR WAGE-STOPPED (THOUSANDS)

| year | in full time work | | | in full time work and wage-stopped | | |
	families	people	(children included)	families	people	(children included)
1960*	85	370	(200)	—	—	—
1966 (June)†	95	470	(280)	110	552	(332)
1968‡	73	334	(188)	102	500	(296)
1969‡	96	527	(335)	122	677	(433)
1970‡	74	336	(188)	105	505	(295)

sources: *B. Abel-Smith and P. Townsend, *The poor and the poorest*, Bell, 1965, †*Circumstances of families*, HMSO, 1967, ‡DHSS, Statistical Report Series No. 14, *Two parent families*, HMSO, 1971 (tables 2, 10a and 10b). The self-employed below the supplementary benefit level were in fact excluded from the tables in the DHSS report for 1968, 1969 and 1970 and an estimate equivalent to the proportion of the employed below the level substituted. In this table an estimate for the self-employed has been restored to allow comparisons with the 1960 and 1966 figures. In the absence of actual information this estimate for 1968, 1969 and 1970 is based on the number found in the *Circumstances of families* survey (i.e. 11,500 additional families in each case).

allowances, national insurance benefits and supplementary benefit rates. Certainly there is little comfort in them for Labour supporters. Moreover they do not reflect differential changes in the cost of living and withdrawal of subsidies. When Labour increased family allowances in 1968 part of the increase was intended to balance the increase in charges for school meals and welfare milk.

The failure to increase family allowances in 1970 and the Conservative Government's new policy of cuts and charges mean that the numbers are bound to increase quite sharply in 1971. Even on the Conservative Government's most optimistic assumption the FIS scheme will not reduce poverty even to the proportions of the late 1960s.

the growth of the social services

The third perspective is public versus private investment, the expansion of public services, and especially social services including education, housing, social security, health and welfare. Expenditure increased rapidly in absolute terms from a grand total of £5,668 million in 1964 to £9,145 million in 1969. As a percentage of GNP expenditure rose from 19.3 per cent to 23.7 per cent (or from 11.3 to 13.2 per cent if transfer income is excluded.

Expansion of expenditure on the social services is partly a consequence of demographic change and rising demand for sixth form and university or college education and expensive new drugs and forms of surgery. For these reasons we would expect their growth to be faster than of the economy as a whole. All industrial societies for which there is information are rapidly increasing the proportion of GNP devoted to social services. The rate of expansion has been higher in some other countries than the UK. Excluding education and

EXPENDITURE ON SOCIAL SERVICES AS A PERCENTAGE OF
GNP AT FACTOR COST

year	current expenditure on goods and services	capital expenditure	current and capital	transfer income	all social services
1959	7.2	2.3	9.6	7.5	17.1
1964	7.8	3.5	11.3	8.0	19.3
1969	9.7	3.6	13.3	10.4	23.7

source: *National income and expenditure, 1970*, supplemented by information supplied by the Treasury and the Central Statistical Office.

housing, the latest information from an ILO compilation (see for example J. Wedel's analysis in the *International Labour Review* for December 1970) shows faster growth in Austria, Belgium, Czechoslovakia, France, Italy, Japan, the Netherlands, Sweden, New Zealand, for example, and 12 countries with a higher percentage of GNP. In a recent OECD paper on education Debeauvais noted that between 1955 and 1965 the number of countries spending more relatively on education than the UK increased from 11 to 13.

The rate of expansion also becomes difficult to change, irrespective of change of government. The next table shows that the rate of expansion in 1964-69 was slightly less than in the previous five years at constant prices. Current expenditure on education grew by 4.2 per cent per annum, compared with 3.8 per cent, and on the NHS by 2.8 per cent, compared with 2.5 per cent. Capital expenditure fluctuated with economic vicissitudes and was lower, as the table shows, because of falls in housing and education.

questions about the record

The evidence on three great questions—the reduction of inequality, the abolition of poverty and the controlled betterment of community through the expansion of the social services—has been sketched. It may help to reduce controversy about developments in the last few years. The Government did not diminish inequalities of income, or did not reduce them much, either between families with children and households without children, or household and occupational groups at different levels of income. Considerable poverty remained among the families of the low paid, old people, the unemployed, the disabled and fatherless families. Resources were not steered

PERCENTAGE INCREASE IN EXPENDITURE DURING 5 YEARS
ON SOCIAL SERVICES, 1959-64, COMPARED WITH 1964-69 AT
CONSTANT PRICES

period	current exp. on goods and services	capital exp.	current capital	all	transfer social security only	income all social services	all social services less housing
1959-64	17	81	31	28	27	31	26
1964-69	18	15	17	41	39	27	29

source: *National income and expenditure, 1970*, supplemented by information supplied by the Treasury and the Central Statistical Office.

towards the fulfilment of social objectives by means of what by international and historical standards would have been a really dramatic expansion of social services.

It is impossible not to feel a sense of dismay. How far are these failures attributable to the institutional structure of society, public values, class conflict, planning and administration, or even to the Labour movement, rather than to the men who formed the Government? Were the forces of material greed or of the institutional *status quo* underestimated or unrecognised? Indeed, had they been sapping Labour's strength and resolution from the inside? Historians will go on asking big questions such as these for many years to come. From a planning viewpoint some of the more interesting narrower questions are these:

1. Could more advantage have been taken of the initial momentum of public enthusiasm and support to introduce sweeping reforms and extend democracy? The first hundred days were solemnly documented by *The Guardian* and other papers. Right wing forces were very much on the defensive. Despite its innovations, particularly in the machinery of Whitehall, the Government was expected to be bolder (in terms say, of a wealth tax or extension of public ownership) than it was. The direction taken by a Party in the early days of office tends to become fixed.

2. Why were certain structural reforms postponed or watered down? The Land Commission had a negligible effect. The national superannuation scheme was intended to be a second Beveridge revolution. It could have been on the Statute Book by the end of 1965 or early 1966 and yet was still being discussed in mid-1970. The aim of channelling resources to *existing* as distinct from future pensioners seemed to have been abandoned.

3. Why were insufficient new structural reforms generated as time went on? In general there was little stimulus for new thinking and new policies of a Socialist nature either within the Government or the Labour movement.

4. Despite protestations to the contrary, why did Labour reintroduce charges and extend means testing, so strengthening the socially divisive elements to which traditionally it was opposed? In statement after statement the Party said the personal means test was "repugnant" and that numbers submitting to it would be reduced to the original purpose of a "safety net" by the universal schemes that would be introduced (see, for example, the Labour Party, *New frontiers for social security*, pp18-19, 1964, H. Wilson, *The new Britain*, pp19-20, Penguin Books, 1964). The number of people dependent on supplementary benefit increased from 2¾ million in 1964 to over 4 millions in 1969. New types of means tests, like rate rebates and exemption from prescription charges, were started.

5. Did public attitudes harden towards certain minority groups? Some Ministers tried to educate the public about immigration and race relations. Others condoned public prejudices or felt inhibited from meeting them head on by the turn about in Labour policy in 1965. Prejudice can grow like a cancer and can affect issues other than race relations. Despite fewer available

jobs than there are unemployed men in many districts, and despite the minute evidence of abuse, public references to "scroungers" and the "work-shy" have also increased. In 1968 a half hearted attempt to publicise supplementary benefits to those who were eligible but did not apply for them was neutralised by a simultaneous tightening up of payments to the unemployed. Exaggeratedly harsh views about fatherless families, wandering gypsies, drug addicts, and the homeless who resort to railway stations and churchyards as well as hostels have also become widespread—and may in part contribute to swelling the numbers of such isolated minorities.

6. Why was much of Labour's moral authority in social affairs shed in one fatal step in 1965, when the Government developed a racially discriminatory system of immigration control? The publication of a White Paper on immigration was possibly the most disastrous action—in terms of achieving Labour's traditional objectives—of the $5\frac{1}{2}$ years. The moral precepts weakened many policies far removed from race relations. To a considerable extent the restrictionist policy made community integration and social equality unrealisable. The failure to adopt a genuine policy of integration in the White Paper also had a disruptive effect generally on housing policy and the chances of a viable policy for community development.

7. Why were social priorities and social planning so poorly formulated? In view of Labour's detailed planning in the late 1950s the comparative dearth of planning came as a surprise. Perhaps the universities and research institutes offered weak support and insufficient harassment. Perhaps central ministries contain too few professional social scientists, and are insufficiently reminded of the effects upon consumers of changes in central policies.

8. Why was social planning attached as an appendage to economic planning and the creative relationship between the two not perceived? Admittedly there are two schools of thought, but Labour's history and traditional sources of support favour the adoption of a newer social perspective. There are those who argue that economic growth depends on generating the savings and the incentives needed for investment, innovation and higher productivity from certain managerial, property owning and skilled manual groups, and then using increased wealth to bring about equality. But there are those who argue that greater equality, by raising low incomes, would foster national morale and drive, contribute to higher labour output and efficiency and involve more of the population in general industrial and social development. Some of the subtleties of growth before redistribution versus redistribution before growth were argued in the 1970 Fabian autumn lectures by Anthony Crosland (*A social democratic Britain*, Fabian tract 404) and J. K. Galbraith (*The US left and some British comparisons*, Fabian tract 405). Gunnar Myrdal is one who has adopted the "social" thesis (see his *Asian drama*, particularly vol 2, p754 ff).

9. At a time of growing concern about community rights and environment why was the opportunity not seized to establish better complaints procedures (particularly in health, welfare and supplementary benefit services), welfare rights offices, co-operative housing schemes, and consumer responsibilities for different community projects?

10. Did Labour require more administrative support in depth? How far did ministers lack skilled advisers to counter obstructionist civil servants' briefs? How far were they able to put creative proposals into operational reality?

11. Why did the Labour movement fail to do more to control, or to support, the Labour leadership? The influence upon events of the Party conference, Transport House, the constituency parties, the PLP, the Parliamentary left and even the TUC could for most of the time be said to be surprisingly small. There was little dialogue and even contact, despite strenuous efforts by a few ministers. An elitist leadership lost touch with the mainsprings of its power. It requires that contact to maintain its own strength and resolution.

the lessons for planning—incomes policy

Questions of policy are, as I have tried to show, inextricably bound up with questions of political machinery and legislation, but the analysis of policy over the last few years provides a number of lessons. The objectives to diminish inequalities, abolish poverty and promote social development through the public social services are interrelated. Incomes, fiscal and social service policies interlock, as our evidence showed.

The three will be examined briefly in turn. Economic objectives were paramount in the Labour Government's policy and, perhaps because they were paramount, that policy failed. The only incomes policy that seems likely to work is one with clear social objectives applying to the whole population. In a carefully argued pamphlet Thomas Balogh leads up to this conclusion but does not properly examine it—largely because he does not set out the social context within which incomes policy operated. He rightly concludes that "a peaceful transition to a more balanced social system demands a policy package of which incomes policy is one of the most essential elements" (*Labour and inflation*, Fabian tract 403, October 1970). But he does not try to spell out the reasons for the distrust with which the trade unions came to view Labour's policy.

The policy aimed to do little more than control wage increases in order to curb inflation. Salaries, dividends and profits escaped the same tight control. Wealth was not taxed, and industry was left largely free to determine prices. In these circumstances it is not surprising that the policy was felt to be socially unfair. Indeed, large awards of extra pay had been made to ministers, MPs, judges, senior civil servants and general practitioners just before the unions were asked to limit wage demands to between 3 and 4 per cent per annum. It was difficult for intelligent trade unionists not to conclude from this that there was one law for the rich and another for the poor.

The problems of the low paid attracted little serious attention. No detailed policy to help them was worked out, even at the time of devaluation. A national survey of earnings was carried out in 1968, but the collection of information about the industrial and family situation of the low paid, and then only for a few industries, was not put in hand until 1970. The reports were among the last to be published by the NBPI before its demise in April 1971. The existing machinery of wages councils, which cover three million workers, was not reviewed. The challenging task of finding practical methods of introducing a minimum wage was not seriously tackled and instead of appointing an enthusiastic but knowledgeable group of social scientists, trade unionists and labour specialists the Government passed it on to an inter-departmental committee. This was like asking the Board of Inland Revenue to investigate the desirability of its reconstruction.

The unions themselves bear some responsibility for not pursuing the implications—for wage policy as a whole—of commitment to a minimum wage. It is frankly impossible to have an incomes policy for the low paid which works without having one also for the high paid. But it must be admitted that the unions received very little hard evidence of the government really giving the priority traditionally accorded by Labour to the underdog. And this applied to the non-working poor as well as the working poor, as the evidence on social security benefits attests.

If a full history of these events were to be written it would of course be complex. The limitations of our existing state of knowledge and capacities for planning have to be recognised. Nonetheless, it is fair to conclude that success in one area of policy seems to depend more on success in others than had been believed hitherto, and is probably contingent on overall planning. Had the Labour Government attempted systematically, or been allowed, to relate in its policy-making the different sources of income; had the unions been given more tangible evidence of efforts to limit salaries, dividends and profits; or had the public been convinced of the Government's determination to give priority to people with low incomes, the outcome might have been very different. The principles on which income differentials (wages, salaries and social security benefits) are based might have begun to be discussed. But none of this would have been possible without more deliberate policies of intervention. Socialism depends on applying collective principles to an increasing extent, not just through public ownership but through the private sector, by means of supervision, encouragement, control and setting minimum as well as maximum standards, for example, for salaries, bonuses and fringe benefits.

the lessons for planning—fiscal policy

Our second example is taxation in relation to social policy. The functions of fiscal policy are surprisingly under researched. The social implications of alternative budget strategies are not fully worked out, nor the consequences of each budget examined. The best data are those produced by the Central Statistical Office, based on the Family Expenditure Survey. These show that poor and rich families pay very similar proportions of gross incomes in tax. This suggests the need for a more progressive tax system, achieved partly by replacing flat rate by graduated national insurance contributions and by making earned income relief absolute in amount rather than proportional. The publication of the Tory Government's reconstruction of personal direct taxation as early as April 1971 forces one to ask why Labour did not introduce a socialist equivalent during its six years of office.

Taxation policy inevitably reinforces, or conflicts with, social service policies. In particular, action to introduce or adjust tax allowances helps to redistribute resources from those without to those with dependants. In general, direct payments are preferable to tax allowances as a means of helping people with dependants, since the poorest do not benefit fully or at all from the latter. The Labour Government acted on the advice of the Child Poverty Action Group to reduce tax allowances when increasing family allowances in order to reduce the gross cost of such increases and concentrate their value on the poorest families. Unhappily the measures were not synchronised and the implications for tax equity were not grasped. The Group had originally proposed that family allowances should be tax-free, so that one of the functions of children's tax allowances, to create a different tax threshold for men with different numbers of children, could be restored.

The right policy for a future Labour government to adopt (to complete what was begun in 1968) would be to abolish child tax allowances, to raise family allowances substantially (introducing them also for the first child) and to free them of tax.

Tax relief on allowances must also be treated as a form of public expenditure, as in parts of Scandinavia. They should come under the scrutiny of those in charge of social policy, along with national insurance benefits, family allowances, rent rebates and the rest. The Tory Government has adopted a deliberate policy of reducing public subsidies and increasing charges and rents on the flimsy pretext that help can be redistributed from the better off to those in need. But the evidence so far suggests that the situation of the latter has been even further imperilled by the measures adopted, while the relative living standards of the manual and non-manual workers and their families have been allowed to become more unequal. Although the tax relief received by a mortgagee is more on average than the average subsidy received by council tenants, the latter and not the former are being reduced. Yet the withdrawal of certain tax allowances would be a perfectly respectable and indeed effective form of "charging", since it does not affect the poorest families.

Tax relief on mortgages is greater the more costly the house and the higher the income of the owner occupier. The withdrawal of part or all of the allowance would save up to £220 million (the value in 1969-70). Such a sum would help to finance a flat rate housing subsidy of £2 per week for every disabled person (of all ages) and every family with three or more children and still leave scope for meeting other exceptional needs.

the lessons for planning—expansion of social services

Finally the social services. In its early period of office the distressing but far-reaching decisions made by the Heath Government in education, housing subsidies and social security, as well as in personal direct taxation, throw into stark relief the timidity of the Labour Government and its failure to adopt a controlled, long-term strategy to reduce inequality and poverty and improve the quality of community life. Both governments have been obsessed by the problem of controlling expenditure, as if it were a problem of reducing or stabilising such expenditure relative to national income instead of one of finding criteria for the rate and priorities of growth of expenditure and relating growth of public expenditure to control of private consumption.

Under both Labour and Tory Governments cuts in public expenditure have been made by introducing or raising charges for goods and services which were previously free or cheap because they were subsidised, and by cutting back on planned expansion, especially capital expenditure. The relationship between projected public expenditure and projected private consumption has not been examined. Yet the economic, tax and incentive grants policies which affect and shape the latter are at least as important in achieving social objectives as more direct government intervention in the public social services. The Labour Government seemed to be unaware of this in re-introducing prescription charges and shaping its social policies at different stages of economic crisis, and unaware even in its first, and only, attempt to set out a comprehensive National Plan in 1965. A modern government can of course decide to limit the manufacture of special varieties of sports cars and of the more garish motor accessories in the interest say, of producing more specially designed vehicles for the disabled, as well as home aids, surgical aids and appliances, and special forms of surgery for both the disabled and hospitalised.

Neither has the relationship between the different components of expenditure *within* the public sector been examined. This involves more than the question of giving priority, say, to education rather than to the health service. One example would be whether to spend relatively more resources on community care and relatively less on long-stay hospitals, or more on probation and the supervision of parole than prisons. Another example would be whether to allocate extra resources to staff of different services, through salaries and fringe benefits, rather than to the consumers of those services, through benefits and general amenities. The point is that a change of priority in one service has implications for others and they need to be formulated. Certain kinds of changes have implications more for the conditions of employment of staff than for the standard of life of consumers.

Such questions are sometimes decided unconsciously. There are of course double standards which operate in assessing salaries and wages in the public sector. On the one hand, there is the principle of comparing earnings with those of people in similar types of employment in the private sector. On the other, there is the principle of public thrift. The idea that public service is a vocation which need not be properly rewarded or for which there are other kinds of rewards, including security of employment, is very commonly accepted, even in collective bargaining. The government of the day frequently decides to sacrifice one or other group of public employees in pursuing its policies. The case of the post office workers is a particularly notorious example under the Heath Government. Under Labour some groups of professional workers, including doctors, teachers and nurses, gained substantial awards, though this may have been partly attributable to their improved organisation. But the consequences for public expenditure as a whole of this up-grading was never discussed. Although salaries and wages accounted for the vast bulk of current expenditure on education, health and welfare no determined attempt was made at various stages to review the distribution of future work between different kinds or grades of staff, or even to compare the living standards of staff and consumers in the same group of services. Instead restraints were imposed on expansion of staff numbers and consumer standards were reduced directly or indirectly through the introduction or raising of charges and the deferment of capital rebuilding. In effect, it might be argued that recent efforts to "save" public expenditure have been inefficient in the sense that they have reduced consumer standards in the short term without tackling the major problems of uneconomical staffing structures and wasteful private consumption.

Increases in pay are also unrelated to increases in benefit. In the summer of 1970 the Kindersley Committee recommended a pay award, costing £83 million a year for about 60,000 doctors (of which the Labour Government conceded £59 million). Increases in allowances costing £70 million in a full year for about 4,000,000 persons dependent in whole or in part upon the Supplementary Benefits Commission were announced at about the same time. These kind of decisions are related to each other and to the objectives being pursued implicitly or explicitly by the Government and more effort might be made to discuss them in conjunction. Incomes as well as manpower policies should be part of any strategy for "controlling" public expenditure.

Another limitation upon planning has been the current vogue for gamesmanship economics in the Treasury and other central departments. Instead of confronting the problems of translating the Labour Government's objectives into operational terms; coordinating a social strategy; providing ministers and the public with a running commentary on inequalities in relation to events; offering advance warning of the inequitable short term and long term repercussions of some decisions and generally developing socially sensitive antennae, a number of the departments have been experimenting, to the exclusion of other techniques, with cost-benefit analysis, performance budgeting, functional costing, output-budgeting and programme budgeting. The Treasury, for example, has published a number of accounts of output budgeting and cost-benefit analysis since 1967 in a series of occasional papers based on the Centre for Administrative Studies. Responsibility for publishing later papers in the series was passed to the Civil Service Department. The Department of Education and Science published its first Education Planning Paper on *Output budgeting for the* DES: *report of a feasibility study* in 1970, and a highly controversial article on "The economic return on investment in higher education in England and Wales" by Vera Morris and Adrian Ziderman, was published in *Economic Trends* in May 1971. As number 2 in its series of Manpower Papers the DEP published in 1970 *Cost benefit aspects of manpower retraining* by James J. Hughes.

The techniques are useful in management accounting and may have a part to play in some planning. But it is a very small part indeed and the importance of the techniques in planning is far less than the measurement of need. Like all specialised techniques and languages, they can be employed to undermine the confidence of the uninitiated, especially politicians. It would be a mistake to regard them as offering more than an alternative means of laying out the arguments leading to some types of decisions. They tend to exaggerate the importance of considerations which can be quantified in monetary terms and values are placed on some things like health, security and scholarship which are either priceless or arbitrary, according to one's point of view. The techniques also apply more easily to what a Government is doing than what it is not but should be doing. Some of those who have pressed the virtues of these techniques strongly, like Professor Alan Williams, formerly the Director of Economic Studies at the Treasury Centre for Administrative Studies, have become much more cautious in recent years (compare papers 4 and 11 which he has contributed to the Centre's series of occasional papers series). "Even if economic efficiency in the narrowest sense were conceded paramountcy, cost-benefit analysis would not provide the administrator with a means of relieving himself of critically important decisions. In fact decision makers might well beware of experts who 'helpfully' simplify their job by making implicit decisions in the course of their analysis; these may include some which later turn out to be wholly unrealistic or unacceptable." Some questions "can be settled ultimately only by administratively or politically determined criteria. Indeed the most fundamental choice of all—which items should be counted as costs and which as benefits —depends upon the point of view of the client" (H. G. Walsh and A. Williams, *Current issues in cost benefit analysis,* Centre for Administrative Studies occasional papers, 11, September 1969, p19). The absurd lengths to which the Royal Commission on the third London airport was prepared to pursue these techniques have however jolted many civil servants into a sceptical awareness of their limitations.

The Labour administration was expected to put social planning into operational effect and many of its own supporters were surprised by its slow progress. Adventurous planning gave way to restrictive Treasury control over public expenditure. Under the previous Conservative Government in the early sixties, ten year plans for the hospital and community care services were developed and published; the Robbins report on higher education had a major influence; research and statistical units were established at some, though not all, of the social service ministries; and better statistical reviews, like that of the National Assistance Board, were published. Labour had ambitious plans for streamlining the administrative machinery of government, particularly in organising the economy, and there were also policies like those on comprehensive schools and national superannuation which suggested the consolidation of planning.

What was put into effect? The Department of Economic Affairs and the NBPI were set up. The Ministries of Health and Social Security were amalgamated and the services of the Central Statistical Office reorganised under Claus Moser. But there was comparatively little forward planning of a concerted kind on the allocation of resources. The National Plan of 1965 was quietly shelved in response to economic events. In social and historical terms astonishingly narrow judgements were displayed in it. The promised series of plans on hospitals and community care was stopped and though surveys of the living standards of pensioners and of families with two or more children were carried out no effort was made at any time to present a general review of future plans in social security in relation to social needs and particularly poverty. This was during a period of growing public awareness of the extent of homelessness, deprivation and poverty. In fact the quantity and quality of information about some services—such as supplementary benefits—actually declined. Each of the annual reports of the SBC for 1967-69 can be compared, for example, with the annual report of the

National Assistance Board for 1965. Ministers such of R. H. S. Crossman had expected the information and planning services to grow, not shrivel (see his Fabian essay "Socialism and Planning" in *Socialism and Affluence*, Fabian Society, 1967).

Little more remained of central social planning than the series of White Papers on public expenditure. The White Paper of December 1969 proposed a rate of growth in the social services of four per cent per annum up to 1972 and only three per cent from 1972-74. Despite some qualifications that were attached these estimates were irreconcilable with previous experience. At constant prices the rate of growth for social services excluding housing had been over 5 per cent during the previous ten years, and even for education, health and welfare had been 4.6 per cent. The Labour Government was planning a smaller rate of expansion of the social services at the beginning of 1970 than it had achieved during the economic stress of the previous five years or than the previous Conservative administration had achieved during 1959-64. This was difficult to understand or explain. An annual increase of three per cent was allowed to education, but in relation to existing commitments this figure implied that the expansion of further and higher education would have had to be cut back drastically and the plans to raise the school leaving age and reduce class sizes deferred.

That public expenditure on the social services is growing proportionately, in Britain as in other countries, is a fact that has to be recognised. Even without any improvement of standards spending will have to grow to accommodate the growing proportion of dependants in the population—principally retirement pensioners, children and the disabled. This is not a problem peculiar to the future or to Britain; it has been a long standing feature of nearly all highly industrialised societies. The expensive impact of science and technology on the social services, particularly health and education, also tends to raise spending disproportionately. New drugs, new types of surgery and methods of rehabilitation and new aids for the disabled as well as in schools, are pushing up costs. Professional staff attach a lot of importance to these innovations and popular support for them is easy to attract. In political terms they are difficult to resist and in Britain it would be very difficult without a vast upheaval of the health and education systems and re-orientation of public values, as well as undesirable, to make them available only to those who can pay for them.

Another long term influence upon public spending is the increase in the proportion of the population in search of upward social mobility. The growth of the secondary school population, soon to be strengthened by the increase from 15 to 16 in the age to which all children have to stay at school; the slow introduction of comprehensive schools and the expansion of further and higher education are contributing to the remorseless rise in public expenditure. A more controlled strategy of expansion in educational expenditure is badly needed. Resources have to be equalised between colleges and universities and training for the professions related to manpower needs. There should be more short courses for the middle aged and young staff of junior rank. More doctors, teachers, nurses and social workers might be persuaded to work with assistants in teams. This would be a more effective and and economical use of manpower and would help to bridge or reduce salary and wage differentials. The uncontrolled expansion of higher education can be wasteful in at least three senses. More people might be financed for a longer period of training than is necessary for professional and managerial manpower needs. The type of higher education may be inappropriate. And a large supply of graduates may lead to a number of professions demanding top-heavy staffing structures in order to preserve their advantages in remuneration and conditions of employment. A large share of the benefits of national economic growth could in fact be absorbed not only by the increasing costs of higher education but by the salaries to which they are expected to lead. All this would be at the expense of those on low incomes.

This suggests how important it is for resources to be allocated in conformity with a widely though carefully drawn social plan. In scope the plan needs to be extended far beyond the traditional boundaries of the social services. Just as incomes policy makes no sense if it is confined to wages and not also salaries and profits, social planning makes no sense if it is confined to the public health, welfare, education, housing and social security services, and not also industrial welfare services and the social aspects of incomes, taxation, environmental and manpower policies.

After the publication of a White Paper in October 1970 on *The reorganisation of central government* the Tory Government transferred the administration of children's services from the Home Office to the Department of Health and Social Security. But the nation is far from having a federal department which amalgamates the Department of Education and Science, the Ministry of Housing and the Department of Health and Social Security. A multi-disciplinary central policy review unit has been set up by Mr. Heath under Lord Rothschild but there is little sign in its membership or management of a creative approach to social planning. What is needed is a strong research, information and planning unit, perhaps under a Social Advisory Council, with direct responsibility to the Prime Minister, which has the job of converting the social objectives of government into an operational programme. This unit would undertake research on social conditions and needs, monitor the social effects of changes in fiscal, incomes and social service policies and produce forward plans.

conclusion

Really big structural reforms eluded the Labour Government. The Government strayed from moral authority over race and withdrew from the obstinate pursuit of socialist objectives. Its social achievements were much smaller than claimed or believed at the time by Labour ministers. Major onslaughts on inequality and poverty were required but not mounted. Although support for the social services was maintained during severe economic difficulties that support was not exceptional in scale nor was it inspired by one of a number of possible socialist strategies—to develop and integrate the local community, (for example, through local employment policies, a public housing repairs and environmental improvement scheme, and services, like housing, for people of different races), establish an effective system of civil and welfare rights as a basis for wider democratic control, or extend those essential educational, health and welfare services which should be available free of charge to the whole population.

There were important reforms but they tailed off in the last two years. As Thomas Balogh remarked after a long period at the Cabinet Office, "Some at least of the difficulties of the Labour Government in its last two years arose because fewer and fewer people believed that a steadfast redistribution of income was one of its main policy planks" (T. Balogh, *op cit,* p45).

Some early policies of the Heath Government help to place the shortcomings in perspective. For example, Labour's half-hearted experiments with new forms of means tested services and its introduction or re-introduction of welfare charges paved the way for the more comprehensive selectivist policies upon which the new Tory Government has now embarked. Certainly the Government's plan to re-structure housing subsidies, its veiled opposition to comprehensive education and its reform of direct taxation must give Labour gradualists pause. In these fields of policy, they must ask, why were not Labour's reforms fierce and sustained?

But two major qualifications have to be attached to this uncomfortable but inescapable conclusion. The new Tory Government is pursuing social policies which are far more reactionary, short sighted and socially divisive than those of the previous Tory Government of 1959-64. To what extent they will actually be put into effect remains to be seen. But these policies are far removed from the timid but moderate reformist approach of 1965-70. Secondly, responsibility for change does not rest solely or even primarily with government. The shortcomings of other Labour institutions and groups, as well as the underlying if not declared opposition of different vested interests and a volatile public opinion have to be analysed and understood. In order to set the seal to social reconstruction democratic socialist governments must depend on favourable trends in social beliefs and values. They must also depend on support in depth from their own movements, in providing the information, the critical research and discussion, the staffing of new types of organisation and the fostering of local enthusiasm, all of which are required to bring about structural change of the right kind. If Labour can ponder constructively about these kind of matters democratic socialism can be shown to lead to the peaceful transformation of society instead of peripheral amelioration of the worst excesses of capitalism. The fundamental question left unanswered by Labour's rule is whether democratic socialism can be effective.

Labour's handling of the problems of inequality, poverty and the growth of the social services suggest certain major lessons—of the need to establish a concerted social policy, with clearly formulated objectives and priorities; an effective system of administration and communication to put that policy into effect; a political control system to ensure that it is put into effect, and a receptive and involved public opinion to legitimise the whole operation.

The working out and adoption of a comprehensive social plan could help the Labour movement to identify its middle-range objectives, sort out priorities and create the conditions for a sustained effort when Labour next takes office. These conditions would include new planning machinery, an edequate public communications network, the need for sufficient staff and consultants in central departments who are sympathetic to the party's objectives and who can advise and support Ministers and, most controversial of all, better methods of consulting Labour members and groups to keep in close touch with rank and file opinion.

The kind of social plan for which I have argued would not be limited to the five social services—social security, education, health, housing and community welfare. It would cover the social aspects of incomes, fiscal, manpower and industrial relations policies too. Certain individual policies have been suggested or implied. They are a wealth tax; a minimum wage; an incomes gains tax for the highly paid; substantially higher family allowances; legislation to make industrial fringe benefits compulsory; abolition of certain tax allowances; pensions for the partly disabled (including a percentage pension for those at work) as well as the wholly disabled, and including the elderly; one parent family benefits; flat rate housing subsidies for the disabled and for families with more than two or three dependants; housing schemes by which groups of poor housing needing renovation would be taken into cooperative or community ownership; the development of professional teams, using assistants, in medicine, teaching, nursing and social work; the further democratisation of the local community, perhaps through the establishment of community Boards to supervise projects to improve welfare and environment; independent information and welfare rights offices in every area; and community employment and welfare programmes. A programme of such scope could be spelt out in great detail long before the next election.

In the short term, such a plan is needed to restore stability and cohesion (in employment, race relations and housing, for example) from which greater national vitality and higher productivity might develop; to provide a rationale for the allocation of national resources and the controlled growth of public expenditure; and to make incomes policy more acceptable to the unions and hence economic problems more manageable.

In the long term, some such plan is required to prevent the strong from gaining most of the fruits of economic growth at a time when the weak are increasing in proportion to total population. More positively, it is needed to construct a just society when powerful multi-national corporations and trading areas, expensive technology and arrogant professionalism, are increasingly liable to undermine traditional democratic procedures and endanger individual and community rights.

chronology

October 1964	Creation of Department of Economic Affairs.
November 1964	Protection from Eviction Act.
February 1964	National Board for Prices and Incomes set up.
February 1965	Allen Committee on rates shows that large numbers eligible for national assistance not claiming.
March 1965	Milner Holland report on housing in London.
July 1965	Circular 10/65 on comprehensive schools.
August 1965	White Paper on immigration policy.

September 1965	National Plan published.
November 1965	Rent Act, including provision for fair rents to be laid down by rent officer or rent tribunal.
April 1966	Rate rebates introduced.
June 1966	Report of financial circumstances of retirement pensioners shows large proportion eligible for national assistance but not claiming.
August 1966	Ministry of Pensions and National Assistance Board amalgamated.
October 1966	Earnings-related supplements for unemployed and sick.
November 1966	Supplementary Benefits Commission, replacing the National Assistance Board, begins work after the Social Security Act is passed.
January 1967	Plowden report on children in primary schools published.
June 1967	Report on circumstances of families with two or more children published, showing a million children in poverty or on its margins.
July 1967	Resignation of Minister of Social Security, Miss Peggy Herbison.
November 1967	Devaluation.
January 1968	Cuts in public expenditure and reintroduction of prescription charges.
March 1968	Urban aid programme announced.
April 1968	Educational Priority Areas programme.
April 1968 to October 1968	Family allowances increased in two steps with introduction of "clawback."
July 1968	Rejection by Minister of Health of allegations of cruelty in geriatric hospitals.
July 1968	New rule terminating supplementary benefits for some unemployed.
July 1968	Seebohm Committee's report published.
July 1968	First Green Paper on NHS reorganisation.
July 1968	Report of Public Schools Commission.
October 1968	Race Relations Act.
October 1968	Ministries of Health and Social Security amalgamated.
November 1968	Community Relations Commission set up.
January 1969	White Paper on national superannuation and social security.
January 1969	Interdepartmental working party report on a minimum wage.
March 1969	Report on allegations of ill-treatment of patients at Ely Hospital.
April 1969	Green Paper on Public Expenditure.
July 1969	Report of Committee on public participation in planning.
October 1969	Amalgamation of housing, transport and planning and appointment of Secretary of State for Local Government and Regional Planning.
December 1969	White Paper on Public Expenditure.
January 1970	Memo on poverty and the Labour Government presented to Secretary of State for Social Services by the CPAG.
February 1970	Second Green Paper on reorganisation of the NHS.
June 1970	Local Authority Social Services Act passed.

some abbreviations

ACE	Advisory Council for Education.
AUEW	Amalgamated Union of Engineering Workers.
AEGIS	Aid to the Elderly in Government Institutions.
AFDC	Aid to Families and Dependent Children.
BMA	British Medical Association.
CPAG	Child Poverty Action Group.
CSC	Comprehensive Schools Committee.
CSO	Central Statistical Office.
DEP	Department of Employment and Productivity.
DHSS	Department of Health and Social Security.
FES	Family Expenditure Survey.
EPA	Educational Priority Area.
FIS	Family Income Supplement.
GNC	General Nursing Council.
GNP	Gross National Product.
GP	General Practitioner.
HP	Hire Purchase.
IMTA	Institute of Municipal Treasurers and Accountants.
JAHA	Journal of the American Hospital Association.
LCC	London County Council.
LEA	Local Education Authority.
MHLG	Ministry of Housing and Local Government.
MPNI	Ministry of Pensions and National Insurance.
NAB	National Assistance Board.
NBPI	National Board for Prices and Incomes.
NCCL	National Council for Civil Liberties.
NFER	National Foundation for Educational Research.
NHS	National Health Service.
NUM	National Union of Mineworkers.
NUT	National Union of Teachers.
PEP	Political and Economic Planning.
PPBS	Planning, Programming, Budgeting System.
SBC	Supplementary Benefits Commission.
SCPR	Social and Community Planning Research.
SET	Selective Employment Tax.
SRN	State Registered Nurse.
SSRC	Social Science Research Council.
T & GWU	Transport and General Workers Union.
TUC	Trades Union Congress.
UCCA	University Central Council for Admissions.
UGC	University Grants Committee.
UN	United Nations.
USA	United States of America.
WRVS	Women's Royal Voluntary Service.
WTE	Whole Time Equivalent.

notes about contributors

A. B. Atkinson is professor of economics at the University of Essex. He is author of *Poverty in Britain and the reform of social security* (CUP, 1969) and of *Unequal shares—the distribution of wealth in Britain* (Allen Lane, Penguin Press, forthcoming). He is grateful to Mr. G. Homewood for assistance with the calculations.

Nicholas Bosanquet is a lecturer in economics at the London School of Economics. He worked for the National Board for Prices and Incomes as an industrial relations adviser from 1967 to 1969. He is a governor of University College Hospital and is currently doing research on manpower problems in the NHS.

Rosalind Brooke is a lecturer in social administration at the London School of Economics, and was formerly legal adviser to CPAG. She is a member of the executive committee of NCCL.

Muriel Brown is a lecturer in social administration at the London School of Economics and was previously a lecturer in social administration at the University of Manchester. She wrote *Introduction to social administration in Britain* (Hutchinson University Library, 1969).

Colin Crouch is a research student at Nuffield College, Oxford and was formerly a lecturer in sociology at the London School of Economics. He wrote *The student revolt* and *Politics in a technological society* (Young Fabian pamphlet 23).

Howard Glennerster is a lecturer in social administration at the London School of Economics and was one of the authors of the Fabian pamphlet *Planning for education in 1980*. He was research consultant to the Public Schools Commission and wrote *Paying for private schools* (Allen Lane, Penguin Press, 1970).

Peter Hall is professor of geography and chairman of the School of Planning Studies at the University of Reading. He wrote *London 2000* and other books.

Michael Hill is a research officer at the Department of Social and Administrative Studies, University of Oxford and was previously a lecturer at Reading University and an executive officer with the National Assistance Board. He also served on the Reading Borough Council's housing committee for three years.

John Hughes is vice-principal of Ruskin College, Oxford, where he lectures on economics and industrial relations and is also director of the Trade Union Research Unit established there. He is author of six Fabian pamphlets.

Peter Kaim-Caudle is senior lecturer in social administration at the University of Durham and was until recently research professor at the Economic and Social Research Institute, Dublin. He is a member of the Durham County Council's Social Services Committee and Durham Executive Council (NHS). He wrote *Pharmaceutical services in Ireland* (Economic and Social Research Institute, Dublin).

Dennis Marsden is a lecturer in sociology at the University of Essex and wrote *Mothers alone* and, with Brian Jackson, *Education and the working class*.

Michael Meacher is Member of Parliament for Oldham West and was previously a lecturer in social administration at the University of York and at the London School of Economics. He wrote "The future of community care" in *The fifth social service* (Fabian Society, 1970) and *Taken for a ride: special residential homes for the elderly mentally infirm* (Longmans, 1972).

Peter Townsend is professor of sociology at the University of Essex. He is author of *The family life of old people* and *The last refuge*, and co-author of *The poor and the poorest* (with Brian Abel-Smith), *Old people in three industrial societies* (with Ethel Shanas and others) and *The aged in the welfare state* (with Dorothy Wedderburn). He is chairman of the Child Poverty Action Group.

A. J. Walsh works for the City of Sheffield social services department and was formerly a Douglas Knoop research fellow in the Division of Economic Studies, at the University of Sheffield. He is indebted to the Douglas Knoop Research Fund for making this study possible, to the Inland Revenue authorities for providing him with a great deal of information, to Mr. R. J. Nicholson for explaining to him the use of certain statistical techniques, and to his colleagues in the Division of Economic Studies, in particular Mr. E. B. Butler, Mr. P. K. Else, Mr. R. W. Houghton and Mr. B. J. McCormick.

Dorothy Wedderburn is reader in Industrial Sociology at the Imperial College of Science and Technology. She wrote *Redundancy and the railwaymen* (CUP, 1965) and *The aged in the welfare state* jointly with Peter Townsend.

Martin Wolf is a research student at Nuffield College, Oxford.